T0339656

Public Goods and Market Failures

Public Goods and Market Failures

A Critical Examination

Edited by
Tyler Cowen

Routledge
Taylor & Francis Group

LONDON AND NEW YORK

Originally published in 1988 by The Cato Institute, George Mason University Press.

First published 1992 by Transaction Publishers

Published 2018 by Routledge
2 Park Square, Milton Park, Abingdon, Oxon OX14 4RN
52 Vanderbilt Avenue, New York, NY 10017, USA

Routledge is an imprint of the Taylor & Francis Group,
an informa business

Library of Congress Catalog Number: 91-23739

Library of Congress Cataloging-in-Publication Data

Theory of market failure
    Public goods and market failures: a critical examination/[edited by] Tyler Cowen.
    p.   cm.
    Reprint. Originally published: The theory of market failure. Fairfax, Va.: George Mason University Press, c1988.
    Includes bibliographical references.
    ISBN: 1-56000-570-X (pbk.)
    1. Public goods. 2. Externalities (Economics).   I. Cowen, Tyler.   II. Title.
[HB846.5.T46   1991]
363—dc20   91-23739
                                                                                 CIP

ISBN 13: 978-1-56000-570-4 (hbk)

Contents

Introduction

1. Public Goods and Externalities: Old and New Perspectives

Tyler Cowen

The assertion of market failure is probably the most important argument for governmental intervention. At one time or another nearly every sector of the American economy has been branded as a market failure. Such assertions are usually based upon the theory of public goods and externalities, a central part of modern welfare economics and the theory of economic policy.

This book contains many of the developments of Paul Samuelson's theory of public goods and externalities. The common feature of those developments is that they challenge the market failure conclusion that many economists and policymakers have drawn from Samuelson's theory. Throughout the 1960s and the 1970s the doctrine of market failure was questioned by such prominent economists as Ronald Coase, Harold Demsetz, and James Buchanan. Those writings, however, had never been collected in a single volume. (Since the completion of the manuscript for this volume a number of important new articles on public goods theory have appeared. See Oakland 1987 and Cornes and Sandler 1986 for a survey and analysis of recent developments.)

The articles in this volume were selected for their readability and their likely impact on future research. The volume contains both theoretical articles and case studies covering the private provision of public goods. Although many of them are recognized classics, a number of lesser-known articles (and two previously unpublished papers) were included in order to fill gaps in the literature.

No attempt was made to collect the numerous criticisms and defenses of public sector methods of providing public goods. Such issues form the focus of public choice economics, which, despite its importance, is beyond the scope of this book. It is thus difficult

1

to draw policy conclusions from the contents of this volume, for it examines only one method of public goods provision: the market. Deriving a complete picture would require comparing public and private sector alternatives.

Introduction to Section 1

The book opens with two classic statements of the theory of market failure: Paul A. Samuelson's "The Pure Theory of Public Expenditure" (1954) and Francis M. Bator's "The Anatomy of Market Failure" (1958). These articles are considered landmarks because they clearly and concisely introduced the fundamentals of the market failure argument to modern economic theory. The key concepts in the Samuelson and Bator articles are discussed very briefly below. Readers who are already familiar with the fundamentals of market failure theory are advised to skip to the introduction to section 2.

Relevant Terms

Externalities

An externality exists whenever one individual's actions affect the utility of another individual. Positive externalities are those that benefit others; negative externalities are those that make others worse off. Improving the fire safety of one's house may confer a positive externality on one's neighbors, for example, whereas painting one's house pink may confer a negative externality.

The notion of externality can be further refined by assigning externalities to various categories: pecuniary or nonpecuniary, marginal or inframarginal, Pareto-relevant or Pareto-irrelevant, and so on. See Buchanan and Stubblebine 1962 as well as the 1958 Bator article reprinted in this volume for expositions of those (and other) important distinctions.

Transactions Costs

Transactions costs receive a number of different definitions in the relevant literature (see, for example, Coase 1960 and the 1979 Carl Dahlman article reprinted in this volume), many of which conflict. In this discussion, transactions costs are defined as any obstacles to market exchanges that interfere with or discourage the process of transacting. Examples include the costs of writing contracts, the costs of finding parties with whom to trade, the costs of enforcing agreements, and the costs of bargaining. Many transactions costs are informational in character.

In the presence of transactions costs, externalities are often considered a source of market failure. If a shipping company erects a lighthouse for its ships, other shipping companies will benefit from the use of the light. In the absence of transactions costs, therefore, an entrepreneur who wishes to build a lighthouse will contract with all of the relevant ship owners to ensure that they will pay their share of the expenditures for the lighthouse. If transactions costs prevent such an arrangement, however, a lighthouse may not be built, even though its benefits would exceed its costs.

Public Goods

A public good involves two elements: nonexcludability and nonrivalrous consumption.

"Nonexcludability" refers to the impossibility of preventing non-paying individuals from enjoying the benefits of a good or service; the term is used to characterize an externality. A lighthouse is a classic example of a nonexcludable public good. Each shipping company owner knows that if another shipping company erects a lighthouse, it will effectively serve his ships as well. Thus, each ship owner will likely try to shirk paying his share of the costs and thereby "free-ride" off the efforts of others. Even if the benefits of a lighthouse would exceed the costs, the market may not provide it, because there is no way of excluding nonpayers from enjoying those benefits. Thus, markets will underproduce goods and services whose provision would entail positive externalities. Likewise, goods and services whose provision would entail negative externalities will be overproduced in the presence of transactions costs.

The revelation of preferences, another problem in the provision of public goods, is sometimes classified under the heading of nonexcludability and is sometimes considered simply an instance of imperfect information. Many economists, including Coase (1960), interpret the difficulty as a transactions cost. If shipping companies are bargaining over the possibility of jointly producing lighthouses, each company may underrepresent the benefits it would receive from the lighthouses in order to lower its share of the total costs. Preference revelation as a general problem of choice mechanisms is discussed in Tideman and Tullock 1976 and in Craven 1983.

The scope of the externalities/nonexcludability issue is vast. Nearly every concern of economic policy, from environmental considerations to research and development, involves externality problems. No one would claim that every instance of an externality warrants state intervention. There is no doubt, however, that the existence of externalities is one of the most powerful arguments for public sector involvement in the provision of public goods.

"Nonrivalrous consumption" refers to cases wherein individuals' ability to consume a good or service is not diminished by allowing additional individuals to consume it. A movie theater provides an example of nonrivalrous consumption. Up to the point of crowding, it is possible to allow additional individuals to enter a theater and watch the movie without infringing upon the consumption of those already in the audience. Because one individual's consumption of a movie (unlike, say, a banana or a pair of eyeglasses) does not prevent another individual from consuming the same good, it is nonrivalrous. Of course, nonrivalrous consumption may be a matter of degree—virtually all public goods experience crowding at sufficiently high levels of use.

The theory of public goods and externalities implies that nonrivalrous consumption may give rise to pricing inefficiencies even when it is possible to exclude those who do not pay for a good or service (however, see Demsetz 1964 and 1970, reprinted in this volume and discussed below). Assume that it is possible to allow additional individuals to enter the movie theater at zero or negligible marginal social cost. Charging a profit-maximizing price might exclude some of them. If the profit-maximizing price is $4, then anyone who would like to see the movie but is not willing to pay $4 will be "inefficiently" excluded.

Like externalities, nonrivalrous consumption is not a problem in the absence of transactions costs. If transactions such as a movie theater's were costless, a private firm could charge each individual a separate entrance price just slightly below his marginal valuation (Demsetz 1970).

Among the industries whose goods and services are often considered to entail some degree of nonrivalrous consumption are transportation, communications, and public utilities. Many economists argue that such industries' pricing inefficiencies can be alleviated by having the government supply the goods and services at marginal cost and financing them through taxation.

Introduction to Section 2

The articles in section 2 are developments of the theory of public goods and externalities stated by Samuelson and Bator. Most of those developments raise possibilities for the private production of public goods, and many of them open the policy implications of public goods theory to serious criticism or caveat.

Kenneth D. Goldin's "Equal Access vs. Selective Access: A Critique of Public Goods Theory" (1977) focuses on the fact that most (if not all) goods can be supplied in two different ways. The first method, which involves what Goldin calls "equal access," allows all consumers of the good to enjoy it free of charge. Examples include a concert in a large public park and a police patrolman walking the beat. In each case, all consumers have equal access to the service in question (music or safety) and externality problems exist. The second method, which involves what Goldin calls "selective access," permits nonpayers to be excluded. Music can be supplied by a private recital, and safety can be supplied by locks and burglar alarms.

Goldin's article surveys many of the classic examples of public goods and describes how it might be possible to supply those goods through selective access. If it is indeed possible, then the free-rider problem loses some of its importance and it becomes necessary to compare the costs of equal and selective access. The provision of goods through selective access must be cost-effective for Goldin's point to have policy relevance. Goldin's article can thus be read as a program for empirical research on the private provision of public goods. What are the costs of the various institutional structures that underlie the provision of such goods and services? Many of the case studies in the final section of this book are directed at that question.

Goldin also draws an interesting parallel between private and public goods. If a public good cannot be adequately produced by the market, he maintains, it is only because the current state of technology makes the exclusion of nonpayers economically unfeasible. The production of private goods, however, suffers from an analogous problem—at certain points in time the production of light bulbs and television sets was either impossible or too costly because the necessary technologies were not available.

One of the frontier areas of economic theory is to incorporate technological change into the comparative institutional analysis of public goods. Although Goldin's article represents a step in that direction, the area is a fertile one for future research. The significant role of technology in determining the publicness or privateness of a good is well known. New recording technologies have made radio broadcasts more "public," whereas sophisticated building-specific sprinkler systems have made fire protection more "private." Computer software is another example of a good that successively becomes more or less public in response to changes in the relative ingenuity of its buyers and sellers. No sooner do computer buffs develop new means of pirating software than computer companies develop new safeguards to prevent piracy.

The importance of comparative institutional analysis can be summarized in the following principle: even if a selective access mode of production is very costly at a given moment, one must be cautious about drawing long-run policy conclusions from that fact. The unavailability of a suitably cost-effective exclusion technology may be due to the public sector's monopolization of the provision of the good or service. Boudewijn Bouckaert of the University of Ghent is currently developing the interesting hypothesis that the "publicness" of many of the goods and services supplied by the public sector is a *result* of their public provision, not a cause of it (Bouckaert 1987). Public sector monopolization may have stifled the incentive to develop exclusion technologies. When we examine the nature of such goods and services, their public provision appears necessary because exclusion technologies are either too costly or completely unimaginable (just as exclusion technologies for many modern private goods—and the goods themselves—were unimaginable in the 18th century).

The second article in section 2, Earl R. Brubaker's "Free Ride, Free Revelation, or Golden Rule?" (1975), also deals with nonexcludability problems. Whereas Goldin discusses achieving exclusion through various technologies, Brubaker points out that simply not producing a good is always a means of exclusion. The possibility that a good will not be produced might give an entrepreneur sufficient leverage to collect preproduction commitments to pay for the good. Brubaker's article largely consists of an examination of that possibility.

Before characterizing preproduction contracting schemes, Brubaker questions the free-rider hypothesis in view of the frequent occurrence of cooperative behavior. Such behavior may be due to altruism, ethical beliefs, conventions, ignorance, or even subtle forms of self-interest (see the 1981 Andrew Schotter excerpt reprinted in this volume and discussed below for an examination of some of those factors). When the free-rider hypothesis was tested in laboratory experiments (Smith 1982), free-riding behavior proved to have considerably less impact than public goods theory leads us to expect. Brubaker thus questions whether the assumption that such behavior is universal ought to be reflected in public goods theory.

Brubaker's paper outlines a method that might be used to overcome free-rider problems. Assume that an entrepreneur wants to build a dam but would have no way of charging for its benefits. The entrepreneur might offer the following deal: if a certain percentage of the community will precommit themselves to contributing a minimum payment for the dam, he will undertake production. If enough signatures are not collected, the dam will not be built and no one will have to pay.

Given a limiting case wherein the entrepreneur can truly precommit himself because everyone in the community places the same value on the dam and the entrepreneur knows that marginal valuation, an effective precommitment contract is easy to design. The entrepreneur will simply refuse to produce the dam until everyone signs the contract, which will give everyone an incentive to do so. If any individual holds out, the dam will not be produced and he will be worse off, whereas if he signs the contract, he will receive dam services whose value will exceed the service fee he will be required to pay.

Problems arise, however, if individuals in the community place different valuations on the dam and the entrepreneur does not have perfect information about their preferences. Assume, for instance, that 1 percent of the individuals in the community do not value the dam, but the entrepreneur cannot identify them. He therefore cannot require that everyone sign the contract, because 1 percent would refuse and the potentially profitable dam would not be built. If the entrepreneur requires that only 99 percent of the individuals in the community sign the contract, another problem arises: the preference revelation problem. Even those who want the dam might attempt to pass themselves off as part of the indifferent 1 percent in order to shirk payment. Again it is possible that everyone will try to shirk and that an insufficient number will sign the contract. This possibility may be one reason that Brubaker questions the validity of a very strict interpretation of the free-rider hypothesis: that individuals will always free-ride as much as possible.

Of course, if the entrepreneur has complete information about the valuations of the potential consumers and there is thus no preference revelation problem, exclusion will again be feasible provided that transactions costs do not prevent him from drawing up a more complicated contract. This suggests that exclusion is an informational problem—given perfect information and costless contracting, the Brubaker method will always be effective. One of the most interesting research questions is to what extent a Brubaker solution can be implemented in the presence of imperfect information and transactions costs. Ethical and altruistic motives, social and community pressures, and economic incentives (such as tying abstention from free-riding to participation in some form of "club") might all serve to encourage the supply of public goods.

The assumption of a multiplicity of entrepreneurs, each offering his own deal to the community, creates complications. On one hand, the competition among the entrepreneurs might split the community and prevent each of them from garnering a sufficiently large number of signatures. On the other hand, the entrepreneurs might have an agreement to pool their resources once the signatures were collected. Linking each entrepreneur's share in the profits to the number of precommitment signatures he gathers would provide him with a strong incentive to discover new ways of inducing preference revelation. One can even imagine next-door neighbors running to each other's homes, trying to collect signatures in return for shares of stock in the enterprise. Brubaker does not discuss the possibility of multiple entrepreneurs, but that possibility and the resultant complications may eventually be incorporated in developments of the theory of precontracting. An extension of Brubaker's analysis can be found in Schmidtz 1987.

The third article in section 2, Harold Demsetz's "The Private Production of Public Goods" (1970), is considered one of the classics of modern public goods theory. Unlike Goldin and Brubaker, however, Demsetz examines the problem of pricing inefficiency in situations where it is possible to prevent nonpayers from consuming public goods. A movie theater and a road are examples. He points out that it is possible for an entrepreneur to charge each consumer a price set slightly below that consumer's marginal valuation of a good. In that case, there will not be inefficient exclusion, and the entrepreneur will be able to collect revenue and perhaps turn a profit.

In practice, price discrimination is unlikely to be perfect. Movie theaters do not charge a different price for each consumer because they do not have enough information to discern everyone's marginal valuation of a given movie. (In addition, legal restrictions significantly curtail their ability to implement price discrimination.) Many movie theaters do, however, charge lower prices for children and senior citizens. That can be considered a partial implementation of a Demsetzian solution. If the marginal valuations of film viewers were thought to vary with other social categories, movie theaters would attempt to identify those groups in order to develop additional means of price-discriminating. The last 50 years of antitrust law have demonstrated that a virtually unlimited number of ingenious forms of price discrimination are available to the entrepreneur who can segment his market and prevent resale.

After the publication of Demsetz 1970 many economists concluded that nonexcludability is generally the only serious problem in the provision of public goods. That conclusion, however, was challenged by such economists as Borcherding (1978) and Ekelund and Hulett (1973), who drew upon the earlier arguments of Samuelson (1969). Samuelson points out that in trying to charge each consumer a price approaching his marginal valuation, an entrepreneur faces a game-theoretic problem. Each consumer knows that if he refuses the offer (even though it would benefit him), the entrepreneur may make him a better offer. After all, it would cost the entrepreneur little or nothing to let him into the movie theater. So if an initial offer of $5 is refused, the entrepreneur may lower his price to $4, then to $3, and so on. Not only does each consumer know that, but each entrepreneur knows it, and each knows that the other knows. What will be the result?

Samuelson 1969 suggests that a substantial quantity of resources will be wasted in costly bargaining between consumers and entrepreneurs. Unfortunately, the topic does not receive sufficient attention elsewhere in the public goods literature. Many authors of articles in the game theory tradition (such as Schelling 1960, Lewis 1969, and Herzenberger 1978) have argued that social conventions, imperfect information, frictions, focal points, tacit understandings, or "first mover advantages" may lead to stable equilibria in situations or games that appear unstable. Those insights, however, have never been adequately applied to the problem of providing public goods.

The second Demsetz article in this volume, "The Exchange and Enforcement of Property Rights" (1964), contains intriguing suggestions for the private provision of public goods, two of which involve tying arrangements and the nature of marginal cost pricing.

A tying arrangement links the provision of a private good to the purchase of a public good. Eighteenth-century British lighthouses (Coase 1974, reprinted in section 3 of this volume) furnish a classic example. Although lighthouses are a public good (and suffer from both nonexcludability and nonrivalrous consumption), port space is a private good. It was thus possible to charge ships for their use of a lighthouse by charging them for their use of the port. In such cases, free-riding behavior may still exist—some ships may use a lighthouse's services without docking at the port. Nonetheless, in the classic case that Coase discusses, the port tolls were more than sufficient to pay for the lighthouses.

Shopping malls and condominiums are other examples of the use of tying arrangements for public goods supply. In the case of shopping malls, public goods such as streets and security are paid for through the provision of private goods such as shoes, clothing, and books. The stores in a mall bargain with the mall owner to split the proceeds derived from the complementarity of the private and public goods. In the case of condominiums, the private good is living space and the public goods may range from fire protection to well-kept recreation facilities. The provision of such public goods is reflected in the rent or selling price of a condominium.

One of the most serious problems with tying arrangements is that they are vulnerable to being disrupted by outsiders' entry into the market for the private good. If an entrepreneur attempts to tie the provision of fire protection to the purchase of oranges, a higher price will have to be charged for oranges, which will ensure that the arrangement will not last. Some other entrepreneur will invade the orange market and sell nontied oranges for a lower price. Consumers who want oranges and fire protection can buy the lower-priced oranges and free-ride on fire protection.

There has never been a systematic effort to ascertain the exact conditions under which public goods tying arrangements will be both stable and beneficial. It is apparent that the tied products must be complementary in some way (the streets near a mall, for instance, provide shoppers with convenient access to the private goods being sold). In addition, barriers to entry into the market for the private good seem favorable to tying arrangements. If every store that wishes to enter a shopping center is permitted to do so, a tying arrangement may not be sustainable. The entire topic deserves further investigation, to which the theory of contestable markets in Baumol 1982 may be applicable. Baumol outlines the conditions under which multiproduct firms will be invulnerable to threats of entry from potential competitors. Klein (1987) also analyzes a number of the relevant issues.

As noted earlier, the theory of public goods and externalities implies that if a good is characterized by nonrivalrous consumption, allowing additional individuals to consume it entails zero marginal cost. Demsetz's arguments (1964; 1970) imply that this is only true in the presence of perfect information. Otherwise, allowing additional individuals to consume a good free of charge results in the abandonment of the price system in that sphere of activity. Since the publication of Hayek 1945, the role of prices in communicating information has been well known. In the provision of public goods as well as private goods, sacrificing such information may entail significant costs.

Assume that the owner of a movie theater eliminates ticket sales because he can finance his operation through lump-sum taxation. Even in the absence of crowding and congestion, admitting additional people to the theater will not involve zero marginal social cost. In forsaking the use of the price system, the owner has forsaken valuable information: How much money should be invested in the renovation and maintenance of the theater? Which movies are blockbusters and which are bombs? Although ticket sales and profit and loss statements are not the only sources of answers to such questions, they are among the most important sources. Profit and loss statements also tell the theater owner whether he is putting his resources to their most highly valued uses. Perhaps it would be better to convert the theater to a two-screen facility or even close it down altogether and open a racquetball club in the building.

In light of such considerations, the case for marginal cost pricing (in the narrow sense in which it is defined by the public goods theory) becomes less persuasive. In a world of change and imperfect information, there are significant costs to not using the price mechanism. Any discussion of the inefficiencies of private sector provision should take that factor into account (Minasian 1964).

The next selection in section 2, an excerpt from Andrew Schotter's book *The Economic Theory of Social Institutions* (1981), summarizes much of the literature that investigates the role of institutions in the solution of coordination problems. Schotter begins by discussing the state-of-nature method utilized by Nozick (1974) and Hayek's analysis of the invisible hand or spontaneous order. The latter holds that many social institutions arose spontaneously and were not planned or designed. The state-of-nature analysis starts by assuming that such institutions do not exist and attempts to demonstrate how self-interested actions by individuals could give rise to them in the absence of any overall plan.

Each of the social institutions analyzed by that method is shown to have arisen from a set of rules that would solve or alleviate recurrent coordination problems with a minimum amount of resources. Among Schotter's examples are the evolution of money, the evolution of the seven-day week, and the evolution of cooperative solutions to the prisoner's dilemma game.

In his discussion of the prisoner's dilemma, a game-theoretic problem, Schotter examines the role of coordination points in recurrent situations. The critical feature of the prisoner's dilemma game is that each player will be best off if his opponent cooperates and he is able to cheat or free-ride. Because of that feature of the game, each player may be afraid to cooperate lest his opponent free-ride. One possible result is that the players will be unable to coordinate their actions and both will cheat, which will make both worse off. Schotter's central point is that the existence of an equilibrium mode of behavior or a convention will help individuals avoid the recurrence of the inefficient outcomes of cheating or free-riding. Such conventions may be ethical precepts, regularities imposed by institutions, or simply fixed rules of thumb for individual behavior.

Robert Axelrod (1984; excerpted in section 3 of this volume) has run a number of computer tournaments at which some computers were programmed to abide by cooperative conventions and others were not. In the overwhelming majority of cases, the most successful programs were the ones that allowed considerable scope for cooperative behavior. That result can be interpreted as evidence that cooperative, non-free-riding behavior has long-run efficiencies that will foster its survival in a market economy. As in Axelrod's simulations, individuals who free-ride may find themselves the target of free-riding behavior from other individuals.

The summaries and extensions in Schotter 1981 are crucial for fleshing out many of the issues discussed in other papers in this volume. For instance, in the presence of change and imperfect information, some form of institutional coordination is required for successful implementation of both the Demsetz 1970 and Brubaker 1975 models for the private production of public goods. Schotter's analysis indicates that conventions and rules evolved through an invisible hand process can generate cost-effective market solutions to such coordination problems.

In addition, conventions and rules may place limitations upon bargaining and haggling, thus diminishing the game-theoretic problems that Samuelson (1969) attributes to the Demsetz model. Rules and conventions may also play a crucial role in eliminating the free-rider problem. Even if free-riding is economically profitable in the short run, it may violate rules and conventions and may therefore result in either short-run psychic inconveniences (such as a guilty conscience) or long-run monetary losses. The latter, for example, may arise if the actions of one individual set a precedent for the actions of others. Another possibility is that individuals will follow rules of thumb that call for cooperating with cooperators and not cooperating with free-riders.

The Schotter 1981 excerpt serves as an introduction to the literature on invisible hand mechanisms and coordination games. For more detailed discussions of those topics, see Schotter's excellent bibliography.

The next two selections in section 2 of this volume discuss the nature of local public goods. Because such goods, by definition, can be provided to only a segment of a nation or community, determining which individuals will receive them becomes part of the economic problem. Once club or community membership becomes endogenous, many of Samuelson's conclusions do not hold.

Charles M. Tiebout's "A Pure Theory of Local Expenditures" (1956) examines a case in which each community supplies local public goods to all of its citizens. Although such an arrangement may seem to involve all of the inefficiencies that usually result when public goods theory is applied, Tiebout argues that this need not be the case.

Tiebout claims that in the presence of perfect mobility and a sufficiently large number of communities, a decentralized system is capable of achieving Paretian optimality. The essence of Tiebout's model is simple: if the mountain (a public good) cannot come to Mohammed, then Mohammed must go to the mountain. Attempting to produce "mountains" for specific groups of Mohammeds will entail all of the usual inefficiencies. Instead, communities can simply offer bundles of public goods, and individuals can express their preferences by voting with their feet.

The Tiebout model avoids the preference revelation problem; an individual's preferences are revealed by his choice of location. It also avoids the free-rider problem; those who choose to belong to a given community are subject to the taxes or user fees that finance the provision of goods. Nor is pricing inefficiency a problem. If an individual is inefficiently excluded from the use of a public good or service, he can simply move to a community where that exclusion is not practiced.

Many economic theorists were quick to criticize the Tiebout model because of the extreme conditions that it assumes. When the assumption of perfect mobility is eliminated, for instance, it is difficult for a set of decentralized communities to attain the Pareto optimal solution. Stiglitz (1977) also points out other problems with the Tiebout equilibria, including economies and diseconomies of scale, the potentially large number of communities required, and potential matching problems—having the wrong groups in the wrong communities. Stiglitz demonstrates that the optimal reshuffling might require either that everyone move at the same time or that one group compensate another for relocating.

Tiebout's article does not hold out the promise that Paretian optimality can be attained in the real world. Nonetheless, individual mobility may play an important role in alleviating many of the public goods problems raised by Samuelson and may often provide a second-best solution. The possibility of implementing Tiebout's solution does not arise in Samuelson's model because the public goods considered in the latter are national or global, which implies that there is only one community and that it has a fixed membership. Most real-world public goods, however, are local.

Most economists, including Tiebout himself, have envisioned Tiebout's communities as city and state governments. Buchanan and Goetz (1972), however, offer the intriguing suggestion that Tiebout's model is better suited to analyses of public goods provision through proprietary communities. Perhaps condominiums are exemplary. For one thing, they may be a case in which the assumptions of large numbers of communities and individuals' mobility have greater scope. More important, however, a condominium owner has an entrepreneurial incentive to provide innovative and efficient packages of public goods for the residents. A municipal government, on the other hand, does not have a direct profit incentive to provide the best package of public goods possible. In the absence of perfect mobility, that difference may be crucial.

Whereas Tiebout's article considers local communities, the next article in section 2, James M. Buchanan's "An Economic Theory of Clubs" (1965), discusses private, voluntary associations formed for the purpose of providing public goods. Trade associations, lecture series, golf clubs, charities, and swimming clubs are all examples.

In Buchanan's model, as in Tiebout's, the critical factor is the relationship between the provision of a public good and membership conditions. The Samuelson and Bator articles in section 1 describe two problems that create inefficiencies in the provision of public goods: nonexcludability and nonrivalrous consumption. The work of Tiebout and Buchanan focuses on another problem: obtaining the best mix and number of individuals in each community or club. That is one of the most important considerations in a comparative institutional study of public goods provision, but many public goods models obscure the issue.

Shopping malls and condominiums may be examples of the private sector provision of public goods in which the efficiency gains from optimal groupings outweigh the efficiency losses from nonexcludability and nonrivalrous consumption. Such efficient groupings of individuals and businesses may yield significant savings and flexibility in the production of the public goods.

The driving force behind such arrangements is the private entrepreneur (Kirzner 1973), who has a profit incentive to discover and implement the most effective combinations of resources and consumers possible. The formation of groups does not require a once-and-for-all allocation of resources. Rather, the requirement is for institutions to produce groups that are flexible and responsive to change, because changes in tastes and technology will continually alter the optimal composition and size of such groups.

The theories of group formation provided by Tiebout and Buchanan imply that user fees or prices for local public goods may actually be more efficient than lump-sum taxation (which supposedly excludes no one, but see Cowen and High 1987). If it is assumed that the optimal community is fairly large and contains both child-plentiful and childless families, that heterogeneity may lead to economies of scale elsewhere. If education is financed through lump-sum taxation or any other method in which payment is not directly related to use, childless individuals will have an incentive to leave the community. In the presence of interregional mobility, even lump-sum taxation will affect the real allocation of resources.

The departure of childless individuals will cause the community to fall below its optimal size and lose its optimal mixture, which will make everyone worse off. Financing education through user fees, however, may involve the pricing inefficiencies discussed by Samuelson and Bator. Those losses may be outweighed by the gains achieved by not encouraging childless individuals to leave the community.

The inability or unwillingness of the private sector to use the supposed "first best" pricing scheme, marginal cost pricing, cannot be interpreted as prima facie evidence of the scheme's inefficiency. Market prices may be one of the means used to achieve efficient group allocations and reshufflings. Both Tiebout's article and Buchanan's have given rise to enormous bodies of literature. For an examination of responses to Tiebout's work, see Zodrow 1983; for a survey of recent developments in the theory of clubs, see Cornes and Sandler 1986.

The final article in section 2, Carl J. Dahlman's "The Problem of Externality" (1979), presents a methodological critique of assertions of market failure. Coase (1960) argues that in the absence of transactions costs, externalities are not a source of market failure, because the relevant parties can bargain their way to the optimum. That argument, however, does not eliminate the possibility that the presence of transactions costs should be considered a source of market failure.

Dahlman's article questions the validity of citing transactions costs in market failure arguments by examining the nature of such costs. Although transactions costs can prevent the attainment of mutually beneficial trades, market failure is not necessarily a result. Transportation costs can also prevent the attainment of mutually beneficial trades, but no one argues that they are a source of market failure. One could push the argument further and claim that the existence of any sort of cost can prevent the achievement of a superior solution. Why are transactions costs singled out as an indication of market failure?

One could also argue that transactions costs are different from other costs because governments and other central authorities can sometimes lower or eradicate them by reassigning property rights. That assertion, however, begs the question, as Dahlman demonstrates, in an argument extended by Levy (1985) and Toumanoff (1984). If a central authority could make everyone better off (and no one worse off) simply by reassigning property rights, then why has the reassignment not taken place? Either it would make someone worse off (perhaps agents of the government itself), or it would be hindered by transactions costs. In either case we are back where we started.

Dahlman's argument, along with Levy's and Toumanoff's extensions, illustrates a tension between positive and normative economics. Most economists believe that universal rationality must be postulated in explanatory and predictive theories. Invoking that postulate, however, may make it impossible to claim that observed economic outcomes are ever inefficient. At the moment of choice that produced such an outcome, each actor was engaged in *ex ante* optimization—no individual could have done better for himself, nor could the system as a whole have done better. If a Pareto improvement had been possible, it would have been achieved. If it was prevented by transactions costs, the observed outcome was nonetheless efficient relative to the constraints in force at the time.

The argument summarized above is sometimes attributed by noneconomists to a naive, Panglossian optimism and mischaracterized as an assertion that everything is for the best. But the view that observed outcomes are always optimally efficient does not imply a corresponding attitude of moral approval. Consider the old anecdote about an inveterate optimist who, like Candide's tutor, asserted that we are living in the best of all possible worlds, whereupon an equally inveterate pessimist expressed complete agreement.

That anecdote is an important reminder that optimality can only be defined in relation to a set of constraints. An outcome might be optimal by one such standard but undesirable by another.

Introduction to Section 3

Because a comprehensive examination of the private production of public goods involves not only economic theory but also empirical evidence, case studies have been included in this volume. The following discussion offers a brief overview of how some of the research presented in section 3 is related to the theoretical arguments presented in the first two sections.

The first selection in section 3, a chapter from Robert Axelrod's *The Evolution of Cooperation* (1984), is discussed in the introduction to section 2 because, as noted there, Axelrod's simulations of the prisoner's dilemma game tend to support the Schotter 1981 excerpt's conclusions about the efficacy of cooperative, non-free-riding behavior.

The next case study in section 3, Ronald H. Coase's "The Lighthouse in Economics" (1974), is probably the best-known instance of public goods theory revisionism. As Coase points out, numerous economists, from John Stuart Mill to Samuelson, have considered lighthouses the paradigm of a public good whose efficient provision requires state intervention. Coase, however, demonstrates that the private sector in Britain had been adequately supplying lighthouses since the 17th century. He notes:

> The early history shows, that contrary to the belief of many economists, a lighthouse service can be provided by private enterprise. . . . The lighthouses were built, operated, financed and owned by private individuals. . . . The role of the government was limited to the establishment and enforcement of property rights in the lighthouse.

As mentioned earlier, the case discussed in Coase 1974 may be of special interest to those wishing to pursue Demsetz's analysis of tying arrangements in public goods provision (1964; reprinted in section 2)—payment for the use of British lighthouses was exacted by collecting tolls in nearby ports.

The next case study, Steven N. S. Cheung's "The Fable of the Bees: An Economic Investigation" (1973), is also a well-known piece of theory debunking. Both Pigou (1932) and Bator (1958; reprinted in section 1) claim that the externalities affecting bee-keepers and apple growers are a source of market failure. They argue that an apple grower benefits from the presence of bees because they pollinate his apple blossoms, which leads to an underinvestment in beekeeping because the benefit cannot be internalized.

Like Coase, Cheung undertook a detailed study of relevant institutions. He found that in Washington State, a leading apple-growing state, there was a long history of contractual arrangements (both explicit and implicit) between apple growers and beekeepers. Through those contracts, which provided for beekeepers to be compensated for the marginal contribution that bees made to the apple crop, the externality problems were largely overcome.

Cheung also provides an interesting analysis of a related problem: the externalities that an apple grower received from the "hired bees" of other apple growers. The apple growers made an implicit agreement that each would keep the same number of bees in order to prevent some growers from free-riding off the bees of others (an externalities problem due to the mobility of bees). Apple growers who did not abide by that convention were ostracized and subjected to "inconvenient treatment" by the others. As a result, free-riding was not a serious problem, which can be considered an example of how social conventions discourage free-riding behavior, as discussed in Schotter 1981.

Cheung's article is followed by two chapters from a 1980 book by Robert W. Poole, Jr., *Cutting Back City Hall*. Poole, an acknowledged expert on local government, has long advocated the privatization of many municipal services, and his book offers evidence that such privatization is cost-effective. One of the chapters reprinted in section 3 of this volume covers fire protection, the other leisure and recreation.

Poole argues that most of the fire protection service in the United States is supplied by the private sector. Among the examples he cites are volunteer fire departments, subscription services, private contractors, and fire suppression devices such as fire extinguishers. Poole's evidence suggests that those alternatives are usually more efficient and innovative than municipal fire protection services.

Poole's discussion of fire prevention and suppression devices may be of special interest in light of the discussion of equal access vs. selective access in Goldin 1977 (reprinted in section 2). Fire extinguishers, building sprinkler systems, and other technological advances are considerably less "public" than fire trucks and hydrants.

Poole's chapter on leisure and recreation discusses libraries, parks, and museums. In each case, Poole maintains that it is possible to charge fees for admission and to exclude nonpayers. Even in the absence of the nonexcludability problem associated with public goods provision, though, pricing inefficiencies may exist if consumption is nonrivalrous. Poole argues, however, that the private sector has many ways of implementing a Demsetzian solution, price discrimination. He discusses such possibilities as maintaining differential fee structures, subsidizing fees for low-income groups through charity, adjusting the fee structure according to a neighborhood's income level, and accepting labor or equipment donations in lieu of fees.

The final two case studies were previously unpublished. In the first, "Private Solutions to Conservation Problems" (1988), environmental consultant Robert J. Smith examines private ownership as a means of species conservation. Smith points out that this alternative has already enjoyed considerable success in practice—one might ask, why were buffaloes threatened with extinction but not cattle? Smith also details private conservation projects that were made possible by the creation of property rights in scarce resources. The intriguing discussion of a private turtle farm in the Cayman Islands is perhaps the most memorable section of his article.

Although Smith concentrates on endangered species, his work is applicable to nearly all "common pool" problems. Without private ownership of a scarce resource, there is no incentive to choose an optimal rate of use for that resource or to take steps to maintain or enhance its quality. If private ownership is allowed, however, there is a profit incentive to take such measures.

This implies that many public goods and externalities problems are actually property rights problems. In the absence of property rights, for instance, each individual has an incentive to hunt down or trap endangered species as quickly as possible. Maintaining those species will prove unprofitable because the benefits of doing so will quickly be exhausted by other hunters and trappers. That external effect, however, can be internalized by allowing individual ownership of animal colonies and other resource stocks.

Those insights are most commonly associated with the "new resource economics" of such economists as Terry Anderson, John Baden, and Richard Stroup. Among the issues to which the property rights theory of externalities has been applied are strip mining, timber and water resources, and pollution. (See Baden and Stroup 1983 for a survey of the relevant literature.)

In "The Private Supply of Education: Some Historical Evidence" (1988), Jack High and Jerome Ellig argue that in both Great Britain and the United States the private sector was providing an adequate supply of education before the advent of school subsidies and compulsory education. Afterward, unsubsidized private education often proved to be a viable alternative to tax-supported public education, largely because it was more flexible, diverse, and consumer-oriented.

The work of High and Ellig can be considered an application of the theory of clubs stated in Buchanan 1965 (reprinted in section 2). Even if private education did not completely internalize the external benefits of education, it may have led to the formation of "clubs" that were more flexible, diverse, and efficient than their public sector counterparts.

New Developments

The private production of public goods is a viable and important research topic. Economists who address the theory of market failure, however, are faced with the challenge of moving beyond refinements of models that have already been developed. In the next several years two hitherto-neglected topics may form the basis of new developments: information as a public good and institutional and constitutional structures as public goods.

Information as a public good is discussed in two articles reprinted in this volume, Goldin 1977 and Demsetz 1964, but neither draws out all of the difficult issues involved. The literature on the economics of information, on the other hand, is not explicitly concerned with the private production of public goods.

Introducing information as a public good into standard economic models leads to enormous complications. Because the production of any private good requires information about market-related factors (such as supply, demand, and production techniques), the production of a public good—information—can be considered a prerequisite for the production of all private goods. Thus, public goods theory and private goods theory may be far more intertwined than the literature suggests.

That difficulty cannot be resolved simply by acknowledging the production function; the maximization problems generally posited by public and private goods theory cannot even be defined without specifying informational prerequisites. Most formal analyses of such problems include the requirement that preferences and the state of technology, for instance, be well defined and known to all the relevant individuals.

If information and knowledge are both the result of an endogenous process of discovery and communication (Lavoie 1985; Arrow and Hurwicz 1977), maximization problems cannot be considered elemental to a theory of market failure or market success. Such problems are themselves the outcome of the prevailing state of knowledge, and accounting for that state of knowledge through a standard maximization process might result in an infinite regress (Winter 1975).

Moreover, the production of both public and private goods involves a simultaneity with the generation of information—one of the "commodities" being generated is also one of the determinants or definers of the usual maximization problems. Thus, both private and public goods production may partake of a class of problems involving self-generating orders for which there are more unknowns than determinants or equations (Hayek 1973; Lavoie 1985; Cowen 1985; Nelson and Winter 1982). That approach to economic problems is still in its infancy and has not yet been applied to public goods problems. A better understanding of self-generating orders may someday permit more specific policy conclusions to be drawn from public goods theory. Although the existing models illuminate various facets of the public goods problem, many of the variables that they take as given (such as the state of knowledge) are among the most important determinants of institutional success or failure.

As noted earlier, the second topic on which new developments may be based is institutional and constitutional structures as public goods. All of the selections in this book simply assume the existence or nonexistence of markets. Yet doing so does not answer the crucial question of why some societies come to rely largely upon markets, others develop a mixed economy, and still others turn to centralized planning. The practice of taking most institutional or constitutional structures as given has hampered economists' ability to understand the evolution of those structures.

Economists who wish to examine laws, constitutions, or property rights assignments as public goods must go beyond existing public goods theory. Instead of taking an institutional structure as given, they must posit a situation in which the structure and its results interact. Significant progress has already been made in analyzing situations that involve a marginal assignment of property rights or a marginal change in the law (see Posner 1972 for an overview of the "partial equilibrium" law and economics approach). Far less progress has been made in analyzing the political and institutional structure of an entire society as a public good, although Buchanan (1977), Olson (1982), Kalt (1981), and Hayek (forthcoming) have made pioneering efforts in that direction.

Viewing constitutional and institutional structures as either public or private goods, however, only pushes the question one step further back—which structures produced those goods? Attempts to ascribe either publicness or privateness to the factors underlying those structures may result in an infinite regress. Thus, treating constitutional and institutional structures as public goods may involve the same logic problem as treating information as a public good: the standard theory of public and private goods contains more unknowns than determinants, and if it is applied in an attempt to account for all the determinants, an infinite regress may result.

Both Buchanan and Hayek suggest developing a theory of self-generating orders that can handle the problems of constitutional choice and societal evolution. Further developments in that area are eagerly awaited; they may help explain why some societies prosper and others fail.

References

Arrow, Kenneth J., and Leonid Hurwicz, eds. 1977. *Studies in Resource Allocation Processes.* Cambridge: Cambridge University Press.

Axelrod, Robert. 1984. *The Evolution of Cooperation.* New York: Basic Books.

Baden, John A., and Richard L. Stroup. 1983. *Natural Resources: Bureaucratic Myths and Environmental Management.* Cambridge, Mass.: Ballinger.

Bator, Francis M. 1958. "The Anatomy of Market Failure." *Quarterly Journal of Economics* 72 (August): 351–79.

Baumol, William J., John C. Panzar, and Robert D. Willig. 1982. *Contestable Markets and the Theory of Industry Structure.* New York: Harcourt Brace Jovanovich.

Borcherding, Thomas E. 1978. "Competition, Exclusion and the Optimal Supply of Public Goods." *Journal of Law and Economics* 21 (April): 111–32.

Bouckaert, Boudewijn. 1987. "Public Goods and the Rise of the Nation State." Manuscript.

Brubaker, Earl R. 1975. "Free Ride, Free Revelation, or Golden Rule?" *Journal of Law and Economics* 18 (April): 147–61.

Buchanan, James M. 1965. "An Economic Theory of Clubs." *Economica* 32 (February): 1–14.

———. 1977. *Freedom in Constitutional Contract: Perspectives of a Political Economist.* College Station: Texas A&M University Press.

Buchanan, James M., and Charles Goetz. 1972. "Efficiency Limits of Fiscal Mobility: An Assessment of the Tiebout Model." *Journal of Public Economics* 1 (April): 25–43.

Buchanan, James M., and William Craig Stubblebine. 1962. "Externality." *Economica* 29 (November): 371–84.

Cheung, Steven N. S. 1973. "The Fable of the Bees: An Economic Investigation." *Journal of Law and Economics* 16 (April): 11–33.

Coase, Ronald H. 1960. "The Problem of Social Cost." *Journal of Law and Economics* 3 (October): 1–44.

———. 1974. "The Lighthouse in Economics." *Journal of Law and Economics* 17 (October): 357–76.

Cornes, Richard, and Todd Sandler. 1986. *The Theory of Externalities, Public Goods, and Club Goods.* Cambridge: Cambridge University Press.

Cowen, Tyler. 1985. "Public Goods Problems: A Reconceptualization." Manuscript.

Cowen, Tyler, and Jack High. 1987. "Lump Sum Taxation as a Welfare Ideal." Manuscript.

Craven, John. 1983. "Social Choice and Telling the Truth." *Journal of Public Economics* 21 (August): 359–75.

Dahlman, Carl J. 1979. "The Problem of Externality." *Journal of Law and Economics* 22 (April): 141–62.

Demsetz, Harold. 1964. "The Exchange and Enforcement of Property Rights." *Journal of Law and Economics* 7 (October): 11–26.

———. 1970. "The Private Production of Public Goods." *Journal of Law and Economics* 13 (October): 293–306.

Ekelund, Robert, and Joseph Hulett. 1973. "Joint Supply, the Taussig-Pigou Controversy, and the Competitive Provision of Public Goods." *Journal of Law and Economics* 16 (October): 369–87.

Goldin, Kenneth D. 1977. "Equal Access vs. Selective Access: A Critique of Public Goods Theory." *Public Choice* 29 (Spring): 53–71.

Hayek, Friedrich A. 1945. "The Use of Knowledge in Society." *American Economic Review* 35 (September): 519–30.

———. 1973. *Law, Legislation and Liberty.* Vol. 1, *Rules and Order.* Chicago: University of Chicago Press.

Herzenberger, Hans G. 1978. "Coordination Theory." In *Foundations and Applications of Decision Theory,* edited by C. A. Hooker, J. J. Leach, and E. F. McClennan. Boston: D. Reidel.

High, Jack, and Jerome Ellig. 1988. "The Private Supply of Education: Some Historical Evidence." In *The Theory of Market Failure: A Critical Examination,* edited by Tyler Cowen. Fairfax, Va.: George Mason University Press.

Kalt, Joseph P. 1981. "Public Goods and the Theory of Government." *Cato Journal* 1 (Fall): 565–84.

Kirzner, Israel M. 1973. *Competition and Entrepreneurship.* Chicago: University of Chicago Press.

Klein, Daniel. 1987. "Tie-Ins and the Market Provision of Collective Goods." *Harvard Journal of Law and Public Policy* 10 (Spring): 451–74.

Lavoie, Don. 1985. *Rivalry and Central Planning: A Reexamination of the Socialist Calculation Debate.* Cambridge: Cambridge University Press.

Levy, David K. 1985. "Is an Observed Monopoly Inefficient?" Manuscript.

Lewis, David. 1969. *Convention: A Philosophical Study.* Cambridge: Harvard University Press.

Minasian, Jora R. 1964. "Television Pricing and the Theory of Public Goods." *Journal of Law and Economics* 7 (October): 71–80.

Nelson, Richard R., and Sidney G. Winter. 1982. *An Evolutionary Theory of Economic Change.* Cambridge: Harvard University Press.

Nozick, Robert. 1974. *Anarchy, State and Utopia.* New York: Basic Books.

Oakland, William. 1987. "Theory of Public Goods." In *Handbook of Public Economics*, vol. 2, edited by A. Averbach and M. Feldstein. New York: North Holland Press.

Olson, Mancur. 1982. *The Rise and Decline of Nations.* New Haven: Yale University Press.

Pigou, Arthur C. 1932. *The Economics of Welfare.* 4th ed. London: Macmillan.

Poole, Robert W., Jr. 1980. *Cutting Back City Hall.* New York: Universe Books.

Posner, Richard A. *Economic Analysis of Law.* Boston: Little, Brown.

Samuelson, Paul A. 1954. "The Pure Theory of Public Expenditure." *Review of Economics and Statistics* 36 (November): 387–89.

———. 1969. "Contrast between Welfare Conditions for Joint Supply and for Public Goods." *Review of Economics and Statistics* 51 (February): 26–30.

Schelling, Thomas. 1960. *The Strategy of Conflict.* Cambridge: Harvard University Press.

Schmidtz, David. 1987. "Contracts and Public Goods." *Harvard Journal of Law and Public Policy* 10 (Spring): 475–503.

Schotter, Andrew. 1981. *The Economic Theory of Social Institutions.* Cambridge: Cambridge University Press.

Smith, Robert J. 1988. "Private Solutions to Conservation Problems." In *The Theory of Market Failure: A Critical Examination*, edited by Tyler Cowen. Fairfax, Va.: George Mason University Press.

Smith, Vernon. 1982. "Microeconomic Systems as an Experimental Science." *American Economic Review* 72 (December): 923–55.

Stiglitz, Joseph E. 1977. "The Theory of Local Public Goods." In *The Economics of Public Services*, edited by Martin S. Feldstein and Robert P. Inman. New York: Halsted Press.

Tideman, Nicholas, and Gordon Tullock. 1976. "A New and Superior Process for Making Social Choices." *Journal of Political Economy* 84 (December): 1145–60.

Tiebout, Charles M. 1956. "A Pure Theory of Local Expenditures." *Journal of Political Economy* 64 (October): 416–24.

Toumanoff, Peter. 1984. "A Positive Analysis of the Theory of Market Failure." *Kyklos* 37, fasc. 4: 529–41.

Winter, Sidney. 1975. "Optimization and Evolution in the Theory of the Firm." In *Adaptive Economic Models*, edited by Richard Day and Theodore Groves. New York: Academic Press.

Zodrow, George, ed. 1983. *Local Provision of Public Services: The Tiebout Model after 25 Years*. New York: Harcourt Brace Jovanovich.

Section I

The Theory of Market Failure

2. The Pure Theory of Public Expenditure

Paul A. Samuelson

Assumptions

Except for Sax, Wicksell, Lindahl, Musgrave, and Bowen, economists have rather neglected the theory of optimal public expenditure, spending most of their energy on the theory of taxation. Therefore, I explicitly assume two categories of goods: ordinary *private consumption goods* $(X_1, \cdots, X_n)$ which can be parcelled out among different individuals $(1, 2, \cdots, i, \cdots, s)$ according to the relations $X_j = \sum_1^s X^i_j$; and *collective consumption goods* $(X_{n+1}, \cdots, X_{n+m})$ which all enjoy in common in the sense that each individual's consumption of such a good leads to no subtraction from any other individual's consumption of that good, so that $X_{n+j} = X^i_{n+j}$ simultaneously for each and every ith individual and each collective consumptive good. I assume no mystical collective mind that enjoys collective consumption goods; instead I assume each individual has a consistent set of *ordinal preferences* with respect to his consumption of all goods (collective as well as private) which can be summarized by a regularly smooth and convex utility index $u^i = u^i(X^i_1, \cdots, X^i_{n+m})$ (any monotonic stretching of the utility index is of course also an admissible cardinal index of preference). I shall throughout follow the convention of writing the partial derivative of any function with respect to its jth argument by a j subscript, so that $u^i_j = \partial u^i / \partial X^i_j$, etc. Provided economic quantities can be divided into two groups, (1) *outputs* or goods which everyone always wants to maximize and (2) inputs or factors which everyone always wants to minimize, we are free to change the algebraic signs of the latter category and from then on to work only with "goods," knowing

Reprinted, by permission, from *Review of Economics and Statistics* 36 (November 1954) : 387–89.

that the case of factor inputs is covered as well. Hence by the convention we are sure that $u^i_j > 0$ always.

To keep production assumptions at the minimum level of simplicity, I assume a regularly convex and smooth production-possibility schedule relating totals of all outputs, private and collective; or $F(X_1, \cdots, X_{n+m}) = 0$, with $F_j > 0$ and ratios F_j/F_n determinate and subject to the generalized laws of diminishing returns.

Feasibility considerations disregarded, there is a *maximal* (ordinal) *utility frontier* representing the Pareto-optimal points—of which there are an $(s - 1)$ fold infinity—with the property that from such a frontier point you can make one person better off only by making some other person worse off. If we wish to make normative judgments concerning the relative ethical desirability of different configurations involving some individuals being on a higher level of indifference and some on a lower, we must be presented with a set of ordinal interpersonal norms or with a *social welfare function* representing a consistent set of ethical preferences among all the possible states of the system. It is not a "scientific" task of the economist to "deduce" the form of this function; this can have as many forms as there are possible ethical views; for the present purpose, the only restriction placed on the social welfare function is that it shall always increase or decrease when any one person's ordinal preference increases or decreases, all others staying on their same indifference levels: mathematically, we narrow it to the class that any one of its indexes can be written $U = U(u^1, \cdots, u^s)$ with $U_j > 0$.

Optimal Conditions

In terms of these norms, there is a "best state of the world" which is defined mathematically in simple regular cases by the marginal conditions

$$\frac{u^i_j}{u^i_r} = \frac{F_j}{F_r} \quad (i = 1, 2, \cdots, s; r, j = 1, \cdots, n) \text{ or} \tag{1}$$

$$(i = 1, 2, \cdots, s; r = 1; j = 2, \cdots, n)$$

$$\sum_{i=1}^{s} \frac{u^i_{n+j}}{u^i_r} = \frac{F_{n+j}}{F_r} \quad (j = 1, \cdots, m; r = 1, \cdots, n) \text{ or} \tag{2}$$

$$(j = 1, \cdots, m; r = 1)$$

$$\frac{U_i u^i_k}{U_q u^q_k} = 1 \quad (i, q = 1, \cdots, s; k = 1, \cdots, n) \text{ or} \tag{3}$$

$$(q = 1; i = 2, \cdots, s; k = 1).$$

Equations (1) and (3) are essentially those given in the chapter on welfare economics in my *Foundations of Economic Analysis*. They constitute my version of the "new welfare economics." Alone (1) represents that subset of relations which defines the Pareto-optimal utility frontier and which by itself represents what I regard as the unnecessarily narrow version of what once was called the "new welfare economics."

The new element added here is the set (2), which constitutes a pure theory of government expenditure on collective consumption goods. By themselves (1) and (2) define the $(s - 1)$ - fold infinity of utility frontier points; only when a set of interpersonal normative conditions equivalent to (3) is supplied are we able to define an unambiguously "best" state.

Since formulating the conditions (2) some years ago, I have learned from the published and unpublished writings of Richard Musgrave that their essential logic is contained in the "voluntary-exchange" theories of public finance of the Sax-Wicksell-Lindahl-Musgrave type, and I have also noted Howard Bowen's independent discovery of them in Bowen's writings of a decade ago. A graphical interpretation of these conditions in terms of *vertical* rather than *horizontal* addition of different individuals' marginal-rate-of-substitution schedules can be given; but what I must emphasize is that there is a different such schedule for each individual at each of the $(s - 1)$ fold infinity of different distributions of relative welfare along the utility frontier.

Impossibility of Decentralized Spontaneous Solution

So much for the involved optimizing equations that an omniscient calculating machine could theoretically solve if fed the postulated functions. No such machine now exists. But it is well known that an "analogue calculating machine" can be provided by competitive market pricing, (a) so long as the production functions satisfy the neoclassical assumptions of constant returns to scale and generalized diminishing returns and (b) so long as the individuals' indifference contours have regular convexity and, we may add, (c) so long as all goods are private. We can then insert between the right- and left-hand sides of (1) the equality with uniform market prices p_j/P, and adjoin the budget equations for each individual

$$p_1 X^i_1 + p_2 X^i_2 + \cdots + p_n X^i_n = L^i \tag{1}'$$

$$(i = 1, 2, \cdots, s),$$

where L^i is a lump-sum tax for each individual so selected in algebraic value as to lead to the "best" state of the world. Now note, if there were no collective consumption goods, then (1) and (1)' can have their solution enormously simplified. Why? Because on the one hand perfect competition among productive enterprises would ensure that goods are produced at minimum costs and are sold at proper marginal costs, with all factors receiving their proper marginal productivities; and on the other hand, each individual, in seeking as a competitive buyer to get to the highest level of indifference subject to given prices and tax, would be led as if by an Invisible Hand to the grand solution of the social maximum position. Of course the institutional framework of competition would have to be maintained, and political decision-making would still be necessary, but of a computationally minimum type: namely, algebraic taxes and transfers $(L^1, \cdots L^s)$ would have to be varied until society is swung to the ethical observer's optimum. The servant of the ethical observer would not have to make explicit decisions about each person's detailed consumption and work; he need only decide about generalized purchasing power, knowing that each person can be counted on to allocate it optimally. In terms of communication theory and game terminology, each person is motivated to do the signalling of his tastes needed to define and reach the attainable-bliss point.

Now all of the above remains valid even if collective consumption is not zero but is instead *explicitly set* at its optimum values as determined by (1), (2), and (3). *However no decentralized pricing system can serve to determine optimally these levels of collective consumption.* Other kinds of "voting" or "signalling" would have to be tried. But, and this is the point sensed by Wicksell but perhaps not fully appreciated by Lindahl, now it is in the selfish interest of each person to give *false* signals, to pretend to have less interest in a given collective consumption activity than he really has, etc. I must emphasize this: taxing according to a benefit theory of taxation can not at all solve the computational problem in the decentralized manner possible for the first category of "private" goods to which the ordinary market pricing applies and which do not have the "external effects" basic to the very notion of collective consumption goods. Of course, utopian voting and signalling schemes can be imagined. ("Scandinavian consensus," Kant's "categorical imperative," and other devices meaningful only under conditions of "symmetry," etc.) The failure of market catallactics in no way denies the following truth: given sufficient knowledge the optimal decisions can always be found by scanning over all the attainable states of the world and selecting the one which according to the postulated ethical welfare function is best. The solution "exists"; the problem is how to "find" it.

One could imagine every person in the community being indoctrinated to behave like a "parametric decentralized bureaucrat" who *reveals* his preferences by signalling in response to price parameters or Lagrangean multipliers, to questionnaires, or to other devices. But there is still this fundamental technical difference going to the heart of the whole problem of *social* economy: by departing from his indoctrinated rules, any one person can hope to snatch some selfish benefit in a way not possible under the self-policing competitive pricing of private goods; and the "external economies" or "jointness of demand" intrinsic to the very concept of collective goods and governmental activities makes it impossible for the grand ensemble of optimizing equations to have that special pattern of zeros which makes *laissez-faire* competition even *theoretically* possible as an analogue computer.

Conclusion

To explore further the problem raised by public expenditure would take us into the mathematical domain of "sociology" or "welfare politics," which Arrow, Duncan Black, and others have just begun to investigate. Political economy can be regarded as one special sector of this general domain, and it may turn out to be pure luck that within the general domain there happened to be a subsector with the "simple" properties of traditional economics.

3. The Anatomy of Market Failure

Francis M. Bator

What is it we mean by "market failure"? Typically, at least in allocation theory, we mean the failure of a more or less idealized system of price-market institutions to sustain "desirable" activities or to stop "undesirable" activities.[1] The desirability of an activity, in turn, is evaluated relative to the solution values of some explicit or implied maximum-welfare problem.

It is the central theorem of modern welfare economics that under certain strong assumptions about technology, tastes, and producers' motivations, the equilibrium conditions which characterize a system of competitive markets will exactly correspond to the requirements of Paretian efficiency.[2] Further, if competitively imputed incomes are continuously redistributed in costless lump-sum fashion so as to achieve the income-distribution implied by a social welfare function, then the competitive market solution will correspond to the one electronically calculated Pareto-efficient solution which maximizes, subject only to tastes, technology and initial endowments, that particular welfare function.[3]

Reprinted, by permission, from *Quarterly Journal of Economics* 72 (August 1958): 351–79.

[1] "Activities" broadly defined, to cover consumption as well as production.

[2] I.e., to the conditions which define the attainable frontier of maximal utility combinations with given preference functions, resource endowments and technology. A community is on its Paretian frontier if it is impossible to make anyone better off (in terms of his own ordinal preference function) without making someone else worse off. Associated with the utility possibility frontier, in turn, is a production possibility frontier denoting maximal alternative output combinations. (Cf. my "Simple Analytics of Welfare Maximization," *American Economic Review*, XLVII (Mar. 1957), 22–59, and references therein.)

[3] In other words, given the "right" lump-sum taxes, markets will match the allocation called for by the point of tangency of the relevant W-function with the utility-possibility frontier, i.e., by the "bliss point." The W-function need not, of course, be explicit—it could be implicit in the political power-configuration which characterizes a community. On the other hand, it cannot be just any kind of function. It has to have some special characteristics which reflect a number of ethic-loaded restrictions, e.g., that individuals' preference functions are to count, and to count positively (cf., *ibid.*, and Section V below).

Many things in the real world violate such correspondence: imperfect information, inertia and resistance to change, the infeasibility of costless lump-sum taxes, businessmen's desire for a "quiet life," uncertainty and inconsistent expectations, the vagaries of aggregate demand, etc. With most of these I am not here concerned: they have to do with the efficiency of "real life" market institutions operated by "real life" people in a nonstationary world of uncertainty, miscalculation, etc.

What follows is an attempt, rather, to explore and order those phenomena which cause even errorless profit- and preference-maximizing calculation in a stationary context of perfect (though limited) information and foresight to fail to sustain Pareto-efficient allocation. I am concerned, in other words, with the decentralizing efficiency of that regime of signals, rules and built-in sanctions which defines a price-market system.[4]

Specifically, Section I sets out the necessary conditions for efficiency of decentralized price-profit calculations both in a "laissez-faire" and in a "socialist" setting of Lange-Lerner civil servants. Section II is a brief digression on an often discussed mode of failure in these conditions: neoclassical external economies. It is concluded that the modern formulation of the doctrine, in terms of "direct interaction," begs more questions than it answers; further, that the usual emphasis on "divorce of scarcity from effective ownership" is misplaced. Section III, then, suggests a comprehensive ordering of types of market failure, with generalized indivisibility, public goods, and, last and least, nonappropriability as the villains of the piece. Section IV consists of some comments on the Meade and Scitovsky classifications of external economies; on the analytical link between indivisibility and public goods; on the significance of "exclusion"; on organizational arrangements designed to offset externality; and on blends of the various types of

---

[4]In most of what follows, I shall assume that individual preferences, though not necessarily sensitive only to own-consumption, are representable by strictly convex indifference surfaces (i.e., by an ordering (one for each individual) such that all points on a straight line connecting two equivalent points x and y are preferred to x (hence to y)). But convexity is too restrictive. It excludes not only such characteristics of man's psyche as violate the "usual" regularities—these I do want to exclude—but also such physical and topographical facts as lumpy consumption-goods. Rather than attempt a specification of preferences with convex-like properties where choice must be made among discrete bundles, I dodge the problem by attributing lumpiness only to inputs (including, however, inputs that are intermediate outputs).

market failure. Section V concludes with some cautionary notes on the relevance of market-efficiency for choice of institutions.

I. The Conditions of Market Efficiency

The central theorem of modern welfare economics, the so-called *duality theorem*, asserts a correspondence between Pareto efficiency and market performance. Its analytical essence lies in the remarkable fact that with all-round convexity, independence of tastes, etc., the technocratically formulated, institutionally neutral, Paretian maximum-of-welfare problem has embedded within it a set of constants: "duals," Lagrangean multipliers, shadow-prices, which have all the analytical characteristics of prices, wages, rents, interest rates.[5] Correspondence between Pareto-efficiency and market performance implies, at the least, that decentralized decisions in response to these "prices" by atomistic profit- and satisfaction-maximizers sustain just that constellation of inputs, outputs and commodity-distribution, that the maximum of the specified social welfare function calls for. It implies, in other words, that decentralized market calculations correctly account for all "economic" costs and benefits to which the relevant W-function is sensitive.[6]

Duality can fail in many ways. Specifically, and in a statical and "laissez-faire" context:[7]

[5]The theorem holds for the statical steady-state flow model of the Walrasian sort where the solution values are stationary time-rates; it holds, also, for dynamical systems involving capital formation (given, still, convexity throughout). For these last, the solution values are time paths of inputs, outputs, prices, etc. (A set of points is convex if, and only if, the straight lines connecting all possible pairs do not anywhere pass outside the set. The set of feasible output points bounded by a production possibility curve is convex, for instance, if the curve itself is concave-to-the-origin or a straight line. On all this, see Section V of "Simple Analytics," *ibid.*)

[6]Given, again, optimal lump-sum redistribution of as-imputed incomes. While I make use of the lump-sum transfer device throughout this paper to abstract from the income distribution problem and permit exclusive attention to Pareto efficiency, it is well to note that this involves a measure of sleight-of-hand. No decentralized price-market type "game" can reveal the pattern of taxes and transfers that would maximize a particular welfare function. "Central" calculation—implicit if not explicit—is unavoidable. Moreover, since distribution (hence correct redistribution) of numeraire-incomes interdepends with allocation in production and exchange, the supposedly automatic, nonpolitical character of market mediation is a myth on the strictest neoclassical assumptions. This is not to say, even on our stratospheric levels of abstraction, that markets are "useless." Where they do compute well we are saved an awful lot of calculation.

[7]With optimal redistribution.

1. Duality will fail unless the Pareto-efficient (a) input-output points (production) and (b) associated commodity distribution points (exchange) which associate with the maximum of the welfare function in hand are characterized by a complete set of marginal-rate-of-substitution (*MRS*) equalities (or limiting inequalities) which, in turn, yield a set of price-like constants. Where no such constants exist, reference will be to *failure of existence*.[8]

2. Should such an associated set of Lagrangean parameters exist, duality would nevertheless fail, specifically in production, unless the bliss configuration of inputs and outputs, evaluated in terms of these price parameters, will yield: (a) a local profit-maximum position for each producer, rather than, as possible, a profit minimum; (b) non-negative profits for all producers from whom production is required; (c) maximum profits-in-the-large for each producer. Failure on counts (a) and (c) will be labeled *failure by signal*, that on count (b) *failure by incentive*.[9]

3. Even if all efficient production configurations, or the one which maximizes a particular welfare-function, coincide with points of maximum and non-negative producers' profits, market mediation may fail in production. If prices are determined by market forces, they will not correspond to a Paretian maximum unless self-policing perfect competition obtains in all markets. Self-policing competition requires "very many" producers in every market.[10] If, then, for whatever reason, some markets are saturated

[8]We could consider, instead, the configuration which associates with the initial pattern of ownership of endowment. Or we could play it safe and extend the conditions to cover each and every Pareto efficient configuration. But this would be overly strict, since many efficient situations have no relevance either to any interesting *W*-functions or in terms of the initial distribution of scarcities.

It may be worth noting, incidentally, that "existence," as used above, is not the same as existence in the sense of, e.g., Arrow and Debreu (in "Existence of an Equilibrium for a Competitive Economy," *Econometrica*, Vol. 22 (July 1954), pp. 265–90). They use the term to denote the complete set of conditions which defines competitive equilibrium, and this includes, in addition to all that is implied by (1) above, conditions akin to my conditions (2), and some analogous conditions on consumers.

[9]This is slightly misleading: as we shall see, failure on count (c) leads both to signaling and to incentive troubles. Anyway, the labels are only for expository convenience.

[10]Or at least the potentiality of very many producers, ready and able to "enter the fray" instantaneously. This may be sufficient in the constant-cost case, where the equilibrium number of firms per industry is indeterminate.

by a few firms of "efficient" scale, the full welfare-maximum solution of inputs, outputs *and prices* will not be sustained. There will be *failure by structure*.

4. Finally, even if all above is satisfied, market performance could still fail, and fail in a statical sense, due to arbitrary legal and organizational "imperfections," or feasibility limitations on "keeping book," such as leave some inputs or outputs "hidden," or preclude their explicit allocation or capture by market processes (e.g., the restriction, unless I go into baseball, on the sale of the capitalized value of my lifetime services). Failure is *by enforcement*.

All the above are germane to duality in its usual sense, to the statical Pareto-efficiency of laissez-faire markets with genuine profit- and satisfaction-seekers.[11] Conditions (1), (2) and (4) are relevant, also, to the decentralizing efficiency of a Lange-Lerner type organizational scheme. In its "capitalist" version, with profit-motivated operation of privately-owned means of production where it is simply an anti-monopoly device to assure parametric take-prices-as-given behavior, conditions (1), (2) and (4) are all necessary for efficiency. Of course condition (3): self-policing competition, no longer matters.

In its true socialist version, a Lange-Lerner system can afford to "fail" also "by incentive," (2b). Socialist civil servants, under injunction to maximize profit (in the small) in terms of fixed centrally-quoted prices, care or should care not at all about absolute profitability. By assumption the scheme can dispense with the built-in incentive of positive profit: the lure of bureaucratic advancement, the image of Siberia, or the old school tie presumably substitute for the urge to get rich. But if prices and the injunction to maximize profit are to be used to decentralize, condition (1): existence, and (2a) and (2c): correct and unambiguous signals, remain crucial.[12] So does condition (4): the solution of quantities

---

[11]The mathematically minded will object that (3) and (4), at least, do not really violate "duality" in its strict mathematical sense; the dual minimum problem still yields Lagrangean constants. True, yet I think it suggestive to use "duality" rather more loosely as a label for the general welfare theorem, particularly as this does not lead, in this context, to any ambiguity.

[12]It is tempting, but wrong, to suggest that in a true Lange-Lerner world totals do not matter and only margins count. It is true that the non-negativeness of profits is immaterial. Where there is any sharing of shadow-price sets by two or more production points, however, totals necessarily become a part of the signaling system and if 2(c) does not hold they may lead down the garden path.

and prices need not be profitable and self-enforcing, but it does have to be enforceable. If the nectar in apple blossoms is scarce and carries a positive shadow price, it must be possible to make every beekeeper pay for his charges' meals.

It warrants repetition that this has to do with whether a decentralized price-market game will or will not *sustain* a Pareto-efficient configuration. The word sustain is critical. There exists a host of further considerations which bear on dynamical questions of adjustment, of "how the system gets there." (E.g., will some "natural" price-market type computational routine of price-quantity responses with a meaningful institutional counterpart tend to track the solution?) These are not here at issue. We shall be concerned only with the prior problem of whether a price-market system which finds itself at the maximum-welfare point will or will not tend to remain there.[13]

The relevant literature is rich but confusing. It abounds in mutually reinforcing and overlapping descriptions and explanations of market failure: external economies, indivisibility, nonappropriability, direct interaction, public goods, atmosphere, etc. In a sense, our problem is simply to sort out the relations among these. In doing so, it is appropriate and useful to begin with a brief review of the neoclassical doctrine of external economies and of its modern formulation in terms of "direct interaction."

---

[13]More precisely, whether the point of maximum welfare is or is not a point of self-policing and "enforceable" market equilibrium, where, following common usage, equilibrium is defined to subsume both the first-order and the second-order inequalities for a maximum. A firm, for instance, is taken to be in equilibrium only at a point of maximum profit. This way of defining equilibrium does bring in issues of stability, hence some implicit dynamics. In particular, the word "sustain" is taken to imply some scanning or reconnaissance by producers and consumers at least in the neighborhood of equilibrium. But I do not think it does any harm to subsume this much stability in the equilibrium notion. The possibility of a firm in *unstable* "equilibrium," i.e., in equilibrium at a point of minimum profit, is hardly likely to be of import.

On the other hand, correspondence between Pareto-efficiency and the equilibrium state of perfectly competitive markets is not sufficient to insure market efficiency. It is the burden of "failure by structure" that markets may fail to be competitive, and of "failure by enforcement" that legal or institutional constraints may prevent competitive markets from allocating efficiently, even though there does exist a competitive equilibrium for each Pareto-efficient configuration. "Existence" in the sense of Arrow and Debreu (*op. cit.*) is necessary but not sufficient for market-efficiency in the present context.

II. Neoclassical External Economies: A Digression

By Way of Some History

Marshall, as has often been pointed out, proposed the external economy argument to explain, without resort to dynamics, the phenomenon of a negatively sloped ("forward falling") long-run industry supply curve in terms consistent with a horizontal or rising marginal cost curve (MC) in the "representative" firm. The device permits—in logic, if not in fact—long-run competitive equilibrium of many firms within an industry, each producing at its profit maximum price-equal-to-a-rising-MC position, without foreclosing the possibility of a falling supply price with rising industry output.[14]

The mechanism is simple. It is postulated that an expansion in the output of the industry as a whole brings into play economies which cause a downward shift of the cost curves of all the component firms. These economies, however, are not subject to exploitation by any one of the myriad of tiny atomized firms. Their own MC curves, at $p = MC$, rise both before and after the shift, due, presumably, to internal diseconomies associated with the entrepreneurial function which defines the firm. Even the modern formulation is not entirely without ambiguity—institutional ambiguity is intrinsic to the device of parametrization: how many firms does it take for the demand curve of each to be perfectly horizontal?—but it does provide a means for "saving" the competitive model, of ducking the monopoly problem.

Marshall, and also Professor Pigou, "preferred," as it were, the other horn of what they perhaps saw as a dilemma. The external economy device, while saving competition, implies a flaw in the efficacy of the "invisible hand" in guiding production.[15] "Price equal to MC" is saved, but wrong. Market forces, they argued, will not give enough output by industries enjoying external economies and will cause industries with rising supply curves to overexpand. Hence the Marshall-Pigou prescription: to harmonize private production decisions with public welfare, tax the latter set of industries and subsidize the former.

---

[14]This refers to a so-called Marshallian supply curve. It has nothing whatever to do with the Walrasian "maximum quan'ity supplied at a given price type schedule.

[15]That there are difficulties also with income distribution was by that time generally recognized.

It took the better part of thirty years, and the cumulative powers of Allyn Young, and Messrs. Robertson, Knight, Sraffa, and Viner, to unravel the threads of truth and error which run through the Marshall-Pigou argument.[16] The crucial distinction, which provides the key to it all, is between what Viner labeled technological external economies, on the one hand, and pecuniary external economies on the other. The latter, if dominant, cause the long-run supply curve of an industry, say A, to decline because the price of an input, B, falls in response to an increase in A's demand for it. The technological variety, on the other hand, though also a reversible function of industry output, consists in organizational or other improvements in efficiency which do not show up in input prices.[17]

As regards pecuniary external economies, Robertson and Sraffa made it clear that in a sense both the Marshall-Pigou conclusions were wrong. For one thing, no subsidy is called for. The implied gains in efficiency are adequately signaled by the input price, and profit-maximizing output levels by the A-firms are socially efficient. Second, monopoly troubles may be with us, via, as it were, the back door. For what causes the price of B to drop in response to increased demand? We are back where we started: a declining long-run supply curve.

In the end, then, if *internal* technological economies of scale are ruled out, we are left with only *technological* external economies. All pecuniary external economies must be due to technological economies somewhere in the system.[18] It is true—and this is what remains of the original Marshall-Pigou proposition—that technological externalities are not correctly accounted for by prices, that they violate the efficiency of decentralized market calculation.

[16]The strategic articles, with the exception of Young's ("Pigou's *Wealth and Welfare*," *Quarterly Journal of Economics*, XXVII (1913), 672–86), as well as Ellis and Fellner's 1943 treatment, have all been reprinted in American Economic Association, *Readings in Price Theory*, ed. Stigler & Boulding. For an excellent modern discussion, see R. L. Bishop, *Economic Theory* (to appear).

[17]Note, however, that there need be nothing about an organizational improvement to make it obvious in advance whether it will turn out to be technological or, through "internalization," pecuniary. Many trade-association type services which are justified by the scale of an industry could as well be provided commercially, and vice versa.

[18]Pecuniary diseconomies, in contrast, need have no technological counterpart. Finite-elastic supplies of unproduced inputs are a sufficient cause. Recall, incidentally, that only narrowly statical reversible phenomena are admissible here.

The Modern Formulation[19]

In its modern version, the notion of external economies—external economies proper that is: Viner's technological variety—belongs to a more general doctrine of "direct interaction." Such interaction, whether it involves producer-producer, consumer-consumer, producer-consumer, or employer-employee relations, consists in interdependences that are external to the price system, hence unaccounted for by market valuations. Analytically, it implies the nonindependence of various preference and production functions. Its effect is to cause divergence between private and social cost-benefit calculation.

That this is so, is easily demonstrated by means of a simplified variant of a production model suggested by J. E. Meade.[20] Assume a world of all-round perfect competition where a single purchasable and inelastically supplied input, labor ($\bar{L}$), is used to produce two homogeneous and divisible goods, apples (A) and honey (H), at nonincreasing returns to scale. But while the output of A is dependent only on $L_A : A = A(L_A)$, honey production is sensitive also to the level of apple output: $H = H(L_H, A(L_A))$. (Professor Meade makes pleasurable the thought of apple blossoms making for honey abundance.)[21]

By solving the usual constrained maximum problem for the production-possibility curve, it can be shown that Paretian production efficiency implies

$$p_H \frac{\partial H}{\partial L_H} = w \tag{1}$$

$$p_A \frac{dA}{dL_A} + p_H \frac{\partial H}{\partial A} \frac{dA}{dL_A} = w \tag{2}$$

where p_H, p_A, and w represent the prices, respectively, of honey,

[19]While this section makes some slight use of elementary calculus, the reader uninterested in technicalities may avoid, without loss of continuity, all but some simple notation.

[20]*Economic Journal*, LXII (Mar. 1952). Meade uses a two factor model and, while he does not explicitly solve the Paretian maximum problem, shows that market imputed rates of remuneration will not match marginal social product.

[21]Both functions are assumed homogeneous of degree one. Moreover, apple blossoms (or the nectar therein) are exhaustible, rationable "private" goods: more nectar to one bee means less to another. On the need for this assumption, see Section III-3 below.

apples and labor.[22] Equation (1) is familiar enough and consistent with profit maximizing. Each competitive honey producer will do for profit what he must for efficiency: hire labor until the value of its social as well as private marginal product equals the wage rate. Not so the apple producers; unless $\frac{\partial H}{\partial A} = 0$—unless the cross effect of apples on honey is zero—their profit-maximizing production decisions will be nonefficient. Specifically, if apples have a positive external effect on honey output, market-determined L_A will be less than is socially desirable.[23]

A different way to see this is to examine the relations of private to social marginal cost. The marginal money cost of apples to the competitive apple producer is $\frac{w}{dA/dL_A}$; that of honey to the bee-keeper, $\frac{w}{\partial H/\partial L_H}$. It is the ratio of the two: $\frac{\partial H/\partial L_H}{dA/dL_A}$, that competitive market-mediation brings into equality with the equilibrating con-figuration of relative prices. Markets will be efficient if, and only if, this *private* marginal cost ratio reflects the true marginal cost to society of an extra apple in terms of foregone honey: the marginal rate of transformation between H and A.

What is *MRT* in the model? Differentiating (totally) the two production functions and dividing the value of one derivative into the other, we get, in absolute (cost) terms:

---

[22]Assuming internal tangencies and all-round convexity (the last is implicit in constant returns to L: the A-effect on H reinforces convexity), as well as non-satiation and nonredundancy ($\bar{L} = L_A + L_H$), the maximization of $p_A A + p_H H$, subject to the production functions and the supply of labor, is equivalent to finding a critical value for the Lagrangean expression, $F = p_A A(L_A) + p_H H[L_H; A(L_A)] + w(\bar{L} - L_A - L_H)$. To do so, differentiate F with respect to L_A and L_H, treating p_A, p_H and w as arbitrary constants and set the resulting first order partial derivatives equal to zero. This will give exactly (1) and (2). (Needless to say, the value weights can be varied at will, or taken as given.)

[23]To see this, rewrite (2) to read $\dfrac{dA}{dL_A} = \dfrac{w}{p_A + p_H\dfrac{\partial H}{\partial A}}$ and match it against the profit-

maximizing rule, $\dfrac{dA}{dL_A} = \dfrac{w}{p_A}$. Clearly, $\dfrac{\partial H}{\partial A} \leq 0. \rightarrow$

$$\left(\frac{dA}{dL_A}\right) \text{Private} \leq \left(\frac{dA}{dL_A}\right) \text{Social}$$

$$MRT \equiv \left| \frac{dH}{dA} \right| = \frac{\partial H/\partial L_H}{dA/dL_A} - \frac{\partial H}{\partial A}.$$

If, then, $\dfrac{\partial H}{\partial A} > 0$, the true marginal *social* cost of an "extra" apple, in terms of honey foregone, is less than the market-indicated private cost. It is less precisely by the amount of positive "feedback" on honey output due the "extra" apple.

By combining (1) and (2), eliminating w, and dividing through by p_H and $\dfrac{dA}{dL_A}$, we get the condition for Pareto efficiency in terms of private MC's: $\dfrac{\partial H/\partial L_H}{dA/dL_A} = \dfrac{p_A}{p_H} + \dfrac{\partial H}{\partial A}$.

Clearly, price equal to private marginal cost will not do. Further, if prices are market-determined, they will diverge from true, *social* marginal cost.

Any number of variations on the model suggest themselves. As Meade pointed out, interactions can be mutual and need not be associated with the outputs. Even in the above case, it is perhaps more suggestive to think of L_A as producing some social value-product both in the A industry and the H industry. In the most general formulation, one can simply think of each production function as containing all the other variables of the system, some perhaps with zero weight. Moreover, by introducing two or more nonproduced inputs one can, as Meade does, work out the consequences for income distribution and input proportions.[24]

Some Queries

The modern formulation of the doctrine of external economies, in terms of direct interaction, is not only internally consistent: it also yields insight. Yet one may well retain about it some dissatis-

---

[24]The question of whether technological external economies involve shifts of each other's production functions, or mutually induced movements along such functions, is purely definitional. If one chooses so to define each producer's function as to give axes only to inputs and outputs that are purchased and sold, or at least "controlled," and the effects of everything else impinging on production (e.g., of humidity, apple blossoms, etc.) are built into the curvature of the function, then it follows that externalities will consist in shifts of some functions in response to movements along others. On the other hand, if, as in our apple-honey case, it seems useful to think of the production function for H as having an A-axis, then, clearly, induced movement along the function is a signal of externality.

faction. There is no doubt that the Robertson-Sraffa-Viner distinction between the technological and the pecuniary sort gets to the nub of what is the matter with the original Marshallian analysis. It cuts right through the confusion which led Marshall and Pigou to conclude that the price mechanism is faulty in situations where in truth it is at its best: in allocating inputs in less than infinitely elastic supply between alternative productive uses. It also facilitates unambiguous formulation of the more difficult "falling supply price" case. But in a sense it only begs the fundamental question: what is it that gives rise to "direct interaction," to short circuit, as it were, of the signaling system?

Most modern writers have let matters rest with the Ellis-Fellner type explanation: "the divorce of scarcity from effective ownership."[25] Does nonappropriability then explain all direct interaction? In a sense it does, yet by directing attention to institutional and feasibility considerations which make it impracticable for "real life" market-institutions to mimic a price-profit-preference computation, it diverts attention from some deeper issues. Surely the word "ownership" serves to illuminate but poorly the phenomenon of a temperance leaguer's reaction to a hard-drinking neighbor's (sound insulated and solitary) Saturday night, or the reason why a price system, if efficient, will not permit full "compensation," in an age of electronic scramblers, for an advertisement-less radio program, or for the "services" of a bridge.[26]

It may be argued, of course, that at least the two latter examples are out of order, that radio programs and bridges do not involve "direct," i.e., non-price, interaction. But is this really so? Does not the introduction of a new program directly affect my and your consumption possibilities, in ways other than by a change in relative prices? Does not a bridge, or a road, have a direct effect on

---

[25]*Op. cit.*

[26]Moreover, in the one sense in which nonappropriability fits all cases of direct interaction, it explains none. If all it denotes is the failure of a price-market game properly to account for (to appropriate) all relevant costs and benefits, then it is simply a synonym for market failure (for generalized externality), and cannot be used to explain what causes any particular instance of such failure. I use it in a much narrower sense, to mean the inability of a producer of a good or service physically to exclude users, or to control the rationing of his produce among them. In my sense not only bridges but also, say, television programs are fully appropriable: it is always possible to use scramblers.

the production possibilities of neighboring producers, in precisely the sense in which apples affect the possibilities of beekeepers?[27]

True, perhaps bridges and roads are unfair: they violate the neoclassical assumption of perfect divisibility and nonincreasing returns to scale. But they surely do involve non-price interaction. In fact, lumpiness and increasing returns are perhaps the most important causes of such interaction. Are they to be denied status as externalities? More generally, are we to exclude from the class of externalities any direct interaction not due to difficulties with "effective ownership," any failures other than "by enforcement"?

It would be, of course, perfectly legitimate to do so—tastes are various. But I think it more natural and useful to broaden rather than restrict, to let "externality" denote any situation where some Paretian costs and benefits remain *external to* decentralized cost-revenue calculations in terms of prices.[28] If, however, we do so, then clearly nonappropriability[29] will not do as a complete explanation. Its concern with the inability of decentralized markets to sustain the solution-prices and quantities called for by a price-profit-preference type calculation, as computed by a team of mathematicians working with IBM machines, tends to mask the possibility that such machine-calculated solution q's may well be nonef-

---

[27]It is possible, of course, to interpret these examples as involving very large changes in price: from infinity to zero. But it does not help to do so. The shared characteristic of bridges and programs is that there is no price which will efficiently mediate both supply and demand.

I have puzzled over ways of limiting the notion of "direct interaction" to something less than all instances where there is some interaction not adequately signaled by price. Robert Solow has suggested to me that this might be done by distinguishing situations where something is not subject to a market test at all from instances where no single price constitutes a correct test for both sides of a transaction (e.g., where the correct ration price for the services of an expensive facility is zero). I am inclined, rather, to drop the attempt to use "direct interaction" as an explanation of market failure; it is best used, if at all, as yet another synonym for such failure.

[28]Recall that it is the existence of such "externality," of residue, at the bliss-point, of Pigouvian "uncompensated services" and "incidental uncharged disservices" that defines market failure. It may be objected that to generalize the externality notion in this way is to rob it of all but descriptive significance. But surely there is not much to rob; even in its strictest neoclassical formulation it begs more than it answers. In its generalized sense it at least has the virtue of suggesting the right questions.

[29]As defined in fn. 26.

ficient.[30] It explains failure "by enforcement," but leaves hidden the empirically more important phenomena which cause failure by "nonexistence," "signal," and "incentive." Section III is designed to bring these deeper causes of generalized externality into the foreground.

III. Statical Externalities: An Ordering

If nonappropriability is, by itself, too flimsy a base for a doctrine of generalized (statical) externality, what broader foundation is there? Section I's hierarchy of possible modes of market failure suggests a fivefold classification. If, however, one looks for an organizing principle not to modes of failure but to causes, there appear to be three polar types: (1) Ownership Externalities, (2) Technical Externalities,[31] and (3) Public Good Externalities. These are not mutually exclusive: most externality phenomena are in fact blends. Yet there emerges a sufficient three-cornered clustering to warrant consolidation.[32]

Type (1): Ownership Externalities

Imagine a world which exhibits generalized technological and taste convexity, where the electronically calculated solution of a Paretian maximum-of-welfare problem yields not only a unique set of inputs, outputs and commodity-distribution, but where initial endowments plus lump-sum transfers render income distribution optimal in terms of the community's social welfare function. Assume, further, that everything that matters is divisible, conventionally rationable, and either available in inelastic total supply,[33]

---

[30]Or that the algorism may break down for lack of a consistent set of p's.

[31]I should much prefer "technological," but since this would necessarily confuse my Type (2) with Professor Viner's "technological" I fixed on "technical."

[32]In effect, we end up with a five-by-three ordering of types of "failure": five "modes" vs. three "causes." Its relation to Meade's categories (*op. cit.*) and to Tibor Scitovsky's classification (in "Two Concepts of External Economies," *Journal of Political Economy*, LXII, April 1954) is discussed in Section IV below. I have had the benefit of reading, also, William Fellner's "Individual Investment Projects in Growing Economies," *Investment Criteria and Economic Growth* (Proceedings of a Conference, Center for International Studies, Massachusetts Institute of Technology, 1955) and an unpublished paper by Svend Laursen, "External Economies and Economic Growth."

[33]The supply of such nonproduced scarcities need not, of course, remain constant. On the other hand, their ownership distribution must not be so concentrated as to preclude competitive rationing. There must exist no "indivisible" lake full of fish, etc., such as might be subject to monopolization, but thousands of lakes, all perfect substitutes.

or producible at constant returns to scale; also that tastes are sensitive only to own-consumption. We know, then, from the duality theorem, that the bliss point implies a unique[34] set of prices, wages and rents, such as would cause atomistic profit- and preference-maximizers to do exactly what is necessary for bliss. In particular, all required production points give maximum and non-negative producer's profits.

This is an Adam Smith dream world. Yet it is possible that due to more or less arbitrary and accidental circumstances of institutions, laws, customs, or feasibility, competitive markets would not be Pareto-efficient. Take, for instance, the Meade example of apples and honey. Apple blossoms are "produced" at constant returns to scale and are (we assumed) an ordinary, private, exhaustible good: the more nectar for one bee, the less for another. It is easy to show that if apple blossoms have a positive effect on honey production (and abstracting from possible satiation and redundancy) a maximum-of-welfare solution, or any Pareto-efficient solution, will associate with apple blossoms a positive Lagrangean shadow-price.[35] If, then, apple producers are unable to protect their equity in apple-nectar and markets do not impute to apple blossoms their correct shadow value, profit-maximizing decisions will fail correctly to allocate resources (e.g., L) at the margin. There will be failure "by enforcement."

This is what I would call an *ownership* externality. It is essentially Meade's "unpaid factor" case. Nonappropriation, divorce of scarcity from effective ownership, is *the* binding consideration. Certain "goods" (or "bads") with determinate non-zero shadow-values are simply not attributed. It is irrelevant here whether this is because the lake where people fish happens to be in the public domain, or because "keeping book" on who produces, and who gets what, may be impossible, clumsy, or costly in terms of resources.[36] For whatever legal or feasibility reasons, certain variables which have positive or negative shadow value are not "assigned" axes. The

---

[34]Or, where there are corners, only inessentially indeterminate.

[35]Set up a variant of the Apple-Honey model of Part II, introducing apple blossoms, B, explicitly. Add a production function, $B = B(L_A)$, and substitute $B(L_A)$ for $A(L_A)$ as the second input in honey production. The solution will give out a positive Lagrangean shadow price for B, and profit-maximizing producers of the joint products: A and B, will push L_A to the socially desirable margin.

[36]Though on this last, see Section IV, first paragraph.

beekeeper thinks only in terms of labor, the orchard-owner only in terms of apples.

The important point is that the difficulties reside in institutional arrangements, the feasibility of keeping tab, etc. The scarcities at issue are rationable and finely divisible and there are no difficulties with "total conditions": at the bliss-configuration every activity would pay for itself. Apple nectar has a positive shadow price, which would, if only payment were enforceable, cause nectar production in precisely the right amount and even distribution would be correctly rationed. The difficulty is due exclusively to the difficulty of keeping accounts on the nectar-take of Capulet bees as against Montague bees.[37]

Many of the few examples of interproducer external economies of the reversible technological variety are of this type: "shared deposits" of fish, water, etc.[38] Much more important, so are certain irreversible dynamical examples associated with investment. For instance, many of Pigou's first category of externalities: those that arise in connection with owner-tenant relationships where durable investments are involved, have a primarily organizational quality.[39] Perhaps the most important instance is the training of nonslave labor to skills—as distinct from education in a broader sense (which partakes more of Type (3)). In the end, however, and in particular if restricted to reversible statical cases, it is not easy to think of many significant "ownership externalities" pure and simple. Yet it turns out that only this type of externality is really due to nonappropriability.

Type (2): Technical Externalities

Assume, again, that all goods and services are rationable, exhaustible, scarcities, that individual ordinal indifference maps are

[37]More generally, it could as well be due to difficulty in knowing who "produced" the "benefit"—oil wells drawing on the same pool are an example. The owner cannot protect his own; in fact it is difficult to know what one means by "his own." Moreover, in the case of *diseconomies*, at least, it may be that both the source and the recipient of the "bad" are identified: one factory producing soot and nothing but one laundry in the neighborhood, yet it is difficult to see how a price can be brought to bear on the situation. Presumably the laundry can pay for negative units of smoke.

[38]Though indivisibility elements enter into some of these. Why can't somebody "own" part of a lakeful of fish?

[39]When not simply due, in a world of uncertainty, to inconsistent expectations.

convex and sensitive only to own-consumption and that there exist no ownership "defects" of Type (1). If, then, the technology exhibits indivisibility or smooth increasing returns to scale in the relevant range of output, these give rise to a second and much more important type of market failure: "technical externality."[40]

The essential analytical consequence of indivisibility,[41] whether in inputs, outputs or processes, as well as of smooth increasing returns to scale, is to render the set of feasible points in production (input-output space) nonconvex. A connecting straight line between some pairs of feasible points will pass outside the feasible set. Nonconvexity, in turn, has a devastating effect on duality.[42]

In situations of pure "technical externality" there does, of course, still exist a maximal production possibility frontier (FF); and with a Samuelson-type social indifference map (SS)—i.e., a map "corrected" for income distribution which provides a ranking for the community as a whole of all conceivable output

[40]Again, this is not the same as Viner's "technological." Note, incidentally, that the above formulation unabashedly begs the question of whether smooth increasing returns to scale could or could not arise without indivisibility somewhere. The issue is entirely definitional: it is conceptually impossible to disprove either view by reference to empirical evidence. (Cf. "Simple Analytics," loc. cit., fn. 37 and references.)

The pioneer work on decreasing cost situations is Jules Dupuit's remarkable 1844 essay, "On the Measurement of Utility of Public Works," translated in International Economic Papers, No. 2, ed. A. T. Peacock, et al. Harold Hotelling's "The General Welfare in Relation to Problems of Taxation and of Railway and Utility Rates," in the July 1938 issue of Econometrica, is the originating modern formulation. Cf., also, references to work by R. Frisch, J. E. Meade, W. A. Lewis and others in Nancy Ruggles' excellent survey articles on marginal cost pricing (Review of Economic Studies, XVII (1949–50), 29–46, and 107–26).

[41]Indivisibility means lumpiness "in scale" and not the kind of indivisibility-in-time we call durability. (Durability, as such, does not violate convexity.) Lumpiness has to do with the impossibility to vary continuously, e.g., the capacity service-yield per unit time of such things as bridges.

[42]The best known and perhaps most important variety of nonconvexity occurs where isoquants are properly convex, but returns to scale are increasing, hence the full set of feasible input-output points is nonconvex. (In a two-input, one-output situation, slices by (vertical) planes through the origin perpendicular to the input plane will cut the production surface in such a way as to give a nonconvex boundary.) A production point lying in an "increasing returns" region of a production function implies that (1) the associated average cost curve (AC) is downward sloping at that level of output; (2) the associated marginal cost curve (MC), while it may be rising, could as well be falling and will certainly lie below AC; and (3) the production possibility curve of the community may be nonconvex. On all this, see Part V of "Simple Analytics," loc. cit.

combinations[43]—it is possible, in concept, to define a bliss point(s).[44] Also, where indivisibility is exhibited by outputs, and only outputs, or, stronger, where smoothly increasing returns to scale is the only variety of nonconvexity—isoquants for one, are properly convex—the locus of efficient output combinations can be defined in terms of conditions on marginal-rates-of-input-substitution.[45] Moreover, bliss could possibly occur at a point where SS is internally tangent to FF, perhaps to a convex FF. But even in the least "pathological," most neoclassically well-behaved case, where there exists a meaningfully defined set of shadow prices associated with the bliss point, genuinely profit-seeking competitive producers, responding to that set of prices, would fail to sustain optimal production. At best, even if at the bliss-configuration all MC's are rising, some producers would have to make continuing losses, hence would go out of business; market calculations would necessarily fail "by incentive." If, in turn, prices are not centrally quoted but permitted to set themselves, monopoly behavior will result. There will be failure "by structure."

Further, bliss may require production at levels of output where losses are not only positive, but at a constrained maximum;[46] $p = MC$ may be correct, though MC at that point is falling. If so, the embedded Lagrangean constants may still retain meaning as marginal rates of transformation, but they will fail to sustain efficient production even by Lange-Lerner civil servants who care only about margins and not about absolute totals. There will be failure "by signal": producers under injunction to maximize profit (in the small) will not remain where they ought to be.

If, moreover, we drop the assumption of smooth increasing returns to scale and permit indivisibilities such as give scallop-like effects and kinks in cost curves and in the production-possibility curve, things get even more complicated. Bliss could require production at points of positive but locally minimum profit, where

[43]Cf. P. A. Samuelson, "Social Indifference Curves," *Quarterly Journal of Economics* LXX (Feb. 1956), 1–22. Such a function presumes that *numeraire*-incomes are continuously redistributed so as to maximize in utility space over the community's operative social welfare function.

[44]This is saying very little, of course, except on the level of metaphysics.

[45]Inequalities due to kinks and corners are as good as equalities where all is smooth.

[46]Subject to the requirement that total cost for that level of output be a minimum, i.e., that each producer be on his least-cost expansion path.

MC exceeds AC but is falling. Worse, even if bliss should occur at points where production functions are locally convex and MC (greater than AC) is rising, prequoted prices may still not sustain the solution unless production functions are in fact convex throughout. Though positive and at a local maximum, profits may not be at their maximum-maximorum: other hills with higher peaks may induce producers with vision at a distance to rush away from bliss. Alternatively, if prices are not administered, competition may not be self-policing and markets could fail "by structure."[47]

On the other hand, given our assumptions, the Paretian contract locus of maximal (ordinal) utility combinations which is associated with any one particular output point is defined, as in the trouble-free neoclassical model, by the usual subjective, taste-determined, marginal-rate-of-substitution equalities (or, at corners, inequalities). These MRS equalities, in turn, imply a set of shadow-prices which, if centrally quoted, would efficiently ration among consumers the associated (fixed) totals of goods. In the sphere of exchange, then, a decentralized price system works without flaw.

In what sense do these Type (2) situations exhibit "externality"? In the (generalized) sense that some social costs and benefits remain external to decentralized profitability calculations. With Type (1) externalities, though it is not feasible to police the bliss values of all quantities and prices, there exists embedded in the solution a set of prices whose use for purposes of decentralized signaling would sustain, if only appropriation or exclusion were feasible, both itself and the maximum welfare configuration of inputs, outputs, and distribution. This is not the case here. In

---

[47]Where sharp indivisibility gives a nonconvex production possibility curve with corners and kinks, duality may fail even if there exists a price vector in terms of which decentralized producer-calculations would sustain the bliss-point output mix. The existence of such a vector does not assure that it will coincide with the price-vector which would efficiently ration that bill of goods among consumers. The point is that there may not exist a *single* set of prices which will at the same time keep both consumers and producers from rushing away from where they ought to be. The prices which will effectively mediate production may cause consumers' calculations to go wrong and vice versa.

It should be noted, incidentally, that none of the above takes space and distance considerations into account. For some interesting effects of plant-indivisibility where there are interplant flows and transport takes resources, see T. C. Koopmans and M. Beckmann, "Assignment Problems and the Location of Economic Activities," *Econometrica*, Vol. 25 (Jan. 1957).

Type (1) situations, at the bliss point there is complete correspondence between social and private pay-off, both at the margin and in totals.[48] Profits are at their maxima and non-negative throughout. Here there is no such correspondence; there may well be divergence, either at the margin: bliss-profits may be at a "minimum," or in *totals*. The private totals in terms of which producers in an (idealized) market calculate—total revenue minus total cost—will not reliably signal the social costs and benefits implied by the relevant social indifference curves.[49] Hence at the set of prices which would correctly ration the bliss point bill of goods, that bill of goods may not be produced by profit seekers, or even by Lange-Lerner civil servants.[50]

A point to note, in all this, is that in relation to "technical externalities" the nonappropriability notion, as generally conceived, tends to miss the point. Strictly speaking, it is, of course, true that price mediation, if efficient, cannot be counted on to "appropriate" the full social benefits of activities showing increasing returns to scale or other types of indivisibility to those engaged in them. But the existence of such "uncompensated services" has in this case nothing whatever to do with "divorce of scarcity from ownership," with feasibility limitations on "exclusion." It is entirely feasible to own a bridge and profitably ration crossings; indeed, a private owner would do so. The point is, rather, that such profitable rationing, such "compensation" for services rendered, would inefficiently misallocate the "output" of bridge crossings. If in terms of scarce resource inputs the marginal cost of an

[48]More correctly, there would be such correspondence, if only the p's could be policed.

[49]This is particularly awkward since the very nonconvexities which cause a divergence between private and social total conditions render output-mix calculations based on margins alone wholly inadequate. Even if bliss gives all local profit maxima, there may be several such open to any one producer, hence he must make total calculations in order to choose.

[50]There is one qualification to be made to the above. It may be that the bliss configuration gives unique and positive profit maxima throughout, though some production functions exhibit nonconvexities at a distance. It was to exclude this case that we assumed that increasing returns or indivisibility obtain in the "relevant ranges." Should this happen, no "externality" divergence of social and private calculation will occur, at least in a statical context. But unless all is convex throughout, the existence of such a locally stable tangency cannot be taken as evidence that the point is in fact the bliss-point—a difficulty of considerable significance for dynamical efficiency.

additional crossing is zero, any positive toll will, in general, have the usual monopolistic effect: the resulting output configuration will not be efficient.[51]

This, incidentally, is where most pecuniary external economies lead: a supplier is required to produce in a range of declining AC due to internal technological economies of scale and hence cannot make "ends meet" at the socially correct price. The crucial associated difficulty at the level of social organization is monopoly.

Can we leave matters at that? Not quite. There is a third kind of externality, recently emphasized by Professor Samuelson, caused by so-called "public goods."

Type (3): Public Good Externalities

In some recent writings on public expenditure theory, Samuelson has reintroduced the notion of the collective or public good. The defining quality of a pure public good is that "each individual's consumption of such a good leads to no subtractions from any other individual's consumption of that good . . .",[52] hence, "it differs from a private consumption good in that each man's consumption of it, X_2^1 and X_2^2 respectively, is related to the total X_2 by a condition of *equality* rather than of summation. Thus, by definition, $X_2^1 = X_2$ and $X_2^2 = X_2$."[53]

As Samuelson has shown, the form of the marginal rate of substitution conditions which define the Pareto-efficient utility possibility frontier in a world where such public goods exist, or at least where there are outputs with important "public" qualities, renders any kind of price-market routine virtually useless for the computation of output-mix and of distribution, hence, also, for organizational decentralization. Where some restraints in the maximum problem take the form: total production of X *equals* consumption by Crusoe of X *equals* consumption of X by Friday, Pareto efficiency requires that the marginal rate of transformation in production between X and Y equal not the (equalized) MRS of each

[51]Of course, if at bliss the bridge were to be used "to capacity," it is possible that the Lagrangean ration price (now positive) would make commercial operation profitable. If so, an administered price setup would efficiently mediate the demand and supply of crossings. But while a Lange-Lerner system would work fine, laissez-faire markets would fail "by structure."

[52]P. A. Samuelson, *Review of Economics and Statistics*, XXXVI (Nov. 1954), 387.

[53]P. A. Samuelson, *Review of Economics and Statistics*, XXXVI (Nov. 1955), 350.

separate consumer, but rather the algebraic *sum* of such *MRS*'s. This holds, of course, in what in other respects is a conventionally neoclassical world: preference and production functions are of well-behaved curvature, all is convex.

If, then, at the bliss point, with Y as numeraire, Px is equated to the marginal Y-cost of X in production (as is required to get optimal production), and X is offered for sale at that p_x, preference-maximizing consumers adjusting their purchases so as to equate their individual *MRS*'s to p_x will necessarily under-use X. Moreover, a pricing game will not induce consumers truthfully to reveal their preferences. It pays each consumer to understate his desire for X relative to Y, since his enjoyment of X is a function only of total X, rather than, as is true of a pure private good, just of that fraction of X he pays for.

The two Samuelson articles[54] explore both the analytics and the general implications of "public goods." Here the notion is of relevance because much externality is due precisely to the "public" qualities of a great many activities. For example, the externality associated with the generation of ideas, knowledge, etc., is due in good part to the public character of these "commodities." Many interconsumer externalities are of this sort: my party is my neighbor's disturbance, your nice garden is any passerby's nice view, my children's education is your children's good company, my Strategic Air Command is your Strategic Air Command, etc. The same consumption item enters, positively or negatively, both our preference functions. The consumptions involved are intrinsically and essentially joint.

This kind of externality is distinct from either of the other two pure types. Here technological nonconvexities need in no way be involved. In fact the $MRT = \Sigma MRS$ condition is certain to hold true precisely where production takes place at constant or nonincreasing returns, and hence where the production possibility set is necessarily convex. Further, there are no decentralized organizational rearrangements, no private bookkeeping devices, which would, if only feasibility were not at issue, eliminate the difficulty. It is the central implication of the Samuelson model that where

---

[54]And a third unpublished paper, which was read at the 1955 American Economic Association meetings and to a copy of which I came to have access while this paper was being written. For earlier writings on public goods, by Wicksell, Lindahl, Musgrave, Bowen and others see references in the above cited Samuelson articles.

public good phenomena are present, there does not exist a set of prices associated with the (perfectly definable) bliss point, which would sustain the bliss configuration. The set of prices which would induce profit-seeking competitors to produce the optimal bill of goods, would be necessarily inefficient in allocating that bill of goods. Moreover, even abstracting from production, no single set of relative prices will efficiently ration any fixed bill of goods so as to place the system on its contract locus, except in the singular case where at that output and income-distribution MRS's of every individual are identically the same (or zero for all but one). There is failure "by existence."

IV. COMMENTS

Type (1)

In a sense, Type (1) is not symmetrical with the other two categories. One can think of some nontrivial instances where the institutional element does appear to be "binding": skill-training of people, for example. But even there, it could be argued that the crucial elements are durability, uncertainty, and the fact that slavery as a mode of organization is itself in the nature of a public good which enters people's preference functions, or the implicit social welfare function, inseparably from the narrowly "economic" variables. In those instances, in turn, where bookkeeping feasibility appears to be the cause of the trouble, the question arises why bookkeeping is less feasible than where it is in fact being done. In the end, it may be that much of what appears to partake of Type (1) is really a compound of Types (2) and (3), with dynamical durability and uncertainty elements thrown in. At any rate, a deeper analysis of this category may cause it substantially to shrink.

Nonproduced Scarcities

One particular instance where what appears like Type (1) is really Type (2) warrants special mention. Public ownership of nonproduced resources, e.g. the lakes and mountains of national parks, may make it appear that externality is due to statutory barriers to private ownership and commercial rental. But this is missing the point. Take, for instance, a community which has available a single source of fresh water of fixed capacity. Assume that the bliss solution gives out a positive ration-price per gallon such as would make sale of the water commercially profitable. Yet a laissez-faire system would fail, "by structure," to sustain bliss. A private owner of the single indivisible well, if given his head, would take advantage of the tilt in the demand curve. The real cause of externality is not the arbitrary rapaciousness of public authority but the indivisibility of the source of supply. This case, by the way, is akin to where indivisibility or increasing returns to scale within a range allow profitable scope for one or a few efficient producers, but for no more. At the bliss price all will do the right thing, but if prices are not administered, oligopoly or monopoly will result. A capitalist Lange-Lerner system with private ownership but administered prices would work fine, but laissez-faire markets would fail.

Meade's "Atmosphere"

The relation of my tri-cornered ordering to Meade's polar categories is of interest.[55] His first category, "unpaid factors," is identical to my Type (1). But his second, labeled "atmosphere," is a rather curious composite. Meade's qualitative characterization of "atmosphere": e.g., of afforestation-induced rainfall, comes very close to the public good notion.[56] He links this, however, as necessarily bound up with increasing returns to scale in production to society at large, hence a J. B. Clark-like overexhaustion, adding-up problem.[57]

If, following Meade, one abstracts from shared water-table phenomena (let rain-caused water input be rigidly proportional to area) then Farmer Jones' rain is Farmer Smith's rain and we have my Type (3). But nothing in this situation requires that either farmer's full production function (with an axis for rain) need show increasing returns to scale. It may be that returns to additional bundles of non-rain inputs, with given constant rainfall, diminish sharply, and that it takes proportional increases of land, labor *and*

---

[55]*Op. cit.* (This and the next section can be omitted without loss of continuity.)

[56]See esp. bottom of p. 61 and top of p. 62, *op. cit.*

[57]Since his argument is restricted to competitive situations, hence necessarily excludes increasing-returns-to-paid-factors such as would require production at a loss, Meade specifies constant returns to proportional variation of labor and land in wheat farming, though the full production function for wheat, including the atmosphere input (rain), exhibits increasing returns to scale. But the individual farmer does not pay for rain, hence his factor payments just match his sales revenue, by the Euler Theorem.

rain to get a proportional effect on output. If so, Meade's overexhaustion problem will not arise. But all would not be well: the public good quality of rainfall would cause an independent difficulty, one that Meade, if I understand him correctly, does not take into account, i.e., that rain ought to be "produced" by timber growers until its *MC* is equal to the sum of all the affected farmers *MRS's* for rain as an input, whatever may be the curvature of the latter's production functions.[58]

On the other hand, Meade's formal mathematical treatment of "atmosphere," as distinct from his verbal characterization and his example, suggests that it is a nonappropriable, and therefore unpaid, factor which gives rise to increasing returns to scale to society though not to the individual producer. At least this is all he needs for the effect he is looking for: a self-policing though nonoptimal competitive situation, where, because the full production functions (i.e., with an axis for rain) are of greater than first degree, the correction of externality via subsidies to promote the creation of favorable atmosphere requires net additions to society's fiscal burden. If this is the crucial consequence of "atmosphere," then it need have no "public" quality. All this would happen even though Smith and Jones were "competing" for the water from the shared water-table under their subsoil, just like bees competing for nectar.

Scitovsky's "Two Concepts"[59]

Professor Scitovsky, in turn, in his suggestive 1954 article, distinguishes between the statical direct interactions of equilibrium

---

[58]Formally, Meade denotes "atmosphere" as a situation where the production function, e.g., of farmers takes the $X_1 = H_1(L_1, C_1)A_1(X_2)$, with L as labor, C as capital and A the atmosphere effect on X_1 of X_2. The full function exhibits increasing returns to scale but the H function alone, with A constant, is homogeneous of first degree. But why can't this be put in terms of Meade's unpaid factor type function where $X_1 = H_1(L_1 C_1 X_2)$? Example: $X_1 = L_1 C_1^{-a} X_2$. All this has nothing to do with whether $A = A_1 + A_2$ or rather $A = A_1 = A_2$. Unfortunately, the example itself tends to mislead. The fact that exclusion of rain-users (farmers) by producers (timber-growers) is hardly feasible, i.e., that rain is like Type (1), distracts attention from the important point that *if* rain is, as Meade tells us, a public good, then rationing it by price would be inefficient even if it were feasible. (It should be said that Meade concludes his article: "But, in fact, of course, external economies or diseconomies may not fall into either of these precise divisions and may contain features of both of them.")

[59]*Op. Cit.*

theory and the kinds of pecuniary external economies emphasized in the economic development literature. He classifies the former as consumer-consumer, producer-consumer, and producer-producer interactions, labels the last as external economies and asserts that they are rare and, on the whole, unimportant.

While Scitovsky does not raise the question of what gives rise to such producer-producer interactions, both his examples, and his conclusion that they are of little significance, suggest that he is thinking primarily of Type (1): nonappropriability. But this is to ignore public goods—surely a more important cause of interaction. Moreover, by taking full account of these, Scitovsky's "fifth and important case, which, however, does not quite fit into . . . (his) . . . classification . . . , where society provides social services through communal action and makes these available free of charge to all persons and firms," can be made nicely to fall into place.[60]

Samuelson on Types (2) and (3)

While the public good model helps to sort out the phenomena Meade lumped under "atmosphere," Samuelson himself emphasizes the analytical bond between indivisibility and public good situations. In both an explicit "summing in" is required of "all direct and indirect utilities and costs in all social decisions."[61] In Type (2) situations it is the intramarginal consumer's and producer's surpluses associated with various all or nothing decisions "in-the-lump" that have to be properly (interpersonally) weighted and summed, while in Type (3) it is only utilities and costs at the margin that require adding. But, and this is the crucial shared

[60]*Ibid.*, fn. 3, p. 144. Scitovsky, following Meade, restricts his "first concept" of external economies to phenomena consistent with competitive equilibrium. He treats indivisibilities and increasing returns to scale as belonging to his "second concept" which has to do with disequilibrium, investment decisions, and growth. It is, of course, entirely legitimate to restrict analysis to competitive situations. But the Scitovsky treatment must not be taken to imply that lumpiness is irrelevant to statical analysis of stationary solution points. If one is interested in the statical efficiency of decentralized price calculations, they are crucial. But this is carping. Scitovsky's important contribution lies in emphasizing and clarifying the point first hinted at by P. N. Rosenstein-Rodan that in a world of disequilibrium dynamics pecuniary external economies may play an independent role—one distinct, that is, from simply being an unreliable signal of monopoly troubles (*Economic Journal*, LIII, 1943, 202–11).

[61]*Ibid.*, p. 9.

quality of the two categories, both make it necessary to sum utilities over many people.[62]

Exclusion

One more comment may be warranted on the significance, in a public good type situation, of nonappropriability. "Exclusion" is almost never impossible. A recluse can build a wall around his garden, Jones can keep his educated children away from those of Smith, etc. But if thereby some people (e.g., the recluse) are made happier and some (e.g., the passers-by) less happy, any decision about whether to "exclude" or not implies an algebraic summing of the somehow-weighted utilities of the people involved. And if the wall requires scarce resources, the final utility sum must be matched against the cost of the wall. When Type (3) blends with indivisibility in production, as it does in the case of the wall, or in the case of a lighthouse, the comparison has to be made between intramarginal totals. Where no lumpiness is involved (e.g., the decibels at which I play my radio) only MRS and perhaps MC calculations are called for. But the really crucial decision may well be about how much perfectly feasible appropriation and exclusion is desirable.

Arrangements to Offset

It is of interest to speculate what, if any, organizational rearrangements could offset the three categories of externality and avoid the need for centrally calculated tax-subsidy schemes.[63] In concept, Type (1) can be offset by rearrangements of ownership and by "proper" bookkeeping, such as need not violate the struc-

[62]There is one qualification to be made: if all public good and increasing returns to scale industries produce only intermediate products, all externalities may cancel out in intra-business-sector transactions. If so, only total revenues and total costs have to be summed. Incidentally, the exposition may misleadingly suggest another symmetry between Types (2) and (3). In a pure Type (3) situation, *if* there are no public producers' goods, then while prices cannot be used to ration the bliss point output-mix, they can be used efficiently to mediate production. In Type (2), on the other hand, *if* all final consumables are divisible, price calculations, while failing in production, will work in exchange. This symmetry breaks down, of course, as soon as one violates, as does the real world, the two "if's."

[63]For illustrative derivation of the formulas for corrective taxes and subsidies in Type (1) situations, see Meade (*op cit.*).

tural requirements of decentralized competition. Further, no resort to nonmarket tests would be required.[64]

Types (2) and (3) are not so amenable to correction consistent with decentralized institutions. The easiest possible case occurs where increasing returns obtain on the level of single producers'-good plants, much of whose production can be absorbed by a single user firm. Here vertical integration takes care of the problem. Not every process inside a well-run firm is expected to cover its cost in terms of the correct set of internal accounting (shadow) prices. Total profits are the only criterion, and it may pay a firm to build a private bridge between its two installations on opposite sides of a river yet charge a zero accounting price for its use by the various decentralized manufacturing and administrative divisions; the bridge would make accounting losses, yet total company profits will have increased. As long, then, as such integration is consistent with the many-firms requirement for competition, no extra-market tests are required.[65] The private total conditions: TR less TC, correctly account for social gain.

Where a producers'-good firm, required to produce at a stage of falling AC, sells to many customer firms and industries, an adding up of all the associated TR's and TC's at the precalculated "as if" competitive prices associated with the bliss point would again effectively "mop up" all social costs and benefits.[66] But the institutional reorganization required to get correct decentralized calculation involves horizontal and vertical integration, and the monopoly or oligopoly problem looms large indeed. The type (3) case of a pure *producers'* public good belongs here: only input MRS's along production functions require summing.

In the general case of a mixed producer-consumer good (or of a pure consumer good) which is "public" or is produced under conditions of increasing returns to scale, it is impossible to avoid comparison of multiperson utility totals. Explicit administrative

[64] The Emancipation Proclamation could constitute, of course, a substantial barrier.

[65] If, however, the "break even" scale of operation of the integrated firm (i.e., where MC cuts AC from below) is much greater than if the river had not been there to span, or could be spanned by some means of a lower fixed-cost-to-variable-cost ratio, the monopoly problem may simply be "pushed forward" to consumer markets.

[66] Assuming that all consumer goods are finely divisible and require no lumpy decisions by consumers.

consideration must be given, if you like, to consumer's and producer's surpluses for which no market-institution tests exist short of that provided by a perfectly discriminating monopolist. But to invoke perfect discrimination is to beg the question. It implies knowledge of all preference functions, while as Samuelson has emphasized,[67] the crucial game-theoretical quality of the situation is that consumers will not correctly reveal their preferences: it will pay them to "cheat."

Blends

Examination is needed of various blends of Types (2) and (3), such as Sidgwick's lighthouse;[68] or, for that matter, and as suggested by Samuelson, of blends of public and private goods even where all production functions are fully convex. There are many puzzling cases. Do bridge crossings differ in kind from radio programs? Both involve indivisibility and, where variable cost is zero for the bridge, *zero MC's*. The correct price for an extra stroller, as for an extra listener, is clearly zero. Yet bridge crossings have a distinctly private quality: bridges get congested, physical capacity is finite. This is not true of a broadcast. There is no finite limit to the number of sets that can costlessly tune in.[69] Radio programs, then, have a public dimension. Yet, in a sense, so do bridges. While your bridge crossing is not my bridge crossing, in fact could limit my crossings, your bridge is my bridge. What is involved here is that most things are multidimensional and more than one dimension may matter.

V. Efficiency, Markets and Choice of Institutions

All the above has to do with the statical efficiency of price-directed allocation in more or less idealized market situations.

[67]Cf. any of the three "Public Expenditure" articles (*supra*).

[68]Sidgwick, by the way, as also Pigou, thought of a lighthouse as of Type (1). It is, of course, "inconvenient" to levy tolls on ships, but it is hardly impossible to "exclude," for instance by means of "scrambling" devices (though poor Sidgwick could hardly have known about such things). The point is, rather, that it would be inefficient to do so; the marginal cost to society of an additional ship taking directional guidance from the beacon atop the Statue of Liberty is zero, *ipso* price should be zero. In the case of a lighthouse this is twice true: because the beacon is in the nature of a public good: more for the Queen Mary means no less for the Liberté; and because a lighthouse is virtually an all-fixed-cost, zero variable-cost facility.

[69]Richard Eckaus has suggested to me that it is possible to exhaust the space to which the broadcast is limited and that this makes the situation a little more like that of a bridge. Neither of us is entirely satisfied, however.

Relevance to choice of institutions depends, of course, on the prevalence of the phenomena which cause externality and on the importance to be attached to statical efficiency. Space precludes extensive discussion of these important issues, but a few casual comments, in the form of *dicta*, are perhaps warranted.

How important are nonappropriability, nonconvexity and public goods? I would be inclined to argue that while nonappropriability is of small import,[70] the same cannot be said of the other two. True enough, it is difficult to think of many examples of pure public goods. Most things—even battleships, and certainly open air concerts and schools (though not knowledge)—have an "if more for you then less for me" quality. But this is of little comfort. As long as activities have even a trace of publicness, price calculations are inefficient.[71] And it is surely hard to gainsay that some degree of public quality pervades much of even narrowly "economic" activity.

Lumpiness, in turn, and nonlinearity of the increasing returns sort, while in most instances a matter of degree, and, within limits, of choice, are also in the nature of things. The universe is full of singularities, thresholds and nonproportionalities: speed of light, gravitational constant, the relation of circumference to area, etc. As economists we can cajole or bully engineers into designing processes and installations that save on congealed inputs and give smaller maximal service yields, especially when designing for low-income communities. But the economically perhaps arbitrary, not completely physics-imposed quality of indivisibilities associated with standard designs and ways of doing things should not blind. Nonlinearity and lumpiness are evident facts of nature.[72]

More important, at this level of discourse[73]—though perhaps it hardly need be said—is that statical market efficiency is neither sufficient nor necessary for market institutions to be the "preferred" mode of social organization. Quite apart from institutional

[70]Except for labor skills—and these would take us beyond the bounds of reversible statics.

[71]This is not to say that there exist other feasible modes of social calculation and organization which are more efficient.

[72]Their quantitative significance is, of course, very sensitive to scale, to "size" of markets. This explains the particular emphasis on the role of "social overheads" in low income countries.

[73]Where recourse to strategic considerations of feasibility, crucial though they be, is quite out of order.

considerations, Pareto efficiency as such may not be necessary for bliss.[74] If, e.g., people are sensitive not only to their own jobs but to other people's as well, or more generally, if such things as relative status, power, and the like, matter, the injunction to maximize output, to hug the production-possibility frontier, can hardly be assumed "neutral," and points on the utility frontier may associate with points inside the production frontier.[75] Furthermore, there is nothing preordained about welfare functions which are sensitive only to individual consumer's preferences. As a matter of fact, few people would take such preferences seriously enough to argue against any and all protection of individuals against their own mistakes (though no external effects be involved).

All this is true even when maximization is subject only to technological and resource limitations. Once we admit other side relations, which link input-output variables with "noneconomic" political and organizational values, matters become much more complicated. If markets be ends as well as means, their noneffi-ciency is hardly sufficient ground for rejection.[76] On the other hand, efficient markets may not do, even though Pareto-efficiency

[74]That it is never sufficient is, of course, well known. Of the infinite Pareto-efficient configurations at best only one: that which gives the "right" distribution of income in terms of the W-function that is to count, has normative, prescriptive significance. Moreover, most interesting W-functions are likely to be sensitive to "noneconomic" factors, such as are, if not inconsistent, at least extraneous to Paretian considerations. Where such additional values of a political or social nature are separable from input-output values (i.e., where the two sets can be varied independently of each other) one "can" of course separate the overall W-function into a "political" and an "economic" component and maximize separately over each.

[75]This is different from the usual case of consumer sensitivity to the input-output configuration of producers, e.g., factory soot or a functional but ugly plant spoiling the view. Such joint-product "bads" can be treated as inputs and treated in the usual Paretian fashion. It is a different matter that their public quality will violate duality, hence render market calculation inefficient.

[76]This is too crude a formulation. It is not necessary that markets as such be an "ultimate" value. Political and social (non-output) values relating to the configuration of power, initiative, opportunity, etc., may be so much better served by some form of nonefficient market institutions than by possible alternative modes of more efficient organization as to warrant choice of the former. The analytical point, in all this, is that the outcome of a maximization process and the significance of "efficiency" are as sensitive to the choice of side-conditions as to the welfare-function and that these need be "given" to the economist in the same sense that a welfare function has to be given.

is necessary for bliss. Even with utopian lump-sum redistribution, efficiency of the "invisible hand" does not preclude preference for other efficient modes of organization, if there be any.[77]

Yet when all is said, and despite the host of crucial feasibility considerations which render choice in the real world inevitably a problem in the strategy of "second best," it is surely interesting and useful to explore the implications of Paretian efficiency. Indeed, much remains to be done. There is need, in particular, for more systematic exploration of the inadequacies of market calculation in a setting of growth.[78]

[77]The above is still strictly statical. For related dynamical problems, e.g., possible conflict between one-period and intertemporal efficiency, cf., "On Capital Productivity, Input Allocation and Growth," LXXI (Feb. 1957).

[78]The development literature on market failure, while full of suggestive insight, is in a state of considerable confusion. Much work is needed to exhaust and elucidate the seminal ideas of Young, Rosenstein-Rodan, Nurkse and others. For important beginnings, see Scitovsky (op. cit.), M. Fleming, "External Economies and the Doctrine of Balanced Growth," Economic Journal, LXV (June 1955), and Fellner (op. cit.).

The view that we should not turn social historian or what not, that the logic of economizing has some prescriptive significance, rests on the belief that narrowly "economic" efficiency is important in terms of many politically relevant W-functions, and consistent with a wide variety of power and status configurations and modes of social organization. On the other hand, some may feel that the very language of Paretian welfare economics: "welfare function," "utility-frontier," in relation to choice of social institutions, is grotesque. What is at stake, of course, is not the esthetics of language, on which I yield without demur, but abstraction and rigorous theorizing.

Section II

Developments in the Theory of Markets

4. Equal Access vs. Selective Access: A Critique of Public Goods Theory

Kenneth D. Goldin

More than twenty years ago, Samuelson published his "Pure Theory of Public Goods." Few can deny that this is one of the most elegant theories of modern times. For more than twenty years, those who admire this theory have searched for equally elegant real-world examples. But this has been a frustrating search. Case after case, although initially plausible, has failed to fit the framework of public goods theory. Faith in the relevance of Samuelson's theory has remained: if one example doesn't fit, then surely there must be others.

But so many examples have been analyzed, and found wanting, that the time has come to make the opposing argument: the pure theory of public goods is an elegant theory without significant application. Furthermore, it is a dangerously misleading theory if it suggests to the unwary that government services should be handled *as if* they were public goods.

The evidence suggests that we are *not* faced with a set of goods and services which have the inherent characteristics of public goods. Rather we are faced with an unavoidable choice regarding every good or service: shall everyone have *equal access* to that service (in which case the service will be similar to a public good) or shall the service be available *selectively*: to some, but not to others? In practice, public goods theory is often used in such a way that one overlooks this important choice problem. Often it is suggested that a certain service is a public good. And once this suggestion is made, it is usually assumed that the service must be equally available to everyone. But this is seriously misleading as, in general, equal access to government services is neither necessary nor efficient.

Reprinted, by permission, from *Public Choice* 29 (Spring 1977): 53–71.

The author thanks Gordon Tullock and an unidentified referee for comments on an earlier draft.

For example, consumers wishing to control insects may choose to have their local government hire an airplane to spray the entire town. Hence, insect control is often *classified* as a public good. As with other public goods, everyone in town has *equal access* to the airplane spray. The equal access feature can be justified in two ways: excluding anyone from the airplane spray is *impossible*, and since nothing is saved by doing so, exclusion is *inefficient*. But consumers seeking insect control have a choice. (Tullock, 1970) They can each buy spray guns and spray their own yards. Although this may be more costly than airplane spraying, efficiency does not depend on costs alone. Hand spraying allows greater diversity in chemicals, timing, and extent of spraying, and may yield substantially greater benefits. (Cf. Buchanan, 1970) This example is intriguing for two reasons. First, it shows that consumers have a choice of distribution system. They may choose to give everyone equal access to insect control (airplane spraying), or they may choose a distribution system (hand spraying) which allows unequal or *selective access* to insect control. Second, the example forces a closer look at costs. With hand spraying, it is clear that serving more persons has added costs (for additional chemicals, equipment, and labor). Similarly, resources are saved when someone is excluded from insect control. Does a change in distribution system (to airplane spraying) make it costless to serve additional persons (so that "nothing is saved" when someone is excluded)? It may seem at first glance that new residents in the town will get the same protection without added cost, but this will be true only if the new residents live within the existing town boundaries and engage in no insect-attracting activities (such as allowing exposed water or garbage to stand outdoors). If the new residents either live outside the town perimeter, or engage in insect attracting activities, or both, then serving them will involve added costs. Either more airplane time and chemicals must be used (to maintain protection levels), or the same inputs can be used to provide reduced protection (which is a cost to the original residents). Thus, for both distribution systems (equal access and selective access), *it is costly to serve additional persons*, except in the special cases mentioned above. (Airplane spraying to control mosquitos is no longer common in the U.S., but it remains as a textbook case.)

At least for this example, it is pointless to classify the service (insect control) as a public good, as it may be distributed with either equal or selective access. The efficient choice of distribution system is an empirical matter, and cannot be found by a priori classification. This conclusion also holds for many major goods and services, traditionally classified as public goods or externalities. (See Section III: Case Studies) At least for the many cases studied:

1. Consumers have a choice of distribution system. Since it is generally costly to serve additional users, the choice between equal and selective access is not trivial.

2. The normative recommendation, that equal access is efficient, cannot be based on a priori classification. For each service, an empirical comparison of the benefits and costs of equal vs. selective access is necessary to determine efficiency. Such empirical studies do not exist.

3. The simple positive analysis, that there is equal access to goods classified as public, because this is the only possibility, is not adequate. Since there is a choice, it is necessary to explain why equal access is chosen over selective access.

This study suggests that there are *no* goods or services which are *inherently* public goods or externalities; that there is *always* a choice between equal and selective access; and that there is *generally* an additional cost to serve additional persons. But this strong theorem can never be proven, as counter examples may always be found. However, considering the range of case studies in this paper, it seems unlikely that any *important* exceptions will be found.

This paper does *not* deal with the issues of who supplies a good (government vs. business) nor how it is financed (taxation vs. prices). The focus is on the distribution of goods (equal vs. selective). There is a tendency to equate equal access with tax financed government supply, but this need not be the case: government supply often involves user fees and restrictive regulations (i.e., selective access). So arguments in favor of selective access deal only with access; they do not imply a case against either government supply or tax financing.

The traditional interpretation of public goods theory (section I) is followed by a reinterpretation (section II) and case studies (section III).

I. Traditional Scenario

A. Classification

Modern public goods theory begins with Samuelson's sparse and elegant statements. (1954, 1955) Some goods, like national defense, are *classified* as public (or collective) goods. Other goods, like bread, are classified as non-public goods. (Samuelson uses the terms "public" and "collective" interchangeably.) This attempt to classify each good, as either a public good or not a public good, is certainly followed by other economists. Goods like pollution control and crime deterrence are routinely classified as public goods, while most types of food, clothing, shelter and transport are treated as nonpublic goods. Traditionally, then, each good is classified as either a public good or not a public good. Choice between equal and selective distribution for a given service (like airplane vs. hand spraying for insect control) usually is not considered.

B. Equal Access (Normative)

If a service is classified as a public good, then it *should* be distributed in a way which gives everyone equal access. Why? The first reason is *necessity*. By Samuelson's definition, *it is impossible to exclude anyone* from using a public good. If a public good is supplied to one person, it must be equally available to everyone else. Although people may place different values on the good, each and every person has equal access to the service, because exclusion is impossible. Of course, the word "everyone" must be taken with a grain of salt, since few public goods are available to everyone in the world. Rather, public goods are equally available to everyone in a specified group, such as everyone in a nation, state or town, or even to everyone in a two-person neighborhood. Thus, public goods run the gamut from the international level to two-person externalities. (Samuelson, 1969) Since the availability of public goods may be limited to a small group, it is necessary to be more precise about "impossibility of exclusion." For a public good, it is impossible to exclude anyone from *either* the group receiving the service or the service itself. Hence, air pollution in Los Angeles may be classified as a public good, if no one can be prevented from either moving to L.A. or from enjoying L.A.'s pollution control benefits. But a hotel swimming pool is not a public good. Although all hotel guests have equal access to the pool, only selected persons have access to the group (hotel guests) receiving the service.

The egalitarian recommendation of traditional public goods theory also rests on the pillar of *efficiency*. By Samuelson's definition, *everyone consumes the "same" unit of a public good*. If an additional person enters the group to which a public good is supplied, there is "no subtraction from any other individual's consumption of that good. . . ." (Samuelson, 1954) To fit this definition, a public good cannot be subject to congestion. If an additional user did cause (or increase) congestion, then there would indeed be a subtraction from other individuals' consumption. But if everyone can use the same unit of a public good without congestion, then there is no rivalry among consumers. So there are three ways to express this important characteristic of public goods: *everyone consumes the same unit; non-congestable; non-rivalness*. But in terms of economic theory, all three terms have a common meaning: *a zero marginal cost of serving additional persons*. The public good itself is costly, and there is agreement that supplying more of the public good (*e.g.*, more soldiers) has a positive marginal cost. But by definition, the marginal cost of serving additional persons is zero, and herein lies the second basis for recommending equal access. As long as it is costless to serve additional persons, it is inefficient to exclude anyone, no matter how little he values the service. Exclusion reduces benefits without reducing costs. To be more precise, there is no inefficiency in excluding persons who get *no* benefit from the good, and it might be efficient to exclude those persons who dislike the public good (*e.g.*, excluding pacifists from defense). But since exclusion is impossible by definition, the point is trivial.

The traditional scenario, then, is to classify some services as public goods. If these services are worth having at all, then everyone should have equal access, for reasons of necessity (exclusion is impossible) and efficiency (zero marginal cost of serving additional persons). This scenario is based on Samuelson's definition of a public good. Although other definitions of public, or collective goods have appeared, the definition used here is necessary if one is to use the familiar graphic analysis (*e.g.*, Musgrave and Musgrave, 1976, p. 53) In that analysis demand (or marginal benefit) curves are added vertically, which is meaningful only if everyone consumes equal quantities. Also, the marginal cost line (for more units of the public good, *e.g.*, the marginal cost of soldiers) is drawn independently of the number of persons served. This is meaningful only if the marginal costs of serving additional persons is zero.

It is also traditional to note that some activities (like education) yield multiple outputs. If some of these are classified as public, and others nonpublic, then the activity is an *impure* or *quasi* public good. For those outputs which are classified as public, equal access is justified on the basis of necessity and efficiency. That is, although the activity may be impure or quasi, the normative recommendations are *fully* applied to that part of the output which is classified as a public good.

C. *Equal Access (Positive)*

The traditional interpretation of public goods vastly simplifies positive analysis. Why do consumers have equal access to public goods? Because exclusion is impossible. Why has there been growth in the part of output to which consumers have equal access? Because of a shift in consumer preferences towards those services which are classified as public goods. These questions are much more difficult to answer if consumers have a choice of distribution system (equal vs. selective access) for every service.

II. A Reinterpretation

The traditional scenario, then, is that it is useful to classify some goods as public, and that for public goods, equal access is both necessary and efficient. But analysis of a wide range of case studies suggests that equal access is neither necessary nor efficient, so that classification of some goods as public is not useful. Rather, the case studies allow two generalizations:

First, there is a *choice of distribution system*. Goods may be distributed without exclusion, so that everyone has equal access to the service and to membership in the group receiving the service. But it is also possible to distribute goods selectively, by excluding some persons either from the service or from the group to which the service is available. Distributing selectively does not mean adopting a distribution system intended for equal access (such as airplane spraying) and then attempting to exclude people (which may prove impossible). Rather, exclusion may require a distribution system aimed at selective access in the first place (*e.g.*, hand spraying).

Second, except in special, essentially trivial cases, *all* goods and services are congestable, there is *always* rivalry among consumers, and the marginal cost of serving additional persons is *positive*. The exceptions have little real-world relevance. For example, it is costless to serve additional persons if they don't use the service, or if the service is not scarce (i.e., there is more than enough to satisfy everyone).

Clearly there is much empirical work to be done. Those interested in normative policy recommendations may investigate the costs and benefits under the two distribution systems. These will depend on the technology of exclusion devices and the diversity of individual preferences. Both factors change over time: efficiency may dictate equal access now; selective access in the future. The efficient distribution system is not an unchangeable inherent characteristic of each service.[1] Those interested in positive economics may investigate why equal access is chosen for some goods; selective access for others. What is the mechanism leading to these choices? Are the choices efficient?

There is also a need for further theoretical development. When goods and services are congestable, then various *qualities* are possible (such as crowded and uncrowded beaches). Given diverse preferences, efficient resource allocation may dictate the simultaneous availability of two or more qualities. (Goldin, 1972) But the optimal mix of qualities may be difficult to specify, since both demands and costs are likely to be interdependent. (The problem is similar to specifying the optimal *mix*—and not the optimal type!—of fresh, frozen and canned orange juice.) This is a general equilibrium problem, much easier solved in principle than in practice.

III. Case Studies

A. Major Government Services

These services are "major" in the sense of expenditures (defense, education, roads), public interest (police, outdoor recreation), and academic interest (lighthouses). Although many people have equal access to these services, some limitations are common and selective access is sometimes observed. Further, all these services are congestable. To serve more persons *without* increased congestion, it is generally necessary to provide more facilities. Alternatively, more persons can be served using existing facilities, but only by increasing congestion and providing a lower quality service (which is a cost to the existing users). Additional persons may be served *without* additional cost only in what are essentially

[1]Head and Shoup (1969) note that most services can be rendered in either a "marketing" or "non-marketing" mode (i.e., distributed with selective or equal access). But their paper still aims at *classification*: "When a service can be rendered in either the marketing mode or the non-marketing mode it is a public good if it can be rendered more efficiently in the latter mode." (p. 569)

trivial cases: if they don't use the service; or if the service is not scarce (*i.e.*, there are unused services available).

Highways. At first glance, it appears that everyone has equal access to toll-free roads. This isn't quite accurate, since one must first have access to a registered vehicle, licensed driver, and taxed fuel. Still, everyone drives on the same road system. But it is generally costly to serve additional persons. During rush hours, additional freeway users may be served by building additional highway lanes, thus allowing other users to maintain their previous speed. Alternatively, additional rush hour users may be squeezed onto the existing roadway, causing increased congestion, and imposing substantial costs on other users. Even during slack periods, additional users require additional lanes, or they will increase the risk of accidents to other drivers (and either way there is a cost).[2] Even country lanes must be widened for heavier traffic, or there will be a deterioration of safety and speed for other users. There is no cost for serving additional persons only (i) if the additional persons don't drive or (ii) for the first user on an otherwise empty road or bridge. Since costs are generally positive, it may be efficient to exclude those persons whose marginal benefits are less than the marginal cost of serving them. Selective access can also serve to make available a *choice of quality*. Fast lanes and slow lanes can exist, side by side, during rush hours, on urban roads—but only if access to the fast lanes is selective. (With equal access, all lanes become equally congested.) The availability of diverse *qualities* will generally increase the benefits generated by a road system. (Goldin, 1972)

Not all roads are distributed with equal access. Early roads were turnpikes, and today there are some toll roads and toll bridges. Obviously a cash price is one way to make access selective. Another method is to put taxes on complementary products (e.g., fuel, tires and vehicles), although this is widely criticised as an inefficient

---

[2]Mansfield (1975 pp. 497–98) fails to notice this interaction among users. He writes: "Consider an uncrowded bridge. If Mr. Smith crosses the bridge, this does not interfere with Mr. Jones's crossing it. Thus, the use of this bridge is a public good . . . [I]t is perfectly feasible to charge a fee for crossing the bridge . . . it would be inefficient to do so." But there is some likelihood that Smith *will* interfere with (*i.e.*, impose a cost on) Jones, as Smith may be drunk, careless, or forced by bad weather into a collision with Jones. Hence it *may* be efficient to exclude Smith from using the bridge, if his valuation of bridge usage is less than the probable cost he will impose on Jones.

screening device. Access can also be limited by rules. On some California freeways and bridges, special fast lanes are reserved for buses and car pools. This is not to say that these examples of selective access are necessarily efficient. Rather, there is no a priori case for equal access to all roads, because exclusion is clearly possible, and it is generally costly to serve additional persons. Positive economists should explain why we have chosen equal access to most, *but not all roads*.

Education. Schools produce several outputs. One is the education of students, considered here. Other outputs may include research and decisionmaking, and these are considered separately in Part B.

Most American children have equal access to their neighborhood public school (or to other public schools if their parents move to other neighborhoods). Although many children may go to the same school, serving additional students requires additional teachers, books and schoolrooms. Alternatively, additional students can be crowded into existing classes, thereby imposing costs on other students, who now get less attention from the teacher, less play area, etc. There is no cost for serving additional *persons* only (i) if they don't use the public schools, such as families without children, or families who send their children to private school, or (ii) for the first student in any otherwise empty class. Since costs are generally positive, it may be efficient to exclude those students whose marginal benefits are less than the marginal cost of educating them. Selective access can also make available a choice of quality, such as large and small classes.

Not all education is distributed with equal access. Early American schools were mostly private. (West, 1967) Today, some public school districts have special schools for selected students, and private schools charge tuition. Most state colleges use a combination of rules (minimum grades) and fees. These examples of selective access are not necessarily efficient, but clearly there is a choice between equal and selective access. Since it is generally costly to serve additional persons, there is no a priori *efficiency* case for equal access. Of course, one can argue for equal access to schools on *egalitarian* principles. But the traditional public goods theory attempts to justify equal access on efficiency grounds. That argument does not hold for education.

Defense from (Internal) Crime. If policemen are assigned to cruise along every street, check every property, and respond to every call without charge, then everyone has equal access to "defense from crime." But as communities grow, and more residents must be supplied with crime defense, most communities hire more policemen; clearly an increased cost. If more policemen are not hired, then new residents can be served only by decreasing service to others: more streets can be patrolled only if there are fewer patrols per night; more properties can be checked only if each one is checked less thoroughly, and only the more urgent calls can be responded to. Each of these service changes imposes costs on residents. Either they will suffer from more crime, or they will incur the costs of purchasing other types of crime defense. Many types of crime defense are selectively available such as locks, fences, guard dogs, guards, and also alarm companies which respond if the burglar alarm is tripped. And don't overlook private police patrols, which check selected houses on selected streets, as thoroughly and as often as each customer requests, for a fee. Selective access to police patrols is efficient if it excludes those persons with low marginal benefits relative to the marginal cost of serving them. It is costless to serve additional persons, if the additional persons live within existing buildings, and have neither stealable property nor criminal tendencies.

Defense from (External) Attack. If all Americans are equally protected from foreign attack on their persons and possessions, then everyone has equal access to national defense. Although this is substantially the case, there is certainly some variation in protection, especially among cities (regarding protection by missiles) and among Americans who either travel or have property abroad. (While the troops may be sent out to protect some Americans or their property from some foreign seizures (such as the Mayaguez), in other cases no action is taken (tuna boats).) One of the firmly embedded myths of modern public finance is that it doesn't matter if population increases: the costs of defending the U.S. from external attack will not change. But consider two points. First, the new population must live somewhere. If they cause an increase in the U.S. land area, then either more defenses must be provided, or there will be a decrease in the level of protection to earlier residents, and either way the marginal cost of protecting additional persons is positive. (Surely providing equal protection to each of the original 48 states is less costly than providing the *same* level of protection to the 48 states plus Alaska and Hawaii.) Second, even if the new population resides within the existing boundaries, they will generally increase the amount of physical and human wealth which might be coveted by an enemy. That is, foreign attack is (at least partially) an economically motivated action, and is more likely to occur if there is more capital worth capturing. (Coveted capital is basically human capital (above the subsistence level) and productive physical capital. (Thompson, 1974)) Thus new population, by increasing the likelihood of attack, requires the provision of more defenses if the degree of protection is to remain unchanged. To sum up, it is costless to serve additional persons only in the (unlikely) case that additional persons live within the existing national boundaries and cause no increase in the amount of capital that might be coveted by foreigners.

But for defense against foreign attack, is selective access possible? Before the modern era, only a few people had more than subsistence capital, and these lords often had personal armies (to deter both internal crime and foreign attack). Private armies still exist today.[3] These personal armies yield benefits primarily to their owner. (A medieval lord could scarcely be a "free rider" on a neighboring lord's defense efforts. If he did not have his own defenses, he would probably suffer attacks from his neighbor.) Does this imply that every American "should" have his own army? Of course not. For most Americans, equal access to the defenses of a communal army is far more efficient. But even with a communal army, selective exclusion is possible from some aspects of its defenses. It may not be possible to exclude anyone from "protection against massive nuclear attack." But this is not the only service rendered. A military force also protects people from theft of property and kidnapping by foreigners. Exclusion from this service is relatively easy: The military force simply makes no attempt to stop theft or kidnapping of named persons. These persons would either hire their own guards, or suffer the damages of theft or kidnapping by foreigners. (Tullock, 1971, Appendix A) Americans with substantial property abroad or at sea might well prefer to provide their own anti-theft defenses, rather than pay for a com-

---

[3]Robert Vesco is reportedly in Central America with his own army to prevent attack by U.S. agents. In Lebanon, according to Ray Vicker, a group of army officers demanded the president's resignation, "But the president refused to budge from his presidential palace overlooking Beirut, where he is guarded by a 7,000-man private army." (p. 1) Furthermore, writes Vicker, every week the many different religious groups "go to their devotion without incident. The reason is that most of these groups have their own private armies, equipped with machine guns, rockets, tank-piercing recoilless rifles and grenade launchers, to protect the faithful." (p. 29)

munal army which cannot be counted on to protect their property. Although equal access to a communal army may be efficient for most Americans most of the time, this is an empirical, not an a priori conclusion.[4] Contrary to public goods theory, even in this key case of defense from external attack, exclusion is not impossible and the marginal cost of serving additional persons generally is not zero. There is no *a priori* case for equal access to defense, although there is probably an empirical one.

Outdoor Recreation. There are still many forests and beaches to which everyone has equal access. But even in wilderness areas, the marginal costs of serving additional users is not zero. As more users enter a wilderness area, other users complain of a "lower quality" experience. And the congestion at more accessible parks and beaches is obvious. To serve additional users, either more land and facilities must be acquired, or the additional users will impose congestion costs on others. It is costless to serve additional persons only for persons who never use outdoor recreation or for the first person in an otherwise empty facility. Clearly it is efficient to exclude those users with the lowest marginal benefits, and some exclusion is increasingly occurring. Many campsites and day use areas are subject to fees, and many wilderness areas restrict entry to a limited number of permit holders. These exclusion methods are not necessarily efficient. For example, wilderness permits are often issued on a first come, first served basis, and it is not clear that this screens out the lowest-benefit users. But by making access selective, it is possible to have both crowded and secluded facilities, on the same day and in the same general area. Unfortunately, this diversity of quality is not available on most public beaches, as most of them are strictly equal access.

Navigation Aids. Lighthouses are a favorite textbook example of public goods, because most economists cannot imagine a method of exclusion. (All this proves is that economists are less imaginative than lighthousekeepers.) Since lighthouse users are also harbor users, use of harbors can be made dependent on payment of lighthouse fees. The British lights were financed in this way for many years. (Coase, 1974) Modern navigation aids such as radar,

---

[4]An interesting empirical problem is to compare the efficiency of a national military force with that of regional, state or even metropolitan forces. The military forces of some countries protect populations smaller than that of an American city. Are these small armies inefficient?

may be distributed equally or selectively. Airport control towers give everyone equal access to their radar information, whereas radar units (for use on ships or planes) are selectively available to those who buy them.

As to costs, additional persons can use lighthouses only by using the waterways they protect. And it is generally costly for an additional person to use a protected waterway. The additional ship increases the likelihood of collisions (imposing costs on other users), or, if safety standards are to remain unchanged, additional navigation aids must be used (more lights, buoys, shipboard radar, etc.). This is also obvious at airports. Anyone can use the runway markings and lights, but heavier traffic requires more navigation aids (control towers, radar, etc.) to maintain safety. Thus, generally, it is costly to serve additional persons, and it may be efficient to exclude low-benefit users from areas protected by navigation aids. Of course, on sufficiently lonely coasts, the chance of collision may be so small that the additional cost is approximately zero. In these cases, the *threat* of exclusion may be a useful method of extracting payment, even if no one is actually excluded. (The fees for British lights usually applied to only the first few trips each year so that, for most users, the fee for marginal trips was zero.)

B. Thinkers and Ideas

These services (research, T.V., the law and courts) are especially troublesome, because the services are not tangible, like a box of food, but consist, basically, of *ideas*. Yet useful ideas are scarce, and producing them requires very tangible inputs: *thinkers*. Generally, producing ideas for more persons involves the cost of more thinkers, or the cost of reduced idea-production for other persons. That is, the services of thinkers are just as congestable as other services, and there is rivalry among consumers to obtain these services. The exceptions are essentially trivial: it is costless to produce ideas for additional persons, if these additional persons have *no* problems needing thinkers' ideas or if they have the *same* problems as other persons. Since it is generally costly to serve more persons, it *may* be efficient to exclude some persons from access to thinkers. This is generally possible, because ideas are of little use unless distributed to users. *And* most methods of distribution (e.g., books) permit selective access.

Research. Equal access (to both thinkers and ideas) may occur for some types of agricultural research. Government agricultural researchers study a variety of problems, covering all regions, all farm sizes and all crops. The new ideas, once produced, are freely distributed to interested farmers. But equal access is not necessarily efficient. The marginal cost of *producing* new agricultural ideas for additional persons is zero only (i) if they are not farmers or (ii) if they have the *same* unsolved problems as other farmers. But generally, additional farmers will have different problems. Farmers' problems in Hawaii differ from those of mainland farmers. If the USDA is to equally solve problems for all farmers, then it must do more research to serve farmers in 50 states than in 49. If it does not hire more researchers, then Hawaii can be served only at the cost of diminished research for mainland farmers. Either way, it is costly to serve additional persons, and it may be efficient to exclude farmers (from access to researchers) when the marginal cost (of solving their problem) exceeds the marginal benefit (from the solution). The marginal cost of *distributing* ideas to additional persons, by means of publication, demonstrations, etc., is also generally positive. Selective access, to those whose marginal benefits (from using ideas) exceeds the marginal cost (of distributing the ideas) may be efficient.

Generally, access to thinkers and their ideas is selective. The reason selective access is possible is simple. Ideas are of little value unless they distributed and/or used. Selective access to the distribution of ideas is easy (by charging fees for books or demonstrations) and selective access to usage often occurs (when fees are charged for using patented ideas). Thus, most persons or groups have access to researchers only if they are willing to buy the publications, etc., in which the results appear. Other groups do not have access to either the researchers or their results. The observed selective access to research is not necessarily efficient,[5] but there is no *a priori* case for equal access. Indeed, it is the existence of copyrights and patents that indicates that research cannot be classified as a public good: although it is possible to give everyone equal access, it is also possible to give thinkers property

[5]The cost situation is similar to "natural" monopoly, as there is a large production cost (for the new idea) and small marginal distribution costs. A uniform price, if efficient (i.e., equal to marginal distribution costs) may not cover full costs. But multiple pricing (which can be both efficient and adequate to cover full costs) is common. Even economics journals charge different prices to libraries, individuals and students.

rights in their thoughts and allow them to control access to their ideas.

Professors in agricultural schools sometimes give everyone equal access to their results (when their results are distributed freely by the government). At other times, they supply their results selectively (when they patent and license agricultural machines). Hence, it is misleading to classify higher education as a public good because one of its final products is research. The research produced by higher education is indeed a valuable product, but one which may be supplied to users either equally or selectively.

Entertainment. Entertainment involves both the production of new entertainments (by writers, editors, actors, directors, etc.) and their distribution (through publications, performances and broadcasts). Given that tastes differ, it is generally costly to produce new entertainments for additional persons. (A new mystery novel will entertain some people. To entertain additional persons may require a science fiction tale, a children's book, etc.) And with most distribution systems (such as publication or performance) serving additional persons involves additional distribution costs. Since it is generally costly to serve additional persons, there is no *a priori* case against selective access to entertainment. Providing that the costs of exclusion are not too large, it is efficient to exclude some persons from influencing producers, if the marginal cost (of satisfying their particular tastes) exceeds their marginal benefit (from the resulting production). Similarly, it is efficient to exclude some persons from the distribution of existing entertainments, if the marginal cost (of distribution) exceeds their marginal benefits (from consuming the entertainment).

What about television? Can it be classified as a public good? To be a public good, exclusion must be impossible, and it must be costless to serve additional persons. TV fails both these tests. Not only is exclusion possible, but it is generally practiced. Although the charging of a cash price is generally prohibited, viewers must bear the (opportunity) cost of commercials. (Movies on TV are rarely "free" and many people are excluded from watching them because of the high cost of incessant commercials.) The debate over pay-TV is basically a debate over the method of exclusion (commercials vs. cash) rather than its existence. Equal access (without exclusion) means TV without commercials or fees or any other costs to viewers. (Non-commercial government channels, in countries that have them, sometimes impose the cost of propaganda on viewers.) Nor is there an *a priori* case for equal access. Since tastes differ, serving more people requires producing more varied programming, clearly an additional cost. (If everyone had the same tastes, one channel would suffice.) (*Cf.* Minasian, 1964) Even distributing existing programs to additional persons generally has positive costs. New users of a TV signal must live somewhere. If they live at the edge of the city, then a stronger signal must be transmitted to reach them. Alternatively, new users may move within the city, housed on previously vacant land, or in taller buildings. But as buildings are notorious for blocking and distorting TV signals, either a stronger signal must be transmitted, or other users will suffer the costs of inferior reception, or the costs of buying taller or stronger antennas. So TV is neither an example of a public good, nor is there even an *a priori* case for equal access.

Property Rights. For all resources of value there are, de facto, property rights. Changes in preferences and technology may make it desirable to change property rights. To do so requires both thinkers (economic decisionmakers) and their ideas (decisions) about changes in "what" "how" and "whom" (i.e., property rights). In some cases, everyone has equal access to decisionmakers: anyone may petition a zoning board to change *what* land is used for; anyone may petition the FCC for changes in *whom* the spectrum is assigned to; and anyone may petition local government to change the codes on *how* buildings are built. Once made, these decisions equally affect everyone within the decisionmaker's jurisdiction. Making these decisions requires the costly services of mayors and commissioners and their staffs. Additional persons can be served without additional cost only if they have the *same* resource allocation problems as other persons. (Town B can simply use the zoning decisions of Town A if towns A and B have exactly the same land use problems, a rather unlikely situation.) Generally, making changes in property rights for more persons has positive marginal costs: either more decisionmakers must be hired, or else they will make each decision more superficially, placing a type of congestion cost on others. Given positive costs, it may be efficient to exclude some persons from access to economic decisionmakers (i.e., make no change in property rights, even though preferences or technology have changed, if the expected gain (from changed property rights) is less than the cost of making the change).

Most economic decisionmakers do *not* make their services

equally available to everyone, but limit access to their employer (for business decisions) and themselves (for personally used resources). Most private contracts, from simple apartment leases to complex labor-management agreements, specify changes in property rights. These contracts are formulated by decisionmakers to whom there is selective access.

A skilled decisionmaker may work on both a selective-access basis, for his business interests, and on equal access basis, in his role as a public official. It is misleading to say that education is a public good because one of its final products is skill in decision-making. These skills are indeed a valuable product of the educational system, but they may be supplied either equally or selectively.

Adjudication. Settling disputes requires thinkers (judges) and their ideas (rulings). To serve more persons generally requires more judges and more courtrooms. If more facilities are not acquired, additional users will impose costs on others, in the form of longer delays for trial and/or less judicial time spent on each case. It is costless to serve additional persons only if they have no disputes or if they have the same disputes as others, and can therefore simply use rulings from other cases. Since it is costly to serve additional users, it may be efficient to exclude those users whose benefits are not expected to exceed the costs of adjudicating their cases. To some extent this is done even in the public courts. Court fees are charged for most cases. (Generally the fee does not vary with the expected difficulty of the case, and so is not an efficient screening device.) Private arbitrators are also available, selectively, to those parties willing to pay a fee. So, although adjudication is a fundamental service in any society, it does not follow that adjudication is a public good.

C. *Externalities*

Traditionally, external benefits are treated in the same manner as public goods. Some goods are *classified* as having inherently external benefits. Exclusion of people from these external benefits is assumed to be impossible. If, furthermore it is assumed costless to extend the external benefit to more persons, then *equal access* (to the external benefit) is both necessary and efficient. (Since a reduction in an external cost is an external benefit, external costs need not be treated separately.)

Examples of "real" externalities range from cases where only a few persons receive external benefits (bee services) to cases involving very large numbers (urban pollution control). Yet, with only trivial exceptions, it is costly to make these external benefits available to more persons. That is, external benefits are generally congestable. Furthermore, exclusion is possible either from the service itself (bee services) or from the group receiving a service (pollution control). Hence, selective access (which restricts low benefit users) may be efficient.

Although not often discussed by economists, both "pecuniary" externalities and "consumption" externalities are very common. To some writers, this extends the scope of public goods theory to cover almost all of economic reality (see below), but an alternative interpretation is available.

Bee Services. In some cases, bee services may be equally available to a beekeeper (for making honey) and, without exclusion or charge, to his neighboring fruit grower (for pollinating fruit trees). In these cases, bee services are an external benefit (to the fruit grower). (Alternatively, this may be considered as the limiting case of a public good: equal access within a two person neighborhood.) If additional fruit growers move into the neighborhood, is it either necessary or efficient to give them equal access to the beekeeper's bees? First, it is not costless to serve the additional orchards. Either more bees must be used (for proper pollination) or, if the number of bees is not increased, the first orchard will bear the costs of inadequate pollination. (Thus, excluding low benefit users from bee services may be efficient.) Second, beekeepers need not, and generally do not, provide bee services freely to fruit growers. Bees are in fact transported to orchards and rented to growers who need pollination services. (Cheung, 1973) It is pointless to classify bee services as externalities, since access to this service may be either equal or selective. And since it is generally costly to serve additional persons, there is no *a priori* case for equal access.

Pollution Control. Pollution is often referred to as an external cost, and so pollution may be classified as an external benefit. In some cases, everyone has equal access to the benefits. Pollution control for an urban air basin not only benefits everyone presently living in the area, but anyone else is free to visit or move into the area. Similarly, when a U.S. river is cleaned up, everyone has equal access to the benefits: both present river users and anyone else who decides to become a river user. But is equal access to the benefits of pollution control either necessary or efficient? First, it is generally costly to extend pollution control benefits to additional persons. These additional persons will generally engage in polluting activities: they will drive cars, burn heating oil, discharge sewage, etc. Either more population control devices must be used (to maintain air and water standards) or pollution will increase (placing costs on previous residents or users). Either way it is costly to serve additional persons, so excluding some persons from the benefits of pollution control may be efficient. But is exclusion possible? Certainly there is no way to withhold cleaner air from one urban resident while supplying it to everyone else. But exclusion is possible *from the group* which receives the pollution control benefits. Thus private retirement and resort communities control many types of pollution for their residents, such as smoke, odors, noise and visual pollution, but access to the community is selective. (Cf. MacCallum, 1964–65, pp. 57–58) Similarly, owners of Scottish rivers control pollution, but limit access to selected users, such as fishing clubs. (Dales, 1968) So, pollution control is not necessarily an external benefit to which everyone must and should have equal access.

"Consumption" Externalities. Almost any act of consumption *may* have external effects. Smith's smoking a pipe may give other persons pleasure (from the aroma) or displeasure (from the smoke), at least if they are in the same room. Similarly, Smith's houseplants may please or displease others, if they can see them. And, Smith's use of marijuana may please or displease other persons if they are aware of his usage. The prevalence of consumption externalities leads Samuelson to claim an astounding domain for public goods:

> Thus, consider what I have given in this paper as the definition of a public good, and what I might better have insisted upon as a definition in my first and subsequent papers: 'A public good is one that enters two or more persons' utility.' What are we left with? . . . *With a knife-edge pole of the private good case, and with all the rest of the world in the public-good domain* by virtue of involving some 'consumption externality.' (1969, p. 108, emphasis added)

As is traditional, this reflects an attempt to classify goods as being inherently "public goods," overlooking the *choice* between equal and selective access. Does everyone unavoidably have access to the external effects of Smith's acts of consumption? If Smith smokes his pipe in public, then everyone has equal access to the external effects, be they good or bad. But, if Smith smokes at home, there are either no consumption externalities (if he is alone) or they are limited to those persons who have selective access to his home. Similarly if Smith's houseplants are outdoors on the street side of his house, there are consumption externalities to which everyone has equal access; if they are in his study, they may affect no one but himself. Smith's laughter at a funny movie may give others pleasure, if he is watching in a theatre, but will have no influence on others, if he is watching the movie on television at home alone. Finally, Smith's consumption of marijuana may affect others if they know about it. If, as is often the case, Smith keeps his consumption secret, there are no "consumption externalities" on others.

What are we left with? By virtue of involving some "consumption externality," a choice must be made with regard to almost every act of consumption: is there to be equal or selective access to the effects of that consumption act? As in other cases, there is no *a priori* answer. Efficient choice depends on the costs of granting access to more persons; the cost of exclusion; the value of diversity, etc.

Pecuniary Externalities. If Smith changes his preferences, desiring, say, to buy more wheat from Jones, this will affect the price of wheat in the market in which they trade. True, Smith's preference change alone may have an effect too small to measure. But if there are many Smiths buying from many Joneses, their combined preference changes will measurably raise the market price of wheat. This price change doesn't just affect the transactions between these buyers (Smiths) and these sellers (Joneses). It also affects all the non-Smiths and non-Joneses who buy and sell wheat. Since the external effect is solely on price, this is called a pecuniary or price externality.

All those people who buy and sell *in the same market* as the Smiths and the Joneses have equal access to this pecuniary externality: if they choose to continue buying and selling it will be at the higher price, which is seen as a pecuniary external benefit by other sellers and as a pecuniary external cost by other buyers. Thus, pecuniary externalities appear similar to public goods: everyone, or at least everyone in the affected market, has equal access to the pecuniary externalities.

But the catch in this description is the phrase "in the affected market." True, there are world-wide markets in some products. In these cases, any change in preference among one group of consumers yields pecuniary externalities to which everyone else in the world has equal access. But, if a nation insulates itself from foreign markets (via quotas, embargos, currency controls, etc.) then changes in foreigners' preferences may have no effect on domestic buyers and sellers (and vice versa). And in the extreme case of a self-sufficient homestead, a change in the homesteaders' preferences will affect no one but themselves. In other words, for both real and pecuniary externalities, there is equal access to everyone in the affected group, but selective access is possible by means of limiting access to the group. In this case, selective access to pecuniary externalities is possible by limiting access to the market.

But on the matter of costs, real and pecuniary externalities differ. Real externalities involve either a net benefit or a net cost. (Hence, for a real externality, it may be efficient to exclude those persons whose benefit is less than the additional cost of serving them.) But pecuniary externalities always involve both an external benefit and an external cost, with a net benefit, or *net cost of zero*. (A higher wheat price is equally a benefit to wheat sellers and a cost to wheat buyers.)[6] Hence, although selective access to pecuniary externalities is possible, it can never be justified on efficiency grounds. Since the net cost is zero, excluding any transactions (*i.e.*, any pairs of buyers and sellers) is inefficient. But this conclusion, that it is efficient to allow all buyers and sellers access to the market, has been with us since Adam Smith, and does not need the theory of public goods for its justification.[7]

[6]Changes often involve *both* real and pecuniary effects. Removing controls on minimum prices (e.g. milk price controls) will generally increase quantity and reduce price. If the price control was inefficient, then its removal will have positive real benefits, related to the increase in quantity. But since removal of the control lowers selling price, there are pecuniary effects on the original quantity. Buyers receive pecuniary benefits, since they pay a lower price; sellers of this quantity incur pecuniary costs of an equal amount, since they receive a lower price. It is generally hard to find changes which yield *only* pecuniary effects. For one example, assume a quota on a product, such that the same amount is imported both before and after tariff removal. The tariff removal will not affect either retail price or the quantity imported (and thus has no "real" effects). But tariff removal will yield pecuniary benefits to sellers (who now retain more of the selling price) and equal pecuniary costs to taxpayers (who must now pay higher taxes to finance their government services).

[7]Real externalities affect output, while pecuniary externalities do not. Hence economists recommend that decisionmakers consider real externalities and ignore

IV. Conclusions

It is generally misleading to describe goods or services as inherently public goods, or quasi public goods, or externalities. Case studies, covering a wide range of traditional examples, show that methods of exclusion exist and, indeed, are frequently used. In case after case consumers jointly use *congestable* facilities, so that serving more persons requires either more, costly facilities, or imposes a congestion cost on others. Minor exceptions to this conclusion may exist, but must be evaluated carefully. For many years, exclusion from the services of lighthouses and bees was asserted to be impossible, not because it actually was, but because economists lacked the imagination or empirical studies to show otherwise.

For normative analysis, the problem is not classification (as public, quasi-public or otherwise) but the choice between equal or selective access. This choice may involve differences in method of distribution, amount produced and its distribution, as well as quality diversity (such as fast and slow highway lanes, which require selective access to prevent speed equalization). Equal access may be more efficient for some services (*e.g.*, defense from external attack), but this is not an inherent characteristic of the services. Changes in technology or preferences could make selective access more efficient in the future.

The questions remain for positive analysis: Why is equal access chosen in some situations, and not others? Why are some roads free; other toll? Why is crime deterrence increased via (equal access) police patrols in some cases, and via (selective access) alarm systems in others? Is there an invisible hand which guides public choices to the efficient distribution system? Or does equal access simply benefit the majority at the expense of the minority? (Spann, 1974)

Many people have egalitarian preferences. They would like to see income equally distributed, and/or a system of equal access to certain goods and services. Economists who share these egalitarian values have a problem, since most economic theory is based on an individualistic value system. There is usually a conflict between the

---

pecuniary externalities. Unfortunately, real decisions often reflect the opposite considerations. Real externalities are often ignored, yielding pollution problems. Pecuniary externalities are often given considerable attention by sellers, who lobby for, and often secure, public policies which limit competition. (Goldin, 1975)

individualism of economic theory and the egalitarian values of some economists. There have been many attempts to use economic theory to support equalization of income, but these have not been particularly successful. (Blum and Kalven, 1953) Perhaps one reason why public goods theory has been so popular is that it appeared to give the support of economic theory to an egalitarian system of distribution, for a number of important services. As shown by the case studies in this paper, economic theory does *not* give *a priori* support to equal access for these services. This, of course is unlikely to dissuade any egalitarian from the preferences he holds, nor is it intended to. Egalitarian sentiments *are* a basic economic preference, and economists who hold these preferences will no doubt search for other methods to justify equality.

References

Blum, Walter J. and Kalven, Harry, Jr., *The Uneasy Case for Progressive Taxation*, Chicago: Univ. of Chicago, 1953.

Buchanan, James M. "Notes for an Economic Theory of Socialism." *Public Choice*, 8 (Spring, 1970), 29–43.

Cheung, Steven N. S. "The Fable of the Bees: An Economic Investigation." *Jour. Law Econ.*, 16 (April, 1973), 11–33.

Coase, R. H. "The Lighthouse in Economics." *Jour. Law Econ.*, 17 (Oct. 1974), 101–28.

Dales, J. H. *Pollution, Property and Prices*. Toronto: Univ. Toronto, 1968.

Goldin, Kenneth D. "Price Externalities Influence Public Policy." *Public Choice*, 23 (Fall 1975), 1–10.

———. "Roads and Recreation." *Land Econ.*, 48 (May, 1972), 114–24.

Head, John G. and Shoup, Carl S. "Public Goods, Private Goods, and Ambiguous Goods." *Econ. Journ.*, 79 (Sept. 1969), 567–72.

MacCallum, Spencer. "The Social Nature of Ownership." *Modern Age*, 9 (Winter, 1964–65), 49–61.

Mansfield, Edwin. *Microeconomics*, (2nd Edition). New York: Norton, 1975.

Musgrave, Richard A. and Musgrave, Peggy B. *Public Finance in Theory and Practice*, (2nd Edition). New York: McGraw-Hill, 1976.

Samuelson, Paul A. "The Pure Theory of Public Expenditure." *Rev. Econ. Stat.*, 36 (Nov. 1954), 387–89.

———. "Diagrammatic Exposition of a Theory of Public Expenditure." *Rev. Econ. Stat.* 37 (Nov. 1955), 350–56.

———. "Pure Theory of Public Expenditure and Taxation," in Margolis, J. and Guitton, H. (eds.). *Public Economics: An Analysis of Public Production and Consumption and their Relations to the Private Sectors: Proceedings of a Conference held by the International Economics Association*. London: Macmillan, 1969.

Spann, Robert M. "Collective Consumption of Private Goods." *Public Choice*, 20 (Winter, 1974), 63–81.

Thompson, Earl A. "Taxation and National Defense." *Jour. Pol. Econ.*, (July–Aug. 1974), 755–82.

Tullock, Gordon. *Private Wants, Public Means*. New York: Basic, 1970.

———. *The Logic of the Law*. New York: Basic, 1971.

Vicker, Ray. "Our Man in Beirut Finds Only Fatalism Amid Chaos, Danger." *Wall Street Journal*, 94 (Mar. 17, 1976), 1, 29.

West, E. G. "The Political Economy of American Public School Legislation." *Jour. Law Econ.*, 10 (Oct. 1967), 101–28.

5. Free Ride, Free Revelation, or Golden Rule?

Earl R. Brubaker

In recent years a number of writers have contributed to some fundamental advances in understanding collective economic action.[1] As Professor James Buchanan has so aptly put it, however, when relevant theories remain "in a preparadigm stage of development . . . no single treatment or presentation is likely to command universal assent among informed scholars nor is it likely to be free of its own ambiguities, confusions, and contradictions."[2] Yet certain propositions do command wide-spread respect and one of the most famous is the virtually universally accepted free-rider hypothesis. According to it individual consumers will fail to state publicly their full monetary evaluation of a collective good. For our purposes, it will be helpful to distinguish between strong and weak statements of this proposition.

The main purpose of this article is to argue that the dominant position occupied by the free-rider hypothesis in contemporary literature has little empirical scientific basis, and that, in fact, recently available experimental evidence seems much more nearly consistent with some plausible alternatives.

Reprinted, by permission, from *Journal of Law and Economics* 18 (April 1975): 147–61.

[1]A clearly nonexhaustive list of noteworthy recent contributions to the literature in English would include: William J. Baumol, *Welfare Economics and the Theory of the State* (2nd ed., 1965); Peter Bohm, "An Approach to the Problem of Estimating Demand for Public Goods," 73 *Swed. J. Econ.* 55 (1971); *id.*, "Estimating Demand for Public Goods: An Experiment," 3 *Eur. Econ. Rev.* 111 (1972); James M. Buchanan, *The Demand and Supply of Public Goods* (1968); *Public Economics* (Julius Margolis & H. Guitton, eds., Int'l Econ. Ass'n Conf. Proceedings, 1969); Richard A. Musgrave, *The Theory of Public Finance* (1959); *id.*, "Provision for Social Goods in the Market System," 26 *Pub. Fin.* 304 (1971); *Classics in the Theory of Public Finance* (Richard A. Musgrave & Alan T. Peacock, eds., 1967); Paul A. Samuelson, "The Pure Theory of Public Expenditure," 36 *Rev. Econ. & Stat.* 387 (1954); *id.*, "Diagrammatic Exposition of a Theory of Public Expenditure," 37 *Rev. Econ. & Stat.* 350 (1955).

[2]James M. Buchanan, *supra* note 1, at 202.

The most prominent alternative, generally referred to as the free exchange model, asserts that individuals will freely reveal their true evaluations of collective goods. Thus it might well be named the free-revelation hypothesis. Whatever the label, the idea has been in extreme disfavor, essentially, however, on the basis of *a priori* reasoning alone.

In this article still a third behavioral hypothesis, the golden rule of revelation is advanced. Its intimate relation to pre-contract group excludability and the latter's universal feasibility is demonstrated. In Appendix A designs for experiments that might be conducted to test conflicting predictions of the three hypotheses are sketched, and the currently available experimental evidence is examined for implications facilitating evaluation of the competing hypotheses.

Context and Varieties of the Free-Rider Hypothesis

Discussion of demand for a collective good may be set within the framework of an extended Walrasian-style multi-market model. The tastes and technical knowledge of the members of the community, say n in number, are taken as given. The time period of concern is such that the parameters describing tastes and knowledge may be regarded as constant. The basic behavioral assumption is that individuals make decisions in their own self-interest. They possess stocks of goods, suitable inputs into productive and/ or consumption activities, including provision of services, which they are free to exchange at mutually acceptable rates. In any market individuals are potential buyers and sellers.

It will be useful to specify somewhat more exactly one of the services provided, namely, collective-good intermediation. Because of the special difficulties in arranging contracts to which the entire community is a party, some individuals specialize in facilitating the necessary negotiations. Their function is to communicate information about the character of collective goods supply to potential purchasers and information about the character of collective-goods demand to potential sellers in order to find bases for mutually satisfactory exchange. Such intermediation seems a *sine qua non* for effective operation of a market for a pure collective good where the number of participants is large.

The basic extension of the Walrasian model derives from distinction between goods on the basis of two crucial properties, non-exhaustiveness and non-excludability. If the full amount of a good may appear as an argument in the preference function of each and every member of the community, its consumption is referred to as non-exhaustive. Purely non-exhaustive consumption may be regarded as the ultimate in positive externality. The full benefit of the good is available to each individual as a result of the activities of the remainder of the community with an essentially imperceptible participation on his part. Purely exhaustive consumption stands at the other end of the scale. Between these pure, polar cases is a continuum of degrees of externality.

A second pertinent property is the feasibility of exclusion from consumption which also ranges along a continuum, namely, from low marginal cost to high marginal cost. Rising costs are associated, of course, with movement from the concept of privateness toward collectiveness. Thus classification of any specific good can be made according to its position along the two continua.

Let us focus on some basic issues regarding expression of demand for a purely collective good, that is, one characterized by completely nonexhaustive consumption and indefinitely large marginal cost of exclusion.[3] Will individuals reveal their true demand for collective goods? If so, why? If not, why not? Under what conditions, if any, will they express such demand?

The size of the community is of paramount importance. As has been argued quite convincingly, if the community is small, the cost of negotiating and consummating a bargain may not be large relative to the aggregate benefit conferred. Expression of demand will be made jointly following negotiations and bargaining. As the community under consideration grows, however, lines of communication multiply, transactions costs rise correspondingly, and in the large number case the mechanism for expressing demand for the collective good is rendered inoperative.

How large? Let us consider values for n large enough so that any individual's desires will have an imperceptible effect on the quantity of the good that will be made available to the community.[4]

---

[3]Given the strong symmetries in the standard contemporary analysis of productive and consumption activities, one might expect a general theory of collective activity to develop. Here, however, we shall focus on collective consumption. The very concept of a collective good has been the subject of a very substantial literature. See, for example, E. J. Mishan, "The Relationship between Joint Products, Collective Goods, and External Effects," 77 *J. Pol. Econ.* 329 (1969); *id.*, "Joint Products, Collective Goods, and External Effects: Reply," 79 *J. Pol. Econ.* 1141 (1971).

[4]It might be argued that there would need to be conditions on the distribution of wealth and income.

Just as the individual adjusts his purchases of purely private goods in response to a community determined price over which he has no perceptible influence, so he adjusts his own subjective unit evaluation (price) of a community-determined quantity of the collective good.

How can the community determine a level for provision for the collective good? Determination of an optimal allocation of resources to its production would appear to call for submission to the intermediary by each individual of a schedule showing measures of his subjective evaluation of various quantities of the good. Given an aggregate gross benefit schedule derived through vertical summation and the corresponding schedule of costs the optimal allocation could be determined by maximizing the difference between them.

According to many of the prominent writers on the problem, difficulties with the above procedure extend well beyond the formidable effort that would be required to assemble and process the relevant data. Specifically each individual in a large group acting in his own self-interest will have no incentive to express his demand for the collective good. No matter how low the offer he makes, he will enjoy full benefits from the amount of the good ultimately decided upon by the community. There is nothing to prevent the individual from submitting a schedule indicating that no quantity of the good is worth anything at all to him. Thus there is no basis for billing him in proportion to his stated evaluation of the good. If he believes that the other members of the group will contribute an amount necessary to pay for the good, he need contribute nothing, with no significant effect on its availability. Furthermore, the individual free-rider may decide that he is not imposing significantly on society and, in fact, in as much as the costs of his non-participation are distributed equally over the remainder of the individuals in the community, no one of them would be perceptibly affected by his decision not to contribute. If he believes, on the other hand, that others will contribute in aggregate an amount insufficient to pay for the collective good, he, himself, will only lose by supporting a lost cause, so to speak. Thus Buchanan argues, "regardless of how the individual estimates the behavior of others, he must always rationally choose the free-rider alternative. Since all individuals will tend to act similarly, the facility [collective good] will not be constructed [produced] from proceeds of wholly voluntary contributions. . . ."[5]

---

[5]James M. Buchanan, *supra* note 1, at 89 (terms in brackets added).

The "strong" version of the free-rider hypothesis elaborated above may be distinguished from a "weak" version frequently encountered in the literature. The former asserts that the collective good *will not be provided* because of the inadequately expressed individual demands. The weaker version states merely that the allocation of resources to its production will be less than Pareto optimal. Both versions almost invariably are followed by the assertion that the coercive police power of government will be required to induce full expression of demand.[6] Their relative usefulness, both for positive economic investigations and for consideration of policy, will be discussed below.

Pre-Contract Excludability and the Golden Rule of Revelation

In this section it will be argued on *a priori* grounds that contemporary orthodox discussions of incentives for expressing individual desires for collective goods have neglected not only the implications of pre-contract excludability but also the existence and extent of positive individual motivation for revealing preferences. Consideration of such motivation suggests that in certain situations individuals may behave according to a golden rule of revelation with results quite different from those predicted by the standard free-rider hypothesis.

An essential and neglected fact is that no matter how costly individual exclusion may be *after* the creation of a collective good, *prior* to consummation of a contract exclusion of the group, and consequently also of the individual, is *always* very easily accomplished. The producer simply holds no inventories. He works strictly on the basis of pre-paid orders. Lacking a firm contract with the community there will be no collective good for any of its members.

Thus if the possibility of exclusion is the factor that elicits demand, one might suppose that the intermediary would suggest terms that require firm offers from potential purchasers before contract consummation. According to contemporary orthodoxy, however, pre-contract group excludability would not alter the individual's reasoning leading inevitably to the conclusion that the free ride is the only rational course. The individual will still reason

---

[6]Buchanan avoids the strong statement that government *will be required* by suggesting that coercive arrangements *tend to emerge* as part of the behavior of the group.

that if others contribute, the good will be provided no matter what he does. If they don't, it won't. The individual's offer has no effect on whether the good is created or not, so that whether he is excluded or not depends only on decisions other than his own. It still makes no difference if he pays; so why should he? It is also clear that if everyone in the community reasons in this fashion, there will be no offers, and the group, and every individual in it, will suffer exclusion.

At zero provision marginal social benefits may exceed marginal costs by a substantial amount, and, consequently, many potential consumers may be amenable to suggestions about how to avoid group exclusion. The typical individual may decide, in particular, that he would, after all, be quite willing to make an offer reflecting the worth of the good to him, provided only that he receive some assurance that the remainder of the community would make an appropriate "matching" offer, so that he doesn't waste his own scarce resources supporting an ineffectual collective effort. Just as an individual consumer of a private good needs to be assured of its provision in specified quantity and quality before he will be willing to make payment, so a major concern for the individual consumer of a collective good will be a "money back" guarantee that the good as offered will, in fact, be provided.

In sum the individual member of the community may readily contemplate the following outcomes of negotiations for a collective good:

1. the remainder of the community commits sufficient resources and he rides free,

2. he pays with assurance of appropriate matching offers, and

3. the entire community attempts to ride free but is excluded.

Outcome (1) might be highest on his preference scale, but he may doubt its actual realization since others may also attempt the free ride with the consequence that the entire group will be excluded. Outcome (2) would appear to be the distinctly preferred of the remaining outcomes.

Outcome (2) refers, rather vaguely, to "assurance of appropriate matching offers." While it is beyond the scope of the present article to examine exhaustively the possible meanings of this phrase, an essential element may be proposed, namely that sufficient resources be offered to make feasible some specified level of provision of the collective good. Thus it is not the desire to ride free at the expense of the group, but the wish to be assured that the others will make an appropriate contribution that may constitute the dominant motivation.

The intermediary arranging a trade in a collective good cannot give a guarantee that community demand will suffice for its provision. But by describing the good and by stating its estimated cost he can give the individual purchaser not only a concrete notion of the good itself, but also, and perhaps more importantly, an indication of a proposed level of commitment by the remainder of the group. That is, any individual potential purchaser realizes that the community must make that commitment or be excluded.[7] Under these circumstances the individual's offer becomes not merely his payment for the collective good, but also his participation in a commitment to the remaining members of the community. He may fear that they, for whatever reason, be it lack of information, free-riding, lack of faith in the rest of the community, moral depravity, or simply lack of genuine desire, will not commit sufficient resources to bring the project to a meaningful scale. But he may, on the other hand, count on the community to commit itself to the purchase. Since he is counting on the rest of the community for the necessary tender, he may be willing to reciprocate by participating in a commitment to it. He has, after all, little to lose by expressing his demand. If the good is in fact created, he gets his "money's worth," and if it isn't, he gets his money back.

In a word humans may behave according to a golden rule of revelation of demand for collective goods. The individual may commit himself to the assurance of others as he would have them commit themselves to his own. Similarly in as much as the individual benefits from higher levels of provision of the good, he is interested in complete expression of demand by others. Again the golden rule may seem applicable to him, so that he, recognizing that he would benefit from a full expression of demand by others, and consequently hoping for it, will feel constrained to provide an accurate expression of his own. In sum it seems worth proposing an additional rival to the free-rider hypothesis, and for convenience it might be called the golden rule of revelation. It asserts that

[7] If excludability is important, it would seem expedient that the intermediary arrange for simultaneous, or secret, or conditional individual offers so that would-be free riders could not feign disinterest upon learning that others already had committed "sufficient" funds to purchase the good. J. H. Dreze & D. de la Vallee Poussin have elaborated an interesting tatonnement process for collective goods. See "A Tatonnement Process for Public Goods," 38 *Rev. Econ. Stud.* 133 (1971).

under pre-contract group excludability the dominant tendency will be for each individual to reveal accurately his preference for a collective good provided that he has some assurance that others will match his offer in amounts he perceives as appropriate.[8]

Pre-contract excludability is, of course, highly important to the golden-rule line of reasoning. The individual and community offers of commitments are required to avoid exclusion of the group. With the threat of group exclusion removed, motivation for revelation would seem to be diminished. Only the individual's conception of his relation with the community remains to temper inclinations toward free riding.[9]

From one point of view the orthodox assertion of the eminence of the free rider seems to resurrect the old image of economics as the dismal science, for it seems to stress the corruptibility of man. Free-rider behavior involves after all what is frequently referred to as cheating strategy. Each individual, betraying the confidence of his community, engages in deceit to avoid paying the price that he himself regards as an appropriate measure of its value.[10] Thus the hypothesis of decision according to the golden rule of revelation constitutes a more optimistic view of human nature.

There are still further reasons for suspecting nontrivial limits to the extent of free-rider behavior. First, an important characteristic[11]

[8]Given the normative, hortatory connotations usually associated with the golden rule, it might be worth emphasizing that the question being raised here is not "Should humans behave according to the golden rule of revelation?" but "Do they . . . ?"

[9]One might suggest that the golden-rule line of reasoning applies as well to the free-revelation hypothesis. It is true that the golden rule would seem to apply whenever the individual has reason to count on the community. The individual may tend, however, to count more heavily on the community before contract consummation has guaranteed availability of the good, and, therefore, in these circumstances his adherence to the golden rule may be stimulated.

[10]It might be argued that free-rider behavior resembles closely normal behavior in bargaining for private goods. Acting in self-interest individuals normally seek to pay the lowest amount for which potential sellers can be induced to give up a good. Bargaining for a private good differs, however, in that the process culminates in a price that is mutually acceptable to both parties. The potential buyer of a private good may fail to reveal his full evaluation, but he does so with the knowledge that he will eventually "reveal" an amount that will be acceptable to his trading partner, if, of course, an exchange is to take place. There seems no way for the individual potential purchaser of a collective good to adopt a similar approach to the bargaining process.

[11]See Kelvin J. Lancaster, "A New Approach to Consumer Theory," 74 *J. Pol. Econ.* 132 (1966).

with reference to which individuals might rank sets of goods is the method by which they were acquired. For some individuals a higher ranking will be accorded to a specified set of goods if it was acquired via a mutually acceptable bargain rather than via hypocrisy and deceit, however easily accomplished. Especially in the case of collective goods the individual may value the knowledge that his "trading partners" also regard the contract as satisfactory. One can imagine that tricking one's enemies into a disadvantageous exchange may be the source of additional satisfaction above that stemming from the goods involved per se. But in a sense, the free-rider finds himself in an adversary, hypocritical, and cynical relationship with society as a whole. Perhaps for some individuals this may be a matter of significant concern, while for others it may not be. It is a question for positive economics to determine the prevalent attitude.

Secondly, preference functions may be interdependent. The welfare of an individual's friends and neighbors and, therefore, availability of collective goods to them as well as to himself may contribute to higher ranks for his preference function. Then the would-be free-rider must reckon with the risk that his behavior may contribute to less than optimal fulfillment of their desires as well as of his own. The adherent to the golden rule of revelation may derive additional satisfaction from the knowledge that he had "done his part" in contributing toward a community commitment to the good for others as well as for himself.

Third, at low levels of provision of the collective good, marginal rates of substitution between it and closely related items may become very high. Under these circumstances free-rider motivation may recede into the background. For instance in the event of imminent breakdown of law and order the imperative for group action may overwhelm free-rider considerations.[12]

If the free-rider hypothesis is indeed the "true" explanation of group behavior, empirical tests against plausible alternatives can strengthen it. But given all the cogent reasons for expecting some revelation of demand for a collective good, one can be confident that the strong versions of the free-rider hypothesis are not likely to receive support from observation. The weak version will be

---

[12]Christopher M. Douty has provided an excellent discussion of collective action in crisis and post-crisis situations in "Disasters and Charity: Some Aspects of Cooperative Economic Behavior," 62 *Am. Econ. Rev.* 580 (1972).

more difficult to refute. Furthermore there may be a bit of free-rider as well as golden-ruler in each individual. If so, it will be important to discover the relative shares and the conditions under which the various forms of behavior manifest themselves.

The issue cannot be resolved solely, or even principally, by ever more elegantly rigorous refinements of a single logically possible doctrine. Empirical tests[13] will be required to improve scientific decisions about which hypothesis conforms more closely to "reality." Fortunately, we are in the highly enviable position of having ready to hand experimental evidence that sheds considerable light on the matter. Bohm[14] has reported on a truly exceptional, brilliantly conceived and executed experiment in which a premier closed circuit television program was offered to sample groups of individuals under conditions simulating a large community and under various sets of terms, some of which correspond closely to those desirable for testing the alternative behavioral hypotheses.

In sum how did the experimental groups respond? In every group individual offers appear to be related closely to prices of substitutes available through normal market channels. Most importantly, there were no significant difference in expressions of demand whether the good was presented as essentially private or as essentially collective. These experiments show beyond reasonable doubt that conditions exist under which free-riding will not be the dominant response to a request for expressions of demand for a pure collective good. They suggest, therefore, that the substantial confidence so frequently expressed in the free-rider hypothesis may be misplaced and may derive in part from an insufficient

[13]Although evidence on expression of demand for collective goods has been virtually non-existent, there have been some significant straws-in-the-wind. Mancur Olson, *The Logic of Collective Action* (rev. ed., 1971), has collected a considerable amount of anecdotal evidence which he interprets as strongly supporting the free-rider doctrine, and Gordon Tullock, "Public Decisions as Public Goods," 79 *J. Pol. Econ.* 913 (1971), has shown how voter behavior can be interpreted in its favor. Martin & Anita Pfaff, "Grants Economics, An Evaluation of Government Policies," 26 *Pub. Fin.* 275, 295 (1971), on the other hand cite surveys suggesting that in certain communities large percentages of taxpayers have regarded their payments as essentially voluntary. Peter Bohm, "An Approach to the Problem of Estimating Demand for Public Goods," *supra* note 1, has pointed out that through political parties, pressure groups, and opinion polls, potential consumers seem to reveal preferences that may very well overstate their sober and considered evaluations.

[14]Peter Bohm, "Estimating Demand for Public Goods: An Experiment," *supra* note 1.

exploration of the domain of terms available for a freely negotiated, mutually acceptable, multi-lateral agreement for collaboration in the provision of a collective consumption good. Additional experimentation on a larger scale seems highly promising, and could do much to advance our knowledge in this vital area.

Concluding Comments

Undoubtedly the issues raised above are open to debate, but in any event they seem to suggest the propriety of somewhat less enthusiastic endorsement of the free-rider principle, especially in its stronger version, than is apparent in the contemporary orthodox literature. The weaker statement is perforce less vulnerable to refutation. In its weakest form, however, the free-rider hypothesis approaches triviality. Strictly speaking it will be upheld by demonstration of the failure of one individual out of a million to express fully his demand for a collective good. But a demonstration of this sort would seem neither of overwhelming scientific interest nor an adequate basis for instituting the coercive apparatus for collective consumption that many of our most highly sophisticated scholars seem willing to accept.

Further brief consideration of some public policy implications of the foregoing analysis may be of interest. Every set of institutions and policies tends, of course, to have both functional and dysfunctional effects. While regimes based upon free revelation or upon golden-rule revelation may be subject to some underallocation of resources due to free-riding, the apparatus of collective compulsion entails unintended detrimental side effects of its own. Most notably it results in "forced-riding" by individuals who are coerced into expressing nonexistent "demands" for collective goods. Or worse a "good" in fact may be a *bad*, in some views, from which it is economically not feasible for the individual to exclude himself, and for which compensation may be appropriate.[15]

Forced riding might well be regarded as a clear violation of freedom of consumer choice, a principal so fundamental in modern societies that it is pervasive in the arrangements for private consumer goods exchanges in predominantly plan-oriented as well as

[15]See Knut Wicksell, "A New Principle of Just Taxation," in Richard A. Musgrave & Alan T. Peacock, *supra* note 1, at 89; and Vito Tanzi, "A Note on Exclusion, Pure Public Goods and Pareto Optimality," 27 *Pub. Fin.* 75 (1972).

in predominantly market-oriented economies. Furthermore under a system of coerced expression of demand for collective goods, demoralizing illusions of forced riding may exist. That is, even if the level and allocation of expenditure on collective goods remained unchanged in conjunction with a switch from a voluntary to a compulsory mechanism, some individuals may suspect that they had lost a valued opportunity to express effectively their own personal evaluation of priorities for collective action.

A parallel may be drawn in this context to a well known principle of criminal proceedings, where attempts are made to avoid two fundamental types of error, conviction of innocents on the one hand and acquittal of the culpable on the other. Judicial systems are vulnerable, doubtlessly, to errors of both types, and rationality calls for an optimal balance.[16] In the past, mechanisms to avoid the first type of mistake have been emphasized, and the presumption of innocence until "proven" guilty is, of course, a famous example.

Operation of fiscal mechanisms can result in two analogous types of error, "conviction" of the innocent forced rider or "acquittal" of the guilty free rider. The forced rider can be "convicted" incorrectly, and without a trial, of failure to express his demand for the collective good. He is "fined" the difference between his true valuation of the good and his stipulated tax payment. There is no court that can possibly try his case, since no one, not even he himself, may have determined his true demand. If he refuses to pay, he can be deprived of his personal liberty. The forced rider's responses might include costly and uncertain attempts to avoid taxes, to evade them, or to reform fiscal institutions, none of which are normally regarded as prime choices for leisure activities. It generally has been thought that a set of institutions relying on uncoerced contributions would avoid the detrimental effects of forced riding only by suffering the free rider. By electing to employ a fine meshed instrument society catches its would-be free riders but only at the expense of victimizing its innocent forced riders. Curiously given the historic emphasis on the presumption of innocence it has been discarded where rules of the game regarding expression of demand for collective goods is concerned.

Other detrimental effects of coerced "revelation" having poten-

---

[16]See Gary S. Becker, "Crime and Punishment: An Economic Approach," 76 J. Pol. Econ. 169 (1968), for a detailed discussion of optimal balances between variables pertinent to crime and punishment.

tially considerable consequences could be mentioned, but a comprehensive analysis is not possible or necessary here. The essential point is that a careful weighing of such dysfunctional effects in conjunction with design of mechanisms for providing for collective needs may promote significantly the rationality of our choices.

In order to compute accurately the relevant costs and benefits of alternative mechanisms for eliciting individual demand for collective goods, more accurate and complete knowledge of human behavior will be needed. What would be the extent of free riding under a regime of pre-contract excludability and assurance of community commitment? What has been the extent of forced riding under existing institutions? How do the terms under which a collective good is offered affect individual expressions of demand? We need more analysis, and especially more evidence, that will allow us to improve our answers to these and related questions.

In the meantime the case for the fundamental violation of freedom of consumer choice that coerced "revelation of demand" entails has been far from adequately substantiated. Strong versions of the free-rider hypothesis may well be highly inaccurate from a positive economic point of view. The weak version is an essentially irrefutable, virtually untestable, proposition. Either way in its present scientific status this hypothesis seems quite incapable of bearing the ponderous policy conclusions that have been placed upon it.[17]

The opportunities for eliciting more nearly voluntary economic expression of individual priorities for collective goods may be far greater than most of the contemporary orthodox literature suggests. If so, it may be eminently worthwhile to explore more carefully means to expand the scope of voluntary arrangements for provision of collective needs while perhaps in some measure of

[17]Even if the free-rider hypothesis correctly describes behavior, as a practical matter infeasibility of post-contract exclusion hardly seems so prevalent as to constitute an adequate justification for governmental expenditure on the scale observable during recent years in most industrialized countries. Inexpensive devices for exclusion often seem to be available especially when account is taken of collectively contrived tie-in devices such as supplemental charges for gasoline, tires, vehicles, etc., to prevent free riding on highways and byways. As Harold Demsetz has argued persuasively, privately contrived tie-ins also often provide significant private incentives for production of collective goods. See "The Private Production of Public Goods," 13 *J. Law & Econ.* 293, 306 (1970).

correspondence reducing reliance on coercive institutions with their own potentially detrimental effects.

Appendix A

In order to test the arguments of this paper, it would be extremely interesting to design and conduct some appropriate experiments. Suppose, for example, a good were discovered for which appropriate variations in the exclusion property could be contrived. That is, suppose we could offer it to a large[18] group on the alternative bases, respectively, of pre-contract group excludability, pre-contract group nonexcludability, as well as at auction with exclusion of all but the highest bidder. Quite interestingly for purposes of positive economic investigation, it is indeed possible to find useful approximations to such a good.

Consider the following terms under which a theatrical performance might be offered. Suppose that: (1) the members of a potential audience were informed of the total revenue needed to meet expenses for the program, (2) they were asked to make pledges expressing the full amount that they were willing to pay with the additional stipulation that the amount actually to be paid by an individual would be a share, calculated in proportion to his pledge, and (3) if the sum of offers failed to attain the specified amount, there would be no performance. According to the strong statement of the free-rider hypothesis no individual would have an adequate incentive to express his demand. Therefore no contributions would be forthcoming, and the good would not be provided. According to the weaker version, demand simply would be understated. According to the golden-rule hypothesis, on the other hand, the dominant tendency would be for individuals to express their "true" demands.

Now suppose that a second potential audience, identical in every relevant respect, was made an offer differing only in that under no circumstances would any member of the group be excluded from the performance and that the payments according to the individual estimates of the value of a ticket were the only requirement for admission. Under these terms even group pre-contract excludability has been removed as a motivation. The group has been assured that the good will be made available, so that there is no need to ruminate over the dire consequences of extensive free-riding. A

[18]In the technical sense of course.

comparison of expression of demands by these first two groups would provide valuable evidence with regard to the importance of pre-contract group excludability.

Finally, suppose the group is informed that the performance will be given but that only the highest bidder will gain admission. In this way the performance is transformed, from the viewpoint of the potential purchasers, into a private good for which they must compete successfully via their offers or suffer exclusion. Under this third set of terms their expressions of demand should be as unbiased as in their bids for a purely private good at a sealed bidding process.[19] Thus the expression of demand by members of the third group would provide a benchmark approximating full expression of demand against which to measure the offers of groups one and two.

The adjectives in columns two and three of the following matrix summarize the various patterns of predictions about the extent of revelation under the proposed experimental conditions. The free-revelation hypothesis predicts full expression of demand for groups one and two and, therefore, no significant differences from three. The free-rider hypothesis predicts significantly lesser expressions of demand from both groups one and two. Finally the golden rule of revelation predicts a significant shortfall from full expression only in group two.

Bohm[20] has presented the results of experiments in which a closed circuit television premier was offered to several groups under alternative sets of terms (labeled I through VI:2), which

Hypothesis	Experimental Group	
	One (Pre-Contract Excludability)	Two (Pure Non-Excludability)
Free revelation	Full	Full
Free rider	Negligible	Negligible
Golden rule	Full	Negligible

[19]See Peter Bohm, "Estimating Demand for Public Goods: An Experiment," *supra* note 1, at 126 for an elaboration of reasons such as "auction fever" and "views on the proper arrangement of society" for suspecting that bids offered for private goods may deviate from "true" demand.

[20]*Id.*

while differing in important ways from those desirable for present purposes, have, nevertheless, generated some highly useful evidence. It will be sufficient here to focus on the expression of demand under terms II, V, and VI:2 which most closely approximate those of the hypothetical experiments described above. Indeed set II corresponds exactly to the first hypothetical experiment.

Set V seems closely related to experiment two but differs in an essential way. Under set V the program was to be provided if and only if aggregate revealed demand attained the specified costs, but in no event was an *actual* payment necessary from any individual. In effect such conditions imply a curious combination of excludabilities. Each individual knows that terms have been stated that prohibit his exclusion no matter how small his pledge. At the same time he needs to pay nothing no matter how large his bid. But the group *will* be excluded if the expression of total demand is less than the cost of putting on the program. What is the rational strategy for individuals strictly adhering to the proposed conditions but also acting aggressively in their own self-interest? Any one individual could secure the full benefit of the program at no expense to himself by insisting that he alone was willing to pay its full costs. On the other hand set V is similar to experiment two in that the individual is guaranteed admission if the program is shown at all. Thus set V does allow for the possibility of group exclusion, but it requires merely "irresponsibly" high bids (perhaps even only one) to avoid that outcome. We might say that set V approaches a pre-bid assurance of individual and group non-exclusion.

Set VI:2 by stating that only the top ten per cent of the bidders will gain admission to the performance approximates quite closely the conditions specified for experiment three. The notion that only a certain percentage will be granted admission demonstrates the extremely interesting possibility that along the excludability dimension the performance in fact can be transformed along a continuum from a purely private good available only to the highest bidder to a purely collective good available to the entire community. Under these conditions expressions of demand by an individual would involve not only an evaluation of the worth of the good to him but also an estimate of the minimum bid necessary for admission. According to the strong free-rider hypothesis, one might expect that, given a commitment to present the program, the total expressed demand may vary more or less continuously and directly with the percentage excluded until all but the highest bidder are denied admission. In any event Bohm set the arbitrary cutoff at ten per cent, that is, at a level approaching the ultimate in individual excludability.

There was *no significant difference* in the average expression of demand among three sample groups who were offered the program under conditions described respectively by terms II, V, and VI:2.[21] In every case sufficient demand was expressed to cover the costs of presenting the program. It seems worth noting that another form of behavior in the spirit of the free-rider was completely lacking. To wit, as was argued above, under set V any individual who was willing to cheat to see the program could have ensured its provision without a charge to himself simply by stating that its full expense was its worth to him. From a group of thirty-nine[22] individuals not one took this extreme action to advance his own welfare. In fact it might be noted that the average expressed willingness to pay happened to be lower, though ever so slightly, under set V than under set II.

While the experimental evidence clearly contradicts the free-rider hypothesis, thereby strengthening the case for its competitors, the results are less clear-cut regarding a decision between them. On first examination it may appear that the pattern of full expression from all three groups conforms to the prediction of the free-revelation hypothesis. But it must be emphasized that set V did not correspond exactly to the conditions necessary to test free revelation against the golden rule. Pre-contract group excludability was possible. Further experimental tests designed specifically to distinguish between free revelation and golden-rule revelation would appear to be of extraordinary scientific interest. New experiments might be performed to yield evidence relevant to the issue of the effects of pre-contract group excludability as opposed to clear-cut non-excludability. The participants should be involved in a real choice and should not be simultaneously in the role of paid consultant. Goods requiring substantial expense might be the subject of the collective decision, so that the potential gains from successful free-riding become significant relative to family budgets.

[21]In fact Bohm, *id.*, at 125–26 argues effectively against the *behavioral* significance of the only *statistically* significant difference between mean expressions (III and IV) of demand for any pair of terms, I through IV:2.

[22]To ensure individual perception of a large-number situation the groups were led to believe that they were only part of the potential audience.

6. The Private Production of Public Goods

Harold Demsetz

This paper analyzes the production of public goods through private means under conditions that allow nonpurchasers to be excluded from the use of the good. Two conclusions are reached. First, given the ability to exclude nonpurchasers, private producers can produce public goods efficiently. Secondly, the payment of different prices for the same good is consistent with competitive equilibrium if the good is a public good.

The allocation of resources to the production of public goods can be understood with the aid of the model formulated long ago by Alfred Marshall for the analysis of joint supply.[1] Just as the slaughtering of a steer provides goods to both leather users and meat consumers, so the production of a public good, by definition, yields benefits that can be enjoyed by more than one individual, for one person's use of public good services does not prevent simultaneous use by others.

Under competitive conditions the rate at which steers are slaughtered is determined where the sum of the market prices for the

Reprinted, by permission, from *Journal of Law and Economics* 13 (October 1970): 293–306.

The author would like to thank the Lilly Endowment for financial aid received through a grant to the University of California at Los Angeles for the study of property rights.

[1]James M. Buchanan, *The Demand and Supply of Public Goods* (1968), explicitly views the demand for a public good as the demand for a jointly supplied good. I suspect that Samuelson, whose views will be considered later, when criticizing the use of the joint supply model for this purpose had Buchanan's view in mind. Paul A. Samuelson, "Contrast Between Welfare Conditions for Joint Supply and for Public Goods," 51 *Rev. Econ. & Stat.* 26 (1969). The reader who is familiar with Buchanan's book will realize that the present paper extends the use of the joint supply model to problems of supplying public goods. Armen A. Alchian and William R. Allen, *University Economics* 475–77 (2d ed., 1967), discuss the relevance of exclusion costs to joint consumption of both private and public good.

hide and the meat is equal to the cost of slaughtering a steer. The geometry of equilibrium for jointly supplied products is shown in Figure 1. Curve d is the market demand for hides and D is the vertical summation of d and the market demand for meat, hence D-d measures the demand for meat. The vertical summation of the demand prices equals the marginal cost of slaughtering cattle, shown by curve S, at the slaughter rate Q. No special problem arises in the allocation of resources to joint products in this, the standard case, nor does any problem arise in allocating the equilibrium production rates among consumers of meat and hides.

The analytical similarity between the joint product problem and the public good problem is seen most easily in a two-person world

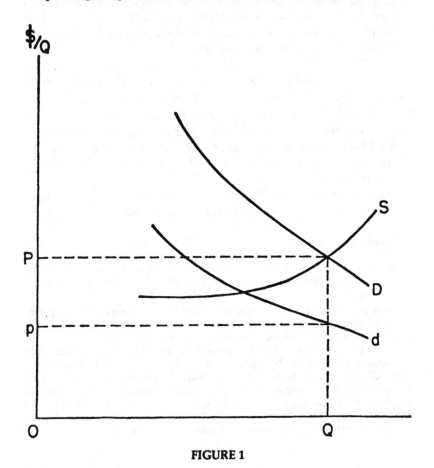

FIGURE 1

in which a unit of the public good can be used to satisfy the demands of both individuals for the good. Thus, a unit of the public good, say, the televising of a taped program, can satisfy the demand of Mr. H and Mr. M, just as the slaughtering of a steer can satisfy the demand for hides and meat. Let curve d be the demand of Mr. H for the public good and let D be the vertical summation of d and the demand of Mr. M for the public good. The appropriate equilibrium rate of output again is given by Q. (The problem of allocating output from a given *inventory* of the public good is discussed later.) Now, just as the number of goods which are supplied jointly (meat, hides, bones, etc.) is not limited to two except for expositional convenience, so the number of persons demanding a public good is not limited to two. With joint supply if the number of goods is increased or with a public good if the number of persons is increased, we will merely have complicated the geometry without changing the analytical similarity of the two cases at all.

What then is the difference between the two cases insofar as rate of output is concerned? There is no difference (an assertion that I plan to defend in more detail), *provided that Mr. H and Mr. M can be excluded from consuming the public good if they fail to pay for it*, which, of course, is implicitly assumed to be true in the joint supply problem.

There is nothing in the public good concept that disallows the ability to exclude. Frequently, there is confusion between the public good concept, as I understand it, which states that it is possible at no cost for additional persons to enjoy the same unit of a public good, and a different concept, that might be identified as a collective good, which imposes the stronger condition that it is *impossible* to exclude nonpurchasers from consuming the good. The technology of modern weaponry may in fact make it difficult to exclude nonpurchasers from benefiting from national defense purchases, and national defense might be termed an "approximate collective good," but it is easy to exclude nonpurchasers from viewing pay TV, an "approximate public good." Ability to exclude nonpurchasers is compatible with both private and public goods.

Although the joint supply model suggests that the rate of production of public goods responds to demand and supply conditions in exactly the same way as jointly produced private goods, there remains the problem of the utilization of an already produced unit of goods. How can market price be used to direct resources into public good production and also to ration the use of existing units of the public good, when the cost of allowing additional persons to use the existing inventory of the public good is zero?

In the case of private goods the existing inventory is rationed by the price mechanism to those who are willing to bid the highest prices. Hides and meat are jointly produced but an individual's use of each of these goods usually precludes its use by others. The price mechanism rations the existing stock according to the dictates of opportunity cost. For in this case the cost associated with the consumption of a unit from the inventory is the foregone opportunity of allowing someone else to consume this same unit. The rationing of the inventory by market price minimizes the loss in value due to others being excluded from consumption (that is, minimizes opportunity cost) by allocating the inventory to those who find it most valuable; those who do not acquire a unit from this inventory fail to do so because the value of a unit of the good to them is less than it is to others. Since the measure of opportunity cost is the value of the good to those who forego it, the market price minimizes the opportunity cost associated with the allocation of an inventory of a purely private good.

If, because demand or supply were forecasted poorly, the existing stock of a private good is so plentiful that the market clearing price falls below the cost of producing more units, then production to replenish inventory will dwindle. The loss in not consuming a unit for those who do not obtain a unit of the good from the existing inventory is less than the production gained elsewhere by not diverting resources from other uses for the purpose of increasing the inventory of this good. Since efficient allocation requires that resources be channeled into their highest value use, this message correctly guides resource allocation. While, if the market price of a unit of good from the existing inventory is above the cost of replenishing the inventory, then resources properly will be moved into the activity of producing more units of this good. The market price of private goods serves efficiently both the function of rationing the existing inventory and rationing resources into replenishment of the inventory.

It would seem that any scheme for pricing the use of a unit of the public good, once an inventory of the good is available, will "unnecessarily" restrain the use of the existing inventory. The burden of the next few paragraphs is to demonstrate that if the cost of excluding nonpurchasers is negligible, then competitive markets can in principle resolve efficiently both the inventory allocation and the rate of output problems. But perhaps the most interesting aspect of the efficient equilibrium to be described below is that it yields for competitive conditions different prices for the "same good."[2]

I assume that the production of the public good is subject to diminishing returns at the level of firm output so that it is possible for the structure of the industry producing the good to conform to the traditional (although, I believe, superficial) view of competition. The production of television tapes for viewing over pay TV might approximate this condition since the production of additional tapes requires more resources while the cost of enlarging the viewing audience for a given telecast can be assumed to impose negligible cost on other viewers. In addition to the assumption that many producers of these tapes compete, I assume also that the cost of excluding nonpurchasers from viewing a telecast is negligible.

I shall consider in the context of pay TV a special case of private production first and then a more general case. Figure 2b shows the market demand for and supply of TV tapes on the assumption either that all individuals have the same demand or that it is too costly to distinguish differences in demands. I assume that buyers are indifferent to the order in which they view first-run TV tapes. D_s is the *vertical* summation of these individual demands so that under the present assumption the height of any single buyer's demand curve is D_s/n where n is the number of buyers. One buyer's demand curve is shown in Figure 2b as D_b. With the stipulated assumptions, private production of TV tapes will yield an equilibrium output equal to q_s (number of TV tapes televised per period). For each viewing of a TV tape, the price paid by each buyer for a "ticket" allowing one person to view the tape is p_b and the total revenue collected for each showing of a TV tape is np_b since each of n viewers pays p_b.

The typical firm, pictured in equilibrium in Figure 2a, produces

[2]The compatibility of competition and different prices for the same good is discussed from a different viewpoint by Earl A. Thompson, "The Perfectly Competitive Production of Collective Goods," 50 *Rev. Econ. & Stat.* 1 (1968). Thompson, however, reaches the contrasting conclusion that these prices characterize an inefficient solution to the production problem. But the model that he employs to reach this conclusion, in my opinion, so strains the concept of competition that a full discussion of the Thompson paper would carry us far beyond our subject.

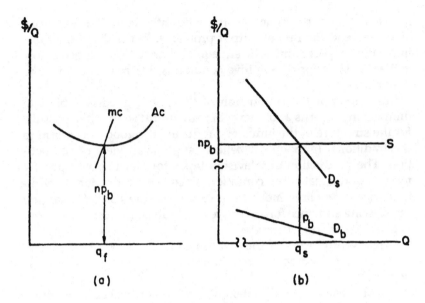

FIGURE 2

tapes at a rate equal to q_f and incurs a marginal cost according to curve mc. The industry, I assume, is subject to constant returns so that curve S shows industry supply. The revenue or aggregate price per program is np_b and this equals mc at q_f. This completes the description of the equilibrium. I now turn to an explanation of just why it is an equilibrium.

There are four tests for competitive equilibrium: (1) each firm should be maximizing profits while taking market price as given, (2) the price should clear the market, (3) there should be no incentive for resources to enter or leave the industry, and (4) buyers should maximize utility while they take the price they face as given. All four conditions are satisfied by the equilibrium just described.

Consider condition (1). Given large numbers of firms producing TV programs, p_b will be taken as given by each firm and, also, since each unit of the public good sold by a firm will be sold to all buyers simultaneously, the firm will earn an aggregate price per unit, np_b, that is equal to marginal cost. Therefore, q_f maximizes profits and no firm seeks to change its output rate. Since profits are zero, resources will neither leave nor enter the industry so that condition (3) also is satisfied. If price p_b persists the market will clear so that condition (2) will be satisfied.

There is no reason for the behavior of sellers to lead to a change in price. Each seller offers TV tapes at rate q_f which means that the tapes of each seller will be available for viewing q_f/q_s fraction of the time. If, in order to conform to the usual notion of competition, I assume that each firm's TV tape is a substitute for that of each other firm (at a particular first viewing, but that once seen it becomes an inferior rerun), then when a specific tape is shown it will be shown to all n buyers because the price to each buyer is reduced to the lowest common level, $mc/n = p_b$, if everyone views the program. Each seller, then, will find the entire viewing audience purchasing telecasts of his tapes q_f/q_s of the viewing time. But since there are many competing bidders for the viewing audience, no single seller can raise his price above p_b without losing his entire audience to some other seller. Moreover, no seller has an incentive to cut price below p_b because he will find that rates of output higher than q_f can be produced only at costs that are too high to be covered by incoming revenues; if one buyer receives a price reduction from p_b equal to Δp then other buyers must in total pay an increment greater than Δp if the new higher marginal cost of the firm is to be covered. But none of the other buyers will accept a price increase since other sellers stand ready to serve them at p_b. Hence, from the viewpoint of sellers the price p_b will persist, especially since any general expansion in output beyond q_s must force price below average and marginal cost and any reduction in output below q_s must attract entrants. Since q_s is the only industry output consistent with zero profit it will be produced and will be made available to all buyers at whatever price it can fetch. The optimum firm size, q_f, determines what fraction of this output will be produced by each firm.

The only difference between the public good case and the private good case is that the sales of each firm receive the exclusive attention of the entire audience. With private goods, it is possible for the outputs of competitive sellers to be consumed simultaneously. With public goods, once a unit is sold to someone there is no cost to selling it to others also. There exist economies of scale in consumption, that is, the price to each buyer is lowered as more buyers purchase the same unit. The various portions of the output produced by different sellers cannot, therefore, be consumed simultaneously. Each producer will sell each of his units of output to the entire market to the exclusion of other sellers. But since all potential sellers compete for this market none can exact a price higher than p_b from each buyer.[3]

Each buyer will take price p_b as given, so that condition (4) also will be satisfied. Each buyer (in the case we are now considering) of course, would like to have the output rate q_s increased, for then, obviously, a price lower than p_b will clear the market. But no buyer will have an incentive to exaggerate his demand for the product in order to bring this about. Nor will a buyer have an incentive to under-reveal his demand. The reason that the buyer takes the price as given in the public good case is the same as the reason that he takes it as given in the private good case. There is no *individual* action that he can take to lower the price that he pays that is *worthwhile* for him to take. The buyer of wheat naturally delights in bumper crops that are large relative to demand because the larger supply can clear the market only at lower prices. But the buyer of wheat does not, therefore, increase the quantity he purchases, for if he did so in significant quantities he would *increase* the price he pays and he would consume units that have a lower value to him than does the payment he makes to purchase them. Similarly, the buyer of wheat would benefit from a collusion among buyers to reduce the demand for wheat relative to the supply of wheat—if the collusion could be policed successfully at little cost to the buyer.

An individual buyer, if he withholds his demand foregoes the viewing of TV tapes that would cost him less to view than the benefit he would derive. Since nonpurchasers are excluded, if an individual did not reveal his demand he would not view TV programs for which the marginal value exceeds the price he would pay. Industry output would, of course, fall as a result and so would the number of producing firms. The price to each remaining buyer would increase since n is reduced. But the same would be true for any overhead cost in the private good case, just as it would be for the case in which private goods are jointly supplied.

It might be thought that an individual buyer could extort other buyers into subsidizing his purchases under the threat that other-

---

[3]This is an excellent example of competition *for the market* as distinct from competition *within the market*, a concept that I have discussed in greater detail in a refutation of the logic of natural monopoly. Harold Demsetz, "Why Regulate Utilities?" 11 *J. Law & Econ.* 55 (1968).

wise he would purchase nothing, for if he purchases nothing, the price to other buyers, because there are fewer of them, must be increased to cover production cost. But similarly, we may ask why a prospective buyer of hides does not threaten to withdraw from the market unless purchasers of meat reward him. Since the reduction in hide demand would result in an increase in the price of meat the incentive for such threats exist in the production of private goods also. A similar incentive exists in the production of private goods subject to scale economies since here, also, the reduction in demand would raise the price paid by other buyers. Conceptually nothing bars such bargaining in the markets for both private and public goods. It just is not worthwhile in most cases. If one purchaser of hides or of TV programs withdraws his demand he raises the cost to others by a magnitude of the order of 1/n of the price that he would have paid. Where n is large it just does not pay to incur the costs of withdrawing one's demand plus the cost of contacting other buyers to exact a reward to reenter the market, especially since these other buyers could utilize their would-be contributions to such a reward to purchase more units for themselves instead. Since the game is seldom worth playing, the problem does not often arise as an empirical matter.

This is not to say that the problem never arises. It does, even in the world of private goods, as when certain landholders hold out for higher prices after other landowners have sold to some land developer. The normal adjustment to the prospect of hold-outs is to enter into contractual arrangements that are conditional upon securing the cooperation of all those who are involved in some relevant way. But in any case, so long as firms are free to compete for the trade of buyers, this issue will reduce to a problem of wealth distribution and not to a problem of efficiency.

I turn now to a consideration of the case in which differences in demand elasticities can be identified at negligible cost. Figure 3b shows the market demand for and supply of TV tapes, with demand segregated into three customer categories, say, single family dwellings, hotels, and other commercial establishments (bars, waiting rooms in movie theatres, etc.). For this second case, I assume that the cost of identifying broad classes of customers is negligible. For each of these categories of customers, the demand curve, either D_1, D_2, or D_3 measures the *vertical* addition of individual demands, and D_s, in turn, measures the vertical sum of D_1, D_2, and D_3. Private production will yield an equilibrium output rate

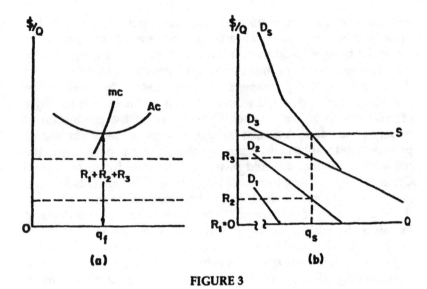

FIGURE 3

equal to q_s, but for each viewing of a show the revenue per show received *from the three subclasses* will be R_1 (= 0), R_2, and R_3. The price per customer for each viewing will be a function of the class to which he belongs (D_1, D_2, or D_3) and the population of that class (denoted, respectively by n_1, n_2, and n_3). The price per viewing per customer, then, is

$$p_1 = \frac{R_1}{n_1} = 0, \; p_2 = \frac{R_2}{n_2}, \; \text{or} \; p_3 = \frac{R_3}{n_3} \; \text{depending on the class to which}$$

he belongs. For ease of exposition solely, let us assume that $n_1 = n_2 = n_3 = 1$ while still retaining the essential behavior of competitive buyers, always understanding that we could have used larger values of n_1, n_2, and n_3 and calculated the appropriate price to each customer. With $n_1 = n_2 = n_3 = 1$, R_3, R_2, and R_1 are the prices per viewing, respectively, facing market classes D_3, D_2, and D_1.

The typical firm producing and marketing TV shows, pictured in equilibrium in Figure 3a, produces shows at a rate equal to q_f and incurs a marginal cost of mc = S = industry supply under conditions of constant returns to industry scale. The revenue or aggregate price per program is equal to $R_3 + R_2 + R_1$ (= 0) = mc. This completes the description of the equilibrium. It now is time to explain just why this is the equilibrium and, in particular, how it can be that the different prices shown can hold simultaneously under competitive conditions.

Again, the four tests for equilibrium are satisfied. Given large numbers of firms producing competitive TV programs, R_1, R_2, and R_3 will be taken as given by each firm and, also, will sum to marginal cost so that each firm will be maximizing profits at q_f. Each firm will be earning zero profits so that entry and exit will not take place as long as R_3, R_2, and R_1 persist. The crucial condition, of course, is the persistence of R_1, R_2, and R_3, for if these prices do persist the market will clear.

The reader surely has some doubts about the persistence of these different prices for the same good under competitive conditions because accepted doctrine teaches us that price discrimination[4] and competition are incompatible. This doctrine is (probably) correct when it is applied in the context for which it was developed—the economics of private goods—but it is incorrect for the marketing of public goods. With private good production, a competitive producer would forego profit if he sold a unit of his output at a price equal to R_2 (or R_1) when the market is offering to him the opportunity to sell at a price of R_3. Price differences for the same good in the world of private goods are inconsistent with perfect competition. *But price differences can be consistent with competition precisely because a firm that sells a unit for R_2 or R_1 in markets D_2 and D_1 does not forego the sale of the same unit to market D_3 at price R_3.* Buyers in each of the submarkets can consume the same unit of the public good simultaneously. When a producer telecasts a tape to markets D_2 and D_1 he does not forego the opportunity of simultaneously telecasting to market D_3.

There is no incentive for price R_3 to be undercut by competitive pressures. If more units than q_s are sold to the D_3 market, R_3 will be forced down and revenues will fail to cover cost. It is no good to say that simultaneously less than q_s will be offered to market D_2 and that this will raise the price in that submarket, because any producer of a program for market D_3, under competition, will not have incentives to hold the program off market D_2. He suffers no loss in revenue from market D_3 nor does he suffer any increase in cost if he makes those programs available to market D_2 that he is selling to D_3. Hence, any rate of output beyond q_s in servicing any

---

[4] I use the phrases "price discrimination" and "different prices for the same good" in the text, but I believe a more detailed analysis of this conceptual problem will show that the different prices described above are not properly called discriminatory.

particular submarket must reduce revenues below cost under competitive conditions and any rate of output less than q_e must lead to entry or output expansion because revenues in excess of costs will be generated. Since q_e is the only industry output consistent with zero profit it will be produced and when this rate of output is produced all of it will be made available to all submarkets at whatever prices it can fetch because doing so does not reduce sales to any particular submarket. Buyers in each of these submarkets will bid up the price of the marginal unit to the value to them of consuming it. The intersection of the supply available to each submarket with that submarket's demand indicates the equilibrium result of this bidding process. The prices that will persist under competitive conditions can be only R_3, R_2, and R_1.

If we turn now to a closer examination of R_1, the zero price that probably has puzzled some readers, our conviction about this conclusion can be reinforced. Assume that q_e is produced but that firms sell only to markets D_2 and D_3 at prices, respectively, of R_2 and R_3. At output q_f each firm maximizes profits and just breaks even. However, at no additional cost each of these firms can sell television programs to D_1 at positive prices since no programs now are being marketed to this class of buyers. Under competition, the price to D_1 must be forced to zero, or if there is a separable cost of delivering a telecast to this submarket the price will be competed down to that cost.

There is no single price that can satisfy all equilibrium requirements under the conditions that have been posited, that is, under the condition that differences in demand prices can be identified at relatively low cost. A single price cannot equal mc since output would then be determined by the intersection of D_3 and S (D_3 being the only market willing to pay a price as high as mc). Each producer would find it in his interest to offer, at no additional cost to him, these same units to markets D_1 and D_2 at prices lower than mc, and buyers in these markets will bid for marginal units until prices equal R_1 and R_2. But this will yield revenues in excess of cost, since for any positive R_2 and for R_1, it must be that mc + R_2 + R_1 > mc. Hence, output must expand until q_e is reached and sold for R_3, R_2, and R_1 respectively, in each submarket. If the single price asked is, say, one third mc, then a shortage will appear in market D_3, at least, and possibly in market D_2, so that prices in these markets will be bid up, output will expand and price to market D_1 will fall. The configuration of variables illustrated in Figure 3 is the only configuration consistent with competition.

The equilibrium depicted above (1) allocates resources efficiently to the production of the public good ($D_s = S$), (2) generates revenues just sufficient to cover costs, and (3) excludes no one from viewing a telecast; those buyers for whom demand price reaches zero to the left of q_s will pay no price and will view as many telecasts as they please, which, because they are easily satiated, is a number less than is available for viewing. An omniscient and efficiency-minded government could do no better.

There is, of course, a policing problem because buyers will attempt to disguise themselves to qualify for the lower price. The same problem is faced if the good is produced by the government. Taxpayers will attempt to disguise themselves as nonbeneficiaries or as poor, or they will use loopholes, in order to reduce the tax burden allotted to them. To the extent that it is costly to police the separate markets, perhaps because some easily identifiable criterion such as age is lacking, to that extent it will be efficient to charge the same price to two groups whose demands may differ. The problem of identifying and separating submarkets, *given the ability to exclude nonpurchasers*, is not any different or any more severe for public goods than it is for the production of private goods. A monopolist who produces private goods and seeks to price discriminate must be able to identify and separate his markets; undoubtedly, he must cope with the problem of those who seek to mislead the monopolist into thinking their demands are more elastic than they truly are. But devices for doing this are available. A monopolistic barber's union is able to use the age of buyers to successfully separate his markets. Similarly, a producer of a public good, a producer who sells exclusively to the market for that fraction of the total supply that he produces, can rely on such devices as age, sex, location, and income to separate his markets. The problem of separating markets is independent of the degree to which the good is private. But what is different is that competitively produced public goods lend themselves to price discrimination whereas competitively produced private goods do not.

The joint supply model clearly is useful for determining the equilibrium that is likely to arise when the private production of public goods conforms closely to the assumptions set out above. As an instrument of positive economics, this application of the joint supply model seems to me to be fully justified and I am led to a conclusion opposite to that which Paul A. Samuelson reached recently:

> The theory of public goods is sometimes confused with the theory of joint production. This is in the nature of a pun, or a play on words for, as I have insisted elsewhere, as we increase the number of persons on both sides of the market in the case of mutton and wool, we can verge in the usual fashion to the conditions of perfect competition. But when we increase the number of persons in the case of a typical public good, we make the problem more *indeterminate* rather than less.[5]

I do not claim to know what Samuelson means by a *typical public good*, but the subset of public goods discussed above is not uninteresting and in that subset (as well as other subsets that I have not discussed here), Samuelson is incorrect in his assertion that the solution to public good production becomes indeterminate as the number of persons is increased. The joint supply model yields predictions as determinate as any to be found in economics.

Samuelson also concludes that it is misleading to characterize the public good problem as a joint supply problem because the vertical addition of demands in the public good case is a summation over people whereas in the joint supply case it is a summation of demands of people for certain goods (hides and meat in my example). Samuelson's paper deduces the technical difference to which this gives rise. The difference is that the public good case yields marginal rates of substitution between the public good and other goods that differ for persons consuming the public good (that is, in our example, the heights of D_1, D_2, and D_3, differ at q_s), while different persons consuming the same good (meat or hides) in the joint supply case will have the same marginal rates of substitution. Calling attention to this difference seems to be the main object of Samuelson's short note.

This technical difference between the two cases is not necessary although it would be highly probable. The very special public good case wherein the demand curves of all individual buyers are of equal height at q_s, as we have seen, would be an exception. But setting this unlikely event aside, what is the implication to be derived from this difference?

[5]Paul A. Samuelson, *supra* note 1, at 26.

A difference between the marginal rate of substitution between buyers of the same *private* good would give rise to further exchange, with the inventory of the good passing from those who value it less to those who value it more. If such exchange did not take place (in the absence of contracting cost), that is, if the differences in the marginal rates of substitution persisted, the allocation of the private good must be inefficient, which, of course, is precisely why exchange will arise. But with public goods, equal marginal rates of substitution, in the general case, are *inconsistent* with the efficient allocation of an inventory among buyers. This is true because extending the use of the public good to those who value it less does not prevent those who value the good more from using it also. Indeed, to require equality in the marginal rates of substitution in the public good case means that those who have "low" demand intensities must be prevented from using as much of the good as is made available to those who have "high" demand intensities. Thus, in Figure 3b, equal marginal rates of substitution are achieved if all buyers are charged the same price. But clearly this leads to an underutilization of the public good by D_2 and D_3 buyers. If title to q_s were given buyers in the D_3 market, they would choose to sell extensions of the use of the good to buyers in the D_2 and D_1 markets even though D_2 and D_1 buyers pay lower prices than did the D_3 buyers because, unlike private goods, the D_3 buyers need not deprive themselves of the use of the good when they sell the right to partake in its use to others. Hence, the difference between the marginal rates of substitution that generally will exist in the equilibrium yielded by the private production of public goods carries with it no implication of inefficiency in the allocation of goods among buyers. This hardly needs to be pointed out to Samuelson, yet in an obscurely worded paragraph, he gives the *impression* that the differences in marginal rates of substitution that would result from the private production of public goods lead to an inefficient allocation of the good among buyers:

> The "externality" involved in the production of wool along with mutton creates no new problems for laissez-faire pricing. . . . [W]e can leave to the invisible hand of the marketplace the determination of optimal resource allocation. . . . There is nothing "pseudo" about the demand functions involved in standard joint products, an intrinsic contrast to the public good case. In this sense I find it misleading to characterize the public case as a case of joint supply.[6]

[6]*Id.* at 30.

I believe that the foregoing analysis shows this statement to be incorrect. For the joint supply model is extremely useful in analyzing both the positive and normative aspects of the private production of public goods, and once we admit that wool and mutton can be substituted at some finite cost in the maintenance of body energy, the differences between the two cases become quantitative and not qualitative. Under the assumptions used here, but not necessarily under only these assumptions, unambiguous statements can be made about the characteristics of equilibrium under private production of public goods.

While private production of public goods seems feasible, the private production of collective goods, for which the cost of excluding nonpurchasers is great, does not seem to be practical. If no consumer can be excluded all may tend to underreveal their true demands for the good. But the conclusion that collective goods cannot be produced in adequate quantities by private firms is too strong, for devices to further such production can be not only conceived, but actually have been used. In many instances it may be possible to tie in the consumption of a second product with consumption of the collective good, and private incentives may very well exist for the production of the tied-in good because exclusion is possible.

Radio and television provide us with classic examples of this procedure. Let us assume, contrary to the previous discussion, that once a show is broadcast the signal can be captured by all who own receivers, and that no owner can be excluded. Yet there are at least two private groups who are willing to pay the cost of broadcasting. One group contains advertisers who have a great interest in getting their messages into all homes; the second group contains producers of radio and television sets, who, even in the absence of advertisers would find it desirable to broadcast popular shows in order to sell the sets they produce. The first group ties in advertising messages with the broadcast signal while the second group ties in sets and signals.

No doubt the tie-in mechanism does not lend itself to the efficient production by private means of some collective goods. But the incantation of a solution in these cases by repeating Government three times merely begs the issue. The demands for a collective good are likely to be misrepresented in the legislature and the taxes levied are unlikely to be related closely to benefits. Whether private or public production yields a better rate of output cannot be determined at this level of discourse.

7. The Exchange and Enforcement of Property Rights

Harold Demsetz

Our economic system, with its specialization of economic activities into separate ownership and decision units, requires both
control over goods and exchange of goods if it is to cope with the
diversity of wants of specialist producers. This paper is concerned
with the fact that the exchange of goods and the maintenance of
control over the use of goods impose costs on traders and owners.
It is also concerned with the cost of government alternatives to the
market place. We seek to establish both the importance and the
wide role of these costs in economic life.

A large part of our argument will be illustrated by two important
controversies in welfare economics in which we will show, on the
one hand, that zero pricing of scarce goods need not result in
inefficiency. The standard criticisms of resource allocation by the
market, which turn on the market's failure to price "external"
effects and on its tendency to price "public" goods, are shown to
be invalid. To do this we extend the well known axiom that there
is no such thing as a free scarce good by including such goods as
markets, government bureaus, and policing devices.

Throughout this paper, our attention is confined to the problem
of efficiency within the framework of smoothly running markets
and governments, in the sense that we assume that persons,
whether in their capacity as civil servants or as private citizens, do
not make arithmetic errors in calculating, or, at least, that they
do not tend to make more errors in one role than in another. We
do not concern ourselves with problems of monopoly by either a
firm or the government, but the problem of imperfect knowledge
is treated.

Reprinted, by permission, from *Journal of Law and Economics* 7 (October 1964):
11–26.

The author wishes to thank Armen A. Alchian, Gary S. Becker, William H.
Meckling, Peter Pashigian, and George J. Stigler for their comments.

Instead of "external effects" or "neighborhood effects" we will use the phrase "side effects" to identify those for which no account *seems* to be taken in the market place. This avoids the flavor of location and of being *necessarily* outside of the market place that seem to be associated with the more common names for these effects.

Exchange Cost

Recent Developments

R. H. Coase,[1] in an important article written recently for this *Journal*, demonstrates that there is, in general, nothing special about side effects that rules out the possibility of their being taken account of by the market. These effects can be taken into account by market transactions between the parties affected once the courts have established who has what right of action. Under competitive conditions and assuming zero exchange costs, these transactions will result in an efficient solution to the scarcity problem. Thus, if ranchers are given the right to allow their cattle to roam and the cattle stray accidentally onto unfenced farm land, it will be in the farmer's interest to bring the damage they cause to the rancher's attention by offering to pay the rancher to reduce the number of cattle foraging nearby. If the rancher disregards this offer, he sacrifices a potential receipt equal to the crop damage. Thus, the crop damage becomes a private cost to the rancher of raising additional cattle and will be taken account of in his calculations. Moreover, Coase points out the efficiency of the solution with respect to the number of cattle and the size of the crops in the absence of exchange costs is independent of whether the farmer or rancher is legally liable for the damage. The party not held liable, of course, acquires the right to act in ways which may have harmful side effects. The assignment of the liability for crop damage to the rancher would lead to a direct accounting for this cost in his operations and he would need to decide whether to reduce his herd or pay the farmer to reduce the crop he plants. Whether the farmer will find it worthwhile to pay enough to the rancher to reduce his herd or whether the rancher can pay enough to the farmer to reduce the area he cultivates depends on whether the value lost because of the crop reduction is greater or less than

[1]Coase, "The Problem of Social Cost," 3 *J. Law & Econ.* 1–44 (1960).

the value lost because the size of the herd is reduced. Whichever way the rights are initially assigned, the outcome of the subsequent bargaining will be that which maximizes the value of output.

Coase has advanced the analysis of the roles that can be played by the market and the government a step beyond its previous position. For now Coase has shown that if exchange costs are positive, it is necessary to ask whether government can take the harmful effects of an action into account at less cost than can the market or, indeed, if the resulting resource realignment is worth the cost of taking the side effects into account at all.

Misapplication of Optimality Theorems

The question which asks whether or not realignment is worthwhile brings to light an improper usage to which we frequently have put our optimality theorems. The cost of using the market relative to the cost of using a political mechanism has seldom been considered explicitly or in detail in the bulk of the theory of welfare economics. This has led to an improper usage of those theorems. As a consequence of the conventional approach to these problems, it has not been recognized that the very conditions under which side effects are believed to lead to inefficiency are those conditions for which the welfare theorems used are inapplicable.

The usual analysis of market inefficiency in such cases attributes the difficulty to the absence of markets in which "appropriate" prices for measuring side effects can be revealed.[2] But absence of a market or of a price can be consistent with efficiency when opti-

[2]*Cf.* Arrow, "Uncertainty and the Welfare Economics of Medical Care," 53 *Am. Econ. Rev.* 941, 944–45 (1963):

> An individual who fails to be immunized not only risks his own health, a disutility which presumably he has weighed against the utility of avoiding the procedure, but also that of others. In an ideal system, there would be a price which he would have to pay to anyone whose health is endangered, a price sufficiently high so that the others would feel compensated; or, alternatively, there would be a price which would be paid to him by others to induce him to undergo the immunization procedure. . . . It is, of course, not hard to see that such price systems could not, in fact, be practical; to approximate an optimal state it would be necessary to have collective intervention in the form of subsidy or tax or compulsion.

and Bator, "The Anatomy of Market Failure," 72 *Q. J. Econ.* 351, 353–54 (1958):

> Pareto-efficient . . . points . . . are characterized by a complete set of marginal-rate-of-substitution . . . equalities (or limiting inequalities) which, in turn, yield a set of price-like constants. Where no such constants exist, reference will be to *failure of existence* (of prices, and hence, of efficiency). (Parenthetic phrase added.)

mality theorems are appropriately interpreted. For produced goods, the optimality theorems require equalities among various marginal rates of substitution. These same optimality conditions, however, do not require such equalities for goods and services that are *not produced* in the final efficient equilibrium; for these we have corner solutions involving inequalities. Thus, a basic premise in requiring equalities is that we are talking about goods which we require to be produced in positive quantities.

We then turn to the competitive model and observe that market prices will often bring about the equalities required for produced commodities and services. But, we ask, what if some goods produce side effects which are not exchanged over a market? We answer that the market fails to provide us with incentives which will guide behavior to take account of the side effects and that, therefore, the required equalities will be absent. The allegation is that even perfectly competitive markets fail to achieve efficiency. But, this reasoning generally fails to take account of the fact that the provision of a market (for the side effect) is itself a valuable and costly service. Where a market, or the political action which would be its counterpart, does not exist, this service is not being produced. If this service is not being produced some *in*equalities (instead of the equalities required for produced goods) among our marginal rates of substitution and marginal rates of transformation may be consistent with efficiency, as will be the case if the cost of taking account of side effects through either the market or the government exceeds the value of realigning resources. In' such cases zero amounts of market pricing or the government equivalent will be efficient. In asking the implications of the nonexistence of some markets, we seem to have forgotten the cost of providing market services or their government equivalent. The existence of prices to facilitate exchange between affected parties has been too much taken for granted. A price for every produced good or service is not a necessary condition for efficiency, so that the absence of a price does not imply that either market transactions or substitute government services are desirable. If we insist either that all actions (services or commodities) be priced in the market or that the government intervene, we are insisting that we do not economize on the cost of producing exchanges or government services. Thus, most welfare propositions concerned with side effects are based on an invalid use of the standard optimality theorems, i.e., they ignore the cost of some of the goods.

Some Examples

We shall consider two examples to illustrate our point. In the first rights of action are clearly defined; in the second they are not.

Our first example is zero-priced parking at shopping plazas in which unpaid-for benefits exist insofar as shoppers, in the prices they pay, confer benefits on nonshopping parkers. Most economists, regardless of their philosophical persuasion, would probably argue that the number of spaces is nonoptimal. But, when we say nonoptimal, we must have some idea of what is the optimal number of spaces. Assuming the absence of increasing returns, the less careful of us are apt to reply that the proper number of spaces is the number that would clear the market when a charge is levied to cover construction cost. A more careful reply would include exchange costs in the charge. *Neither* answer is necessarily correct.

It is true that the setting and collecting of appropriate shares of construction and exchange costs from each parker will reduce the number of parking spaces needed to allow ease of entry and exit. But while we have reduced the resources committed to constructing parking spaces, we have increased resources devoted to market exchange. We may end up by allocating more resources to the provision and control of parking than had we allowed free parking because of the resources needed to conduct transactions. By insisting that the commodity be priced, we may become less efficient than had we allowed persons to ration spaces on a first come, first serve basis. Similarly, rationing by government involves its own costs and may be no better. Those who purchase merchandise and indirectly pay for parking spaces may prefer to substitute the smaller total cost of constructing additional spaces to accommodate free-loaders rather than ration out the nonbuying parkers by paying the required exchange costs minus the savings of constructing fewer parking spaces. Since the cost of providing additional parking spaces depends largely on the price of land, it follows that we should expect to observe free parking allowed more frequently in suburbs than in the center of towns because of the differential prices of land. Given this differential, both methods of allocating parking may be efficient.

Is this example consistent with competition? Will not competing stores open nearby and charge lower prices because their customers use a free parking lot supplied by a competitor? Will they, thereby, force their competitor out of business? The desirability of providing parking spaces implies that we are dealing with a world of finite dimension in which all cars cannot be parked at zero cost on a dimensionless point. For this reason, differential land rent will be taken into account. Owners of land surrounding the free parking lot will enjoy windfall profits, a question of wealth redistribution, but potential competitors will have the advantages of the nearby lot capitalized and included in the rent they pay; they will enjoy no competitive advantage. The equilibrium is a stable competitive one although it gives rise to differential land rent. If the windfall is expected to be large enough to warrant the additional transactions required to purchase surrounding land, the (prospective) owners of the shopping plaza could take account of these gains in their calculations by purchasing the surrounding land before free parking is allowed. This option, which Coase refers to as extending the role of the firm, is alternative to both exchange and government action.[3]

In this particular example, the efficiency of producing this costly but zero-priced parking depends on the supplier being able to recoup the cost by other means, namely in the prices of his merchandise. This method of financing the parking lot becomes economically superior *only* if demand interrelations are such that a sale in combination arrangement reduces exchange costs sufficiently. Both the loose combination sale (not all parkers need to buy merchandise) as well as tighter tie-ins may, in fact, be methods which reduce the cost of allocating and which lead to optimal quantities of goods. We will have more to say on the relevance of this for the problems posed by public goods.

For contrast, our next example, one that has become a favorite, involves neither tie-in arrangements nor defined rights of action. It is the case in which market transactions do not take place in the use of nectar by bees, so that prices do not arise which reflect the

---

[3]The existence of unique locations does not necessarily imply the inefficiency usually associated with monopolistic competition. *Cf.* Demsetz, "The Welfare and Empirical Implications of Monopolistic Competition," 74 *Economic J.* 623–41 (1964). It should also be noted that if the landowners could know of the differential land rents that would result from the superior technology offered by free parking, they would be inclined to enter into an agreement sharing the differential rent accruing to land adjacent to the shopping plaza. If they did not enter into such an agreement there would be an inclination to let the free parking facility be built on the other man's property.

beneficial effects of apple blossoms on the productivity of bees. Clearly, as Coase would probably point out, it is possible for beekeepers and apple growers to strike a bargain over how many trees are to be planted, the bargain taking account of an apple tree's contribution to honey production and a bee's contribution to cross-fertilization of trees. Further, were there significant predictable benefits from the interaction, significant enough to offset any diseconomies of underspecialization, beekeeping and apple growing would be carried on by the same farmer. However, the benefits may be small relative to the costs of forsaking specialization. Merger will not then be the solution. Suppose, also, that estimates of benefits are small relative to estimates of the cost of developing the science of the apple-bee interaction and to either the costs of transacting in the market or providing substitute government services. Then efficiency requires that bees be allowed to "help themselves" on a first come, first serve basis, which is, after all, an alternative arrangement for settling scarcity problems.

Here no combination sales are directly involved. A valuable and costly good, nectar, is provided free of charge because it would be too costly to take account of the indirect benefits to beekeepers. In contrast to the parking and merchandising example, the separate marketing of the two products, apples and blossoms, is costly. Hence a zero-priced good may be efficient even though no combination sale is used. Since no low cost combination sale seems possible, the good (nectar) will be provided free if apples, *per se*, are worth producing. If apples are not worth producing, our recognition of the existence of a benefit to beekeepers will not make the production of apples desirable, for the cost of inducing the apple grower to take this benefit into account is too high to make it worthwhile.

Police Cost

Up to now we have largely limited our attention to situations in which direct bargaining between individuals requires an exchange cost that is larger than the benefits derived from the exchange. To take account of these side effects, the interested parties, therefore, resort to combination sales, to extensions of the firm, or they find it expedient not to modify these effects. All of these alternatives are consistent with efficiency and yet all fail to exhibit a market in the side effect. There are situations, however, which are somewhat different in that the cost of *policing* the effects of actions, rather than the cost of exchange, may be so high as to cause additional complications. The following discussion of these situations is designed to reveal the roles played by police cost and private property and to help clear up some public good problems.

Property Rights and the Valuation Problem

There are two tasks which must be handled well by any acceptable allocative mechanism. These are, firstly, that information must be generated about all the benefits of employing resources in alternative uses, and secondly, that persons be motivated to take account of this information. To the extent that both these tasks are solved by the allocative mechanism, the problem of attaining an efficient allocation of resources reduces to arithmetic. Setting aside the second problem, we turn to the first and, in particular to the necessity for protecting the right to use economically valuable resources if we are to obtain accurate information about benefits.

It is well known that prices can serve as guideposts to where resources are wanted most, and in addition, that exchangeability of goods at these prices can provide incentives for people to follow these guideposts. However, analytical concentration on the price mechanism has kept us from closely examining what it is that is being traded. The value of what is being traded depends crucially on the rights of action over the physical commodity and on how economically these rights are enforced. The enforcement of the accompanying property rights has an important impact on the ability of prices to measure benefits. An emphasis on this aspect or view of the problem, in conjunction with our emphasis on exchange cost, will allow us to unify our treatment of what is now largely a collection of special cases in which our measures of benefits diverge from actual benefits. The petroleum and fishery "pool" problems are good examples of problems created by treating economic goods as free goods. The general conclusion reached by the analysis of pool problems is that a resource, be it petroleum, fish, or game, is too rapidly worked. This conclusion is correct and if we think in terms of producible inventories, the absence of property right enforcement also can be shown to result in too little production of the good, or in too small an increment to the pool or inventory of the good. This is because the prices, which reflect private benefits, fail to measure the whole of the social benefit derived from the good. As a special case of this general proposition, if we assume that it costs nothing to police property rights, it follows that there exists a direct relationship between the degree to which private benefits approach social benefits and the degree to which the conveyed property rights are enforced. This relationship can be illustrated with two examples.

Given any definition of the rights that accompany ownership in an automobile, the price mechanism will ration the existing stock of automobiles. But the total private value of this stock will depend on the degree to which auto theft is reduced by our laws and police. If we pass a law *prohibiting* the arrest and prosecution of auto thieves, and also prohibiting the use of private protection devices, the bids that persons subsequently offer for the purchase of automobiles will fall below the social value of automobiles. The lower bids will result from the reduction in control that a purchaser can expect to exercise over the use of a purchased auto and, in addition, from his ability to "borrow" at no charge those autos which are purchased by others. The bids submitted after the passage of such a law will underestimate the social value of autos, for we can assume for our purposes that the usefulness of an auto remains the same whether it is used by the purchaser or by the legal thief. This is true even though the existing stock of autos is efficiently distributed among owners. The total value of autos will fall below social value and the subsequent increase in the stock of autos will be less than it should.

The lowering of bids that results from our law is similar to the lowering of bids that will take place when high police cost reduces the degree of private control that it is economical to guarantee owners. The provision of national defense provides us with a classic example of the impact of high police cost. Voluntarily submitted bids for defense will be lower than the social value of defense because the bidder can count on being able to enjoy (some of) the defense bought and also enjoyed by his fellow citizen. The effect on bidding is similar to that which takes place in our example of legalized auto theft except that the reason for lack of control is not merely the absence of an appropriate law but, rather, it is the high cost of defending a purchaser from a foreign aggressor while at the same time preventing his neighbors from enjoying protection. The cost of excluding those who have not contracted for benefits from the enjoyment of some of these benefits is so high that a general attitude of letting others bear the cost of defense can be expected. Consequently, voluntarily submitted bids will underestimate the social value of defense.

If a low cost method is available and is used to prevent those who do not contract for defense from benefiting from the defense bought by others, the market would reveal accurate information about the social value of defense. Such information would be extremely useful if the market or the planner is to allocate resources efficiently.

The institution of private property, which attempts to exclude nonpurchasers from the use of that which others have purchased, should, therefore, not be looked upon as either accidental or undesirable. On the contrary, its existence is probably due in part to its great practicality in revealing the social values upon which to base solutions to scarcity problems. This is precisely why we do not worry that bids for, say, candy will fail to reveal the social value of candy. The price of candy is accurate in its measure of social value because reflected in it is the ability of each purchaser to control the use of his purchase, whether that use be for resale or for charity, for his children, or for his own consumption. This valuation function is related to but distinct from the incentives to work provided by a property system, for even in a society where work is viewed as a pleasurable activity, and, hence, where incentives to work are not needed, it would still be necessary to properly value the varieties of alternative output that can be produced.

We have already observed that the value of what is being traded depends upon the allowed rights of action over the physical good and upon the degree to which these rights are enforced. This statement at once raises the question of which rights and which degrees of enforcement are efficient. If changing the mix of property rights that accompany ownership increases the value of property, such a change will be desirable from the viewpoint of wealth maximizing. For example, if the problem is whether to allow automobile owners to increase the speed at which they travel on side streets, one could assess whether there would result an increase in the total value of affected property. Would people be willing to pay higher prices for automobiles? It is by no means clear that they would, for some prospective owners may fear high speed more than they value it. And, if there would result an increase in the price of automobiles, would it be large enough to offset any increase in the cost of insuring life, limb, and home (i.e., the resulting decline in the value of other property)? If a net increase in the total property follows a change in the mix of rights, the change should be allowed if we seek to maximize wealth. Not to allow the change would be to refuse to generate a surplus of value sufficient to compensate those harmed by the change. The process of calculating the net change in value will, of course, involve the taking into account of side effects and this is a problem that we have already discussed. The enforcement of rights can be viewed in the same way. Indeed, we can insist that a proper definition of a right of action include the degree to which the owner or the community is allowed to enforce the right. Enforcement thus becomes the specification of additional rights and can be included in the above analytical framework. The conclusion we have reached depends, of course, upon the existence of competitive entry in the exercise of particular rights. It is therefore necessary to exclude rights which confer monopoly by restricting entry and to insist that all owners have the same rights of action. There are some difficult problems which we do not take up here. For example, since everyone has the right to take out a patent or a copyright on "newly created" goods or ideas, does the granting of this right involve the granting of monopoly power?

It is, of course, necessary to economize on police cost, so that we will not always want to guarantee full control to the purchaser; more will be said below about this aspect of the problem. But, this aspect aside, it is essential to note that the valuation power of the institution of property is most effective when it is most *private*. It is ironic, therefore, that one of the strongest intellectual arguments for expanding the role of government has been based on the alleged necessity for eliminating exclusivity and for allowing free access to the use of certain types of resources. These resources have been given the name "public goods" and they are characterized by their alleged ability to confer benefits on additional persons without thereby reducing the benefits conferred on others. The provision of national defense is a well known example.

The Public Goods Problem

The relevance of what we have been discussing for public goods is that if the cost of policing the benefits derived from the use of these goods is low, there is an excellent reason for excluding those who do not pay from using these goods. By such exclusion we, or the market, can estimate accurately the value of diverting resources from other uses to the production of the public good. Thus, even though extending the use of an existing bridge to additional persons adds nothing to the direct cost of operating the bridge, there is good reason for charging persons for the right to cross the bridge. Excluding those who do not pay for the use of the bridge allows us to know whether a new bridge is likely to generate more benefit than it is likely to cost.[4] Why should we desire information about a new bridge if the direct marginal cost of using the existing bridge is zero? Firstly, the bridge may depreciate with time rather than with traffic, so that the question of replacement remains relevant even though the marginal cost of use is zero. Secondly, there is a private marginal benefit to users of the bridge, at least in lessening their driving costs, and this benefit can be measured by pricing the use of the bridge. Such information would allow us to ascertain whether it is economic to have a new bridge closer to some persons than is the present bridge.

For some goods, air for example, the supply is so plentiful that diversion from some uses is not required to increase the intensity with which they are used elsewhere. Only where scarcity is absent is it *a priori* reasonable to charge a zero price. Superabundance is the only true *a priori* case for a zero-priced public good. All other goods are such that their provision forces us into resource allocation problems. To solve these problems efficiently, we need information which is obtained by excluding nonpurchasers, *provided that the additional information is worth more than the exchange and police costs necessitated*. In cases where the costs are greater, a zero price can be reconciled with efficiency requirements. If we must distinguish among goods, we had best do away with the "public goods" *vs.* private goods dichotomy and instead classify goods according to whether they are truly free or economic and classify economic goods according to whether marketing costs are too high relative to the benefits of using markets and to the costs of substitute nonmarket allocation devices.

Alternative Devices

The use of taxation for the provision of scarce goods must be defended on grounds other than the usual rationale of their being public goods. As we have seen, insofar as efficiency is concerned, the fact that side benefits can be derived by nonpurchasers from

[4]See Coase, "The Marginal Cost Controversy," 13 *Economica* 169–82 (1946), for an early application of this point in reference to the use of multipart pricing in natural monopoly situations. See also Minasian, "Television Pricing and the Theory of Public Goods," 7 *J. Law & Econ.* 71 (1964).

the acquisition by others of these goods is inconclusive. If the planner's or the market's calculation of benefits can be improved by a small expenditure to protect or to confer property rights, the use of price rationing to measure these benefits may be justified. The problem can be viewed as that of determining the degree to which it is desirable to purchase valuation information through the competitive pricing process. A purchase of valuation information reduces the utilization of a public good below the levels that seem to be warranted by the direct cost of extending utilization. If the direct cost of, say, increasing the volume of traffic carried by an existing bridge is zero, it may nonetheless be *undesirable* to charge a zero price because of the indirect costs implied by zero-pricing. These indirect costs are of two kinds.

Firstly, and obviously, valuation information about the bridge is sacrificed. (Is not valuation information one of the most important public goods?) Secondly, the alternative methods of financing the building of bridges may also lead to inefficiency, especially by degrading valuation information elsewhere. This is most easily seen by supposing that an excise tax is levied on other goods to finance bridges. Such a tax will lead to inefficiently small rates of production of these other goods (assuming competitive markets). Alternatively, the levying of an income tax will inefficiently reduce the quantities of income generating activities undertaken by those taxed. A tax on property values, even one on rent, would tend to discourage the seeking out of more valuable uses of property. A head tax would have the least effect because it is not concentrated on particular activities. Even a head tax, one could argue, would alter a person's choice of community, and moreover, a resident who refused to pay the tax might be excluded from use of the bridge. Taxes exclude just as do prices, so that on grounds of exclusion there is not much principle to guide us. Given these indirect costs of alternative methods of financing the provision of public goods, the desirability of zero-pricing is not at all clear, especially if the cost of policing is low.

For some goods, however, it must be recognized that police cost may seem too high to allow the market to generate accurate information on social benefits economically. In these cases taxation *may* be the most practical method of finance and zoning the most practical way of establishing rights, just as subsidies, excise taxes, and government nonprice rationing may be the most practical way of coping with high exchange costs. But it must be remembered that all these devices are "exclusionary" and have costs of their own. At best, they would be second best alternatives to a market in which police and exchange costs are small and in which there is no bias in arithmetic mistakes as between civil servants and others, for these devices are not as likely to turn up correct estimates of the social values of alternative goods.

In a world in which exchange and police cost and the cost of providing alternative political devices are all zero, reliance on the political mechanism of a smoothly run democracy will result in less efficiency than will reliance on the market. Aside from problems of monopoly in government or of errors in calculation, in a one-man, one-vote democracy, where votes are not for sale, the polling place will generate information that is based on majoritarian principles rather than on maximum benefit principles. Thus, suppose some citizens prefer a stronger national defense but that a majority prefer a weaker defense. Left to a vote, the weaker defense will be our chosen policy even though the minority is willing to pay more than the additional cost required to bring defense up to the level they desire (and so, if possible, they may hire private police services). An error in the opposite direction is also possible. The majority of voters may approve of a large space effort even though they would not be able to bid high enough to acquire these resources for space in the absence of forced tax contributions. (Here, however, the minority cannot privately adjust.)

Although taxation is sometimes the most practical way of dealing with the provision of high police costs goods, there are other methods which are likely to arise in the market and which will lower the required police cost. As we have seen, extending the firm and the practice of sale-in-combination may overcome many instances of high exchange cost. These devices can also be used to reduce high police cost.

In the famous railway example, sparks from passing trains destroy some crops. The damage caused was believed to be adequate grounds for the government to take action through one or more of the political devices we have already mentioned. Direct contracting between the farmers and the railroad might take account of this side effect were it not that a bargain struck between a farmer and the railway would automatically confer benefits on all surrounding farmers by reducing spark fall-out on their land. Police costs are too high to allow benefits to be conferred on the contracting farmer without at the same time conferring them on non-contracting farmers. Therefore, it is believed that each farmer will wait for someone else to buy a reduction in spark output. (This conclusion requires two preliminary assumptions. The exchange cost of farmers getting together to submit a joint bid must be high relative to the benefits they will receive so that it is blocked by the expense it entails, and the exchange cost of their getting together to submit a joint bid must be higher than the cost of their organizing politically to lobby for antispark legislation.)

However, once the spatial aspects of the problem are admitted, we must again consider the phenomenon of differential land rent. Presumably, land rents on property adjacent to railways have been suitably depressed to allow farmers to compete with those not affected by sparks. The landowners, who find it in their interest to reduce the railroad's output of sparks, also find themselves not willing to enter into contracts through which other landowners will benefit. To some extent each would wait for the other to transact with the railway for a reduction in spark output. However, the analysis is not yet finished. The railway may realize a profit by purchasing the surrounding land at its depressed price. The purchase of a parcel of land does not confer benefits on neighbors to the same degree as would a purchase of spark curtailment so that this action would not hamper the concluding of similar contracts with other landowners as much as would the sale of a reduction in sparks. After the railroad purchases title to enough land to make it worthwhile, it could take into account the effect of its output of sparks on land values and profitably bring about an adjustment of this output to the socially optimal amount—that which maximizes the joint value of railroading and landowning. The land must, of course, be rented or resold with a contractual agreement requiring a continuance of reduced spark output. The low police cost associated with the purchase of land is substituted for the very high police cost that would be required to eliminate sparks on some land but not on other nearby land. The necessity for purchasing a reduction in spark output is obviated by substituting a purchase of land.

The extension of the firm together with the combination-sale devices that are associated with differential land rent are extremely important alternatives to government action. These devices can extend considerably the usefulness of markets for revealing and measuring the value of many side effects. The sale of land may entail much less exchange and policing cost than the direct exchange of whatever is producing the side effect. The smoke emitted from a nearby factory would, in principle, be subject to solution in the same manner. Now, of course, in many of these cases we do not observe such solutions taking place because exchange and police costs are not reduced sufficiently and because they may require too much underspecialization cost. Governmental devices, say, zoning laws, may help take account of such benefits, however inaccurately, at a lower cost (in which we should include those costs imposed by the rigidities of zoning laws). It may be, however, that both governmental and market solutions are too costly and that the most efficient alternative is not to attempt to take account of some side effects.[5]

There are other indirect devices for internalizing via combination sales. The activities of labeling, branding, and advertising allow

[5]The ability of combination sales to take account of side benefits depends on how closely the value of the tied-in goods reflects the value of the public good. There is a direct and exact correspondence between the value of land and the (negative to farmers) value of spark output. A less exact correspondence between the values of the tied goods, while not a perfect device, can nonetheless be useful in taking account of the value of public goods.

Even the stubborn classic case of providing for the national defense is amenable to some usable tie-in arrangements. The provision of defense again presents us with a situation in which it is in the interest of a beneficiary to let others buy defense since he will benefit from their purchases. Suppose, however, that instead of financing defense with taxes, the government resorts to the sale of insurance to citizens which covers their lives and property in the event of loss arising from war. The tied goods, insurance and defense, are substitutes, but they do not fully correspond in value fluctuations. For a stated premium per thousand dollars of insurance and a stated maximum, citizens would buy more insurance the more likely they thought war and the less able they thought our defense. Those having more at stake would buy more insurance. The premiums could then be used to finance the defense establishment. The side effect is not fully captured, however, because your purchase of insurance, although it fully internalizes your losses in the event of war, also decreases the likelihood of war, and, hence, reduces the amount of insurance others would volunteer to buy. This smaller remaining public aspect of the good could be accounted for by offering the insurance for premiums that are believed to be subsidized.

War, as well as other events, can topple governments, so that to make the insurance credible, the government might need to offer citizens the option of canceling their insurance and receiving all or some of the premiums they have paid. This cancellation option need be effective only up to the date before a war starts. The insurance device is not without dangers. By raising the maximum purchasable insurance (and lowering premiums), the government could induce a more aggressive attitude among the citizens than is warranted by actuarial fair insurance.

for internalization of side effects by tying in the sale of information with other goods. Suppose persons would like their tuna boiled longer before canning. Each canner would find it in his interest to prepare the tuna more carefully except that, in a world without labels, all competitors would enjoy at no cost some of the benefits of the resulting increase in demand. Some, therefore, wait for competitors to act. Underinvestment in tuna boiling (or overinvestment in boiling tuna at home) takes place and government regulations governing canning procedures are instituted.

Suppose we allow each canner to state on the label both his name and the minimum boiling time. The name is required to establish responsibility and thereby to reduce policing cost, which is another way of saying that the cost of exercising the rights acquired by purchasers by reason of the purchase contract is reduced for the buyer. The sale of knowledge jointly with that of tuna allows the value of longer boiling to be taken into account by producers and buyers. Structural market imperfections of the monopolistic competition variety can be ruled out if both longer boiled and less boiled tuna have numerous producers. The demand for each producer's tuna will then be the going market price of the particular quality he produces.[6]

Still other institutional arrangements have been devised to combine extensions of the firm with the sale-in-combination device. Department stores and shopping plazas are organizational devices for overcoming high police cost. The owner of the department store or shopping plaza can provide a general environment that is conducive for shopping, such as pleasant plantings, escalators, and other customer services that merchants who owned their own land might hesitate to pay for, hoping instead that neighboring landowners would incur the necessary expenses from which all would benefit. The enclosing of the land into a single ownership entity which often undertakes to provide services usually provided by government from tax revenues, such as streets, sidewalks, refuse collection, and even police protection, allows the owner to exclude those who refuse to pay rentals which cover the cost of these services. The competition of various plazas and department stores will provide ample opportunity for merchants to select the

[6]It is not really necessary for efficiency to obtain to require that producers take the product price as given and beyond their control. See Demsetz, *op. cit.*, *supra* note 3.

services that they wish to buy without fearing or counting on free-loading. Apartment buildings can also be viewed in the same light, and especially the modern apartment building which combines office and recreational space with living space. The development of these institutional arrangements provides an interesting challenge to political institutions for the provision of many of the services generally presumed to be within the scope of the polling place.

The preceding discussion has taken as given the state of technical arts. The levels of exchange and police costs that are required for effective marketing and the costs of government substitute services depend on how well we master the technology of operating markets and governments. Attention is sometimes called to the fact that emerging technical developments will make the use of markets or governments more economic than they now are. There are surely many instances where this is true. However, our analysis suggests that technological developments can operate in the opposite direction. At the same time that technology is reducing the cost of using these alternative institutional arrangements for economizing, it is also reducing the cost of constructing parking spaces, of developing fire resistant corn, and of mass producing automobiles. Whether or not it pays to increase the extent to which we exchange via markets, protect private property rights, or use alternative government devices depends on how much we will thereby reduce production cost and crop damage. Markets or their government alternatives should come into greater prominence only if technical developments lower the costs of these institutional arrangements more than they reduce the costs of producing parking spaces and cars and the cost of crop damage.

Essentially, we have argued in this paper that there exist no qualitative differences between side effects and what we may call "primary" effects. The only differences are those that are implicitly based on quantitative differences in exchange and police cost. Suppose a factory invents a new more efficient furnace which can burn a cheaper grade of coal than can existing furnaces. The burning of cheap coal, we will assume, dirties homes in the neighborhood. We label this effect as side or neighborhood or external, but its real economic implication is to reduce the wealth of nearby homeowners. If this same factory, by virtue of its new furnace, successfully forces a nearby competing firm out of business, and if the resulting decline in demand for housing reduces the wealth of neighborhood homeowners, we do not become concerned. Why the difference in our attitudes toward these two situations which have the same effect on homeowners?

The decline in wealth which results from the fall in demand for housing is more than offset by an increase in wealth elsewhere. This increase accrues primarily to other homeowners and to persons purchasing the lower priced product produced by the factory. We accept the reallocation, I conjecture, because we feel that the existence of a smoothly operating market will insure that wealth is maximized. In the smoke case, exchange and police costs are high relative to the benefits of marketing smoke and, therefore, we do not have an existing market to rely on for the reallocation, although a potential one always stands ready. If the costs of exchanging and policing smoke contracts were zero (and if the cost of exchanging houses were zero) there would be no reason for distinguishing between the two cases insofar as "remedial" action is concerned. We have already argued that the most efficient arrangement may, in fact, require that nothing be done to prohibit smoke and we will not go into these matters again. Our present purpose is merely to emphasize that there is nothing special or qualitatively different about any of these effects, including the effects which stem from what we ineptly call public goods, and that any special treatment accorded to them cannot be justified merely by observing their presence.

8. State-of-Nature Theory and the Rise of Social Institutions

Andrew Schotter

If economics is going to study the rise and evolution of social institutions, a very simple methodological approach is suggested. We should start our analyses in a Lockean state of nature in which there are no social institutions at all, only agents, their preferences, and the technology they have at their disposal to transform inputs into outputs. The next step would be to study when, during the evolution of this economy, such institutions as money, banks, property rights, competitive markets, insurance contracts, and the state would evolve. Looking at economics this way has distinct pedagogical advantages, because it allows us to connect a highly abstract economic theory with the world as we view it through the institutions we observe in everyday life.

The type of method suggested in this chapter is not new. In political science, theorists have tried to deal with the evolution of the state as a "social contract" among free individuals and, as a result, have depicted the institution of the state as emerging from a state of nature. Recently, Robert Nozick (1975) has used such a state-of-nature approach to study how the state can arise in a noncoercive way or at least in a manner that is consistent with individual liberties. He is, as a matter of fact, convinced that we can learn a great deal about such social institutions as the state by understanding how the institutions could have evolved that way. He states:

> A theory of state-of-nature that begins with fundamental general descriptions of morally permissible and impermissible actions, and of deeply based reasons why some persons in any society would violate these moral constraints, and goes on to describe how a state would arise from that state-of-nature will serve our

Reprinted, by permission, from *The Economic Theory of Social Institutions* (Cambridge: Cambridge University Press, 1981), pp. 20–39, 170–73.

> explanatory purposes, *even if no actual state ever arose that way.*
> . . . State-of-nature explanations of the political realm are funda-
> mental potential explanations of this realm and pack explanatory
> punch and illumination, even if incorrect. We learn much by
> seeing how the state could have arisen, even if it didn't arise that
> way. If it didn't arise that way, we also would learn much by
> determining why it didn't; by trying to explain why the particular
> bit of the real world that diverges from the state-of-nature model
> is as it is. [Nozick 1975, pp. 8–9]

In economics, a fascinating article by Radford (1945) described
the evolution of a wide variety of social institutions in a prisoner-
of-war camp during the Second World War. He demonstrated
convincingly that if all social and economic institutions were destroyed tomorrow and their memory erased from everybody's
mind, the people surviving would proceed to create a new set of
institutions which, although possibly different in form from the
earlier ones, would serve the same function. Social institutions are
human-made, and the only way to destroy them is to destroy
human beings themselves. Short of that, we cannot be prevented
from creating social mechanisms that make our lives more efficient.

If we are to study how institutions evolve from an institutional
state of nature, the institutional form emerging will be an endogenous variable in the model. It emerges without any agent or group
of agents consciously designing it—through human actions but
not human design. This emphasis on the endogenous unplanned
aspect of social institutions is counter to the usual social-scientific
view of institutions as planned or designed mechanisms given
exogenously to the theorist. The role of the social scientists in that
analysis is one of studying the properties of these preordained
institutions and not of studying their "organic" evolution. One of
the few social scientists to have attacked this conventional point of
view is F. A. Hayek, who states:

> It is a mistake to which careless expressions by social scientists
> often give countenance, to believe that their aim is to explain
> conscious action. This, if it can be done at all, is a different task,
> the task of psychology. For the social sciences the types of
> conscious actions are data. . . . The problems which they try to
> answer arise only in so far as regularities are observed which are
> not the result of anybody's design. If social phenomena showed
> no order except in so far as they were consciously designed,
> there would be, as is often argued, only problems of psychology.

> It is only in so far as some sort of order arises as a result of
> individual action but without being designed by any individual
> that a problem is raised which demands theoretical exploration.
> [Hayek 1955, p. 39]

Basically, what Hayek is saying is that if one feels that the task
of social science is to explain planned behavior or consciously
planned social institutions, then all that remains to be studied are
the preferences of the planner. But the study of the origin of
preferences is the study of psychology; hence, if that were true, all
social science would reduce to just that. That may be a fortunate
or an unfortunate state of affairs, but, as Hayek rightly points out,
a possibly more interesting field of endeavor might be to study the
unplanned or unconscious interaction of social agents in order to
investigate the spontaneous or unintended social institutions they
create. I believe that the types of problems that Hayek feels
demand a theoretical explanation can be answered through the
use of what we are calling a "state-of-nature method."

In this chapter I present a wide variety of admittedly extreme
models that employ this state-of-nature methodology to analyze
the evolution of various social institutions. Some of the institutions
studied and their analyses will be familiar, others will probably be
new; some will discuss the creation of empirically significant
institutions, other more frivolous ones. The point will always be
the same, however: to demonstrate the type of problem from which
social institutions emerge as a solution. Consequently, it is important to make clear that this chapter presents neither a formal
theory of social institutions nor a realistic model of the emergence
of any particular one. Rather, in this chapter we merely attempt to
offer some examples of phenomena for which the method just
described would be of value and to classify those situations for
which social institutions are created. The examples presented are
meant only to be illustrative and are in no way complete models of
the phenomena described.

Situations Likely to Lead to the Creation of Social Institutions

Social institutions, as we have stated, are created to help the
agents in an economy solve certain recurrent problems that they
face. From each problem there emerges a different social institution
whose function is to solve the problem with a minimum of social
resources. Consequently, it seems that a simple classification of

social institutions is implied by the types of problems they are created to solve, together with the actual way they are created: organically, as Menger thought, or explicitly, as Commons suggested. In a recent book entitled *The Emergence of Norms* (1978), Edna Ullman-Margalit offers three types of situations or problems from which social institutions (which she calls norms)[1] will emerge. Although these three categories are not exhaustive, Ullman-Margalit feels that they cover the most empirically relevant cases.

In a nutshell, the three categories of problems are:
1. Problems of coordination.
2. Problems of the prisoners' dilemma type.
3. Problems of inequality preservation.

In addition, I will treat a fourth category not covered by Ullman-Margalit, which I call problems of the cooperative-game type. Before we turn to our examples, let us look more closely at these four categories.

Problems of Coordination

A problem is a *coordination problem* if the payoff space of the game it defines is such that at any equilibrium point, not only does no player have any incentive to change his behavior, given the behavior of the other players, but no player wishes that any other player would change either. To understand how such problems are different from other noncooperative game problems—especially prisoners' dilemma problems—consider Matrix 1. Looking at Matrix 1a we notice that at the equilibrium (2, 2) no player has any incentive to deviate given the other players' strategy choice. The point (2, 2) is therefore a Nash equilibrium point. This is also true for the two equilibrium points circled in Matrix 1b, because if both players happened to choose strategy 1 [leading to payoff (6, 4)] or both chose strategy 2 [leading to payoff (3, 7)], neither would have

Matrix 1. (a) Prisoners' dilemma problem (b) Coordination problem

any incentive to change his strategy given the other's choice. The difference between these equilibria and the one in Matrix 1a, however, is that at the equilibrium in Matrix 1a, although neither player has any incentive to deviate, each would certainly like the other player to have chosen differently, because this would increase his payoff from 2 to 8; whereas in Matrix 1b, not only does each player not want to deviate from his chosen strategy, he does not want the other to deviate either. Their preferences are *locally* parallel, although globally divergent.

The strategic problem for each player in this type of game, then, is that he wants to "coordinate" his choice of strategy with his opponents, because for any given choice by his opponent, it is always beneficial to coordinate, yet he is not indifferent as to the exact strategy n-tuple they coordinate on.[2] If a coordination game were a recurrent feature of a given economy or society, rather than trying to solve the game each time it reappears, it would be reasonable to expect the agents in the economy to establish some equilibrium mode of behavior or convention and adhere to it each time the problem arises. Such a convention of behavior, if adhered to, is a social institution and would allow the agents to avoid the occurrence of inefficient nonequilibrium payoffs.

The problem, then, for each agent in a recurrent coordination game is to avoid recurrent nonequilibrium payoffs by always coordinating his activities with those of the others, yet to try to have the n-tuple of coordinated strategies be one that is best for him. In other words, in the game depicted by Matrix 1b, both players clearly prefer the diagonal equilibria to any off-diagonal nonequilibrium payoffs, yet player 1 would prefer the payoff pair (6, 4) and player 2 would prefer (3, 7). [The game is what Thomas Schelling (1960) calls a mixed-motive game.]

Prisoners' Dilemma Games

Prisoners' dilemma games are games in which for any noncooperative equilibrium, there exists at least one payoff vector associated with some *nonequilibrium* pure strategy n-tuple that is Pareto-superior to it. Consequently, if societies faced prisoners' dilemma games recurrently, it would be efficient for them to evolve some regularity of behavior that would avoid the repeated use of equilibrium, but inefficient, strategies. Again, such a regularity would be a social convention that would prescribe behavior for the agents in this recurrent situation and would be adhered to. The institutional rule would specify the use of some nonequilibrium n-tuple to be played recurrently as the game reappears. However, since the game is of the prisoners' dilemma type, at each iteration there is an incentive to deviate from the institutional rule. The consequences of such a deviation must be spelled out in the definition of the institution itself.

As we will see later, it is important that the situations under investigation be recurrent ones because social institutions can best be described as noncooperative equilibria of supergames that involve the repeated play of some particular constituent game, not as features of one-shot games. The institutions that evolve, then, are in equilibrium only with respect to the supergame and its payoff, not with respect to the constituent game making it up. This distinction will concern us later. At present, the relevant point to make is that prisoners' dilemma situations are clearly situations for which we might expect social institutions to emerge.

To illustrate the need for social institutions in the solution to prisoners' dilemma problems, Michael Taylor (1976) has discussed the possibility that stable social institutions (in the form of stable supergame equilibria) may be established to solve public-goods problems modeled as prisoners' dilemma games in order to avoid nonoptimal outcomes. Consider Matrix 2. In this game two agents are being asked to contribute to the construction of a public good. The amount of the good constructed will depend upon the marginal rates of substitution between this good and an all-purpose private good that the agents report to the economy's central planner. The public good is assumed to last only one period, after which it vanishes and the game will have to be played again. The strategies of the two agents in any period are either to lie or to tell the truth to the planner when he asks their marginal rates of substitution. Based on these reports, the planner will determine the amount of public good to provide.

| | II | |
	Give true information	Lie
I Given true information	8, 10	1, 12
Lie	12, 1	3, 3

Matrix 2. Public-goods game

This recurrent problem is clearly a prisoners' dilemma game, and, as is customarily thought, if no binding contracts can be enforced between the agents, a nonoptimal equilibrium will result in which the public good would be underprovided. However, if the game were recurrent and the players realized this, both of them might realize that the repeated use of a lying strategy would be self-destructive, and as the situation is iterated, we might expect a norm of truthful revelation of preferences to be developed upon which the convention of telling the truth would be built. Consequently, we could expect social institutions to evolve to solve recurrent prisoners' dilemma games.[3]

The two types of problems, coordination and prisoners' dilemma, are not necessarily mutually exclusive. Prisoners' dilemma games may have coordination elements associated with them (although the reverse is not true). Consider Matrix 3. Here we have a 6 × 6 game that is composed of three subgames, each of which is a 2 × 2 prisoners' dilemma game. Although each subgame is of the prisoners' dilemma variety, even if no binding contracts could be made that would stabilize the game at the *nonequilibrium* payoff (6, 6), the players still have an incentive to coordinate their actions and choose strategy 6, which determines that *equilibrium* payoff (5, 5) which is Pareto-superior to any other *equilibrium* payoff. The game then includes elements of both the prisoners' dilemma and the coordination variety.

Inequality-preserving Social Institutions

The third type of social institution that Ullman-Margalit considered is what she calls "norms of partiality" and what I call

II

	1	2	3	4	5	6
1	4, 4	1, 8	0, 0	0, 0	0, 0	0, 0
2	8, 1	2, 2	0, 0	0, 0	0, 0	0, 0
3	0, 0	0, 0	5, 5	3, 6	0, 0	0, 0
4	0, 0	0, 0	6, 3	4, 4	0, 0	0, 0
5	0, 0	0, 0	0, 0	0, 0	6, 6	4, 10
6	0, 0	0, 0	0, 0	0, 0	10, 4	5, 5

I (row label)

Matrix 3. A coordination-prisoners' dilemma game

inequality-preserving institutions. Actually, these institutions are really not a separate category because they are a subclass of coordination institutions, as we will soon see. For reasons of taxonomy, however, it does make sense to classify them separately. These are institutions created to preserve a status quo position of inequality among various economic agents. The type of institution envisioned here would be something like a property right or an inheritance law that establishes a convention in which property of certain types, or the right to use such property, is agreed to be safe from theft or violation by others. The important point about the type of situation leading to the creation of such inequality-preserving institutions is that one equilibrium payoff vector in the situation is given special importance by being designated as the status quo, and all of the analysis takes this as a starting point. This sanctification of the status quo is what makes the situation different from a coordination problem or a prisoners' dilemma problem.

To understand this type of problem more thoroughly, consider Matrix 4 (Ullman-Margalit's Matrix 4.16). Assume that this game is a recurrent game in which the same 2×2 matrix game is played over and over again by the same two players. As such, it appears to be a simple coordination game in which there are two noncooperative equilibria (R_1, C_1) and (R_2, C_2), each favoring a different player. From what we said about coordination games and institutions, we can expect that, if this game were iterated, the players would create some convention of behavior for themselves that would specify which one of these equilibria they would adhere to in every iteration of the game.

In situations leading to the formation of inequality-preserving institutions, the problem is identical to the one described above except that one equilibrium outcome, the one circled, is specified "historically" as the status quo. Consequently, the question under investigation is *not* which equilibrium will emerge as the societally agreed upon social convention, but rather whether the historically

II

	C_1	C_2
R_1	(2, 1)	0, 0
R_2	0, 0	1, 2

I

Matrix 4. Inequality preservation games: coordination game with a status quo predetermined convention prescribing an unequal distribution of utility will be adhered to or whether the unfavored party will try to deviate from it. To understand why an incentive for deviation exists, consider Matrix 4 and the game at the iteration in which the equilibrium (R_1, C_1) has been played for $t - 1$ periods and is by now an institutional fact of life or established convention of behavior (in the sense of Lewis). At the time it may be rational for the column player to try to change the equilibrium (or status quo) from (R_1, C_1) to (R_2, C_2), because as far as he can see, the game is symmetric and there is no reason why the historically fossilized convention (which is unfavorable to him) is any more justifiable than (R_2, C_2), in which case he would be doing better. Consequently, we can expect (as Ullman-Margalit argues) the column player to try to break this noncooperative equilibrium and move it from (R_1, C_1) to (R_2, C_2). He will do this by (as Schelling describes it) trying to commit himself totally to choosing C_2, in which case the row chooser is forced into choosing between the payoff associated with (R_1, C_2) and the payoff associated with (R_2, C_2). Here the row chooser would prefer (R_2, C_2), which is better for the column chooser than (R_1, C_1), the status quo. The column chooser's hope is that if he can inflict a low payoff on the row chooser often enough in the iteration of the game, he can convince him that he is totally committed to C_2 and can thereby break the previously established convention. If the convention is well defined, however, such an attempt would be impossible because, by definition, the institutional rule supporting (R_1, C_1) not only specifies (R_1, C_1) as the accepted mode of behavior, but also specifies punishing behavior for the column chooser if he tries to deviate. This punishing behavior involves having the row chooser continue to choose R_1 no matter what. Consequently, social institutions emerge and perpetuate historically determined but possibly unequal distributions of utility, and to that extent they are inherently conservative.

Although we have classified these situations as distinct and separate circumstances leading to the creation of social conventions, we will not treat them separately, because the distinction between inequality-preserving institutions and institutions created to solve coordination problems is artificial. This is true because by separately classifying each of these situations, we are merely drawing a distinction between the analysis of a coordination problem before and after a social institution has been created. In other words, if we started with a coordination problem and a convention evolved establishing (R_1, C_1) as the socially agreed upon and stable social institution, then, once established, the situation immediately becomes one requiring an inequality-preserving institution. However, such an inequality-preserving institution has already been established, because it is included in the institution created to solve the coordination problem. Consequently, if stable institutions are created that, as is often the case, determine unequal distributions of income, the policing strategies defined by the institution are, in and of themselves, inequality-preserving institutions. There is no need to create a separate category here, and consequently we will not formally treat such situations here.

Explicitly and Organically Determined Social Institutions in
Cooperative Game Contexts

One common characteristic of the type of situation leading to the creation of social institutions in the cases described above is that all of the games specified are played noncooperatively or without communication among the agents. They emerge organically by human action but not by human design and are the result of individual but not collective human behavior. Now, of course, many social institutions are created in one stroke by a social planner or by the agents of society meeting in a face-to-face manner and bargaining about the type of institution they would like to see created. Here the exact form of the institution that emerges is the result of explicit human design (in the case of a planner) or multilateral bargaining (in the case of a legislature). Probably the best example of such institutions is presented by James Buchanan and Gordon Tullock (1962) in their classic book, *The Calculus of Consent*, where they discuss how various characteristics of state constitutions are determined. Here such social conventions or institutional rules as the majority needed to pass bills are explicitly set and bargained for, and the constitution creation game is played cooperatively, with communication.

We will not discuss these types of institutions, for two reasons. First, if the social institutions we are investigating are created by a social planner, their design can be explained by maximizing the value of some objective function existing in the planner's mind. Such an exercise, as Hayek (1955) has pointed out, is of less theoretical interest and need not warrant our consideration here, unless the problem of preference revelation exists, which we will discuss later. On the other hand, if the form of the social institution created is the outcome of a multilateral bargaining process, a bargaining theory would be required. Such an analysis, however, is probably best left to others. What remains is the study of social institutions created to help solve those societal problems that exist and are created organically or spontaneously. It is to these that we devote our attention.

This does not mean that the study of explicitly or consciously defined social institutions is not an interesting topic. Quite the contrary is true, as Leonid Hurwicz (1973a) has demonstrated. In fact, the design of desirable social institutions can be considered one of the major contributions of game theory to economics, as has been argued by Schotter and Schwödiauer (1980). The point made by Hurwicz and others is that each social institution can be considered as a set of rules that specify or constrict the behavior of agents in various social and economic situations. If these situations can be specified as games of strategy whose equilibria can be calculated, then, if the planner can indicate the type of outcomes he desires to see emerge from the game, the proper institutional structure (rules of the game) can be determined that yields these outcomes as equilibria. Such a study becomes the study of the creation of optimal rules of games.

This view of social institutions, as embodied in the rules of the game, is different from the view presented here because here we view social institutions not as various sets of rules but as various and alternative standards of behavior (strategy n-tuples) that are elements of the equilibrium of the game. In other words, our social institutions are not part of the rules of the game but part of the solutions to iterated games of strategy. It is for this reason that we do not consider what we have called explicitly created social institutions.

There are, however, social institutions that emerge organically from a social situation equivalent to cooperative n-person games which are not the product of human design but appear as properties of the equilibrium solution to the game under investigation. Here the institutions are created through the interaction of individual and group maximizing behavior, none of which has as its purpose the creation of a social institution. One of the best examples of such an institution is given by Robert Nozick (1975) in his explanation of how the state can emerge from a Lockean state of nature without an agent actually planning it and without the players being coerced to accept it. As we will see, the state in

Nozick's analysis is a property of the core of what we will call the *state-of-nature theft game*. The important point to keep in mind, however, is that although the agents who create the state are able to speak with each other and bargain in a face-to-face manner, the type of institutional arrangements that emerge from these negotiations may be totally unintended and qualify completely as what Menger called organically created social institutions.

Since we are interested in all organically created social institutions, we will pay some attention to these types of cooperative game institutions as well. However, the attention will be limited to the one example we offer below.

As a result of our discussion, we can construct a 4 × 2 classification of social institutions (see Table 1) according to the way they are created (organically or explicitly) and the type of problem they

Table 1
CLASSIFICATION OF SOCIAL INSTITUTIONS

| | Method of Creation | |
Type of problem	Organically	Deliberately
Coordination problem	Studied here	Bargaining problem—not studied here
Prisoners' dilemma problem	Studied here	The creation of binding and explicit contracts—not studied here
Inequality-preserving problem	Not studied here (part of the coordination institution)	Unequal distribution of income enforced by the state or some coercive force—not studied here
Cooperative game problem	Studied here, but limited to one example	Problems of planning—not studied here

solve (coordination, prisoners' dilemma, inequality-preserving, or cooperative).

From this description it is clear why we will limit ourselves to the analysis of institutions that are created to solve either noncooperative coordination problems or problems of the prisoners' dilemma type and take the form of noncooperative equilibria to infinitely repeated supergames or cooperative game problems in which the social institution created is a feature of the solution concept used. Although this admittedly leaves out a wide variety of social institutions, it does include many that are of extreme empirical significance and, in addition, treats those cases that are of the most interest theoretically.

To give a better picture of the type of analysis envisioned, let us turn to a series of examples presented to illustrate the type of real-world situation that requires the creation of a social institution, together with a demonstration of what we have called a state-of-nature method. It must again be pointed out that these examples are not meant to be realistic models of social phenomena as much as motivating examples illustrating an institution-generating problem. As Nozick states, we can learn a great deal about social institutions by studying how they could have evolved from a state of nature even if, in fact, they did not evolve that way. Consequently, although we do not claim that the social institutions used to illustrate our approach actually did evolve to solve the exact problem described, we can learn a great deal about social institutions by studying the type of situation that cries out for the creation of one. This is what I hope to do in the remainder of this chapter. I apologize if at times the presentation of the examples seems too formal for the purposes of illustration. I have tried, whenever possible, to make the examples as intuitive as possible while remaining precise. It has not always been an easy task.

Some Examples

Now that we know the type of situation for which social institutions are created, let us investigate a series of real-world problems that have been settled by the development of some social institutions. We will classify the examples into the four categories discussed above.

Coordination Problems and Coordination Institutions

The Evolution of the Week. It is interesting to contemplate why time is divided into weeks.[4] Clearly, this is an arbitrary division, because there is no natural event, such as the rotation of the moon, which corresponds to the week. Yet in almost all parts of the world, time is divided into weeks, usually consisting of 5 or 6 working days and 2 or 1 day of leisure, respectively.[5] The division of time into weeks is clearly a man-made social convention or institution; it is an artifact of human existence.

What facts explain the existence of the week? What function does it serve? To answer these questions, we shall assume that we are observing an agrarian society in which time is totally undifferentiated except for its division into days—a society that has not yet evolved the concept of the week as a social institution.

To offer a possible explanation of how the week evolved, let us assume that the society described above is composed of a set of n farmers and that the farms they inhabit are arranged in a circle around a central city (Figure 1).

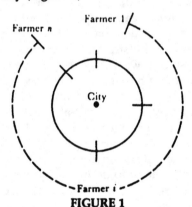

FIGURE 1
Coordination of distribution in an agrarian society.

To help our analysis, let us make some fanciful assumptions that will serve to highlight the coordination problem of interest to us in this chapter. First, assume that each farmer grows only one crop on his soil, so that farmer i grows only crop x_i, and that all farmers have a utility function of the following type:

$$U_i = Ax_1^{a_1}x_2^{a_2} \cdots x_{i-1}^{a_{i-1}}x_{i+1}^{a_{i+1}} \cdots x_n^{a_n}$$

Notice that each farmer gains no utility from the consumption of his own crop but most consume every other crop in positive amounts to obtain any utility at all. Next, assume that there is no disutility or utility to be derived from work and that the amount of crop available to be harvested by farmer i at time t is

$$x_i^t = \psi^i(\bar{t}_i)$$

where $\bar{t}_i$ is the amount of time that has elapsed since the last harvest of i's crop and ψ^i is a concave, twice-differentiable function of $\bar{t}_1$. Finally, assume that all trade must take place in the city; that there are transportation costs c_i involved for farmer i each time he brings a crop to the city; and that, after harvesting, crops cannot be stored but must be consumed during that market day or they will spoil. Each farmer must bring his produce to the city to be sold (because he gains no utility from the consumption of the crop that he alone produces), but each trip to the market is costly.

When a farmer brings his goods to the city, he takes them to a marketing institution that we assume evolved at an earlier time, whose function it is to allocate the goods brought to it each day. Consequently, at the end of any given day, each farmer must decide if he wants to travel to the city with his crop. We assume that if he goes, he takes all of his harvestable crop with him; therefore, the game we will describe will not include quantity as a strategic variable. The only strategic variable for each farmer is when to go to the city. When all the farmers who have decided to go on a given day arrive, they hand over all their produce to the central marketing agent, whose existence is assumed and not explained, and who is fully informed about the utility functions of all farmers. This central marketing agent then defines a set of equilibrium prices based on the supplies that have been brought to the market and upon the known utility functions of the farmers, from which he derives his demand functions. At these prices he calculates the utility-maximizing bundle for each farmer and allocates the bundles accordingly. All farmers then consume the bundles allocated to them.

Some things are now obvious. First, unless all farmers arrive in the city on the same day, all prices must be zero. This is true because unless a farmer can consume positive amounts of each good, he will be unwilling to demand any good at a positive price. However, because a farmer's income can be positive only if the good he produces receives a positive price, his income will be zero on any day in which not all farmers come to the city. On those days the farmer's utility from consumption must be zero and his final payoff from traveling to the city on that day will be $-c_i$, because it cost him c_i to travel to the city and yet he gained no utility when he got there.

More generally, it is possible to express the payoff to player i when he arrives at the market simultaneously with all other farmers as being strictly a function of $\bar{t} = (\bar{t}_1, \ldots, \bar{t}_n)$ or $P_i = \xi^i(\bar{t})$, because any vector $\bar{t}$ determines the supply of goods available on a given day, which, when juxtaposed to the demand curves derived, determines the equilibrium prices and allocations. The problem that results is a simple coordination problem in which all agents must tacitly agree to arrive in the city on the same day if any agent is to receive a positive payoff. Consequently, a recurrence pattern must be specified that indicates the number of days between market days. Such regularity in behavior or recurrence pattern, if unanimously adhered to, is exactly what Lewis has called a social convention and what we are calling a social institution. The length of time between market occurrences is the week, and the institution of the week is a coordination equilibrium, because no agent would choose to deviate from it or have anyone else deviate.[6]

In describing the normal form of the game, we can think of the game being played as follows. Starting on day 1, each farmer will choose some number in the interval $[0, \infty]$, which we will call his recurrence time in the city. This time will specify the number of days that he will allow to elapse between visits to the city. Consequently, the strategy space for our game will be the product set $T = \Pi_{i=1}^{n} [0, \infty]$, and an n-tuple $t = (t_1, \ldots, t_n)$ will represent a vector of choices, one for each farmer. The payoffs to any farmer when a given vector $t = (t_1, \ldots, t_n)$ is chosen, that is, when he chooses the recurrence pattern t_i and all other players choose the recurrent pattern $\bar{t}_i = (t_1, \ldots, t_{i-1}, t_{i+1}, \ldots, t_n)$, is

$$\Pi_i = \sum_{t \in T_i^*} \alpha_i^{t-1}[\xi_i(\bar{t}) - c_i] - \sum_{t \in \bar{T}_i} \alpha_i^{t-1}[c_i]$$

where α_i is the discount rate for farmer i; T_i^* is the set of time periods in which, given the vector of recurrence times $t = (t_1, \ldots, t_i, \ldots, t_n)$, farmer i arrives in the city and all other farmers are there; and $\bar{T}_i$ is the set of time periods during which farmer i travels to the city and not all farmers are there.

What this payoff function tells us is that on those days in which farmer i goes to the city and all other farmers are there (those $t \in T_i^*$), he will receive a payoff of $\xi_i(\bar{t}) - c_i$, whose discounted value is $\alpha_i^{t-1}[\xi_i(\bar{t}) - c_i]$; whereas in those periods in which farmer i travels to the city and not all other farmers are there (those $t \in \bar{T}_i$), his payoff is $-c_i$, whose present discounted value is $\alpha_i^{t-1}[-c_i]$.

As a result, we can define the payoffs to the farmers in the recurrence game in normal form, strictly in terms of the n-tuple of recurrence times chosen by the farmers, as $\Pi_i = \Pi_i(t)$. In addition, we can specify utility functions, production functions, and discount rates such that for all i, any vector for which $t_1 = t_2 = \ldots t_n = t^*$ determines a greater payoff for him than does a vector for which he or anyone else deviates and sets $t_i \neq t^*$.

The problem, then, is a pure recurrent coordination problem that is best looked upon as a supergame in which each player must decide upon an infinite sequence of 0s and 1s, in which each 1 would indicate a choice to go to the city on a given day and each 0 would indicate a choice to stay at home. The week would be institutionalized when all the sequences of the players are identical. In addition, assumptions can be made in the simple model presented, such that it is in every farmer's interest to establish the week and every t^* days to stop work and go to the city. The possibility that the week might have actually evolved for the purpose of solving a marketing coordination problem is perhaps suggested by the fact that in Brazil the days of the week are called "first market day," "second market day," and so on.

Although every agent in the economy has some interest in establishing the week, the preferences of the players over the actual length of the week are certainly not identical. Depending on the parameters that characterize the farmer, the optimal length of the week may differ very greatly. More precisely, if each farmer could control the length of the week, he would determine a length that would maximize the following expression:

$$\max_{t_1, \ldots, t_n} \Pi_i(t_1, \ldots, t_n; c_i, \alpha_i)$$

In other words, each farmer, if he were allowed to choose the length of the week, might actually choose a different optimal length. The preferences of the players are then identical in establishing the existence of the week, but their preferences are conflicting in determining its length.

The relevant questions at this point in our analysis are: How long will the week that is established actually be, and how many periods can be expected to pass until it is established? A successful theory of social institutions would have to answer these questions in a rigorous manner. [However,] it is clear that any analysis that gives a determinate answer to such a question cannot be valid. The exact form of any social institution can be specified only probabilistically. The development of the week will be greatly influenced by the coincidence with which people start to converge on the city and see each other. What develops is a snowballing effect in which people come to the city in a particular pattern, see that other people are also following this pattern, and continue to return or not, according to whether their pattern is popular. Eventually, a universal pattern is established and institutionalized, but the exact pattern that is institutionalized is actually randomly determined.

As we will see in our formal model, the history or path of the game will have a dramatic influence upon the type of institution that is created, and to the extent that different coincidental paths occur, different institutions are possible. The problem is clearly a dynamic one, however, and can only be modeled in extensive form or as a supergame with dynamic properties.

Finally, it is clear that the size of the week that finally evolves from a given society may not be Pareto-optimal.[7] For instance, consider the two-person society shown by Matrix 5, in which the players have to play the recurrence game explained above but the number of days from which they can choose is limited to three. Here we see that although each farmer would rather have a week established no matter what its length, farmer 1 would prefer its length to be 3 days, then 2 days, and then 1 day, whereas farmer 2 would prefer it to be 2 days, then 3 days, then 1 day. Notice, however, that there exists a length of week—the 1-day week—that is Pareto-inferior to the 2- and 3-day weeks but may still evolve as an equilibrium pattern. Consequently, the efficiency of the institutions that evolve from a given situation may be rather low.

The Evolution of Money. Money, like the invention of the week, is a man-made artifact. There is nothing in nature that says that corn or gold or silver shall function universally as money or that money should exist at all. To the extent that these commodities do function

| | | Farmer 2 | | |
		Every day	Every 2 days	Every 3 days
	Every day	6, 5	3, 4	2, 3
Farmer 1	Every 2 days	5, 5	8, 10	0, 0
	Every 3 days	3, 2	0, 0	9, 6

Matrix 5. The week game

as a means of exchange, they do so because of a tacit (or explicit, in the case of fiat money) agreement among the agents in the economy to accept these goods as payments for other goods and services. Menger states

> that every economic unit in a nation would be ready to exchange his goods for little metal disks apparently useless as such, or for documents representing the latter is a procedure so opposed to the ordinary course of things. . . . The problem, which science has here to solve consists in giving an explanation of a general homogeneous course of action pursued by human beings when engaged in traffic which taken concretely makes unquestionably for the common interest and which seems to conflict with the nearest and immediate interest of contracting individuals. [Menger 1892, pp. 239–40]

In a recent article in the *Journal of Political Economy*, Robert Jones (1976) presents a probabilistic model of the evolution of a medium of exchange in which he derives stable solutions for an economy in which full monetization, full barter, and intermediate amounts of monetization or trade evolve. As such, it is a prime example of a model that employs the type of methodology being called for here. However, since Jones's model is non-game-theoretical, we attempt our own simple game-theoretical model here, which, I hope, will highlight the salient aspects of the problem, whose solution lies in the creation of money.

To begin, consider the agrarian economy studied above, which, at present, has two institutions—a week of duration t^* and a marketing institution. Assume that a technological breakthrough has occurred and it is now possible for the marketing agent to pick up each farmer's goods on market day and deliver them to a central warehouse at zero cost. Consequently, any farmer i no longer need incur a cost of c_i when he wants to deliver his goods to the market, but need only incur a cost of g_i to transport himself there, with $g_i < c_i$ for all farmers in the economy. Further assume that every week, the marketing agent arrives, picks up the supplies of goods, deposits them in his warehouse, and, given the known and fixed utility functions of the agents, calculates what would be the competitive equilibrium price vector for the economy if competitive markets existed.

Because the week is always the same length, all crops grow in a stationary manner according to $x_i^i = \psi^i(t_i^*)$, all utility functions are unchanging, and there is no capital investment, the economy is in a stationary state in which the set of equilibrium prices determined each week is identical, as are the resulting incomes of the farmers and their weekly bundles. Hence each week each farmer would receive the same utility from transacting in the market. There is one problem, however, which we will assume is that the marketing agent is not actually capable of executing trades and consequently must rely on an external mechanism to do this. To discover how the evolution of money might solve this problem, let us assume that in addition to the crops existing in the economy, there are also m different plastic chips, each of a different color, in which all trade must take place but which yield no utility. Consequently, once the equilibrium prices are announced each week, each trader takes a number of chips equal to his equilibrium income with him to the city and attempts to buy his equilibrium bundle at those prices. (Each chip of any color is given an exogenously determined price of 1 so that they can all function as the *numéraire* in the economy.) Consequently, at the recurrent set of equilibrium prices, each farmer i will take with him to the city a number K_i of possible m different colored chips (indexed $m = 1, 2, \ldots, M$) equal to $K_i = p_i^* \psi(t_i^*)$, where p_i^* is the equilibrium price for the good he produces and $\psi(t_i^*)$ is the amount that he recurrently brings to the market. Each period, the distribution of income is given by $K = (K_1, \ldots, K_n)$ and each farmer chooses a distribution of chips to take to the market, $d^i = (d_1^i, \ldots, d_j^i, \ldots, d_m^i)$, $d_j^i \geq 0$ and $\Sigma_j d_j^i = K_i$.

At any given week, then, there exists a set of n farmers each with income K_i and each with a portfolio of chips represented by d^i. When in the city, the farmers conduct trade as follows. There are n trading booths at which the n goods are traded. The prices of the goods are known by all farmers and they calculate their optimal bundles on these prices, so that the only strategic problem involved is one of actually executing the set of equilibrium trades. To do this, each farmer must make two decisions. One concerns how he wants to be paid for the goods he sells (i.e., in what chip or what combination of chips he will accept payment) and the other concerns how he will decide to pay for the goods he wants to buy. In other words, each farmer must decide upon a pair of distributions $s_i = (f^i, r^i)$ in which $f^i = (f_{11}, \ldots, f_{Mn-1})$ is an $n - 1 \times M$ dimensional vector in which f_{mj} indicates the amount of chips m brought to the city by farmer i that he wants to allocate in purchasing good j. Feasibility requires that $d_m^i \geq \Sigma_j f_{mj}$ for all m. In other words, a farmer cannot decide to pay for goods in a way that requires him to use more of any color plastic chip than he has brought to the city, and $\Sigma_m \Sigma_j f_{mj} \leq K_i$. In addition, the farmer must decide upon an M-dimensional vector $r^i = (r^i_1, \ldots, r^i_M)$ that defines the way he wants to be paid for the goods he supplies. By feasibility, $\Sigma^M_{m=1} r^i_m \leq K_i$—a farmer cannot ask to be paid in such a way that the sum of payments to him are greater than his income.

Clearly, we have defined a recurrent game that the set of farmers play with each other each week when they arrive in the city and try to execute trades. The game can be described as follows. Time starts at the market day defined in week 1. At that time all supplies of crops are collected and brought to the city and all prices and incomes are determined. At these prices all farmers calculate the equilibrium bundles and then attempt to purchase them. To do this each farmer makes a choice of a pair of vectors $s_i = (f^i, r^i)$ such that $\Sigma_m \Sigma_j f_{mj} \leq K_i$ and $\Sigma_m r^i_m \leq K_i$. Letting S_i be the set of all such feasible strategy choices for player i (a closed compact convex set), the strategy space for the game is $S = \Pi^n_{i=1} S_i$. To determine the payoffs of the game, let us look at player j. Assume that he supplies good j. Then he will agree to sell all of his good only if he is paid in the way he specifies [i.e., according to $r^i = (r^i_1, \ldots, r^i_M)$]. This will be true if $r^i_m = \Sigma_{i \neq j} f_{mj}$ for all m. Consequently if $r^i_m = \Sigma_{i \neq j} f_{mj}$ holds for all j and m, it will be true that the manner in which all farmers have specified that they want to be paid exactly balances the paying plans of each of the others. In this case all goods brought to the market will actually be sold, and a Pareto-optimal equilibrium payoff will be determined. If, however, for farmer j, $r^i_m > \Sigma_{i \neq j} f_{mj}$, for any chip m, in which case the farmers fall short by $e^i_m = r^i_m - \Sigma_{i \neq j} f_{mj}$ of paying farmer j the r^i_m chips m he specified, farmer j will refuse to sell $b^j = E^j/p^*_j$ units in the market, where $E^j = \Sigma^m_{m=1} e^i_m$. In other words, if E^j is the sum of farmer j's shortfalls on the m types of chips, then at price p^*_j for his goods he will hold E^j/p^*_j units from sale. As a result, because there is a shortage of the right kind of chips being offered for good j at trading booth j, a limited supply of the good will be allocated by giving each of the $n-1$ farmers demanding the product a fraction of the available supply $J = \psi_j(t^*_j) - b^j$ equal to

$$Z_i = \frac{\displaystyle\sum_{m=1}^{M} f_{mj}}{\displaystyle\sum_m \sum_i f_{mj}} \; (J)$$

This means that if the manner in which the farmers want to pay for good j does not coincide with the manner in which farmer j

wants to be paid (i.e., not in the chip or chips he will accept for payment), the resulting shortfall in supply is allocated in such a way that farmer i receives a fraction of the available supply equal to his fraction of the demand for that good at the equilibrium.[8]

From this description we can clearly see that we have defined a recurrent coordination game in normal form in which the strategy space for each player is a pair of vectors $s_i = (f_i, r^i)$ such that $\Sigma_j \Sigma_m f_{mj} \leq K_i$ and $\Sigma_m r^i_m \leq K_i$ and the payoff function is a mapping $\gamma: \Pi^n_{i=1}: S_i \rightarrow R^N$ describing the vector of utility payoffs determined for each n-tuple of pairs $s = (s_1, \ldots, s_n)$. It is the solution to this problem for which the convention of money emerges, because if each farmer agreed to receive his income in one and only one type of chip and to pay all other farmers in exactly the same type of chip, and all other farmers chose to do the same, then the equilibrium conditions specified above would be trivially satisfied in each period, and in each period the farmers would receive the payoffs associated with the competitive equilibrium of the economy. If this occurred, the economy would be fully monetized and there would emerge a chip that would function as *the* medium of exchange. However, it may be that the farmers recurrently decide to bring a mix of colored chips to the market and ask to be paid with a mix of chips and yet our equilibrium conditions are still satisfied. (There may exist mixed-strategy equilibria.) In this case, although the economy would execute all equilibrium trades in each period, we could not say that *a* money exists for the economy, and trade would not be considered fully monetized. The question of which chip will evolve as *the* chip of exchange in this economy and what the probability is that one actually will emerge is typical of the types of questions that we hope to answer in this book.

In conclusion, although our model is admittedly abstract and highly stylized, I feel that it presents the type of problem that has historically led to the evolution of money. Most succinctly, the problem is one of executing trade in the least costly manner, and this can be done only if the agents in the economy will accept one particular good in exchange when they trade. The problem is, of course, that they have to agree implicitly on the same good (or chip), and it is in tracing how this one good gets established as money that our problem takes on its intellectual interest.

Prisoners' Dilemma Problems and Social Institutions

Many social situations can be represented as prisoners' dilemma games. The metaphor has become so commonplace, in fact, that it is a standard phrase in the vocabulary of social scientists. But prisoners' dilemma games as described in textbooks rarely exist in the real world. This is so because the classic prisoners' dilemma situation is a static one-shot situation in which the players face each other one and only one time and must choose strategies for that one play only. Most real-world situations of any interest, however, are *repeated situations* in which a set of players *repeatedly* face each other in the same situation. This is clearly true in international relations, where countries repeatedly test each other in situations of conflict in various parts of the world. It is also true in military conflicts, because each side in a conventional war knows that this will not be the only such war they will fight in the course of their history and therefore will realize that their behavior now will affect the type of behavior they can expect in future wars. Consequently, their behavior is likely to be different from what it would be in a one-shot war game.

The distinctive characteristic of all these situations is that in all of them there is a learning process going on in which the players learn the type of behavior they can expect from each other and build up a set of commonly held norms of behavior. It is upon these commonly established norms that a social convention of behavior or institution is established that prescribes behavior for each participant in the conflict. Consequently, countries that fight conventional wars in the world today do not use certain types of strategies (germ warfare, infanticide, nuclear weapons, the bombing of civilian population centers, etc.), because they know that if they introduce such tactics, and future wars occur, the present value of the payoffs associated with the fighting of the future wars would be so low that they would be better off to fight the present war without them than to introduce such tactics. Similarly, oligopolists must concern themselves with the effects their present actions will have on the set of industry norms and realize that although a low-price strategy now may be beneficial in the short run, in the long run it could lead to a protracted price war that would be mutually damaging to all members of the industry. Consequently, in these recurrent prisoners' dilemma games, we can expect some type of social convention to be established by the players in the game that will allow them to avoid the payoffs predicted by the one-shot analysis.

Footnotes

[1]What we mean when we talk about a norm is not the same as what we mean when we talk about a social institution, because a norm is merely a shared belief

among agents that allows the agents to assess the probability of each other's behavior, whereas a social institution is something that is built upon a set of norms and is a rule prescribing behavior in various recurrent situations. In other words, the norm "honor among thieves" does not tell you how to behave in a prisoners' dilemma game if you are forced to play one recurrently; it merely gives you some information about how you might expect others to behave, and you will act upon this information.

[2]A. Sen (1967) describes the following type of coordination game, which he calls an "assurance game."

Player II

		1	2	3
	1	6, 6	0, 0	2, 2
Player I	2	1, 1	4, 4	3, 3
	3	2, 2	3, 3	5, 5

What Sen discusses is the fact that in this game, as opposed to prisoners' dilemma games, each player, in order to choose strategy 1, needs only the assurance that the other will choose strategy 1; he need not have a binding contract to that effect. This assurance will be built up among the players as they iterate the game and begin to trust each other. They will build up a norm of cooperation, and it is upon this norm that the institution of always choosing strategy 1 in this game will evolve.

[3]Another approach to the problem of preference revelation would be for the planner to change the rules of the game or its payoff function in such a way that telling the truth was either a dominant strategy for each player or at least determined a Nash equilibrium for the game. Such schemes have been devised by Theodore Groves (1973) and Groves and Ledyard (1977) and others, and have been experimentally tested by Vernon Smith (1978a). The problem with these mechanisms and the experimental evidence supporting them is that they are static theories with static experimental support. As a result, it has not been established that such schemes are actually required in order to elicit the truthful responses from agents in such situations if the players know that they will play the same game repeatedly. In such cases, the players might establish the convention of telling the truth by themselves and thereby obviate the need for an explicit or imposed preference revelation scheme.

[4]This example was offered to me by Carlos Varsavsky both in conversation and in the first chapter of his most interesting manuscript, *Why Seven Days in a Week?* (1978, unpublished manuscript). A similar analysis can be found in a book entitled *The Week: An Essay on the Origin and Development of the Seven Day Week*, by Francis Colson (1926).

[5]The 7-day week is by no means universal, however. Many different societies have had weeks of other than seven days. For instance, in Peru the Incas established a 10-day week, and in ancient Mexico the week had 5 days. The most common length has been 7 days, however. [These facts are from Varsavsky (1978).]

'To understand this situation more formally, consider the following description of the extensive form of the game being played by the farmers. Time starts on day 1. At the end of the day each farmer must decide, in isolation, whether to go to the city, G, or stay at home, S. On day 1 his payoffs if he goes to the city are

$$P_i = \begin{cases} \mathcal{E}(1) - c_i & \text{if } |s| = N \\ -c_i & \text{if } |s| < N \end{cases}$$

where $|s|$ is the number of farmers in the city at the end of day 1. Whether or not he has gone to the city on day 1, on day 2 he faces the same problem and must decide again, at which time his payoff is

$$P_i = \begin{cases} \mathcal{E}(\bar{t}) - c_i & \text{if } |s| = N \\ -c_i & \text{if } |s| < N \end{cases}$$

where $\bar{t}$ in this case is a vector of either 1s or 2s. Consequently, on every day, each farmer must decide whether or not he will go to the city on that day. The game shown in Figure N.1 in extensive form is determined.

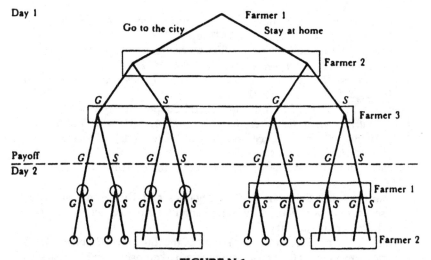

FIGURE N.1.

Farmer coordination problem: the week game-three farmer extensive form representation. Notice that the information sets indicate that if a farmer decides to go to the city on a given day, he is able to observe who else decided to go on that day. Consequently, when he makes his next move he has this information at his disposal.

The game described by this tree is very simple. On day 1 all farmers must decide in isolation whether they will go to the city. Because this is the first time period, all decisions are made in ignorance of past choices. But on day 2 we can assume that their decision is eased by the knowledge of who was present on day 1. This additional information is indicated by the circle at the information sets of the players on day 2. If a farmer does not go to the city on day 1, he must make his decision whether to go on day 2 in total ignorance of what occurred on day 1. Such is the case for all days $t \geq 1$, in that all farmers are assumed to be able to see when they go to the market who else decided to go on that day, but when they are there they are not allowed to communicate with each other about when they want to return. The game is strictly noncooperative.

[7]Varsavsky (1978), in *Why Seven Days in a Week?*, argues that the 7-day week, which is virtually universal today, is not an efficient size for the week and that a 9-day "continuous work-week" is preferable because it fits the technological facts of today's life better than does the conventional week.

[8]The total demand for chips by a farmer must not exceed his income, so that we need not specify what happens if $r'_m < \Sigma_{i=1}^n f_{mj}$.

Bibliography

Arrow, Kenneth. "Political and Economic Evaluation of Social Effects and Externalities." In *The Analysis of Public Output*, (Julius Margolis, ed.). New York: National Bureau of Economic Research–Columbia University Press, 1970.

———. "Vertical Integration and Communication," *The Bell Journal of Economics*, vol. 6, no. 1, Spring 1975, pp. 173–84.

Arrow, Kenneth, and Debreu, G. "Existence of Equilibrium for a Competitive Economy," *Econometrica*, vol. 22, 1954, pp. 265–90.

Arrow, Kenneth, and Hahn, Frank. *General Competitive Analysis.* San Francisco: Holden-Day, 1971.

Aumann, R. "Acceptable Points in General Cooperative n-Person Games." In *Contributions to the Theory of Games*, vol. 4, Annals of Mathematics Study no. 40 (R. D. Luce and A. W. Tucker, eds). Princeton, N.J.: Princeton University Press, 1959.

Barash, David P. *Sociobiology and Behavior.* Amsterdam: North-Holland, 1977.

Berman, S., and Schotter, A. "Supergames and Diffusion Processes." Discussion paper 79–01, C. V. Starr Center for Applied Economics, New York University, January 1979.

Berman, S., and Schotter, A. "When Is the Incentive Problem Real?" Paper presented at the Oskar Morgenstern Symposium on Mathematical Economics, May 28–30, 1980, Vienna.

Billingsley, P. *Convergence of Probability Measures.* New York: Wiley, 1968.

Brandt, R. B. "Utilitarianism and the Rules of War." In *War and Moral Responsibility* (M. Cohen, T. Nagel, and T. Scanlon, eds.). Princeton, N.J.: Princeton University Press, 1974.

Buchanan, James. *The Limits of Liberty: Between Anarchy and Leviathan.* Chicago: University of Chicago Press, 1975.

Buchanan, James, and Tullock, Gordon. *The Calculus of Consent: Logical*

Foundations of Constitutional Democracy. Ann Arbor, Mich.: University of Michigan Press, 1962.

Clarke, E. "Multipart Pricing of Public Goods," *Public Choice*, vol. 11, Fall 1971, pp. 17–33.

Colson, Francis. *The Week: An Essay on the Origin and Development of the Seven Day Week.* Cambridge: Cambridge University Press, 1926.

Commons, John. *Institutional Economics.* Madison, Wis.: University of Wisconsin Press, 1961 (first published in 1934).

Cyert, R., and March, J. *A Behavioral Theory of the Firm*, Englewood Cliffs, N.J.: Prentice-Hall, 1963.

Debreu, Gerhard. *The Theory of Value.* New York: Wiley, 1959.

Debreu, G., and Scarf, H. "A Limit Theorem on the Core of an Economy," *International Economic Review*, vol. 4, 1963, pp. 234–46.

Demsetz, H. "Exchange and Enforcement of Property Rights," *Journal of Law and Economics*, vol. 7, October 1964, pp. 11–26.

——. "Toward a Theory of Property Rights," *American Economic Review*, vol. 57, May 1967, pp. 347–73.

Dynkin, E. B., *Markov Processes*, vol. 1. New York: Academic Press, 1965.

Edgeworth, Francis Y. *Mathematical Psychics.* London: Kegan Paul, 1881.

Feller, W. "The Parabolic Differential Equations and the Associated Semi-groups of Transformations," *Annals of Mathematics*, 55, 1952, pp. 468–519.

——. "Generalized Second Order Differential Operators and Their Lateral Conditions," *Illinois Journal of Mathematics*, vol. 1, 1957, pp. 495–504.

——. *An Introduction to Probability Theory and Its Applications*, vol. 1, 3rd ed. New York: Wiley, 1968.

Foley, Duncan, "Problems versus Conflicts: Economic Theory and Ideology," *American Economic Association Papers and Proceedings*, vol. 65, May 1975, pp. 231–7.

Fredlund, Melvin. "Wolves, Chimps and Demsetz," *Economic Inquiry*, vol. 45, no. 2, June 1976, pp. 279–291.

Friedman, J. W. *Oligopoly and the Theory of Games.* Amsterdam: North-Holland, 1977.

Green, J., and Laffont, J. J. *Incentives in Public Decision-Making.* Amsterdam: North-Holland, 1979.

Groves, Theodore. "Incentives in Teams," *Econometrica*, vol. 41, July 1973, pp. 617–31.

Groves, T., and Ledyard, J. "Optimal Allocation of Public Goods: A Solution to the 'Free Rider' Problem," *Econometrica*, vol. 45, 1977, pp. 783–809.

Hare, R. M. "Rules of War and Moral Reasoning." In *War and Moral Responsibility* (M. Cohen, T. Nagel, and T. Scanlon, eds.). Princeton, N.J.: Princeton University Press, 1974.

Harsanyi, John C. "The Tracing Procedure: A Bayesian Approach to Defining a Solution for *n*-Person Non-cooperative Games," *The International Journal of Game Theory*, vol. 4, issue 1, 1975, pp. 61–95.

——. *Rational Behavior and Bargaining Equilibrium in Games and Social Situations*, Cambridge: Cambridge University Press, 1976.

Hayek, Friedrich A. "The Use of Knowledge in Society," *American Economic Review*, vol. 35, September 1945, pp. 519–30.

——. *The Counterrevolution of Science*. New York: Free Press, 1955.

Hildebrand, W., and Kirman, A. P. *Introduction to Equilibrium Analysis*. Amsterdam: North-Holland, 1976.

Hume, David. *Treatise on Human Nature*. New York: 1911 (first published in 1734).

Hurwicz, Leonid. "The Design of Mechanisms for Resource Allocation," *American Economic Review*, Papers and Proceedings, vol. 63, no. 2, May 1973a.

——. "On the Concept and Possibility of Information Decentralization," *American Economic Review*, vol. 59, May 1973b, pp. 513–54.

Jones, Robert. "The Origin and Development of a Medium of Exchange," *Journal of Political Economy*, vol. 84, no. 4, pt. 1, August 1976, pp. 757–76.

Kirzner, Israel M. *Competition and Entrepreneurship*. Chicago: University of Chicago Press, 1973.

Kuhn, H. W. "Extensive Games and the Problem of Information." In *Contributions to the Theory of Games*, vol. 2, Annals of Mathematics Study, no. 28 (H. W. Kuhn and A. W. Tucker, eds). Princeton, N.J.: Princeton University Press, 1953.

Kurz, M. "Altruistic Equilibrium." In *Economic Progress, Private Values and Public Policy* (B. Balassa and R. Helson, eds.). Amsterdam: North-Holland, 1977.

Laughlin, C. D., and d'Aquili, E. G. *Biogenetic Structuralism*. New York: Columbia University Press, 1974.

Levy, P. *Processus stochastiques et mouvement Brownien*, 2nd ed. Paris: Gauthier-Villars, 1965.

Lewis, D. *Convention: A Philosophical Study*. Cambridge, Mass.: Harvard University Press, 1969.

Marschak, J., and Radner, R. *The Economic Theory of Teams*. New Haven, Conn.: Yale University Press, 1972.

Marshall, Alfred. *Principles of Economics*. 8th ed. London: Macmillan, 1920.

Menger, Karl. *Untersuchungen über die Methode der Sozialwissenschaften und der politischen Ökonomie insbesondere* (1883). Translated by Francis J. Nock as *Problems in Economics and Sociology*. Urbana, Ill.: University of Illinois Press, 1963.

——. "On the Origins of Money," *Economic Journal*, vol. 2, June 1892, pp. 239–55.

————. *Principles of Economics* (J. Dingwall and B. F. Hoselitz, trans.). Glencoe, Ill.: Free Press, 1950 (first published 1923).

Morgenstern, Oskar. "Thirteen Critical Points in Contemporary Economic Theory: An Interpretation," *Journal of Economic Literature*, vol. 10, no. 4, December 1972, pp. 1163–89.

————. "Pareto Optimum and Economic Organization." In *Selected Writings of Oskar Morgenstern* (Andrew Schotter, ed.) New York: New York University Press, 1976.

Nozick, Robert. *Anarchy, State and Utopia*. New York: Basic Books, 1975.

Owen, G. *Game Theory*, Philadelphia: Saunders, 1968.

Parzen, E. *Stochastic Processes*. San Francisco: Holden-Day, 1962.

Radford, R. A. "The Economic Organization of a P.O.W. Camp," *Economica*, vol. 12, 1945, pp. 189–201.

Rawls, John. *A Theory of Justice*. Cambridge, Mass.: Harvard University Press (Belknap), 1971.

Robbins, Lionel. *On the Nature and Significance of Economic Science*. London: Macmillan, 1935.

Roberts, Blaine, and Bob Holdren. *Theory of Social Process*. Ames, Iowa: University of Iowa Press, 1972.

Schelling, Thomas C. *The Strategy of Conflict*. New York: Oxford University Press, 1960.

Schotter, A., and Schwödiauer, G. "Economics and the Theory of Games: A Survey," *Journal of Economic Literature*, vol. 18, June 1980, pp. 479–527.

Selten, R. "A Re-examination of the Perfectness Concept for Equilibrium Points," *International Journal of Game Theory*, vol. 4, issue 1/2, 1975, pp. 25–55.

Sen, Amartya. "Isolation Assurance and the Social Rate of Discount," *Quarterly Journal of Economics*, vol. 81, 1967.

Shannon, C. E. "A Mathematical Theory of Communication," *Bell Systems Technical Journal*, vol. 27, 1948, pp. 379–423, 623–56.

Shapley, L., and Shubik, M. "Trade Using One Commodity as a Means of Payment," *Journal of Political Economy*, vol. 85, no. 5, October 1977, pp. 937–69.

Shubik, Martin. "Edgeworth Market Games." In *Annals of Mathematics Study* no. 40 (A. W. Tucker and R. D. Luce, eds.). Princeton, N.J.: Princeton University Press, 1959, pp. 267–79.

————. "The General Equilibrium Model Is the Wrong Model and a Noncooperative Strategic Process Model Is a Satisfactory Model for the Reconciliation of Micro and Macroeconomic Theory," *Cowles Foundation Discussion Paper 365*, November 1973.

————. "A Trading Model to Avoid Tatonnement Metaphysics." In *Bidding and Auctioning for Procurement and Allocation* (Y. Amihud, ed.). New York: New York University Press, 1974.

Simon, Herbert. "Rational Decision Making in Business Organizations," *American Economic Review*, vol. 69, no. 4, September 1979, pp. 493–514.

Smith, Maynard. "The Theory of Games and the Evolution of Animal Conflicts," *Journal of Theoretical Biology*, vol. 47, 1974, pp. 209–21.

Smith, Vernon. "Experimental Mechanisms for Public Choice." *Game Theory and Political Science* (Peter Ordeshook, ed.). New York: New York University Press, 1978a.

————. "Incentive Compatible Experimental Processes for the Provision of Public Goods," NBER Conference on Decentralization, Northwestern University, April 23–25, 1976. To appear in *Research in Experimental Economics*. Greenwich, Conn.: J. A. I. Press, 1978b.

Taylor, Michael. *Anarchy and Cooperation*. New York: Wiley, 1976.

Telser, Lester. *Competition, Collusion and Game Theory*. Chicago: Aldine, 1972.

————. *Economic Theory and the Core*. Chicago: University of Chicago Press, 1979.

Theil, Henri. *Economics and Information Theory*. Chicago: Rand McNally, 1967.

Thompson, G. "Bridge and Signalling." In *Contributions to the Theory of Games*, vol. 2, Annals of Mathematics Study no. 28 (H. W. Kuhn and A. W. Tucker, eds.). Princeton, N.J.: Princeton University Press, 1953a.

————. "Signalling Strategies in *n*-Person Games." In *Contributions to the Theory of Games*, vol. 2, Annals of Mathematics Study no. 28 (H. W. Kuhn and A. W. Tucker, eds.). Princeton, N.J.: Princeton University Press, 1953b.

Tideman, T. N., and Tullock, G. "A New and Superior Process for Making Social Choices," *Journal of Political Economy*, vol. 84, December 1976, pp. 1145–59.

Ullman-Margalit, Edna. *The Emergence of Norms*. New York: Oxford University Press, 1978.

Varsavsky, Carlos. *Why Seven Days in a Week?* 1978 (unpublished manuscript).

Veblen, Thorstein. "Why Is Economics Not an Evolutionary Science?" *Quarterly Journal of Economics*, vol. 12, 1898.

von Neumann, J., and O. Morgenstern. *The Theory of Games and Economic Behavior*, 2nd ed. Princeton, N.J.: Princeton University Press, 1947.

Weinberger, H. F. *A First Course in Partial Differential Equations with Complex Variables and Transform Methods*. Waltham, Mass.: Blaisdell, 1965.

Wentzell, A. D. "On Boundary Conditions for Multidimensional Diffusion Processes" (in Russian), *Teoriya Verojatnostei i Ee Primeneniya*, vol. 4, 1959, pp. 172–85.

————. "General Boundary Problems Connected with Diffusion Processes" (in Russian), *Uspehki Matematicheskikh Nauk*, vol. 15, no. 2 (92), 1960, pp. 202–4.

Williamson, O. *Markets and Hierarchies: A Study in the Economics of Internal Organization*. New York: Basic Books, 1975.

Wilson, Edward. *Sociobiology: The New Synthesis*. Cambridge, Mass.: Harvard University Press (Belknap), 1975.

9. A Pure Theory of Local Expenditures

Charles M. Tiebout[1]

One of the most important recent developments in the area of "applied economic theory" has been the work of Musgrave and Samuelson in public finance theory.[2] The two writers agree on what is probably the major point under investigation, namely, that no "market type" solution exists to determine the level of expenditures on public goods. Seemingly, we are faced with the problem of having a rather large portion of our national income allocated in a "non-optimal" way when compared with the private sector.

This discussion will show that the Musgrave-Samuelson analysis, which is valid for federal expenditures, need not apply to local expenditures. The plan of the discussion is first to restate the assumptions made by Musgrave and Samuelson and the central problems with which they deal. After looking at a key difference between the federal versus local cases, I shall present a simple model. This model yields a solution for the level of expenditures for local public goods which reflects the preferences of the population more adequately than they can be reflected at the national level. The assumptions of the model will then be relaxed to see what implications are involved. Finally, policy considerations will be discussed.

Reprinted, by permission, from *Journal of Political Economy* 64 (October 1956): 416–24.

[1] I am grateful for the comments of my colleagues Karl de Schweinitz, Robert Eisner, and Robert Strotz, and those of Martin Bailey, of the University of Chicago.

[2] Richard A. Musgrave, "The Voluntary Exchange Theory of Public Economy," *Quarterly Journal of Economics*, LII (February 1939), 213–17; "A Multiple Theory of the Budget," paper read at the Econometric Society annual meeting (December 1955); and his forthcoming book, *The Theory of Public Economy*; Paul A. Samuelson, "The Pure Theory of Public Expenditure," *Review of Economics and Statistics*, XXXVI, No. 4 (November 1954), 387–89, and "Diagrammatic Exposition of a Pure Theory of Public Expenditure," *ibid.*, XXXVII, No. 4 (November 1955), 350–56.

The Theoretical Issue

Samuelson has defined public goods as *"collective consumption goods* $(X_n + 1, \ldots, X_n + n)$ which all enjoy in common in the sense that each individual's consumption of such a good leads to no subtraction from any other individual's consumption of that good, so that $X_n + j = X_n^i + j$ simultaneously for each and every *i*th individual and each collective good."[3] While definitions are a matter of choice, it is worth noting that "consumption" has a much broader meaning here than in the usual sense of the term. Not only does it imply that the act of consumption by one person does not diminish the opportunities for consumption by another but it also allows this consumption to be in another form. For example, while the residents of a new government housing project are made better off, benefits also accrue to other residents of the community in the form of the external economies of slum clearance.[4] Thus many goods that appear to lack the attributes of public goods may properly be considered public if consumption is defined to include these external economies.[5]

A definition alternative to Samuelson's might be simply that a public good is one which should be produced, but for which there is no feasible method of charging the consumers. This is less

---

[3]"The Pure Theory . . .," *op. cit.*, p. 387.

[4]Samuelson allows for this when he states that "one man's circus may be another man's poison," referring, of course, to public goods ("Diagrammatic Exposition . . .," *op. cit.*, p. 351).

[5]There seems to be a problem connected with the external-economies aspect of public goods. Surely a radio broadcast, like national defense, has the attribute that A's enjoyment leaves B no worse off; yet this does not imply that broadcasting should, in a normative sense, be a public good (the arbitrary manner in which the level of radio programs is determined aside). The difference between defense and broadcasting is subtle but important. In both cases there is a problem of determining the optimal level of outputs and the corresponding level of benefits taxes. In the broadcasting case, however, A may be quite willing to pay more taxes than B, even if both have the same "ability to pay" (assuming that the benefits are determinate). Defense is another question. Here A is not content that B should pay less. A makes the *social judgment* that B's preference *should* be the same. A's preference, expressed as an annual defense expenditure such as $42.7 billion and representing the majority view, thus determines the level of defense. Here the A's may feel that the B's *should pay* the same amount of benefits tax.

If it is argued that this case is typical of public goods, then, once the level is somehow set, the voluntary exchange approach and the benefit theory associated with it do not make sense. If the preceding analysis is correct, we are now back in the area of equity in terms of ability to pay.

elegant, but has the advantage that it allows for the objections of Enke and Margolis.[6] This definition, unfortunately, does not remove any of the problems faced by Musgrave and Samuelson.

The core problem with which both Musgrave and Samuelson deal concerns the mechanism by which consumer-voters register their preferences for public goods. The consumer is, in a sense, surrounded by a government whose objective it is to ascertain his wants for public goods and tax him accordingly. To use Alchian's term, the government's revenue-expenditure pattern for goods and services is expected to "adapt to" consumers' preferences.[7] Both Musgrave and Samuelson have shown that, in the vertically additive nature of voluntary demand curves, this problem has only a conceptual solution. If all consumer-voters could somehow be forced to reveal their true preferences for public goods, then the amount of such goods to be produced and the appropriate benefits tax could be determined.[8] As things now stand, there is no mechanism to force the consumer-voter to state his true preferences; in fact, the "rational" consumer will understate his preferences and hope to enjoy the goods while avoiding the tax.

The current method of solving this problem operates, unsatisfactorily, through the political mechanism. The expenditure wants of a "typical voter" are somehow pictured. This objective on the expenditure side is then combined with an ability-to-pay principle on the revenue side, giving us our current budget. Yet in terms of a satisfactory theory of public finance, it would be desirable (1) to force the voter to reveal his preferences; (2) to be able to satisfy them in the same sense that a private goods market does; and (3)

[6]They argue that, for most of the goods supplied by governments, increased use by some consumer-voters leaves less available for other consumer-voters. Crowded highways and schools, as contrasted with national defense, may be cited as examples (see Stephen Enke, "More on the Misuse of Mathematics in Economics: A Rejoinder," *Review of Economics and Statistics*, XXXVII [May 1955], 131–33; and Julius Margolis, "A Comment on the Pure Theory of Public Expenditure," *Review of Economics and Statistics*, XXXVII [November 1955], 247–49.

[7]Armen A. Alchian, "Uncertainty, Evolution, and Economic Theory," *Journal of Political Economy*, LVIII (June 1950), 211–21.

[8]The term "benefits tax" is used in contrast to the concept of taxation based on the "ability to pay," which really reduces to a notion that there is some "proper" distribution of income. Conceptually, this issue is separate from the problem of providing public goods and services (see Musgrave, "A Multiple Theory . . . ," *op. cit.*).

to tax him accordingly. The question arises whether there is any set of social institutions by which this goal can be approximated.

Local Expenditures

Musgrave and Samuelson implicitly assume that expenditures are handled at the central government level. However, the provision of such governmental services as police and fire protection, education, hospitals, and courts does not necessarily involve federal activity.[9] Many of these goods are provided by local governments. It is worthwhile to look briefly at the magnitude of these expenditures.[10]

Historically, local expenditures have exceeded those of the federal government. The thirties were the first peacetime years in which federal expenditures began to pull away from local expenditures. Even during the fiscal year 1954, federal expenditures on *goods and services exclusive of defense* amounted only to some 15 billions of dollars, while local expenditures during this same period amounted to some 17 billions of dollars. There is no need to quibble over which comparisons are relevant. The important point is that the often-neglected local expenditures are significant and, when viewed in terms of expenditures on goods and services only, take on even more significance. Hence an important question arises whether at this level of government any mechanism operates to insure that expenditures on these public goods approximate the proper level.

Consider for a moment the case of the city resident about to move to the suburbs. What variables will influence his choice of a municipality? If he has children, a high level of expenditures on schools may be important. Another person may prefer a community with a municipal golf course. The availability and quality of such facilities and services as beaches, parks, police protection, roads, and parking facilities will enter into the decision-making process. Of course, non-economic variables will also be considered, but this is of no concern at this point.

---

[9]The discussion that follows applies to local governments. It will be apparent as the argument proceeds that it also applies, with less force, to state governments.

[10]A question does arise as to just what are the proper expenditures to consider. Following Musgrave, I shall consider only expenditures on goods or services (his Branch I expenditures). Thus interest on the federal debt is not included. At the local level interest payments might be included, since they are considered payments for services currently used, such as those provided by roads and schools.

The consumer-voter may be viewed as picking that community which best satisfies his preference pattern for public goods. This is a major difference between central and local provision of public goods. At the central level the preferences of the consumer-voter are given, and the government tries to adjust to the pattern of these preferences, whereas at the local level various governments have their revenue and expenditure patterns more or less set.[11] Given these revenue and expenditure patterns, the consumer-voter moves to that community whose local government best satisfies his set of preferences. The greater the number of communities and the greater the variance among them, the closer the consumer will come to fully realizing his preference position.[12]

A Local Government Model

The implications of the preceding argument may be shown by postulating an extreme model. Here the following assumptions are made:

1. Consumer-voters are fully mobile and will move to that community where their preference patterns, which are set, are best satisfied.

2. Consumer-voters are assumed to have full knowledge of differences among revenue and expenditure patterns and to react to these differences.

3. There are a large number of communities in which the consumer-voters may choose to live.

4. Restrictions due to employment opportunities are not considered. It may be assumed that all persons are living on dividend income.

5. The public services supplied exhibit no external economies or diseconomies between communities.

Assumptions 6 and 7 to follow are less familiar and require brief explanations:

6. For every pattern of community services set by, say, a city manager who follows the preferences of the older residents of the

[11]This is an assumption about reality. In the extreme model that follows the patterns are assumed to be absolutely fixed.

[12]This is also true of many non-economic variables. Not only is the consumer-voter concerned with economic patterns, but he desires, for example, to associate with "nice" people. Again, the greater the number of communities, the closer he will come to satisfying his total preference function, which includes non-economic variables.

community, there is an optimal community size. This optimum is defined in terms of the number of residents for which this bundle of services can be produced at the lowest average cost. This, of course, is closely analogous to the low point of a firm's average cost curve. Such a cost function implies that some factor or resource is fixed. If this were not so, there would be no logical reason to limit community size, given the preference patterns. In the same sense that the average cost curve has a minimum for one firm but can be reproduced by another there is seemingly no reason why a duplicate community cannot exist. The assumption that some factor is fixed explains why it is not possible for the community in question to double its size by growth. The factor may be the limited land area of a suburban community, combined with a set of zoning laws against apartment buildings. It may be the local beach, whose capacity is limited. Anything of this nature will provide a restraint.

In order to see how this restraint works, let us consider the beach problem. Suppose the preference patterns of the community are such that the optimum size population is 13,000. Within this set of preferences there is a certain demand per family for beach space. This demand is such that at 13,000 population a 500-yard beach is required. If the actual length of the beach is, say, 600 yards, then it is not possible to realize this preference pattern with twice the optimum population, since there would be too little beach space by 400 yards.

The assumption of a fixed factor is necessary, as will be shown later, in order to get a determinate number of communities. It also has the advantage of introducing a realistic restraint into the model.

7. The last assumption is that communities below the optimum size seek to attract new residents to lower average costs. Those above optimum size do just the opposite. Those at an optimum try to keep their populations constant.

This assumption needs to be amplified. Clearly, communities below the optimum size, through chambers of commerce or other agencies, seek to attract new residents. This is best exemplified by the housing developments in some suburban areas, such as Park Forest in the Chicago area and Levittown in the New York area, which need to reach an optimum size. The same is true of communities that try to attract manufacturing industries by setting up certain facilities and getting an optimum number of firms to move into the industrially zoned area.

The case of the city that is too large and tries to get rid of residents is more difficult to imagine. No alderman in his right political mind would ever admit that the city is too big. Nevertheless, economic forces are at work to push people out of it. Every resident who moves to the suburbs to find better schools, more parks, and so forth, is reacting, in part, against the pattern the city has to offer.

The case of the community which is at the optimum size and tries to remain so is not hard to visualize. Again proper zoning laws, implicit agreements among realtors, and the like are sufficient to keep the population stable.

Except when this system is in equilibrium, there will be a subset of consumer-voters who are discontented with the patterns of their community. Another set will be satisfied. Given the assumption about mobility and the other assumptions listed previously, movement will take place out of the communities of greater than optimal size into the communities of less than optimal size. The consumer-voter moves to the community that satisfies his preference pattern.

The act of moving or failing to move is crucial. Moving or failing to move replaces the usual market test of willingness to buy a good and reveals the consumer-voter's demand for public goods. Thus each locality has a revenue and expenditure pattern that reflects the desires of its residents. The next step is to see what this implies for the allocation of public goods at the local level.

Each city manager now has a certain demand for n local public goods. In supplying these goods, he and $m - 1$ other city managers may be considered as going to a national market and bidding for the appropriate units of service of each kind: so many units of police for the ith community; twice that number for the jth community; and so on. The demand on the public goods market for each of the n commodities will be the sum of the demands of the m communities. In the limit, as shown in a less realistic model to be developed later, this total demand will approximate the demand that represents the true preferences of the consumer-voters—that is, the demand they would reveal, if they were forced, somehow, to state their true preferences.[13] In this model there is no attempt on the part of local governments to "adapt to" the preferences of

[13]The word "approximate" is used in recognition of the limitations of this model, and of the more severe model to be developed shortly, with respect to the cost of mobility. This issue will be discussed later.

consumer-voters. Instead, those local governments that attract the optimum number of residents may be viewed as being "adopted by" the economic system.[14]

A Comparison Model

It is interesting to contrast the results of the preceding model with those of an even more severe model in order to see how these results differ from the normal market result. It is convenient to look at this severe model by developing its private-market counterpart. First assume that there are no public goods, only private ones. The preferences for these goods can be expressed as one of n patterns. Let a law be passed that all persons living in any one of the communities shall spend their money in the particular pattern described for that community by law. Given our earlier assumptions 1 through 5, it follows that, if the consumers move to the community whose law happens to fit their preference pattern, they will be at their optimum. The n communities, in turn, will then send their buyers to market to purchase the goods for the consumer-voters in their community. Since this is simply a lumping together of all similar tastes for the purpose of making joint purchases, the allocation of resources will be the same as it would be if normal market forces operated. This conceptual experiment is the equivalent of substituting the city manager for the broker or middleman.

Now turn the argument around and consider only public goods. Assume with Musgrave that the costs of additional services are constant.[15] Further, assume that a doubling of the population means doubling the amount of services required. Let the number of communities be infinite and let each announce a different pattern of expenditures on public goods. Define an empty community as one that fails to satisfy anybody's preference pattern. Given these assumptions, including the earlier assumptions 1 through 5, the consumer-voters will move to that community which *exactly* satisfies their preferences. This must be true, since a one-person community is allowed. The sum of the demands of the n communities reflects the demand for local public services. In this model the demand is exactly the same as it would be if it were determined by normal market forces.

[14]See Alchian, *op. cit.*
[15]Musgrave, "Voluntary Exchange . . .," *op. cit.*

However, this severe model does not make much sense. The number of communities is indeterminate. There is no reason why the number of communities will not be equal to the population, since each voter can find the one that exactly fits his preferences. Unless some sociological variable is introduced, this may reduce the solution of the problem of allocating public goods to the trite one of making each person his own municipal government. Hence this model is not even a first approximation of reality. It is presented to show the assumptions needed in a model of local government expenditures, which yields the same optimal allocation that a private market would.

The Local Government Model Re-examined

The first model, described by the first five assumptions together with assumptions 6 and 7, falls short of this optimum. An example will serve to show why this is the case.

Let us return to the community with the 500-yard beach. By assumption, its optimum population was set at 13,000, given its preference patterns. Suppose that some people in addition to the optimal 13,000 would choose this community if it were available. Since they cannot move into this area, they must accept the next best substitute.[16] If a perfect substitute is found, no problem exists. If one is not found, then the failure to reach the optimal preference position and the substitution of a lower position becomes a matter of degree. In so far as there are a number of communities with similar revenue and expenditure patterns, the solution will approximate the ideal "market" solution.

Two related points need to be mentioned to show the allocative results of this model: (1) changes in the costs of one of the public services will cause changes in the quality produced; (2) the costs of moving from community to community should be recognized. Both points can be illustrated in one example.

Suppose lifeguards throughout the country organize and succeed in raising their wages. Total taxes in communities with beaches will rise. Now residents who are largely indifferent to beaches will be forced to make a decision. Is the saving of this added tax worth the cost of moving to a community with little or

---

[16]In the constant cost model with an infinite number of communities this problem does not arise, since the number of beaches can be doubled or a person can find another community that is a duplicate of his now filled first choice.

no beach? Obviously, this decision depends on many factors, among which the availability of and proximity to a suitable substitute community is important. If enough people leave communities with beaches and move to communities without beaches, the total amount of lifeguard services used will fall. These models then, unlike their private-market counterpart, have mobility as a cost of registering demand. The higher this cost, *ceteris paribus*, the less optimal the allocation of resources.

This distinction should not be blown out of proportion. Actually, the cost of registering demand comes through the introduction of space into the economy. Yet space affects the allocation not only of resources supplied by local governments but of those supplied by the private market as well. Every time available resources or production techniques change, a new location becomes optimal for the firm. Indeed, the very concept of the shopping trip shows that the consumer does pay a cost to register his demand for private goods. In fact, Koopmans has stated that the nature of the assignment problem is such that in a space economy with transport costs there is *no* general equilibrium solution as set by market forces.[17]

Thus the problems stated by this model are not unique; they have their counterpart in the private market. We are maximizing within the framework of the resources available. If production functions show constant returns to scale with generally diminishing factor returns, and if indifference curves are regularly convex, an optimal solution is possible. On the production side it is assumed that communities are forced to keep production costs at a minimum either through the efficiency of city managers or through competition from other communities.[18] Given this, on the demand side we may note with Samuelson that "each individual, in seeking as a competitive buyer to get to the highest level of

[17]Tjalling Koopmans, "Mathematical Groundwork of Economic Optimization Theories," paper read at the annual meeting of the Econometric Society (December 1954).

[18]In this model and in reality, the city manager or elected official who is not able to keep his costs (taxes) low compared with those of similar communities will find himself out of a job. As an institutional observation, it may well be that city managers are under greater pressure to minimize costs than their private-market counterparts—firm managers. This follows from (1) the reluctance of the public to pay taxes and, what may be more important, (2) the fact that the costs of competitors—other communities—are a matter of public record and may easily be compared.

indifference subject to given prices and *tax*, would be led as if by an Invisible Hand to the grand solution of the social maximum position."[19] Just as the consumer may be visualized as walking to a private market place to buy his goods, the prices of which are set, we place him in the position of walking to a community where the prices (taxes) of community services are set. Both trips take the consumer to market. There is no way in which the consumer can avoid revealing his preferences in a spatial economy. Spatial mobility provides the local public-goods counterpart to the private market's shopping trip.

External Economies and Mobility

Relaxing assumption 5 has some interesting implications. There are obvious external economies and diseconomies between communities. My community is better off if its neighbor sprays trees to prevent Dutch elm disease. On the other hand, my community is worse off if the neighboring community has inadequate law enforcement.

In cases in which the external economies and diseconomies are of sufficient importance, some form of integration may be indicated.[20] Not all aspects of law enforcement are adequately handled at the local level. The function of the sheriff, state police, and the FBI—as contrasted with the local police—may be cited as resulting from a need for integration. In real life the diseconomies are minimized in so far as communities reflecting the same socioeconomic preferences are contiguous. Suburban agglomerations such as Westchester, the North Shore, and the Main Line are, in part, evidence of these external economies and diseconomies.

Assumptions 1 and 2 should be checked against reality. Consumer-voters do not have perfect knowledge and set preferences, nor are they perfectly mobile. The question is how do people actually react in choosing a community. There has been very little empirical study of the motivations of people in choosing a community. Such studies as have been undertaken seem to indicate a surprising awareness of differing revenue and expenditure patterns.[21] The general disdain with which proposals to integrate

[19]"The Pure Theory . . .," *op. cit.*, p. 388. (Italics mine.)

[20]I am grateful to Stanley Long and Donald Markwalder for suggesting this point.

[21]See Wendell Bell, "Familism and Suburbanization: One Test of the Choice Hypothesis," paper read at the annual meeting of the American Sociological Society, Washington, D.C., August 1955. Forthcoming in *Rural Sociology*, December 1956.

municipalities are met seems to reflect, in part, the fear that local revenue-expenditure patterns will be lost as communities are merged into a metropolitan area.

Policy Implications

The preceding analysis has policy implications for municipal integration, provision for mobility, and set local revenue and expenditure patterns. These implications are worth brief consideration.

On the usual economic welfare grounds, municipal integration is justified only if more of any service is forthcoming at the same total cost and without reduction of any other service. A general reduction of costs along with a reduction in one or more of the services provided cannot be justified on economic grounds unless the social welfare function is known. For example, those who argue for a metropolitan police force instead of local police cannot prove their case on purely economic grounds.[22] If one of the communities were to receive less police protection after integration than it received before, integration could be objected to as a violation of consumers' choice.

Policies that promote residential mobility and increase the knowledge of the consumer-voter will improve the allocation of government expenditures in the same sense that mobility among jobs and knowledge relevant to the location of industry and labor improve the allocation of private resources.

Finally, we may raise the normative question whether local governments *should*, to the extent possible, have a fixed revenue-expenditure pattern. In a large, dynamic metropolis this may be impossible. Perhaps it could more appropriately be considered by rural and suburban communities.

Conclusion

It is useful in closing to restate the problem as Samuelson sees it:

> However, no decentralized pricing system can serve to determine optimally these levels of collective consumpion. Other kinds of "voting" or "signaling" would have to be tried. . . . Of course utopian voting and signaling schemes can be imagined. . . . The failure of

[22]For example, in Cook County—the Chicago area—Sheriff Joseph Lohman argues for such a metropolitan police force.

market catallactics in no way denies the following truth: given sufficient knowledge the optimal decisions can always be found by scanning over all the attainable states of the world and selecting the one which according to the postulated ethical welfare function is best. The solution "exists"; the problem is how to "find" it.[23]

It is the contention of this article that, for a substantial portion of collective or public goods, this problem *does have* a conceptual solution. If consumer-voters are fully mobile, the appropriate local governments, whose revenue-expenditure patterns are set, are adopted by the consumer-voters. While the solution may not be perfect because of institutional rigidites, this does not invalidate its importance. The solution, like a general equilibrium solution for a private spatial economy, is the best that can be obtained given preferences and resource endowments.

Those who are tempted to compare this model with the competitive private model may be disappointed. Those who compare the reality described by this model with the reality of the competitive model—given the degree of monopoly, friction, and so forth—*may* find that local government represents a sector where the allocation of public goods (as a reflection of the preferences of the population) need not take a back seat to the private sector.

---

[23]"The Pure Theory . . .," *op. cit.*, pp. 388–89.

10. An Economic Theory of Clubs

James M. Buchanan[1]

The implied institutional setting for neo-classical economic theory, including theoretical welfare economics, is a régime of private property, in which all goods and services are privately (individually) utilized or consumed. Only within the last two decades have serious attempts been made to extend the formal theoretical structure to include communal or collective ownership-consumption arrangements.[2] The "pure theory of public goods" remains in its infancy, and the few models that have been most rigorously developed apply only to polar or extreme cases. For example, in the fundamental papers by Paul A. Samuelson, a sharp conceptual distinction is made between those goods and services that are "purely private" and those that are "purely public."[3] No general theory has been developed which covers the whole spectrum of ownership-consumption possibilities, ranging from the purely private or individualized activity on the one hand to purely public or collectivized activity on the other. One of the missing links here is "a theory of clubs," a theory of co-operative membership, a theory that will include as a variable to be determined the extension of ownership-consumption rights over differing numbers of persons.

Reprinted, by permission, from *Economica* 32 (February 1965): 1–14.

[1] I am indebted to graduate students and colleagues for many helpful suggestions. Specific acknowledgement should be made for the critical assistance of Emilio Giardina of the University of Catania and W. Craig Stubblebine of the University of Delaware.

[2] It is interesting that none of the theories of Socialist economic organization seems to be based on explicit co-operation among individuals. These theories have conceived the economy either in the Lange-Lerner sense as an analogue to a purely private, individually oriented social order or, alternatively, as one that is centrally directed.

[3] See Paul A. Samuelson, "The Pure Theory of Public Expenditure," *Review of Economics and Statistics*, vol. xxxvi (1954), pp. 387–89; "Diagrammatic Exposition of a Theory of Public Expenditure," *Review of Economics and Statistics*, vol. xxxvii (1955), pp. 350–55.

Everyday experience reveals that there exists some most preferred or "optimal" membership for almost any activity in which we engage, and that this membership varies in some relation to economic factors. European hotels have more communally shared bathrooms than their American counterparts. Middle and low income communities organize swimming-bathing facilities; high income communities are observed to enjoy privately owned swimming pools.

In this paper I shall develop a general theory of clubs, or consumption ownership-membership arrangements. This construction allows us to move one step forward in closing the awesome Samuelson gap between the purely private and the purely public good. For the former, the optimal sharing arrangement, the preferred club membership, is clearly one person (or one family unit), whereas the optimal sharing group for the purely public good, as defined in the polar sense, includes an infinitely large number of members. That is to say, for any genuinely collective good defined in the Samuelson way, a club that has an infinitely large membership is preferred to all arrangements of finite size. While it is evident that some goods and services may be reasonably classified as purely private, even in the extreme sense, it is clear that few, if any, goods satisfy the conditions of extreme collectiveness. The interesting cases are those goods and services, the consumption of which involves some "publicness," where the optimal sharing group is more than one person or family but smaller than an infinitely large number. The range of "publicness" is finite. The central question in a theory of clubs is that of determining the membership margin, so to speak, the size of the most desirable cost and consumption sharing arrangement.[4]

In traditional neo-classical models that assume the existence of purely private goods and services only, the utility function of an individual is written,

$$(1) \qquad U^i = U^i(X_1^i, X_2^i, \ldots, X_n^i),$$

where each of the X's represents the amount of a purely private good available during a specified time period, to the reference individual designated by the superscript.

[4]Note that an economic theory of clubs can strictly apply only to the extent that the motivation for joining in sharing arrangements is itself economic; that is, only if choices are made on the basis of costs and benefits of particular goods and services as these are confronted by the individual. In so far as individuals join clubs for camaraderie, as such, the theory does not apply.

Samuelson extended this function to include purely collective or public goods, which he denoted by the subscripts, $n + 1, \ldots, n + m$, so that (1) is changed to read,

(2) $U_i = U^i (X_1^i, X_2^i, \ldots, X_n^i; X_{n+1}^i, X_{n+2}^i, \ldots X_{n+m}^i).$

This approach requires that all goods be initially classified into the two sets, private and public. Private goods, defined to be wholly divisible among the persons, $i = 1, 2, \ldots, s$, satisfy the relation

$$X_j = \sum_{i=1}^{s} X_j^i,$$

while public goods, defined to be wholly indivisible as among persons, satisfy the relation,

$$X_{n+j} = X_{n+j}^i.$$

I propose to drop any attempt at an initial classification or differentiation of goods into fully divisible and fully indivisible sets, and to incorporate in the utility function goods falling between these two extremes. What the theory of clubs provides is, in one sense, a "theory of classification," but this emerges as an output of the analysis. The first step is that of modifying the utility function.

Note that, in neither (1) nor (2) is it necessary to make a distinction between "goods available to the ownership unit of which the reference individual is a member" and "goods finally available to the individual for consumption." With purely private goods, consumption by one individual automatically reduces potential consumption of other individuals by an equal amount. With purely public goods, consumption by any one individual implies equal consumption by all others. For goods falling between such extremes, such a distinction must be made. This is because for such goods there is no unique translation possible between the "goods available to the membership unit" and "goods finally consumed." In the construction which follows, therefore, the "goods" entering the individual's utility function, the X_j's, should be interpreted as "goods available for consumption to the whole membership unit of which the reference individual is a member."

Arguments that represent the size of the sharing group must be included in the utility function along with arguments representing goods and services. For any good or service, regardless of its ultimate place along the conceptual public-private spectrum, the utility that an individual receives from its consumption depends upon *the number of other persons with whom he must share its benefits.* This is obvious, but its acceptance does require breaking out of the private property straitjacket within which most of economic theory has developed. As an extreme example, take a good normally considered to be purely private, say, a pair of shoes. Clearly your own utility from a single pair of shoes, per unit of time, depends on the number of other persons who share them with you. Simultaneous physical sharing may not, of course, be possible; only one person can wear the shoes at each particular moment. However, for any finite period of time, sharing is possible, even for such evidently private goods. For pure services that are consumed in the moment of acquisition the extension is somewhat more difficult, but it can be made none the less. Sharing here simply means that the individual receives a smaller quantity of the service. Sharing a "haircut per month" with a second person is the same as consuming "one-half haircut per month." Given any quantity of final good, as defined in terms of the physical units of some standard quality, the utility that the individual receives from this quantity will be related functionally to the number of others with whom he shares.[5]

Variables for club size are not normally included in the utility function of an individual since, in the private-goods world, the optimal club size is unity. However, for our purposes, these variables must be explicitly included, and, for completeness, a club-size variable should be included for each and every good. Alongside each X_j there must be placed an N_j, which we define as the number of persons who are to participate as "members" in the sharing of good, X_j, including the ith person whose utility function is examined. That is to say, the club-size variable, N_j, measures the number of persons who are to join in the consumption-utilization arrangements for good, X_j, over the relevant time period. The sharing arrangements may or may not call for equal consumption on the part of each member, and the peculiar manner of sharing will clearly affect the way in which the variable enters the utility function. For simplicity we may assume equal sharing, although

---

[5]Physical attributes of a good or service may, of course, affect the structure of the sharing arrangements that are preferred. Although the analysis below assumes symmetrical sharing, this assumption is not necessary, and the analysis in its general form can be extended to cover all possible schemes.

this is not necessary for the analysis. The rewritten utility function now becomes,

$$(3) \qquad U^i = U^i[(X_1^i, N_1^i), (X_2^i, N_2^i), \ldots, (X_{n+m}^i, N_{n+m}^i)].[6]$$

We may designate a numeraire good, X_r, which can simply be thought of as money, possessing value only as a medium of exchange. By employing the convention whereby the lower case u's represent the partial derivatives, we get u_j^i/u_r^i, defined as the marginal rate of substitution in consumption between X_j and X_r for the ith individual. Since, in our construction, the size of the group is also a variable, we must also examine, $u_{N_j}^i/u_r^i$, defined as the marginal rate of substitution "in consumption" between the size of the sharing group and the numeraire. That is to say, this ratio represents the rate (which may be negative) at which the individual is willing to give up (accept) money in exchange for additional members in the sharing group.

We now define a cost or production function as this confronts the individual, and this will include the same set of variables,

$$(4) \qquad F = F^i[(X_1^i, N_1^i), (X_2^i, N_2^i), \ldots, (X_{n+m}^i, N_{n+m}^i)].$$

Why do the club-size variables, the N_j's, appear in this cost function? The addition of members to a sharing group may, and normally will, affect the cost of the good to any one member. The larger is the membership of the golf club the lower the dues to any single member, given a specific quantity of club facilities available per unit time.

It now becomes possible to derive, from the utility and cost functions, statements for the necessary marginal conditions for Pareto optimality in respect to consumption of each good. In the usual manner we get,

$$(5) \qquad u_j^i/u_r^i = f_j^i/f_r^i.$$

Condition (5) states that, for the ith individual, the marginal rate of substitution between goods X_j and X_r, in consumption, must be

---

[6]Note that this construction of the individual's utility function differs from that introduced in an earlier paper, where "activities" rather than "goods" were included as the basic arguments. (See James M. Buchanan and Wm. Craig Stubblebine, "Externality," *Economica*, vol. xxxi (1962), pp. 371–84.) In the alternative construction, the "activities" of other persons enter directly into the utility function of the reference individual with respect to the consumption of all other than purely private goods. The construction here incorporates the same inter-dependence through the inclusion of the N_j's although in a more general manner.

equal to the marginal rate of substitution between these same two goods in "production" or exchange. To this acknowledged necessary condition, we now add,

(6) $$u_{Nj}^i/u_r^i = f_{Nj}/f_r.$$

Condition (6) is not normally stated, since the variables relating to club size are not normally included in utility functions. Implicitly, the size for sharing arrangements is assumed to be determined exogenously to individual choices. Club size is presumed to be a part of the environment. Condition (6) states that the marginal rate of substitution "in consumption" between the size of the group sharing in the use of good X_j, and the numeraire good, X_r, must be equal to the marginal rate of substitution "in production." In other words, the individual attains full equilibrium in club size only when the marginal benefits that he secures from having an additional member (which may, and probably will normally be, negative) are just equal to the marginal costs that he incurs from adding a member (which will also normally be negative).

Combining (5) and (6) we get,

(7) $$u_j^i/f_j = u_r^i/f_r = u_{Nj}^i/f_{Nj}.$$

Only when (7) is satisfied will the necessary marginal conditions with respect to the consumption-utilization of X_j be met. The individual will have available to his membership unit an optimal quantity of X_j, measured in physical units and, also, he will be sharing this quantity "optimally" over a group of determined size.

The necessary condition for club size may not, of course, be met. Since for many goods there is a major change in utility between the one-person and the two-person club, and since discrete changes in membership may be all that is possible, we may get,

(7A) $$\left. \frac{u_j^i}{f_j} = \frac{u_r^i}{f_r} > \frac{u_{Nj}^i}{f_{Nj}} \right|_{Nj=1} \; ; \; \left. \frac{u_j^i}{f_j} = \frac{u_r^i}{f^r} < \frac{u_{Nj}^i}{f_{Nj}} \right|_{Nj=2}$$

which incorporates the recognition that, with a club size of unity, the right-hand term may be relatively too small, whereas, with a club size of two, it may be too large. If partial sharing arrangements can be worked out, this qualification need not, of course, be made.

If, on the other hand, the size of a co-operative or collective sharing group is exogenously determined, we may get,

(7B) $$\left. \frac{u_j^i}{f_j} = \frac{u_r^i}{f_r} > \frac{u_{Nj}^i}{f_{Nj}} \right|_{Nj=k}$$

Note that (7B) actually characterizes the situation of an individual with respect to the consumption of any purely public good of the type defined in the Samuelson polar model. Any group of finite size, k, is smaller than optimal here, and the full set of necessary marginal conditions cannot possibly be met. Since additional persons can, by definition, be added to the group without in any way reducing the availability of the good to other members, and since additional members, could they be found, would presumably place some positive value on the good and hence be willing to share in its costs, the group always remains below optimal size. The all-inclusive club remains too small.

Consider, now, the relation between the set of necessary marginal conditions defined in (7) and those presented by Samuelson in application to goods that were exogenously defined to be purely public. In the latter case, these conditions are,

$$(8) \qquad \sum_{i=1}^{s} (u_{n+j}^i/u_r^i) = f_{n+j}/f_r,$$

where the marginal rates of substitution in consumption between the purely public good, X_{n+j}, and the numeraire good, X_r, summed over all individuals in the group of determined size, s, equals the marginal cost of X_{n+j} also defined in terms of units of X_r. Note that when (7) is satisfied, (8) is necessarily satisfied, provided only that the collectivity is making neither profit nor loss on providing the marginal unit of the public good. That is to say, provided that,

$$(9) \qquad f_{n+j}/f_r = \sum_{i=1}^{s} (f_{n+j}^i/f_r^i).$$

The reverse does not necessarily hold, however, since the satisfaction of (8) does not require that each and every individual in the group be in a position where his own marginal benefits are equal to his marginal costs (taxes).[7] And, of course, (8) says nothing at all about group size.

The necessary marginal conditions in (7) allow us to classify all goods only after the solution is attained. Whether or not a particular good is purely private, purely public, or somewhere between these extremes is determined only after the equilibrium values for

---

[7] In Samuelson's diagrammatic presentation, these individual marginal conditions are satisfied, but the diagrammatic construction is more restricted than that contained in his earlier more general model.

the N_j's are known. A good for which the equilibrium value for N_j is large can be classified as containing much "publicness." By contrast, a good for which the equilibrium value of N_j is small can be classified as largely private.

The formal statement of the theory of clubs presented above can be supplemented and clarified by geometrical analysis, although the nature of the construction implies somewhat more restrictive models.

Consider a good that is known to contain, under some conditions, a degree of "publicness." For simplicity, think of a swimming pool. We want to examine the choice calculus of a single person, and we shall assume that other persons about him, with whom he may or may not choose to join in some club-like arrangement, are identical in all respects with him. As a first step, take a facility of one-unit size, which we define in terms of physical output supplied.

On the ordinate of Figure 1, we measure total cost and total

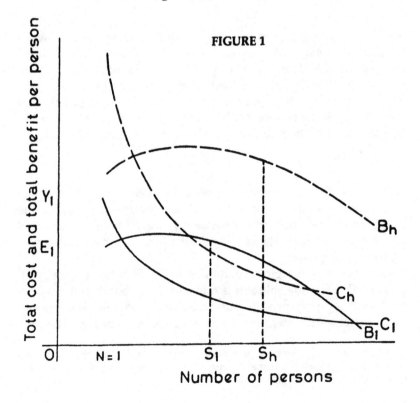

FIGURE 1

benefit per person, the latter derived from the individual's own evaluation of the facility in terms of the numeraire, dollars. On the abscissa, we measure the number of persons in possible sharing arrangements. Define the full cost of the one-unity facility to be Y_1, and the reference individual's evaluation of this facility as a purely private consumption good to be E_1. As is clear from the construction as drawn, he will not choose to purchase the good. If the single person is required to meet the full cost, he will not be able to enjoy the benefits of the good. Any enjoyment of the facility requires the organization of some co-operative-collective sharing arrangement.[8]

Two functions may now be traced in Figure 1, remaining within the one-unit restriction on the size of the facility. A total benefit function and a total cost function confronting the single individual may be derived. As more persons are allowed to share in the enjoyment of the facility, of given size, the benefit evaluation that the individual places on the good will, after some point, decline. There may, of course, be both an increasing and a constant range of the total benefit function, but at some point congestion will set in, and his evaluation of the good will fall. There seems little doubt that the total benefit curve, shown as B_1, will exhibit the concavity property as drawn for goods that involve some commonality in consumption.[9]

The bringing of additional members into the club also serves to reduce the cost that the single person will face. Since, by our initial simplifying assumption, all persons here are identical, symmetrical cost sharing is suggested. In any case, the total cost per person will fall as additional persons join the group, under any cost-

[8]The sharing arrangement need not be either co-operative or governmental in form. Since profit opportunities exist in all such situations, the emergence of profit-seeking firms can be predicted in those settings where legal structures permit, and where this organizational form possesses relative advantages. (Cf. R. H. Coase, "The Nature of the Firm," *Economica*, vol. IV (1937), pp. 386–405.) For purposes of this paper, such firms are one form of club organization, with co-operatives and public arrangements representing other forms. Generally speaking, of course, the choice among these forms should be largely determined by efficiency considerations.

[9]The geometrical model here applies only to such goods. Essentially the same analysis may, however, be extended to apply to cases where "congestion," as such, does not appear. For example, goods that are produced at decreasing costs, even if their consumption is purely private, may be shown to require some sharing arrangements in an equilibrium or optimal organization.

sharing scheme. As drawn in Figure 1, symmetrical sharing is assumed and the curve, C_1, traces the total cost function, given the one-unit restriction on the size of the facility.[10]

For the given size of the facility, there will exist some optimal size of club. This is determined at the point where the derivatives of the total cost and total benefit functions are equal, shown as S_1 in Figure 1, for the one-unit facility. Consider now an increase in the size of the facility. As before, a total cost curve and a total benefit curve may be derived, and an optimal club size determined. One other such optimum is shown at S_h, for a quantity of goods upon which the curves C_h and B_h are based. Similar constructions can be carried out for every possible size of facility; that is, for each possible quantity of good.

A similar construction may be used to determine optimal goods quantity for each possible size of club; this is illustrated in Figure 2. On the ordinate, we measure here total costs and total benefits confronting the individual, as in Figure 1. On the abscissa, we measure physical size of the facility, quantity of good, and for each assumed size of club membership we may trace total cost and total benefit functions. If we first examine the single-member club, we may well find that the optimal goods quantity is zero; the total cost function may increase more rapidly than the total benefit function from the outset. However, as more persons are added, the total costs to the single person fall; under our symmetrical sharing assumption, they will fall proportionately. The total benefit functions here will slope upward to the right but after some initial range they will be concave downward and at some point will reach a maximum. As club size is increased, benefit functions will shift generally downward beyond the initial non-congestion range, and the point of maximum benefit will move to the right. The construction of Figure 2 allows us to derive an optimal goods quantity for each size of club; Q_k is one such quantity for club size $N = K$.

---

[10]For simplicity, we assume that an additional "membership" in the club involves the addition of one separate person. The model applies equally well, however, for those cases where cost shares are allocated proportionately with predicted usage. In this extension, an additional "membership" would really amount to an additional consumption unit. Membership in the swimming club could, for example, be defined as the right to visit the pool one time each week. Hence, the person who plans to make two visits per week would, in this modification, hold two memberships. This qualification is not, of course, relevant under the strict world-of-equals assumption, but it indicates that the theory need not be so restrictive as it might appear.

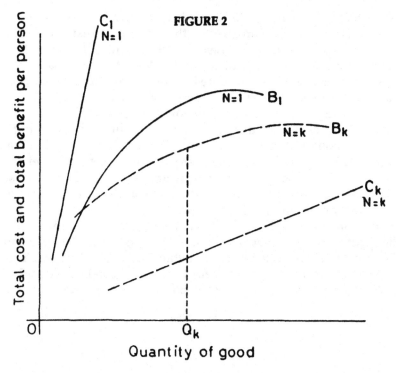

FIGURE 2

The results derived from Figures 1 and 2 are combined in Figure 3. Here the two variables to be chosen, goods quantity and club size, are measured on the ordinate and the abscissa respectively. The values for optimal club size for each goods quantity, derived from Figure 1, allow us to plot the curve, N_{opt}, in Figure 3. Similarly, the values for optimal goods quantity, for each club size, derived from Figure 2, allow us to plot the curve, Q_{opt}.

The intersection of these two curves, N_{opt} and Q_{opt}, determines the position of full equilibrium, G. The individual is in equilibrium both with respect to goods quantity and to group size, for the good under consideration. Suppose, for example, that the sharing group is limited to size, N_k. The attainment of equilibrium with respect to goods quantity, shown by Q_k, would still leave the individual desirous of shifting the size of the membership so as to attain position L. However, once the group increases to this size, the individual prefers a larger quantity of the good, and so on, until G is attained.

Figure 3 may be interpreted as a standard preference map

depicting the tastes of the individual for the two components, goods quantity and club size for the sharing of that good. The curves, N_{opt} and Q_{opt}, are lines of optima, and G is the highest attainable level for the individual, the top of his ordinal utility mountain. Since these curves are lines of optima within an individual preference system, successive choices must converge in G.

It should be noted that income-price constraints have already been incorporated in the preference map through the specific sharing assumptions that are made. The tastes of the individual depicted in Figure 3 reflect the post-payment or net relative evaluations of the two components of consumption at all levels. Unless additional constraints are imposed on the model, he must move to the satiety point in this construction.

It seems clear that under normal conditions both of the curves in Figure 3 will slope upward to the right, and that they will lie in approximately the relation to each other as therein depicted. This reflects the fact that, normally for the type of good considered in this example, there will exist a complementary rather than a

FIGURE 3

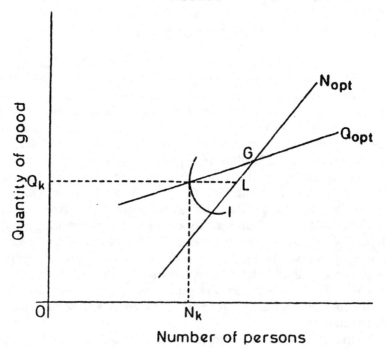

substitute relationship between increasing the quantity of the good and increasing the size of the sharing group.

This geometrical model can be extended to cover goods falling at any point along the private-public spectrum. Take the purely public good as the first extreme case. Since, by definition, congestion does not occur, each total benefit curve, in Figure 1, becomes horizontal. Thus, optimal club size, regardless of goods quantity, is infinite. Hence, full equilibrium is impossible of attainment; equilibrium only with respect to goods quantity can be reached, defined with respect to the all-inclusive finite group. In the construction of Figure 3, the N curve cannot be drawn. A more realistic model may be that in which, at goods-quantity equilibrium, the limitations on group size impose an inequality. For example, in Figure 3, suppose that the all-inclusive group is a size, N_k. Congestion is indicated as being possible over small sizes of facility, but, if an equilibrium quantity is provided, there is no congestion, and, in fact, there remain economics to scale in club size. The situation at the most favourable attainable position is, therefore, in all respects equivalent to that confronted in the base of the good that is purely public under the more restricted definition.

Consider now the purely private good. The appropriate curves here may be shown in Figure 4. The individual, with his income-price constraints is able to attain the peak of his ordinal preference mountain without the necessity of calling upon his fellows to join him in sharing arrangements. Also, the benefits that he receives from the good may be so exclusively his own that these would largely disappear if others were brought in to share them. Hence, the full equilibrium position, G, lies along the vertical from the N = 1 member point. Any attempt to expand the club beyond this point will reduce the utility of the individual.[11]

[11]The construction suggests clearly that the optimal club size, for any quantity of good, will tend to become smaller as the real income of an individual is increased. Goods that exhibit some "publicness" at low income levels will, therefore, tend to become "private" as income levels advance. This suggests that the number of activities that are organized optimally under co-operative collective sharing arrangements will tend to be somewhat larger in low-income communities than in high-income communities, other things equal. There is, of course, ample empirical support for this rather obvious conclusion drawn from the model. For example, in American agricultural communities thirty years ago heavy equipment was communally shared among many farms, normally on some single owner-lease-rental arrangement. Today, substantially the same equipment will be found on each farm,

FIGURE 4

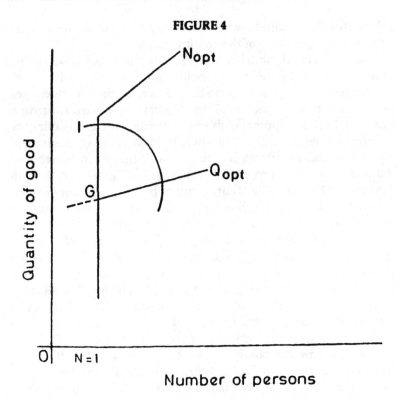

The geometrical construction implies that the necessary marginal conditions are satisfied at unique equilibrium values for both goods quantity and club size. This involves an oversimplification that is made possible only through the assumptions of specific cost-sharing schemes and identity among individuals. In order to generalize the results, these restrictions must be dropped. We know that, given any group of individuals who are able to evaluate both consumption shares and the costs of congestion, there exists some set of marginal prices, goods quantity, and club size that will satisfy (7) above. However, the quantity of the good, the size of

---

even though it remains idle for much of its potential working time.

The implication of the analysis for the size of governmental units is perhaps less evident. In so far as governments are organized to provide communal facilities, the size of such units measured by the number of citizens, should decline as income increases. Thus, in the affluent society, the local school district may, optimally, be smaller than in the poor society.

the club sharing in its consumption, and the cost-sharing arrangements must be determined simultaneously. And, since there are always "gains from trade" to be realized in moving from non-optimal to optimal positions, distributional considerations must be introduced. Once these are allowed to be present, the final "solution" can be located at any one of a sub-infinity of points on the Pareto welfare surface. Only through some quite arbitrarily chosen conventions can standard geometrical constructions be made to apply.

The approach used above has been to impose at the outset a set of marginal prices (tax-prices, if the good is supplied publicly), translated here into shares or potential shares in the costs of providing separate quantities of a specific good for groups of varying sizes. Hence, the individual confronts a predictable set of marginal prices for each quantity of the good at every possible club size, independently of his own choices on these variables. With this convention, and the world-of-equals assumption, the geometrical solution becomes one that is relevant for any individual in the group. If we drop the world-of-equals assumption, the construction continues to hold without change for the choice calculus of any particular individual in the group. The results cannot, of course, be generalized for the group in this case, since different individuals will evaluate any given result differently. The model remains helpful even here, however, in that it suggests the process through which individual decisions may be made, and it tends to clarify some of the implicit content in the more formal statements of the necessary marginal conditions for optimality.[12]

The theory of clubs developed in this paper applies in the strict sense only to the organization of membership or sharing arrangements where "exclusion" is possible. Insofar as non-exclusion is a characteristic of public goods supply, as Musgrave has suggested,[13]

[12]A note concerning one implicit assumption of the whole analysis is in order at this point. The possibility for the individual to choose among the various scales of consumption sharing arrangements has been incorporated into an orthodox model of individual behaviour. The procedure implies that the individual remains indifferent as to which of his neighbours or fellow citizens join him in such arrangements. In other words, no attempt has been made to allow for personal selectivity or discrimination in the models. To incorporate this element, which is no doubt important in many instances, would introduce a wholly new dimension into the analysis, and additional tools to those employed here would be required.

[13]See R. A. Musgrave, *The Theory of Public Finance*, New York, 1959.

the theory of clubs is of limited relevance. Nevertheless, some implications of the theory for the whole excludability question may be indicated. If the structure of property rights is variable, there would seem to be few goods the services of which are non-excludable, solely due to some physical attributes. Hence, the theory of clubs is, in one sense, a theory of optimal exclusion, as well as one of inclusion. Consider the classic lighthouse case. Variations in property rights, broadly conceived, could prohibit boat operators without "light licenses" from approaching the channel guarded by the light. Physical exclusion is possible, given sufficient flexibility in property law, in almost all imaginable cases, including those in which the interdependence lies in the act of consuming itself. Take the single person who gets an inoculation, providing immunization against a communicable disease. In so far as this action exerts external benefits on his fellows, the person taking the action could be authorized to collect charges from all beneficiaries under sanction of the collectivity.

This is not, of course, to suggest that property rights will, in practice, always be adjusted to allow for optimal exclusion. If they are not, the "free rider" problem arises. This prospect suggests one issue of major importance that the analysis of this paper has neglected, the question of costs that may be involved in securing agreements among members of sharing groups. If individuals think that exclusion will not be fully possible, that they can expect to secure benefits as free riders without really becoming full-fledged contributing members of the club, they may be reluctant to enter voluntarily into cost-sharing arrangements. This suggests that one important means of reducing the costs of securing voluntary co-operative agreements is that of allowing for more flexible property arrangements and for introducing excluding devices. If the owner of a hunting preserve is allowed to prosecute poachers, then prospective poachers are much more likely to be willing to pay for the hunting permits in advance.

11. The Problem of Externality

Carl J. Dahlman

I. Introduction

On the modern research agenda externalities occupy a rather prominent position. The increasing complexity of modern technology and society seems to create yet additional unwanted side effects that require classification on a lengthening list of externalities. However, externalities are of interest not only as current policy issues but also from a more theoretical point of view. Using Pigou's terminology, we say that when an externality is present there is a divergence between private and social cost. We interpret this to mean that when all voluntary contractual arrangements have been entered into by market transactors, there still remain some interactions that ought to be internalized but which the market forces left to themselves cannot cope with. This is the basis, for example, for the assertion of Buchanan and Stubblebine that "externality has been, and is, central to the neoclassical critique of market organization."[1] Without interference in the price mechanism, some transactions that would be beneficial are not carried out. Two conclusions follow: first, that since market forces by themselves are unable to eliminate the remaining inefficiencies, some government action is automatically necessitated; second, a conceptually feasible alternative to government action is that, through a suitable

Reprinted, by permission, from *Journal of Law and Economics* 22 (April 1979): 141–62.

I would like to thank the following for helpful discussions or for reading and commenting on earlier drafts of this paper: Kenneth Arrow, Daniel Bromley, John Cogan, Robert Deacon, Harold Demsetz, Stephen Ferris, Robert Haveman, Jack Hirshleifer, David Kiefer, Axel Leijonhufvud, Ezra Mishan, and participants in the Law and Economics Workshop at UCLA and the Applied Welfare Workshop at the University of Wisconsin, Madison. Any remaining errors are, of course, my responsibility.

[1]James M. Buchanan & W. C. Stubblebine, "Externality," 29 *Economica* 371 (n.s. 1962).

establishment of appropriate markets, economic agents can be made to take into account the side effects they generate.[2]

One may then inquire why market transactors are unable to make the emittor of an externality internalize the costs of his actions. The only reason why wealth-maximizing economic agents do not undertake these transactions must be that the cost of carrying out the actual transaction is greater than the expected benefit. Ultimately, the relevance of externalities must lie in the fact that they indicate the presence of some transaction costs. For if there were no costs of transacting, then the potential Pareto improvement could be realized by costless bargaining between self-interested economic agents.[3] Transaction costs are therefore a necessary condition for the persistence of unwanted effects from externalities, for with zero transaction costs side effects will be internalized and will not negatively affect resource allocation. The conclusion is thus unambiguous: in the theory of externalities, transaction costs are the root of all evil. But for transaction costs,

[2]See, for example, Kenneth J. Arrow, "The Organization of Economic Activity: Issues Pertinent to the Choice of Market vs. Non-market Allocation," in *Public Expenditure and Policy Analysis* 59–73 (Robert H. Haveman & Julius Margolis, eds., 1970).

[3]Calabresi puts this point nicely: "Thus if one assumes rationality, no transaction costs, and no legal impediment to bargaining, *all* misallocations of resources would be fully cured in the market by bargains. Far from surprising, this statement is tautological, at least if one accepts any of the various definitions of misallocation. These ultimately come down to a statement akin to the following: A misallocation exists when there is available a possible reallocation in which all of those who would lose from the reallocation could be fully compensated by those who would gain, and, at the end of this compensation process, there would still be someone who would be better off than before. . . . If people are rational, bargains are costless, and there are no legal impediments to bargains, transactions will *ex hypothesis* occur to the point where bargains can no longer improve the situation; to the point, in short of optimal resource allocation. We can, therefore, state as an axiom the proposition that all externalities can be internalized and all misallocations, even those created by legal structures, can be remedied by the market, except to the extent that transactions cost money or the structure itself creates some impediments to bargaining." Guido Calabresi, "Transaction Costs, Resource Allocation, and Liability Rules: A Comment," 11 *J. Law & Econ.* 67, 68 (1968). Stigler's remark on this is worth repeating: "If this proposition strikes you as incredible on first hearing, join the club. The world of zero transaction costs turns out to be as strange as the physical world would be without friction. Monopolies would be compensated to act like competitors, and insurance companies would not exist." George J. Stigler, "The Law and Economics of Public Policy: A Plea to the Scholars." 1 *J. Legal Stud.* 1, 12 (1972).

such perversions of the invisible hand could not even occur much less persist.[4]

However straightforward this may seem, in contemporary literature there appear to be two radically different approaches to the problem of externalities, delineated from each other both by conflicting theoretical foundations and by the policy implications derived from them. On one hand, there is the modern welfare theory, based on general equilibrium analysis, which attempts to evaluate actual economic performance by the measuring rod provided by the maximum welfare solution derived from a Walrasian general equilibrium system. On the other, there is the view of externalities, originating with the Coase theorem, according to which it is neither possible to identify the real source of an externality nor to establish uniquely the fact that there even is an externality if the possibility of bargaining and side payments is taken into account.

The task attempted in this paper is essentially twofold. First, although the role of transaction costs in the generation of externalities is well understood, no systematic analysis as yet exists of exactly what kinds of transaction costs are necessary to generate externalities. Thus, this paper will analyze the concept of transaction costs as it pertains specifically to externalities. Section II attempts a suitable classification of transaction costs, and Section III extends the analysis to the modern general equilibrium approach to externalities. Two major conclusions emerge: first, that it is not possible to specify any class of transaction costs that—given

[4]Francis M. Bator, "The Anatomy of Market Failure," 72 *Q. J. Econ.* 351, 357 (1958), makes a distinction between three classes of market failure: externalities, monopoly, and public goods. It is therefore interesting to note that both monopoly and public goods can be treated as subcategories of externalities. Demsetz makes the following observation: "A world in which negotiating costs are zero is a world in which no monopolistic inefficiencies will be present, simply because the buyer and seller both can profit from negotiations that result in a reduction and elimination of inefficiencies." Harold Demsetz, "Why Regulate Utilities?" 11 *J. Law & Econ,* 55, 61 (1968). Guido Calabresi, *supra* note 3, at 70, makes this same point: "Assuming no transaction costs, those who lose from the relative underproduction of monopolies could bribe the monopolists to produce more." The point is that the negative effects of monopolies occur because market power allows a producer to deviate from the competitive allocation, and the result is a lower level of satisfaction for consumers. This is an externality in consumption: the utility of the consumers is affected by the utility-maximizing behavior of the monopolist and transaction costs prevent a change in the activities of the monopolist. The case is the same with respect to public goods.

individual wealth-maximizing behavior under well-specified constraints that include exchange costs—generate externalities that constitute deviations from an *attainable* optimum; second, that the concept of externalities—insofar as the word is intended to connote, as Buchanan and Stubblebine would have it, the existence of an analytically proven market failure—is void of any positive content but, on the contrary, simply constitutes a normative judgment about the role of government and the ability of markets to establish mutually beneficial exchanges. That is to say, it cannot be shown with purely conceptual analysis that markets do not handle externalities: any such assertion necessitates an *assumption* that the government can do better. That this assumption is valid cannot be proved analytically, and it follows that market failure is an essentially normative judgment.

The second task attempted in this paper is to draw the conclusions implicit in the analysis of Section III about the relationship between the Coase theory of externalities and the standard Pigou tradition. A widespread misconception exists that the Coase analysis implies that no government policy is desirable and that the Pigou tradition shows the optimality of certain taxes. It is shown in Section IV that, if the implications of individual wealth maximization under known constraints are drawn correctly, it is really the Pigou tradition that logically suggests no policy, whereas the Coase analysis does give rise to positive suggestions which could assign an important role to the government.

II. Transaction Costs and Externalities

In view of the crucial role of transaction costs in generating externalities, it is remarkable that no systematic analysis exists of the nature of transaction costs. In recent years the concept has achieved a rather prominent place. On the one hand, it has become a catch-all phrase for unspecified interferences with the price mechanism; on the other, it has been shown that an understanding of this concept is necessary for the foundations of monetary theory.[5] In current literature there appear to be three possible interpretations of the nature of transaction costs: the immediate question is if any or all of these interpretations generate externali-

---

[5]This was brought to the attention of modern eyes by Robert W. Clower, "Foundations of Monetary Theory," reprinted in *Monetary Theory* (Robert W. Clower, ed., 1969), and his introduction to the same.

ties as deviations from an otherwise attainable optimum. We proceed by assuming the existence of some side effects, namely a difference between social and private costs, and ask what sort of transaction costs are consistent with the origination and perpetuation of this situation.

The perhaps most common notion of transaction costs among mathematical economists is one which is comparatively simple to handle with mathematical tools: a fixed proportion of whatever is being traded is assumed to disappear in the transaction itself.[6] This idea is then employed to show that a specific medium of exchange may have lower transaction costs than any other good in the economy so that a smaller amount of real resources is consumed in the exchange process by switching from barter to money.

What is noteworthy about this concept of transaction costs is that in no significant way does it differ from a regular transportation cost. In the process of moving resources from one location to another—in this particular context from one person to another—a certain amount of the goods to be traded is used up. The conditions that are put on transaction costs, in order to prove existence of a transaction-cost-constrained equilibrium, are then just the same as those normally put on transportation costs: a well-defined convex production set is assumed. Just as self-interested individuals will select the cheapest mode of transportation, it is possible to show that they may choose to use a medium of exchange as an alternative to barter if less resources are used as a consequence. It is difficult to see, however, that anything significant is added to the traditional treatment of transportation costs in the already existing literature: the strictly proportional costs of transaction convey nothing of significance that is not already known from earlier analysis. The specific application to money is new, and that is all.

Furthermore, it is difficult to see in what significant way ordinary transportation costs or proportional transaction costs differ from regular costs of production. Moving resources from one

[6]See, for example, Duncan K. Foley, "Economic Equilibrium with Costly Marketing," 2 J. Econ. Theory 276 (1970); F. Hahn, "On Transaction Costs, Inessential Sequence Economies, and Money." 40 Rev. Econ. Stud. 449 (1973); Mordecai Kurz, "Equilibrium with Transaction Costs and Money in a Single Market Exchange," 7 J. Econ. Theory 418 (1974); Jürg Niehans, "Money and Barter in General Equilibrium with Transaction Costs." 61 Am. Econ. Rev. 773 (1971); id., "Interest and Credit in General Equilibrium with Transactions Costs," 63 Am. Econ. Rev. 548 (1975).

location to another or from one person to another will presumably only be done if there is a net increase in the evaluation of the resources at the two different locations. Fundamentally, therefore, both transportation costs and proportional transaction costs are productive in precisely the same way that resources used up in the physical transformation of inputs into outputs are productive—indeed, they could be treated in an identical manner with no loss of information. All that is required is to interpret an exchange as a productive activity requiring certain resources in a specified technological relationship.

Can this notion of transaction costs be shown to generate externalities as well as be a medium of exchange? Consider a simple example: a steel producer generates smoke that fouls the drying linen of a neighboring laundry owner. The laundry owner knows the costs of transacting with the steel producer to make him reduce the smoke outpour, and these costs stand in direct proportion to the amount of smoke reduction desired or, what is the same thing, to the value of the clean laundry the owner estimates he will get from the smoke reduction. Clearly, if these costs are lower than the expected benefits the smoke output will be reduced, otherwise not. Suppose it is not: the laundry owner endures the smoke. Is this a Pareto-relevant externality?[7] Clearly not, for the equilibrium that is reached is already a Pareto optimum—it is too costly to bargain for a reduction of the smoke, and hence the market participants and society are better off if the smoke is left to soil the laundry. This conclusion is unaffected by the problems of small or large number cases: in principle, it does not matter if we talk about the costs of eliminating the smog in the Los Angeles basin, for example. If it is too costly for the smog breathers to pay the smog creators to reduce their emissions, then the observed amount of smog is quite clearly consistent with a Pareto optimum. Hence, we must conclude that, if transaction costs are well known to the agents involved and strictly proportional to the value of the transaction, there will be no externalities in the sense of a deviation from an optimum. Proportional transaction costs do not generate

[7]James M. Buchanan & W. C. Stubblebine, *supra* note 1, make this distinction between Pareto-relevant and Pareto-irrelevant externalities. With the latter they understand side effects that are too costly to remove. They also assert that the modern treatment of externalities is concerned with Pareto-relevant externalities, namely, side effects that can be shown to be removed at a net positive benefit for society.

Pareto-relevant externalities, but only the trivial Pareto-irrelevant variety.

The second version of the notion of transaction costs employed in modern literature is one which is conceptually equal in simplicity to the fixed-proportions variety, but one which is more tricky to handle mathematically. It concerns the idea that a trade may be costless to carry through, but may still require resources to organize: there may be setup costs associated with each exchange. Such a cost is no longer proportional to the trade itself, but is a fixed cost which is independent of the amount to be exchanged. This introduces an important nonconvexity, and havoc is wrought with existence and uniqueness proofs. In dealing with this, mathematical economists have been forced to resort to radical measures. One such measure[8] consists of taking the closed convex hull of the nonconvex set and replacing the problematic nonconvexity with its closest approximation of a well-behaved convex set according to some specified measure. It can then be shown that, if the new convexified set does not differ substantially from the nonconvex one, there will exist an approximate equilibrium in spite of the nonconvexity, and markets will clear except for a negligible fraction. It follows that the resource misallocations resulting from such setup costs are small if the nonconvexities are small in relation to the size of the economy.[9]

Several observations are in order. Although it is nice to know that a problem can be ignored if its consequences are insignificant, it is not clear that this is relevant with respect to fixed setup costs—in fact, mathematical economists would seem to agree on the point that such costs are of great importance. The fact that present mathematical techniques make it impossible to handle this version of the transaction-cost concept does not appear to be of any earth-shattering significance: the economics profession has shown itself quite content with this state of affairs for a long time. For it is difficult to see any significant difference between the setup cost of an exchange, called a transaction cost, and the setup cost of the

[8]As proposed by Walter Perrin Heller, "Transactions with Set-Up Costs," 4 *J. Econ. Theory* 465 (1972).

[9]Although it is possible to give a precise mathematical meaning to the phrase "small in relation to the economy," this has no operational interpretation. Thus we cannot turn to mathematical economists to tell us if setup costs can be neglected in determining policy towards externalities in modern capitalistic economies, for example.

basic unit of production, or the fixed cost of the firm.[10] We have known for a long time that such fixed costs are inconsistent with available existence proofs, and have reconciled ourselves to looking away from the problem of the indeterminate firm size in general equilibrium theory, while retaining the notion of fixed costs in partial equilibrium analysis. Furthermore, the parallel to the fixed cost in production theory points to the significant observation that the fixed setup cost of an exchange is not really fixed at all. Just as the firm can choose any level of its fixed costs, so may the individual transactor choose betwen different trades with different setup costs—that is, the fixed cost in any trade is really endogenously determined as a known and adjusted cost of "producing" the exchange. There is already a well-developed body of economic doctrine that can be brought to bear on this problem, and the difficulties involved seem to concern the limitations of present mathematical techniques rather than the logic of economic ideas.

Can this version of the transaction-cost concept be used to account for the presence of externalities? If an externality exists between two agents but it would cost too much in terms of resources to set up the transaction between them that would make the emittor internalize the costs of the side effects of his actions, then it follows that the externality is a Pareto-irrelevant one. Reverting once again to the simplistic example of the laundry and the steel producer, this means that if it costs the laundry owner too much to get the steel manufacturer to reduce his emissions, he will rather endure the smoke. Again, this is a conclusion that is unaffected by the number of transactors involved. If it costs smog breathers too much to set up the exchange that induces the emittors to reduce the outpour of pollutants, then it follows necessarily that, the funny smell notwithstanding, the optimal level of pollution has been achieved.

Neither of these definitions of transaction costs is then consistent with our accepted ideas of what is to be understood by externalities. However, there is a third line of thought on transaction costs which may be found in Coase's definition:

> In order to carry out a market transaction it is necessary to discover who it is that one wishes to deal with, to inform people that one wishes to deal and on what terms, to conduct negotia-

---

[10]See Jack Hirshleifer, *Price Theory and Applications* 254–58 (1976), for an elaboration on this theme.

tions leading up to a bargain, to draw up the contract, to undertake the inspection needed to make sure that the terms of the contract are being observed, and so on.[11]

Since it would appear that this definition is even more difficult to handle with mathematical tools than the previous one, it is consequently no surprise that this notion is prevalent among nonmathematical writers—notably those who treat issues in law and economics.

It is necessary to take the definition of transaction costs by Coase a little futher. A natural classification of transaction costs consistent with his definition can be obtained from the different phases of the exchange process itself. In order for an exchange between two parties to be set up it is necessary that the two search each other out, which is costly in terms of time and resources. If the search is successful and the parties make contact they must inform each other of the exchange opportunity that may be present, and the conveying of such information will again require resources. If there are several economic agents on either side of the potential bargain to be struck, some costs of decision making will be incurred before the terms of trade can be decided on. Often such agreeable terms can only be determined after costly bargaining between the parties involved. After the trade has been decided on, there will be the costs of policing and monitoring the other party to see that his obligations are carried out as determined by the terms of the contract, and of enforcing the agreement reached. These, then, represent the first approximation to a workable concept of transaction costs: search and information costs, bargaining and decision costs, policing and enforcement costs.

Yet, this functional taxonomy of different transaction costs is unnecessarily elaborate: fundamentally, the three classes reduce to a single one—for they all have in common that they represent resource losses due to lack of information. Both search and information costs owe their existence to imperfect information about the existence and location of trading opportunities or about the quality or other characteristics of items available for trade. The case is the same for bargaining and decision costs: these represent resources spent in finding out the desire of economic agents to participate in trading at certain prices and conditions. What is being revealed in a bargaining situation is information about will-

[11]R. H. Coase, "The Problem of Social Cost," 3 *J. Law & Econ.* 1, 15 (1960).

ingness to trade on certain conditions, and decision costs are resources spent in determining whether the terms of the trade are mutually agreeable. Policing and enforcement costs are incurred because there is lack of knowledge as to whether one (or both) of the parties involved in the agreement will violate his part of the bargain: if there were adequate foreknowledge on his part, these costs could be avoided by contractual stipulations or by declining to trade with agents who would be known to avoid fulfilling their obligations. Therefore, it is really necessary to talk only about one type of transaction cost: resource losses incurred due to imperfect information.

In the modern treatment of uncertainty, the individual is considered to associate his uncertain choice variables with a subjective probability distribution, described by its mean and variance, over all possible states of the world. This treatment of the problem then presupposes that the individual agent has stable probability estimates of finding someone to trade with, of that person being costly to bargain with, of that party being inclined to cheat on the terms of the agreement. In the case of externalities this implies that some unwanted side effects remain because of the uncertainty associated with undertaking the transaction that would eliminate them.

Reverting to our simple laundry-smoke example, the laundry owner in deciding whether to transact with the smoke emittor to curtail his outpour may not be certain about the costs of doing so. We may then envision four cases, defined according to whether the laundry owner (i) has correct or incorrect subjective probability estimates,[12] and (ii) decides to endure or transact away the smoke. This can be illustrated as in Figure 1.

In case I, the laundry owner correctly anticipates the costs of bargaining to be low enough for him to gain from reducing the

FIGURE 1

		Expectations	
		Correct	Incorrect
Smoke	Reduced	I	III
	Endured	II	IV

[12]Strictly speaking, there can be no "correct" or "incorrect" probability estimates when probabilities are purely subjective, but only when there is some objective "truth" that can be ascertained. With correct probability estimates we may then understand stable rather than changing subjective estimates.

smoke outpour from the steel mill: the externality becomes internalized by the steel operator. In case II, he correctly anticipates the cost of smoke reduction would be too high: he thus lives with the smoke. The externality is now internalized by the laundry operator, and there is no inoptimality problem. In case III, the laundry owner decides to bargain for reduction in smoke outpour but finds in the process of bargaining and policing the agreement that it cost him too much to do so.[13] In case IV, he decides to live with the smoke in the belief that it would cost too much to reduce it but is incorrect: he would have gained from reducing it in view of the costs of transacting with the steel operator.

We have already noted that in cases I and II there is no Pareto-relevant externality remaining; the question remains whether there is one in cases III and IV. In case number III there is obviously no Pareto-relevant side effect remaining; on the contrary, there is too little smoke. The laundry owner lost by having the smoke reduced, so total income is lower in case III than it would have been if the smoke had been endured. In case IV, however, the laundry owner should have bargained for a reduction in smoke outpour but failed to do so. This is then the only case that can qualify as a potential externality.

From the point of view of the laundry owner, it would not appear that it is a mistake to endure the smoke: given the information that he has at his disposal, he performs his constrained optimization and does nothing. His information is incomplete or wrong, so he makes the wrong decision: given the correct information there is a loss of income from the enduring of the smoke, and the situation looks very much like what we associate with an externality. Yet that interpretation is fundamentally incorrect, for, with the information that the laundry owner has at his disposal when he makes the decision, he decides correctly, as constrained optimization procedures would have it. It is only later that he may realize that he has made a mistake, in view of additional information that was not available at the time. This can be regarded as an externality only if you assume that "he should have known better" or that there is someone else who does know better. This issue will be dealt with in the next section.

In summary, it would seem, then, that no kind of known

---

[13]For obvious reasons, we may disregard the alternative possibility of the actual costs being lower than the expected.

transaction costs can possibly generate anything looking like a Pareto-relevant externality. Once the logical implications of bargaining under transaction costs are fully accepted, it is seen that all existing side effects are internalized one way or the other. An assertion that externalities represent a deviation from an optimal allocation of resources then implies that the analyst considers himself in possession of superior information than what is available to market transactors: he knows the "true" probabilities, as it were. The issue of whether an alternative and improved allocation of resources exists is then seen to hinge on whether there is available relevant information about better alternatives.

III. Pareto Optimality and Externalities

From a doctrinal standpoint, it would seem to be consistent with the treatments of Marshall and Pigou, the originators of the concept of externality, to conduct the analysis within a strict partial equilibrium context. Yet, in modern treatises, partial equilibrium analysis is not the normal methodology for dealing with externalities. "We are all Walrasians now," almost anybody from outside the University of Chicago might be expected to say with a confident smile on his face.

Exactly how the partial equilibrium approach to externalities came to be grafted on to the trunk of the general equilibrium tree as a branch of its own is an interesting story that will not be pursued here. It might be conjectured that the demise of the social welfare function had something to do with it: for to understand the distinction between social and private cost it is easy to refer to such a function. That is to say, whenever private agents do not take into account the greater social implications of their actions, we may conceive of a loss of social welfare. But we were told that it was not possible even under reasonable conditions to use that notion, and instead we have resorted to the Pareto optimum of the general equilibrium system as our point of reference for discussing the welfare problems associated with externalities. It is of course possible that social cost in the mind of Pigou is the solution to an appropriately constructed Walrasian model, although this has not been shown. However that may be, for modern purposes it is agreed that the negative effects of externalities are associated with the Pareto optimum as a measuring rod.

The impact of externalities is then shown in the following rather simplistic manner. First, assume a general equilibrium system with appropriate shapes of production and utility functions, one that for every initial endowment yields a unique general equilibrium price vector (call that Model I). Given the distribution of resource ownership in our world, this methodology allows us to conceptualize one Pareto-optimal solution, and only one. Secondly, into this system, introduce externalities, and let the auctioneer grind out the new equilibrium price vector (call that Model II). In general, this vector, and its associated equilibrium allocation of resources, will be different from that of Model I. Hence it follows that externalities imply that the Pareto optimum of Model I is not attained.

This is the positive methodology of modern welfare theory. The only normative judgments that appear to be involved in the conclusion that externalities ought to be eliminated are the ones generally accepted by the economics science that (i) individual preferences alone matter and (ii) the notion of Pareto optimality is at least inoffensive from an ethical standpoint. Given this, we can show that externalities unambiguously imply a distortion.

However, there is also one more strong implication of the analysis: private contracting in markets will not lead to the elimination of the negative influences of externalities. This follows from the simple fact that the allocation in Model II above is different from that of Model I. Hence the policy implication: government intervention is necessary to correct the failure of the market forces. Again, this is thought to be an essentially positive conclusion, void of any judgments as to the proper role of government in a free society.

We may now inquire into the role of transaction costs in this framework. It can then be seen that Model II above, the one with externalities, must contain some transaction costs, for otherwise the Walrasian auctioneer would help self-interested economic agents bargain away the negative effects of the externality. On the other hand, Model I cannot contain any transaction costs, for it is a description of a situation in which no externalities exist and a Pareto optimum is reached. Indeed, we may state that the failure of Model II to be an optimum is due to the presence of transaction costs. Thus it can be seen that the policy implication that the government must intervene rests on the implicit comparison of a world with transaction costs with one with zero transaction costs.

The literature on welfare economics abounds with examples of the use of this methodology. For example, the gauge for measuring monopoly problems is the world of perfect competition, that is, implicitly, the Pareto optimum of a suitable Walrasian framework, or Model I above. In the international trade literature, various distortions are measured as against this same point of reference. Signaling theory asserts that, relative to a world in which information is perfect, our world is suboptimal.[14] In judging the ability of markets to handle the public-goods aspect of information, various authors use as a point of reference a world in which information is a perfectly private good, that is, one in which there are no costs of making users of information pay its value in use.[15] And, naturally, this is the basis for the proof of the optimality of the Pigovian tax rules: they can be shown to establish the resource allocation that would rule in a world of perfect information.[16]

However, it is far from obvious that the point of reference for the misallocation effects of externalities and other distortions ought to be Model I (that is, the Pareto optimum of the Walrasian model with zero transaction costs), for it is a rather well-known fact that the world in which we live is plagued with various kinds of transaction costs. Transfer and setup costs are sometimes observed, and bargaining, decision, and policing costs have been known to enter into private contracting and exchange. It is clear, of course, but of no particular consequence for externality problems, that it would be desirable to reduce such transaction costs, of whatever kind, preferably to zero if that were possible, just as it would be desirable to decrease costs of production in a firm.[17] Surely there must be something more of substance in the reference to the Pareto optimum.

[14]See for example, Kenneth J. Arrow, "Higher Education as a Filter," 2 *J. Public Econ.* 193 (1973); or A. Michael Spence, *Market Signaling Theory* (1974).

[15]As in, for example, Kenneth J. Arrow, "Economic Welfare and the Allocation of Resources for Invention," in *The Rate and Direction of Inventive Activity: Social and Economic Factors* (Nat'l Bureau Econ. Res., 1962). Or similarly, Jack Hirshleifer, "The Private and Social Value of Information and the Reward to Inventive Activity," 61 *Am. Econ. Rev.* 561 (1971).

[16]For a recent proof of this proposition, see the lucid exposition of William J. Baumol & Wallace E. Oates, *The Theory of Environmental Policy* (1975).

[17]This is much like stating that a world in which apples are costly to produce is inoptimal compared to one in which apples are a free good. While obviously true, this observation cannot serve as a foundation for any decisions on resource allocation in the apple industry. Or to take a different simile, it is as though a transportation economist who is asked to calculate the optimal fare structure for a railroad company operating between Los Angeles and New York would say: suppose transportation costs did not exist.

Given the actual costs of transacting observed in our world, the immediate problem is whether we should include such costs in the constraints that specify the Pareto optimal solution from which we measure the distortions due to externalities. There are at least two substantive arguments why this would be a correct approach. The first is given by Buchanan and Stubblebine: not all externalities are Pareto relevant.[18] This implies that in the Pareto optimum not all externalities, whether marginal or inframarginal, should be reduced to zero: we are better off keeping some of them at a positive level. This is not the case in Model I above: in the perfectly competitive solution to a Walrasian model, all side effects are either internalized or eliminated. But the simple fact is that, if there are costs of transacting present in our world, then it may be too costly to eliminate all externalities, so we should preserve some of them in order to reach an optimum. Hence, as a suitable reference point, we ought to use a transaction-cost-constrained model that describes the relevant and attainable optimum, not the irrelevant and unattainable solution to a model with zero transaction costs. The second argument why we ought not to use the world of zero transaction costs as a frame of reference is given by Demsetz in a critique of that particular methodology in Arrow's discussion of the public-goods problems associated with inventions.[19] The point is that it is a logical fallacy to use as a frame of reference a world in which transaction costs are zero, for that world is unattainable, given human behavior in our world. Since it is unattainable, it is clearly incorrect to use it as a frame of reference in judging the welfare implications of actions in our own world with its inherent and unavoidable transaction costs.

Both these arguments are compelling, and they have important consequences for all welfare judgments in economics. If we include costs of transacting in the constraints that describe the conditions under which economic agents perform their individual wealth maximization, we would then describe an attainable optimum, and

[18]James M. Buchanan & W. C. Stubblebine, *supra* note 1, at 375–76.

[19]Harold Demsetz, "Information and Efficiency: Another Viewpoint," 12 *J. Law & Econ.* 1 (1969). Demsetz's comment is on the article on inventive activity by Arrow, cited in note 15 *supra*. In showing that Arrow commits the fallacy of skipping from a world of zero transaction costs, where he derives his theorems, to a world of positive transaction costs, where he (incorrectly) applies these results, Demsetz accuses Arrow of "three logical fallacies—the *grass is always greener fallacy, the fallacy of the free lunch,* and *the people could be different fallacy.*" *Id.* at 2.

this is the one we should use in judging optimality and welfare problems. The immediate question is then in what way this alternative, transaction-cost-constrained equilibrium differs from Model II above. The answer is of course that they would not differ in any way, for Model II is precisely the one that describes the allocation of resources in our present world with its attendant transaction costs. This then, ought to be the attainable optimum that we should strive to achieve. However, that description also contains whatever externalities are observed in the real world. It would seem that if side effects persist they must be of the Pareto-irrelevant variety, for otherwise they would not be observed but transacted away by self-interested economic agents.

The conclusion, unpalatable to many economists, would seem to be that if it exists it must be optimal, and if it does not exist it is because it is too costly, so that is optimal too. If you do not like the smell of the air, seek comfort in the knowledge that it would cost you more than it is worth to you to do away with the stench, for, otherwise, would you not do it? Again, the conclusion is the same whether we talk about large or small number cases—the only difference being that in the former case we introduce an important setup cost of the group of bargainers on one side of the market, or both. Conceptually, the problem is the same: if it is too costly to eliminate, the side effect is optimal. If we include transaction costs in the constraints, this appears to be the unavoidable conundrum we end up in: externalities are irrelevant, monopoly problems do not exist, public goods present no difficulties, and so on.[20]

This conclusion seems inherent in the methodology of the general equilibrium treatment: the point of the paradigm is to establish the conditions under which a system of markets can reach equilibrium simultaneously in all markets. Once the constraints in the form of tastes, technology, endowments, information, costs of transacting, and so forth, all have been suitably specified, the logic of the framework leads to a description of a Pareto optimal equilibrium (if it exists). If the constraints describe our world, then we must conclude that the world is optimal relative to those constraints. The very conceptual framework of the model would seem to make it singularly unsuited for treating welfare and optimality problems.

---

[20]For an enjoyable elaboration around this theme, see E. J. Mishan, "Pangloss on Pollution," 73 *Swedish J. Econ.* 113 (1971).

It is difficult to see, then, how it is possible to prove analytically that the presence of externalities imply welfare problems. Once we realize that externalities can remain uninternalized only if there are costs of transacting, and once we include such costs in the constraints on individual and government behavior, then we cannot show that there are any deviations from an attainable optimum. It is possible, of course, to assert or assume that people will not take into account the greater good of their personal actions. As a matter of fact, this is what is normally done in the welfare literature: the divergence between private and social cost is never proved to exist, but always *initially assumed* to exist. Thus, for example, Pigou:

> The essence of the matter is that one person, A, in the course of rendering services, for which payment is made, to a second person, B, incidentally also renders services or disservices to other persons (not producers of like services) of such a sort *that payment cannot be exacted* from the benefited parties *or compensation enforced* on behalf of the injured parties.[21]

Pigou here simply *assumes* that the costs of exacting compensating payments exceed the benefits, but he does not prove that there is a good reason for assuming that somebody else, outside the market, can do it cheaper or better. Again, at a later point he continues:

> There are a number of other (cases) in which, owing to the technical difficulties of enforcing compensation for incidental disservices, marginal net private product is greater than marginal social net product. Thus, incidental uncharged disservices are rendered to third parties.[22]

The difference between private and social cost is simply *postulated*, and it is not shown that an alternative method, an alternative to private contracting through market exchange, can decrease the costs of internalizing the effects on third parties. If the government, or some other nonmarket force, cannot do it at a cheaper cost than the market, then there is no difference at all between private and social cost. From Pigou's assertion that there is such a difference we must infer that he believes that the government can take the social cost into account better than the market can. But, in

[21]A. C. Pigou, *The Economics of Welfare* 183 (4th ed., 1928).
[22]*Id.* at 185.

the absence of an analytical proof that this is the case, it remains an assertion, to be taken on faith.

If this is what the word externality means, it may be noted how utterly normative the concept is. There is no proof that the market, in the presence of costs of transacting, does not attain an optimum, but a simple assertion: the market leads to an inoptimal solution *relative to what the government can attain.* To make this a reasonable proposition we must *assume* that the government can do better than the market can—and this is the implicit point of reference according to which we judge market performance. This is to be taken on faith since there is no well-specified cost-benefit analysis of a particular government policy that can eliminate the externality and equalize private and social cost. Furthermore, it is not a qualified statement: on the contrary, it is a quite general one. It says that, when there are externalities, the market does not work, but the government does—no matter how small or large the externalities, no matter what the structure of transaction costs is, no matter how many agents are involved in the generation of externalities. In the presence of side effects, markets fail.

It may then be seen that *any* kind of transaction cost is capable of generating an "externality." If some transactions do not occur because of a proportional transaction cost, an externality may exist—*if* we can show that the government knows a better way of internalizing the side effect than private parties do. Or if there is a setup cost that prevents internalization, there may be an externality—*if* the government can find a better way than markets. Or if uncertainty and imperfect information prevent certain transactions from occurring, the side effect may be there—*if* we can assume that the government knows better. However, if we cannot assume that the government knows better, then there is no externality.

The conclusion is rather startling: transaction costs per se have nothing to do with externalities. What is involved is a value judgment: if you believe that markets internalize everything, you will believe that externalities do not exist; on the other hand, if you believe that markets do not internalize side effects, you will believe in the persistence of externalities as deviations from an attainable optimum. This is not science; it is metaphysics: value judgments and political goals will enter into the determination of whether externalities occur in our world. You cannot show analytically that the government, in principle and in all cases, handles externalities better than the market; nor can you prove the opposite: it all depends on what point of reference you choose. And *that* is not a question of positive economics. By choosing the appropriate point of reference, the "conclusion" is reached that government intervention (or no government intervention) is optimal. Someone wishing to justify government intervention will choose the competitive equilibrium of Model I as the appropriate point of reference; someone who wants to avoid government intervention will choose Model II instead, with its transaction-cost-constrained equilibrium as the only relevant and attainable optimum. This is not positive economics; it is a political discussion, at least until we can better justify the choice of appropriate reference points.

It is thus doubtful whether the term "externality" has any meaningful interpretation, except as an indicator of the political beliefs and value judgments of the person who uses (or avoids using) the term. However, the further question remains whether we can say anything at all of what kinds of policies, if any, would be desirable to deal with pollution and other matters that economists and politicians alike (and sometimes the two are indistinguishable) are concerned with. This will be dealt with in the next section.

IV. The Policy Issue

The policy implications of the Pigou tradition in modern welfare theory are strong and simple. The argument goes somewhat along the following lines: take as an initial datum the proposition that we can conceptually define a competitive equilibrium, and then demonstrate the fact that in the presence of externalities actual markets, as observed in today's capitalistic economies, for example, do not achieve the Pareto optimum described by the competitive model. Since it can be easily established that in this case markets will not establish an optimum, it follows immediately that the government must do something since there simply is no other alternative.[23] In addition, however, the theory does something more: in the case of externalities, it tells you to impose taxes or

[23]Since there seems to be no alternative, we are prone to take it on faith that the government, with its self-interested bureaucrats and politicians, always is a better decision maker than the individual agent when the invisible hand is performing less than perfectly. The analysis is greatly complicated if we allow for the fact that not all government decisions are Pareto optimal, but are simply acts of utility maximizing agents who have all the policy powers of the government vested in them.

subsidies, of a very special kind, on the emittor of the externality. It can be demonstrated that such a Pigovian tax-subsidy scheme indeed is capable of attaining the equilibrium which is the optimum, at least as long as we assume that it is possible to make the distinction between emittors and recipients.

Modern discussion of tax rules has centered on a different, but equally important, point: with our limited information about production and utility functions, we cannot adequately describe the allocation of the competitive equilibrium so that the Pigovian taxes can be calculated correctly. Given this, the Pigovian taxman must resort to other means to determine the proper rates. Baumol suggests: ". . . given the limited information at our disposal, it is perfectly reasonable to act on the basis of a set of minimum standards of acceptability."[24] Such minimum standards of acceptability can then act as a proxy for the Pareto optimum to be established.

This, of course, dispenses totally with the competitive equilibrium as a point of reference. All that is required is that we tax an activity which we all agree is carried to an extreme, so that we reduce it to an acceptable level. The modern treatment seems to go in this way: first, pretend that there is a competitive equilibrium applicable to our world. Secondly, since we cannot really discern that point of reference, find out by subjective estimation which way the world actually deviates from a perceived optimum; and, thirdly, correct it with taxes to approximate that subjective optimum. However, since that subjective point of reference can only be derived by pure ad hoc value judgments, there can be no *general* proof of the optimality of the implied tax rules. That the tax rules are still optimal follows from the derivation of the "approximate equilibrium": it is defined to comprise "reasonable" standards that we all agree on—and if we all agree on it, it must be optimal. If that is the case one wonders why the notion of the competitive equilibrium is at all necessary—optimality already being presupposed, any method that attains that alternative, attainable resource allocation will necessarily be optimal.

Fortunately, there is another approach to the general problem of externalities that significantly differs from the mainstream analysis. This is the approach originating with Coase,[25] which has

[24]William J. Baumol, "On Taxation and the Control of Externalities," 62 *Am. Econ. Rev.* 318 (1972).

[25]R. H. Coase, *supra* note 11.

introduced several question marks into the standard treatment of externalities. The difficulty lies in finding the exact relationship between the treatment of Coase and that of modern welfare theory with its origins in Pigou. From the discussion of transaction costs in Section II, it is obvious that Coase's notion of this concept is identical to what was labeled transaction costs due to imperfect information. Coase proceeds to show that when there are no costs of transacting, then all externalities will be eliminated, as costless transaction opportunities will allow suitable modifications of trans-actors' behavior so that all undesirable side effects are properly internalized. In this case, it is possible to show that the assignment of liability rules is irrelevant for the allocation of resources in equilibrium, and many authors seem to think this is the most important and controversial conclusion to come out of Coase's treatment. However, it is clear that only an imperfect understanding of the transaction-cost concept can make the nonrelevance of liability rules puzzling. For with zero transaction costs we must now understand zero setup and transfer costs, and also complete and costless information about prices, qualities, and desired transactions, including no cheating and strategic bargaining behavior. That resources in such a case will go to their highest value in use is a trivial consequence: it will not matter who is assigned ownership rights or liability obligations initially, for whoever has the highest relative valuation of any particular resource will offer most for it and will acquire that resource by costless exchange—at least, this will be true insofar as alternative allocations resulting from different wealth distributions may be disregarded. This cannot in any way be a startling result unless the notion of transaction costs is imperfectly understood.[26]

[26]This seems to be the point that Donald H. Regan entirely misses in his "The Problem of Social Costs Revisited," 15 *J. Law & Econ.* 427 (1972). First, he asserts that there is no individual behavior that yields efficient allocation of resources in the presence of externalities. This is clearly wrong, since a Walrasian general equilibrium model with zero transaction costs indeed achieves this result as long as transactors are utility maximizers. Secondly, he asserts that the only context in which Coase's argument makes sense is in a game theoretic setting. He then goes on to show that Coase's results do not hold. What is ironic about this is that he employs no specific definition of transaction costs; however, his examples and his use of game theory show that he implicitly uses the kind of transaction costs that Coase refers to and that we have here labeled information costs. What Regan really does is to show that Coase's results do not hold in the presence of transaction costs—but that is what Coase has said all along. For a formal analysis of these

The important and lasting contribution in Coase's article, in the opinion of this writer, is his focus on the all-important concept of transaction costs as preventing certain trades which otherwise would be mutually beneficial if carried out. This directs the analysis to the heart of the problem rather than to its symptoms: for transaction costs are a necessary condition for deviations from an attainable optimum to persist. The immediate implication, so often overlooked in subsequent writings on Coase's work, is that when there are transaction costs and informational differences between traders, then it may very well matter to whom liabilities and rights are assigned. This directs the analysis to policy matters, which will be taken up after a few observations on the methodological differences between Coase's analysis and modern welfare theory.

It is notable how completely the Coase approach bypasses both the problem of deciding who is the emittor and who is the recipient of an externality and the rather shady distinction between pecuniary and technological externalities so central to the Pigovian tax rules. Perhaps the real significance of the court cases cited by Coase is that the distinction between emittor and recipient of an externality is irrelevant: what matters is whether we achieve a higher-valued output by putting the liability on one or the other of the parties involved, and not who is the "source" of the externality. Since at least two parties are necessarily involved, either may be considered the source. It is noteworthy how the legal profession

---

issues, and for a proof of the invariance proposition, see Kenneth J. Arrow, "The Property Rights Doctrine and Demand Revelation under Incomplete Information" (Technical Report No. 243, Inst. Mathematical Studies Soc. Sci., Stanford Univ., Aug. 1977), esp. at 2–5. Arrow also shows that when information is less than perfect, inoptimalities result. *Id.* at 10–14. Private bargaining can then be shown not to attain the relevant optimum, the solution that Arrow has specified as the optimum. What he seems to disregard, however, is that, if a suboptimal solution is reached, then there will exist incentives for the two parties to exchange, at some positive price, the information that can show why they have reached a suboptimum. It would seem to be implicit in Arrow's treatment—as well as in others—that it is difficult or impossible to make such exchanges, due perhaps to the public-goods aspects of privately owned information or to the problems of authenticating the quality of information for sale. Thus, the reason for the inoptimality is really to be sought in the special characteristics of information as a commodity, bringing us back to the issue that Demsetz, *supra* note 19, has already accused Arrow of mishandling. That is to say, if what Arrow (with the superior information available to the analyst) has chosen as an optimum turns out not to be an optimum at all, then there are no grounds for stating that the outcome of the game is "suboptimal"—for now that point of reference is not allowed any longer.

and the courts have come to grips with this point well before economists. The legal cases referred to by Coase show how courts in the presence of transaction costs have placed the liability sometimes with the "emittor" and sometimes with the "recipient" as these would be identified by an economist trained in modern welfare theory. Nor is the distinction between pecuniary and technological externalities in any way relevant for Coase's arguments: what matters is the role of transaction costs, and how such costs affect the allocation of resources.

Perhaps the distinction between the Coase approach and modern welfare theory can best be understood as being very similar to the one between Walrasian general equilibrium theory and Marshallian partial equilibrium theory. The former uses the reference point of a global Pareto optimum under zero transaction costs, and all externalities are measured as deviations from that optimum. The latter only makes comparative static exercises,[27] and consequently employs marginal analysis in making the judgment of whether resource allocation ought to be changed from some given state or not. Are the costs of altering the current allocation worth the benefits? The answer to this question requires no zero-transaction-cost point of reference.

Many times the Coase analysis has been criticized for seemingly implying that no government action can ever be justified. Yet it is striking that the Coase approach, correctly interpreted, would imply exactly the same results that a correctly amended Pigou analysis would advocate. In the presence of transaction costs, liability assignments and ownership rights will have effects on the allocation of resources. As a consequence, transaction costs may prevent the establishment of a desirable allocation of resources, one that everyone would agree is better than the one attained when transactions are costly. In this case the Coase analysis implies one of two corrective measures: (i) find out if there is a feasible way to decrease the costs of transacting between market agents through government action, or (ii), *if* that is not possible, the analysis would suggest employing taxes, legislative action, standards, prohibitions, agencies, or whatever else can be thought of that will achieve the allocation of resources we have already

---

[27]On these and related issues, see Axel Leijonhufvud, "Varieties of Price Theory: What Microfoundations for Macrotheory?" (UCLA Working Paper, No. 44, 1974); and his forthcoming Marshall lectures.

decided is preferred. The implication of status quo is simply not there: the theory says to find practicable ways of diminishing transaction costs, by whatever kind of action is necessary, including governmental action.[28] In this way, the Coase recommendations arrive at exactly the same policy implications that the correct Pigou analysis does—the one that dispenses with the competitive equilibrium and sets up a "reasonable standards" approach.

There are two advantages in the Coase approach of choosing the transaction-cost-constrained equilibrium of Model II as the attainable optimum, and both are significant. The first is that the Coase line of reasoning does not limit attention to tax rates alone—any government action that achieves either a decrease in the costs of transaction or some other approximation to a desirable course of action is feasible.[29] Not only Pigovian taxes, but all other weapons in the government's arsenal become available as well. Secondly, instead of referring to an imaginary global optimum, the Coase approach *explicitly* requires dealing with marginal concepts in terms of opportunity costs, and always keeps an eye open to the fact that transaction costs are here to stay: the fact that we all agree on the desirability of reducing some externality guarantees that some government action indeed may be desirable since we otherwise could get together and price out of business the beast who creates the disturbance. If the government can make the costs of moving to a preferred allocation lower than the benefits of doing so, there is a guarantee that the result is sanctioned by the Pareto criterion. Any economist who is also a self-interested government consultant ought to embrace the Coase analysis whole-heartedly,

---

[28]Calabresi concurs in this interpretation: "Some may take Coase's analysis to suggest that little or no government intervention is usually the best rule. My own conclusions are quite different. His analysis, combined with common intuition or guesses as to the relative costs of transactions, taxation, structural rules and liability rules, can go far to explain various types of heretofore inadequately justified governmental actions." Guido Calabresi, *supra* note 3, at 73.

[29]This statement is made in blatant disregard of the implications of the theory of second best. Indeed, if some of the rather sweeping assertions of this essay are correct, the conclusion seems to be that the theory of second best is vulnerable to exactly the same criticisms that are here leveled against modern welfare with respect to externalities: for if the competitive equilibrium is not an optimum in the presence of transaction costs, there is no feasible "first best." If we decide that some alternative is preferable to actual resource allocation, then the "reasonable standards" approach would have us identify that point of reference as the first-best alternative. In either case, the theory of second best is irrelevant.

for it would seem to call for more and better cost-benefit analysis by government agencies dealing with pollution and other environmental problems.

V. Conclusion

In the final analysis, therefore, externalities and market failures are not what is the matter with the world, nor is it externalities and market failure that prevent us from reestablishing the Garden of Eden here on earth—our sad state of affairs is rather due to positive transaction costs and imperfect information. It is a very strange feature of modern welfare-policy prescriptions that they propose to do away with externalities, which are only one of the symptoms of an imperfect world, rather than with transaction costs, which are the heart of the matter of what prevents Pareto optimal bliss from ruling sublime. For if we could only eliminate transaction costs, externalities would be of no consequence; and given that there are certain costs of transaction and exchange, it is better to let some side effects remain. What is clear, though, is that it would be consistent with the Pareto criterion if some policy, whatever policy, could be devised that will decrease on net the costs of transacting, whether they be due to setup and transfer costs or imperfect information. This is the important conclusion of the Coase analysis, and the one which makes for its analytical attractiveness. The neatness of the Coase analysis lies in the fact that it dispenses completely with what Demsetz has called "the Nirvana approach" and instead calls for what he labels "the comparative systems approach" which explicitly attempts to ascertain the economic consequences of alternative ways of organizing the allocation of resources. The analysis thus directs attention to the point that institutions fulfill an economic function by reducing transaction costs and therefore ought to be treated as variables determined inside the economic scheme of things. The question then ultimately becomes: how can the economic organization be improved upon by endogenous institutional rearrangements? This is not the outlook of modern welfare theory where the government is seen as a force outside the economic system altogether, which will come to our aid and rectify the havoc wrought by endogenously working market forces, just like the classical *deus ex machina*. Coase opens the door for an economic theory of institutions, whereas modern welfare theory can only gaze into its crystal ball of mathematical abstraction and wisely state that heaven on earth is still far off—which is true, but of no particular consequence either for the correct conduct of economic policy or for the theory of externalities.

Section III

Case Studies

12. The Problem of Cooperation

Robert Axelrod

Under what conditions will cooperation emerge in a world of egoists without central authority? This question has intrigued people for a long time. And for good reason. We all know that people are not angels, and that they tend to look after themselves and their own first. Yet we also know that cooperation does occur and that our civilization is based upon it. But, in situations where each individual has an incentive to be selfish, how can cooperation ever develop?

The answer each of us gives to this question has a fundamental effect on how we think and act in our social, political, and economic relations with others. And the answers that others give have a great effect on how ready they will be to cooperate with us.

The most famous answer was given over three hundred years ago by Thomas Hobbes. It was pessimistic. He argued that before governments existed, the state of nature was dominated by the problem of selfish individuals who competed on such ruthless terms that life was "solitary, poor, nasty, brutish, and short" (Hobbes 1651/1962, p. 100). In his view, cooperation could not develop without a central authority, and consequently a strong government was necessary. Ever since, arguments about the proper scope of government have often focused on whether one could, or could not, expect cooperation to emerge in a particular domain if there were not an authority to police the situation.

Today nations interact without central authority. Therefore the requirements for the emergence of cooperation have relevance to many of the central issues of international politics. The most important problem is the security dilemma: nations often seek their own security through means which challenge the security of others. This problem arises in such areas as escalation of local

Reprinted, by permission, from *The Evolution of Cooperation* (New York: Basic Books, 1984), pp. 3–24.

conflicts and arms races. Related problems occur in international relations in the form of competition within alliances, tariff negotiations, and communal conflict in places like Cyprus.[1]

The Soviet invasion of Afghanistan in 1979 presented the United States with a typical dilemma of choice. If the United States continued business as usual, the Soviet Union might be encouraged to try other forms of noncooperative behavior later on. On the other hand, any substantial lessening of United States cooperation risked some form of retaliation, which could then set off counter-retaliation, setting up a pattern of mutual hostility that could be difficult to end. Much of the domestic debate about foreign policy is concerned with problems of just this type. And properly so, since these are hard choices.

In everyday life, we may ask ourselves how many times we will invite acquaintances for dinner if they never invite us over in return. An executive in an organization does favors for another executive in order to get favors in exchange. A journalist who has received a leaked news story gives favorable coverage to the source in the hope that further leaks will be forthcoming. A business firm in an industry with only one other major company charges high prices with the expectation that the other firm will also maintain high prices—to their mutual advantage and at the expense of the consumer.

For me, a typical case of the emergence of cooperation is the development of patterns of behavior in a legislative body such as the United States Senate. Each senator has an incentive to appear effective to his or her constituents, even at the expense of conflicting with other senators who are trying to appear effective to *their* constituents. But this is hardly a situation of completely opposing interests, a zero-sum game. On the contrary, there are many opportunities for mutually rewarding activities by two senators. These mutually rewarding actions have led to the creation of an elaborate set of norms, or folkways, in the Senate. Among the most important of these is the norm of reciprocity—a folkway which involves helping out a colleague and getting repaid in kind.

---

[1] For useful illustrations of these applications to international politics, see the following sources: the security dilemma (Jervis 1978), arms competition and disarmament (Rapoport 1960), alliance competition (Snyder 1971), tariff negotiations (Evans 1971), taxation of multinational firms (Laver 1977), and communal conflict in Cyprus (Lumsden 1973).

It includes vote trading but extends to so many types of mutually rewarding behavior that "it is not an exaggeration to say that reciprocity is a way of life in the Senate" (Matthews 1960, p. 100; see also Mayhew 1975).

Washington was not always like this. Early observers saw the members of the Washington community as quite unscrupulous, unreliable, and characterized by "falsehood, deceit, treachery" (Smith 1906, p. 190). In the 1980s the practice of reciprocity is well established. Even the significant changes in the Senate over the last two decades, tending toward more decentralization, more openness, and more equal distribution of power, have come without abating the folkway of reciprocity (Ornstein, Peabody, and Rhode 1977). As will be seen, it is *not* necessary to assume that senators are more honest, more generous, or more public-spirited than in earlier years to explain how cooperation based on reciprocity has emerged or proved stable. The emergence of cooperation can be explained as a consequence of individual senators pursuing their own interests.

The approach of this book is to investigate how individuals pursuing their own interest will act, followed by an analysis of what effects this will have for the system as a whole. Put another way, the approach is to make some assumptions about individual motives and then deduce consequences for the behavior of the entire system (Schelling 1978). The case of the U.S. Senate is a good example, but the same style of reasoning can be applied to other settings.

The object of this enterprise is to develop a theory of cooperation that can be used to discover what is necessary for cooperation to emerge. By understanding the conditions that allow it to emerge, appropriate actions can be taken to foster the development of cooperation in a specific setting.

The Cooperation Theory that is presented in this book is based upon an investigation of individuals who pursue their own self-interest without the aid of a central authority to force them to cooperate with each other. The reason for assuming self-interest is that it allows an examination of the difficult case in which cooperation is not completely based upon a concern for others or upon the welfare of the group as a whole. It must, however, be stressed that this assumption is actually much less restrictive than it appears. If a sister is concerned for the welfare of her brother, the sister's self-interest can be thought of as including (among many other things) this concern for the welfare of her brother. But this does not necessarily eliminate all potential for conflict between sister and brother. Likewise a nation may act in part out of regard for the interests of its friends, but this regard does not mean that even friendly countries are always able to cooperate for their mutual benefit. So the assumption of self-interest is really just an assumption that concern for others does not completely solve the problem of when to cooperate with them and when not to.

A good example of the fundamental problem of cooperation is the case where two industrial nations have erected trade barriers to each other's exports. Because of the mutual advantages of free trade, both countries would be better off if these barriers were eliminated. But if either country were to unilaterally eliminate its barriers, it would find itself facing terms of trade that hurt its own economy. In fact, whatever one country does, the other country is better off retaining its own trade barriers. Therefore, the problem is that each country has an incentive to retain trade barriers, leading to a worse outcome than would have been possible had both countries cooperated with each other.

This basic problem occurs when the pursuit of self-interest by each leads to a poor outcome for all. To make headway in understanding the vast array of specific situations which have this property, a way is needed to represent what is common to these situations without becoming bogged down in the details unique to each. Fortunately, there is such a representation available: the famous *Prisoner's Dilemma* game.[2]

In the Prisoner's Dilemma game, there are two players. Each has two choices, namely cooperate or defect. Each must make the choice without knowing what the other will do. No matter what the other does, defection yields a higher payoff than cooperation. The dilemma is that if both defect, both do worse than if both had cooperated. This simple game will provide the basis for the entire analysis used in this book.

The way the game works is shown in Figure 1. One player chooses a row, either cooperating or defecting. The other player simultaneously chooses a column, either cooperating or defecting. Together, these choices result in one of the four possible outcomes shown in that matrix. If both players cooperate, both do fairly well.

[2]The Prisoner's Dilemma game was invented in about 1950 by Merrill Flood and Melvin Dresher, and formalized by A. W. Tucker shortly thereafter.

FIGURE 1
The Prisoner's Dilemma

		Column Player	
		Cooperate	*Defect*
Row Player	Cooperate	R=3, R=3 Reward for mutual cooperation	S=0, T=5 Sucker's payoff, and temptation to defect
	Defect	T=5, S=0 Temptation to defect and sucker's payoff	P=1, P=1 Punishment for mutual defection

NOTE: The payoffs to the row chooser are listed first.

Both get R, the *reward for mutual cooperation*. In the concrete illustration of Figure 1 the reward is 3 points. This number might, for example, be a payoff in dollars that each player gets for that outcome. If one player cooperates but the other defects, the defecting player gets the *temptation to defect*, while the cooperating player gets the *sucker's payoff*. In the example, these are 5 points and 0 points respectively. If both defect, both get 1 point, the *punishment for mutual defection*.

What should you do in such a game? Suppose you are the row player, and you think the column player will cooperate. This means that you will get one of the two outcomes in the first column of Figure 1. You have a choice. You can cooperate as well, getting the 3 points of the reward for mutual cooperation. Or you can defect, getting the 5 points of the temptation payoff. So it pays to defect if you think the other player will cooperate. But now suppose that you think the other player will defect. Now you are in the second column of Figure 1, and you have a choice between cooperating, which would make you a sucker and give you 0 points, and defecting, which would result in, mutual punishment giving you 1 point. So it pays to defect if you think the other player will defect. This means that it is better to defect if you think the other player will cooperate, *and* it is better to defect if you think the other player will defect. So no matter what the other player does, it pays for you to defect.

So far, so good. But the same logic holds for the other player too. Therefore, the other player should defect no matter what you are expected to do. So you should both defect. But then you both get 1 point which is worse than the 3 points of the reward that you both could have gotten had you both cooperated. Individual rationality leads to a worse outcome for both than is possible. Hence the dilemma.

The Prisoner's Dilemma is simply an abstract formulation of some very common and very interesting situations in which what is best for each person individually leads to mutual defection, whereas everyone would have been better off with mutual cooperation. The definition of Prisoner's Dilemma requires that several relationships hold among the four different potential outcomes. The first relationship specifies the order of the four payoffs. The best a player can do is get T, the temptation to defect when the other player cooperates. The worst a player can do is get S, the sucker's payoff for cooperating while the other player defects. In ordering the other two outcomes, R, the reward for mutual cooperation, is assumed to be better than P, the punishment for mutual defection. This leads to a preference ranking of the four payoffs from best to worst as T, R, P, and S.

The second part of the definition of the Prisoner's Dilemma is that the players cannot get out of their dilemma by taking turns exploiting each other. This assumption means that an even chance of exploitation and being exploited is not as good an outcome for a player as mutual cooperation. It is therefore assumed that the reward for mutual cooperation is greater than the average of the temptation and the sucker's payoff. This assumption, together with the rank ordering of the four payoffs, defines the Prisoner's Dilemma.

Thus two egoists playing the game *once* will both choose their dominant choice, defection, and each will get less than they both could have gotten if they had cooperated. If the game is played a known finite number of times, the players still have no incentive to cooperate. This is certainly true on the last move since there is no future to influence. On the next-to-last move neither player will have an incentive to cooperate since they can both anticipate a defection by the other player on the very last move. Such a line of reasoning implies that the game will unravel all the way back to mutual defection on the first move of any sequence of plays that is of known finite length (Luce and Raiffa 1957, pp. 94–102). This reasoning does not apply if the players will interact an indefinite number of times. And in most realistic settings, the players cannot be sure when the last interaction between them will take place. As will be shown later, with an indefinite number of interactions, cooperation can emerge. The issue then becomes the discovery of the precise conditions that are necessary and sufficient for cooperation to emerge.

In this book I will examine interactions between just two players at a time. A single player may be interacting with many others, but the player is assumed to be interacting with them one at a time.[3] The player is also assumed to recognize another player and to remember how the two of them have interacted so far. This ability to recognize and remember allows the history of the particular interaction to be taken into account by a player's strategy.

A variety of ways to resolve the Prisoner's Dilemma have been developed. Each involves allowing some additional activity that alters the strategic interaction in such a way as to fundamentally change the nature of the problem. The original problem remains, however, because there are many situations in which these remedies are not available. Therefore, the problem will be considered in its fundamental form, without these alterations.

1. There is no mechanism available to the players to make enforceable threats or commitments (Schelling 1960). Since the players cannot commit themselves to a particular strategy, each must take into account all possible strategies that might be used by the other player. Moreover the players have all possible strategies available to themselves.

2. There is no way to be sure what the other player will do on a given move. This eliminates the possibility of metagame analysis (Howard 1971) which allows such options as "make the same choice as the other is about to make." It also eliminates the possibility of reliable reputations such as might be based on watching the other player interact with third parties. Thus the only information available to the players about each other is the history of their interaction so far.

3. There is no way to eliminate the other player or run away from the interaction. Therefore each player retains the ability to cooperate or defect on each move.

---

[3]The situations that involve more than pairwise interaction can be modeled with the more complex n-person Prisoner's Dilemma (Olson 1965; G. Hardin 1968; Schelling 1973; Dawes 1980; R. Hardin 1982). The principal application is to the provision of collective goods. It is possible that the results from pairwise interactions will help suggest how to undertake a deeper analysis of the n-person case as well, but that must wait. For a parallel treatment of the two-person and n-person cases, see Taylor (1976, pp. 29–62).

4. There is no way to change the other player's payoffs. The payoffs already include whatever consideration each player has for the interests of the other (Taylor 1976, pp. 69–73).

Under these conditions, words not backed by actions are so cheap as to be meaningless. The players can communicate with each other only through the sequence of their own behavior. This is the problem of the Prisoner's Dilemma in its fundamental form.

What makes it possible for cooperation to emerge is the fact that the players might meet again. This possibility means that the choices made today not only determine the outcome of this move, but can also influence the later choices of the players. The future can therefore cast a shadow back upon the present and thereby affect the current strategic situation.

But the future is less important than the present—for two reasons. The first is that players tend to value payoffs less as the time of their obtainment recedes into the future. The second is that there is always some chance that the players will not meet again. An ongoing relationship may end when one or the other player moves away, changes jobs, dies, or goes bankrupt.

For these reasons, the payoff of the next move always counts less than the payoff of the current move. A natural way to take this into account is to cumulate payoffs over time in such a way that the next move is worth some fraction of the current move (Shubik 1970). The *weight* (or importance) of the next move relative to the current move will be called w. It represents the degree to which the payoff of each move is discounted relative to the previous move, and is therefore a *discount parameter*.

The discount parameter can be used to determine the payoff for a whole sequence. To take a simple example, suppose that each move is only half as important as the previous move, making $w = \frac{1}{2}$. Then a whole string of mutual defections worth one point each move would have a value of 1 on the first move, $\frac{1}{2}$ on the second move, $\frac{1}{4}$ on the third move, and so on. The cumulative value of the sequence would be $1 + \frac{1}{2} + \frac{1}{4} + \frac{1}{8} \ldots$ which would sum to exactly 2. In general, getting one point on each move would be worth $1 + w + w^2 + w^3 \ldots$. A very useful fact is that the sum of this infinite series for any w greater than zero and less than one is simply $1/(1-w)$. To take another case, if each move is worth 90 percent of the previous move, a string of 1's would be worth ten points because $1(1-w) = 1/(1-.9) = 1/.1 = 10$. Similarly, with w

still equal to .9, a string of 3 point mutual rewards would be worth three times this, or 30 points.

Now consider an example of two players interacting. Suppose one player is following the policy of always defecting (ALL D), and the other player is following the policy of TIT FOR TAT. TIT FOR TAT is the policy of cooperating on the first move and then doing whatever the other player did on the previous move. This policy means that TIT FOR TAT will defect once after each defection of the other player. When the other player is using TIT FOR TAT, a player who always defects will get T on the first move, and P on all subsequent moves. The *value* (or *score*) to someone using ALL D when playing with someone using TIT FOR TAT is thus the sum of T for the first move, wP for the second move, w^2P for the third move, and so on.[4]

Both ALL D and TIT FOR TAT are strategies. In general, a *strategy* (or *decision rule*) is a specification of what to do in any situation that might arise. The situation itself depends upon the history of the game so far. Therefore, a strategy might cooperate after some patterns of interaction and defect after others. Moreover, a strategy may use probabilities, as in the example of a rule which is entirely random with equal probabilities of cooperation and defection on each move. A strategy can also be quite sophisticated in its use of the pattern of outcomes in the game so far to determine what to do next. An example is one which, on each move, models the behavior of the other player using a complex procedure (such as a Markov process), and then uses a fancy method of statistical inference (such as Bayesian analysis) to select what seems the best choice for the long run. Or it may be some intricate combination of other strategies.

The first question you are tempted to ask is, "What is the best strategy?" In other words, what strategy will yield a player the highest possible score? This is a good question, but as will be shown later, no best rule exists independently of the strategy being used by the other player. In this sense, the iterated Prisoner's Dilemma is completely different from a game like chess. A chess

---

[4]The value received from always defecting when the other is playing TIT FOR TAT is:

$$V(\text{ALL D}|\text{TFT}) = T + wP + w^2P + w^3P \ldots$$
$$= T + wP(1 + w + w^2 \ldots)$$
$$= T + wP/(1-w).$$

master can safely use the assumption that the other player will make the most feared move. This assumption provides a basis for planning in a game like chess, where the interests of the players are completely antagonistic. But the situations represented by the Prisoner's Dilemma game are quite different. The interests of the players are not in total conflict. Both players can do well by getting the reward, R, for mutual cooperation or both can do poorly by getting the punishment, P, for mutual defection. Using the assumption that the other player will always make the move you fear most will lead you to expect that the other will never cooperate, which in turn will lead you to defect, causing unending punishment. So unlike chess, in the Prisoner's Dilemma it is not safe to assume that the other player is out to get you.

In fact, in the Prisoner's Dilemma, the strategy that works best depends directly on what strategy the other player is using and, in particular, on whether this strategy leaves room for the development of mutual cooperation. This principle is based on the weight of the next move relative to the current move being sufficiently large to make the future important. In other words, the discount parameter, w, must be large enough to make the future loom large in the calculation of total payoffs. After all, if you are unlikely to meet the other person again, or if you care little about future payoffs, then you might as well defect now and not worry about the consequences for the future.

This leads to the first formal proposition. It is the sad news that if the future is important, there is no one best strategy.

Proposition 1. If the discount parameter, w, is sufficiently high, there is no best strategy independent of the strategy used by the other player.

The proof itself is not hard. Suppose that the other player is using ALL D, the strategy of always defecting. If the other player will never cooperate, the best you can do is always to defect yourself. Now suppose, on the other hand, that the other player is using a strategy of "permanent retaliation." This is the strategy of cooperating until you defect and then always defecting after that. In that case, your best strategy is never to defect, provided that the temptation to defect on the first move will eventually be more than compensated for by the long-term disadvantage of getting nothing but the punishment, P, rather than the reward, R, on future moves. This will be true whenever the discount parameter,

w, is sufficiently great.[5] Thus, whether or not you should cooperate, even on the first move, depends on the strategy being used by the other player. Therefore, if w is sufficiently large, there is no one best strategy.

In the case of a legislature such as the U.S. Senate, this proposition says that if there is a large enough chance that a member of the legislature will interact *again* with another member, there is no one best strategy to use independently of the strategy being used by the other person. It would be best to cooperate with someone who will reciprocate that cooperation in the future, but not with someone whose future behavior will not be very much affected by this interaction (see, for example, Hinckley 1972). The very possibility of achieving stable mutual cooperation depends upon there being a good chance of a continuing interaction, as measured by the magnitude of w. As it happens, in the case of Congress, the chance of two members having a continuing interaction has increased dramatically as the biennial turnover rates have fallen from about 40 percent in the first forty years of the republic to about 20 percent or less in recent years (Young 1966, pp. 87–90; Polsby 1968; Jones 1977, p. 154; Patterson 1978, pp. 143–44).

However, saying that a continuing chance of interaction is necessary for the development of cooperation is not the same as saying that it is sufficient. The demonstration that there is not a single best strategy leaves open the question of what patterns of behavior can be expected to emerge when there actually is a sufficiently high probability of continuing interaction between two individuals.

Before going on to study the behavior that can be expected to emerge, it is a good idea to take a closer look at which features of reality the Prisoner's Dilemma framework is, and is not, able to encompass. Fortunately, the very simplicity of the framework makes it possible to avoid many restrictive assumptions that would otherwise limit the analysis:

1. The payoffs of the players need not be comparable at all. For example, a journalist might get rewarded with another inside story, while the cooperating bureaucrat might be rewarded with a chance to have a policy argument presented in a favorable light.

---

[5] If the other player is using a strategy of permanent retaliation, you are better off always cooperating than ever defecting when $R/(1-w) > T T T + wP/(1-w)$ or $w > (T-R)/(T-P)$.

2. The payoffs certainly do not have to be symmetric. It is a convenience to think of the interaction as exactly equivalent from the perspective of the two players, but this is not necessary. One does not have to assume, for example, that the reward for mutual cooperation, or any of the other three payoff parameters, have the same magnitude for both players. As mentioned earlier, one does not even have to assume that they are measured in comparable units. The only thing that has to be assumed is that, for each player, the four payoffs are ordered as required for the definition of the Prisoner's Dilemma.

3. The payoffs of a player do not have to be measured on an absolute scale. They need only be measured relative to each other.[6]

4. Cooperation need not be considered desirable from the point of view of the rest of the world. There are times when one wants to retard, rather than foster, cooperation between players. Collusive business practices are good for the businesses involved but not so good for the rest of society. In fact, most forms of corruption are welcome instances of cooperation for the participants but are unwelcome to everyone else. So, on occasion, the theory will be used in reverse to show how to prevent, rather than to promote, cooperation.

5. There is no need to assume that the players are rational. They need not be trying to maximize their rewards. Their strategies may simply reflect standard operating procedures, rules of thumb, instincts, habits, or imitation (Simon 1955; Cyert and March 1963).

6. The actions that players take are not necessarily even conscious choices. A person who sometimes returns a favor, and sometimes does not, may not think about what strategy is being used. There is no need to assume deliberate choice at all.[7]

The framework is broad enough to encompass not only people but also nations and bacteria. Nations certainly take actions which can be interpreted as choices in a Prisoner's Dilemma—as in the raising or lowering of tariffs. It is not necessary to assume that such actions are rational or are the outcome of a unified actor

---

[6]This means that the utilities need only be measured as an interval scale. Using an interval scale means that the representation of the payoffs may be altered with any positive linear transformation and still be the same, just as temperature is equivalent whether measured in Fahrenheit or Centigrade.

[7]For the implications of not assuming deliberate choice in an evolutionary model of economic change, see Nelson and Winter (1982).

pursuing a single goal. On the contrary, they might well be the result of an incredibly complex bureaucratic politics involving complicated information processing and shifting political coalitions (Allison 1971).

Likewise, at the other extreme, an organism does not need a brain to play a game. Bacteria, for example, are highly responsive to selected aspects of their chemical environment. They can therefore respond differentially to what other organisms are doing, and these conditional strategies of behavior can be inherited. Moreover, the behavior of a bacterium can affect the fitness of other organisms around it, just as the behavior of other organisms can affect the fitness of a bacterium. But biological applications are best saved for chapter 5.

For now the main interest will be in people and organizations. Therefore, it is good to know that for the sake of generality, it is not necessary to assume very much about how deliberate and insightful people are. Nor is it necessary to assume, as the sociobiologists do, that important aspects of human behavior are guided by one's genes. The approach here is strategic rather than genetic.

Of course, the abstract formulation of the problem of cooperation as a Prisoner's Dilemma puts aside many vital features that make any actual interaction unique. Examples of what is left out by this formal abstraction include the possibility of verbal communication, the direct influence of third parties, the problems of implementing a choice, and the uncertainty about what the other player actually did on the preceding move. In chapter 8 some of these complicating factors are added to the basic model. It is clear that the list of potentially relevant factors that have been left out could be extended almost indefinitely. Certainly, no intelligent person should make an important choice without trying to take such complicating factors into account. The value of an analysis without them is that it can help to clarify some of the subtle features of the interaction—features which might otherwise be lost in the maze of complexities of the highly particular circumstances in which choice must actually be made. It is the very complexity of reality which makes the analysis of an abstract interaction so helpful as an aid to understanding.

The next chapter explores the emergence of cooperation through a study of what is a good strategy to employ if confronted with an iterated Prisoner's Dilemma. This exploration has been done in a novel way, with a computer tournament. Professional game theorists were invited to submit their favorite strategy, and each of these decision rules was paired off with each of the others to see which would do best overall. Amazingly enough, the winner was the simplest of all strategies submitted. This was TIT FOR TAT, the strategy which cooperates on the first move and then does whatever the other player did on the previous move. A second round of the tournament was conducted in which many more entries were submitted by amateurs and professionals alike, all of whom were aware of the results of the first round. The result was another victory for TIT FOR TAT! The analysis of the data from these tournaments reveals four properties which tend to make a decision rule successful: avoidance of unnecessary conflict by cooperating as long as the other player does, provocability in the face of an uncalled for defection by the other, forgiveness after responding to a provocation, and clarity of behavior so that the other player can adapt to your pattern of action.

These results from the tournaments demonstrate that under suitable conditions, cooperation can indeed emerge in a world of egoists without central authority. To see just how widely these results apply, a theoretical approach is taken in chapter 3. A series of propositions are proved that not only demonstrate the requirements for the emergence of cooperation but also provide the chronological story of the evolution of cooperation. Here is the argument in a nutshell. The evolution of cooperation requires that individuals have a sufficiently large chance to meet again so that they have a stake in their future interaction. If this is true, cooperation can evolve in three stages.

1. The beginning of the story is that cooperation can get started even in a world of unconditional defection. The development *cannot* take place if it is tried only by scattered individuals who have virtually no chance to interact with each other. However, cooperation can evolve from small clusters of individuals who base their cooperation on reciprocity and have even a small proportion of their interactions with each other.

2. The middle of the story is that a strategy based on reciprocity can thrive in a world where many different kinds of strategies are being tried.

3. The end of the story is that cooperation, once established on the basis of reciprocity, can protect itself from invasion by less cooperative strategies. Thus, the gear wheels of social evolution have a ratchet.

Chapters 4 and 5 take concrete settings to demonstrate just how widely these results apply. Chapter 4 is devoted to the fascinating case of the "live and let live" system which emerged during the trench warfare of World War I. In the midst of this bitter conflict, the front-line soldiers often refrained from shooting to kill—provided their restraint was reciprocated by the soldiers on the other side. What made this mutual restraint possible was the static nature of trench warfare, where the same small units faced each other for extended periods of time. The soldiers of these opposing small units actually violated orders from their own high commands in order to achieve tacit cooperation with each other. A detailed look at this case shows that when the conditions are present for the emergence of cooperation, cooperation can get started and prove stable in situations which otherwise appear extraordinarily unpromising. In particular, the "live and let live" system demonstrates that friendship is hardly necessary for the development of cooperation. Under suitable conditions, cooperation based upon reciprocity can develop even between antagonists.

Chapter 5, written with evolutionary biologist William D. Hamilton, demonstrates that cooperation can emerge even without foresight. This is done by showing that Cooperation Theory can account for the patterns of behavior found in a wide range of biological systems, from bacteria to birds. Cooperation in biological systems can occur even when the participants are not related, and even when they are unable to appreciate the consequences of their own behavior. What makes this possible are the evolutionary mechanisms of genetics and survival of the fittest. An individual able to achieve a beneficial response from another is more likely to have offspring that survive and that continue the pattern of behavior which elicited beneficial responses from others. Thus, under suitable conditions, cooperation based upon reciprocity proves stable in the biological world. Potential applications are spelled out for specific aspects of territoriality, mating, and disease. The conclusion is that Darwin's emphasis on individual advantage can, in fact, account for the presence of cooperation between individuals of the same or even different species. As long as the proper conditions are present, cooperation can get started, thrive, and prove stable.

While foresight is not necessary for the evolution of cooperation, it can certainly be helpful. Therefore chapters 6 and 7 are devoted to offering advice to participants and reformers, respectively.

Chapter 6 spells out the implications of Cooperation Theory for anyone who is in a Prisoner's Dilemma. From the participant's point of view, the object is to do as well as possible, regardless of how well the other player does. Based upon the tournament results and the formal propositions, four simple suggestions are offered for individual choice: do not be envious of the other player's success; do not be the first to defect; reciprocate both cooperation and defection; and do not be too clever.

Understanding the perspective of a participant can also serve as the foundation for seeing what can be done to make it easier for cooperation to develop among egoists. Thus, chapter 7 takes the Olympian perspective of a reformer who wants to alter the very terms of the interactions so as to promote the emergence of cooperation. A wide variety of methods are considered, such as making the interactions between the players more durable and frequent, teaching the participants to care about each other, and teaching them to understand the value of reciprocity. This reformer's perspective provides insights into a wide variety of topics, from the strength of bureaucracy to the difficulties of Gypsies, and from the morality of TIT FOR TAT to the art of writing treaties.

Chapter 8 extends the implications of Cooperation Theory into new domains. It shows how different kinds of social structure affect the way cooperation can develop. For example, people often relate to each other in ways that are influenced by observable features, such as sex, age, skin color, and style of dress. These cues can lead to social structures based on stereotyping and status hierarchies. As another example of social structure, the role of reputation is considered. The struggle to establish and maintain one's reputation can be a major feature of intense conflicts. For example, the American government's escalation of the war in Vietnam in 1965 was mainly due to its desire to deter other challenges to its interests by maintaining its reputation on the world stage. This chapter also considers a government's concern for maintaining its reputation with its own citizens. To be effective, a government cannot enforce any standards it chooses but must elicit compliance from a majority of the governed. To do this requires setting the rules so that most of the governed find it profitable to obey most of the time. The implications of this approach are fundamental to the operation of authority, and are illustrated by the regulation of industrial pollution and the supervision of divorce settlements.

By the final chapter, the discussion has developed from the study of the emergence of cooperation among egoists without central authority to an analysis of what happens when people actually *do* care about each other and what happens when there *is* central authority. But the basic approach is always the same: seeing how individuals operate in their own interest reveals what happens to the whole group. This approach allows more than the understanding of the perspective of a single player. It also provides an appreciation of what it takes to promote the stability of mutual cooperation in a given setting. The most promising finding is that if the facts of Cooperation Theory are known by participants with foresight, the evolution of cooperation can be speeded up.

References

Allison, Graham T. 1971. *The Essence of Decision*. Boston: Little, Brown.

Cyert, Richard M., and James G. March. 1963. *A Behavioral Theory of the Firm*. Englewood Cliffs, N.J.: Prentice-Hall.

Hinckley, Barbara. 1972. "Coalitions in Congress: Size and Ideological Distance." *Midwest Journal of Political Science* 26: 197–207.

Hobbes, Thomas. 1651. *Leviathan*. New York: Collier Books edition, 1962.

Howard, Nigel. 1971. *Paradoxes of Rationality: Theory of Metagames and Political Behavior*. Cambridge, Mass.: MIT Press.

Jones, Charles O. 1977. "Will Reform Change Congress?" In Lawrence C. Dodd and Bruce I. Oppenheimer, eds. *Congress Reconsidered*. New York: Praeger.

Luce, R. Duncan, and Howard Raiffa. 1957. *Games and Decisions*. New York: Wiley.

Matthews, Donald R. 1960. *U.S. Senators and Their World*. Chapel Hill: University of North Carolina Press.

Mayhew, David R. 1975. *Congress: The Electoral Connection*. New Haven, Conn.: Yale University Press.

Ornstein, Norman, Robert L. Peabody, and David W. Rhode. 1977. "The Changing Senate: From the 1950s to the 1970s." In Lawrence C. Dodd and Bruce I. Oppenheimer, eds., *Congress Reconsidered*. New York: Praeger.

Patterson, Samuel. 1978. "The Semi-Sovereign Congress." In Anthony King, ed., *The New American Political System*. Washington, D.C.: American Enterprise Institute.

Polsby, Nelson. 1968. "The Institutionalization of the U.S. House of Representatives." *American Political Science Review* 62: 144–68.

Schelling, Thomas C. 1960. *The Strategy of Conflict*. Cambridge, Mass.: Harvard University Press.

———. 1978. "Micromotives and Macrobehavior." In Thomas Schelling, ed., *Micromotives and Macrobehavior*, 9–43. New York: Norton.

Shubik, Martin. 1970. "Game Theory, Behavior, and the Paradox of Prisoner's Dilemma: Three Solutions." *Journal of Conflict Resolution* 14: 181–94.

Simon, Herbert A. 1955. "A Behavioral Model of Rational Choice." *Quarterly Journal of Economics* 69: 99–118.

Smith, Margaret Bayard. 1906. *The First Forty Years of Washington Society*. New York: Scribner's.

Taylor, Michael. 1976. *Anarchy and Cooperation*. New York: Wiley.

Young, James Sterling. 1966. *The Washington Community, 1800–1828*. New York: Harcourt, Brace & World.

13. The Lighthouse in Economics

Ronald H. Coase

Introduction

The lighthouse appears in the writings of economists because of the light it is supposed to throw on the question of the economic functions of government. It is often used as an example of something which has to be provided by government rather than by private enterprise. What economists usually seem to have in mind is that the impossibility of securing payment from the owners of the ships that benefit from the existence of the lighthouse makes it unprofitable for any private individual or firm to build and maintain a lighthouse.

John Stuart Mill, in his *Principles of Political Economy*, in the chapter "Of the Grounds and Limits of the Laissez-Faire or Non-Interference Principle," said:

> It is a proper office of government to build and maintain lighthouses, establish buoys, etc. for the security of navigation: for since it is impossible that the ships at sea which are benefited by a lighthouse, should be made to pay a toll on the occasion of its use, no one would build lighthouses from motives of personal interest, unless indemnified and rewarded from a compulsory levy made by the state.[1]

Henry Sidgwick, in his *Principles of Political Economy*, in the chapter "The System of Natural Liberty Considered in Relation to Produc-

Reprinted, by permission, from *Journal of Law and Economics* 17 (October 1974): 357–76.

It is with great pleasure that I acknowledge the helpfulness of members of Trinity House and of officials in the Department of Trade and of the Chamber of Shipping in providing me with information on the British lighthouse system. They are not, however, in any way responsible for the use I have made of this information and should not be presumed to share the conclusions I draw.

[1]John Stuart Mill, *Principles of Political Economy*, in 3 *The Collected Works of John Stuart Mill* 968 (ed. J. M. Robson, 1965).

tion," had this to say:

> There is a large and varied class of cases in which the supposition
> [that an individual can always obtain through free exchange
> adequate remuneration for the services he renders] would be
> manifestly erroneous. In the first place there are some utilities
> which, from their nature, are practically incapable of being ap-
> propriated by those who produce them or would otherwise be
> willing to purchase them. For instance, it may easily happen that
> the benefits of a well-placed lighthouse must be largely enjoyed
> by ships on which no toll could be conveniently imposed.[2]

Pigou, in his *Economics of Welfare*, used Sidgwick's lighthouse
example as an instance of uncompensated services, in which
"marginal net product falls short of marginal social net product,
because incidental services are performed to third parties from
whom it is technically difficult to exact payment."[3]

Paul A. Samuelson, in his *Economics*, is more forthright than
these earlier writers. In the section on the "Economic Role of
Government," he says that "government provides certain indispensable *public* services without which community life would be
unthinkable and which by their nature cannot appropriately be left
to private enterprise." He gives as "obvious examples," the maintenance of national defense, of internal law and order, and the
administration of justice and of contracts and he adds in a footnote:

> Here is a later example of government service: lighthouses. These
> save lives and cargoes; but lighthouse keepers cannot reach out
> to collect fees from skippers. "So," says the advanced treatise,
> "we have here a divergence between *private* advantage and money
> cost [as seen by a man odd enough to try to make his fortune
> running a lighthouse business] and true *social* advantage and cost
> [as measured by lives and cargoes saved in comparison with (1)
> total costs of the lighthouse and (2) extra costs that result from
> letting one more ship look at the warning light]." Philosophers
> and statesmen have always recognized the necessary role of
> government in such cases of "external-economy divergence be-
> tween private and social advantage."[4]

Later Samuelson again refers to the lighthouse as a "government

[2]Henry Sidgwick, *The Principles of Political Economy* 406 (3rd ed., 1901). In the first
edition (1883), the sentence relating to lighthouses is the same but the rest of the
wording (but not the sense) is somewhat changed.

[3]A. C. Pigou, *Economics of Welfare* 183–84 (4th ed., 1938).

[4]Paul A. Samuelson, *Economics: An Introductory Analysis* 45 (6th ed., 1964). All
references to Samuelson's Economics will be to the 6th edition.

activit[y] justifiable because of external effects." He says:

> Take our earlier case of a lighthouse to warn against rocks. Its beam helps everyone in sight. A businessman could not build it for a profit, since he cannot claim a price from each user. This certainly is the kind of activity that governments would naturally undertake.[5]

Samuelson does not leave the matter here. He also uses the lighthouse to make another point (one not found in the earlier writers). He says:

> In the lighthouse example one thing should be noticed: The fact that the lighthouse operators cannot appropriate in the form of a purchase price a fee from those it benefits certainly helps to make it a suitable social or public good. But even if the operators were able—say, by radar reconnaissance—to claim a toll from every nearby user, that fact would not necessarily make it socially optimal for this service to be provided like a private good at a market-determined individual price. Why not? Because it costs society *zero extra cost* to let one extra ship use the service; hence any ships discouraged from those waters by the requirement to pay a positive price will represent a social economic loss—even if the price charged to all is no more than enough to pay the long-run expenses of the lighthouse. If the lighthouse is socially worth building and operating—and it need not be—a more advanced treatise can show how this social good is worth being made optimally available to all.[6]

There is an element of paradox in Samuelson's position. The government has to provide lighthouses because private firms could not charge for their services. But if it were possible for private firms to make such a charge they should not be allowed to do so (which also presumably calls for government action). Samuelson's position is quite different from that of Mill, Sidgwick or Pigou. As I read these writers, the difficulty of charging for the use of a lighthouse is a serious point with important consequences for lighthouse policy. They had no objection to charging as such and therefore, if this were possible, to the private operation of light-houses. Mill's argument is not, however, free from ambiguity. He argues that the government should build and maintain lighthouses because, since ships benefitted cannot be made to pay a toll, private enterprise would not provide a lighthouse service. But he

[5]Paul A. Samuelson, *supra* note 4, at 159.
[6]*Id.* at 151.

then adds a qualifying phrase "unless indemnified and rewarded from a compulsory levy made by the state." I take a "compulsory levy" to be one imposed on ships benefitted by the lighthouse (the levy would be, in effect, a toll). The element of ambiguity in Mill's exposition is whether he meant that the "compulsory levy" would make it possible for people to "build lighthouses from motives of personal interest" and therefore for government operation to be avoided or whether he meant that it was not possible (or desirable) for private firms to be "indemnified and rewarded from a compulsory levy" and that therefore government operation was required. My own opinion is that Mill had in mind the first of these alternative interpretations and, if this is right, it represents an important qualification to his view that building and maintaining lighthouses is "a proper office of the government." In any case, it seems clear that Mill had no objection in principle to the imposition of tolls.[7] Sidgwick's point (to which Pigou refers) raises no problems of interpretation. It is, however, very restricted in character. He says that "it may easily happen that the benefits of a well-placed lighthouse must be largely enjoyed by ships on which no toll could be conveniently imposed." This does not say that charging is impossible: indeed, it implies the contrary. What it says is that there may be circumstances in which most of those who benefit from the lighthouse can avoid paying the toll. It does not say that there may not be circumstances in which the benefits of the lighthouse are largely enjoyed by ships on which a toll could be conveniently laid and it implies that, in these circumstances, it would be desirable to impose a toll—which would make private operation of lighthouses possible.

It is, I think, difficult to understand exactly what Mill, Sidgwick and Pigou meant without some knowledge of the British lighthouse system since, although these writers were probably unfamiliar with how the British system operated in detail, they were doubtless aware of its general character and this must have been in the back of their minds when they wrote about lighthouses. However, knowledge of the British lighthouse system not only enables one to have a greater understanding of Mill, Sidgwick and Pigou; it also provides a context within which to appraise Samuelson's statements about lighthouses.

[7]Compare what Mill has to say on tolls in *supra* note 1, at 862–63.

The British Lighthouse System

The authorities in Britain which build and maintain lighthouses are Trinity House (for England and Wales), the Commissioners of Northern Lighthouses (for Scotland) and the Commissioners of Irish Lights (for Ireland). The expenses of these authorities are met out of the General Lighthouse Fund. The income of this Fund is derived from light dues, which are paid by shipowners. The responsibility for making the arrangements for the payment of the light dues and for maintaining the accounts is placed on Trinity House (whether the payments are made in England, Wales, Scotland or Ireland) although the actual collection is made by the customs authorities at the ports. The money obtained from the light dues is paid into the General Lighthouse Fund, which is under the control of the Department of Trade. The lighthouse authorities draw on the General Lighthouse Fund to meet their expenditures.

The relation of the Department of Trade to the various lighthouse authorities is somewhat similar to that of the Treasury to a British Government Department. The budgets of the authorities have to be approved by the Department. The proposed budgets of the three authorities are submitted about Christmas time and are discussed at a Lighthouse Conference held annually in London. In addition to the three lighthouse authorities and the Department, there are also present at the conference members of the Lights Advisory Committee, a committee of the Chamber of Shipping (a trade association) representing shipowners, underwriters and shippers. The Lights Advisory Committee, although without statutory authority, plays an important part in the review procedure and the opinions it expresses are taken into account both by the lighthouse authorities in drawing up their budgets and by the Department in deciding on whether to approve the budgets. The light dues are set by the Department at a level which will yield, over a period of years, an amount of money sufficient to meet the likely expenditures. But in deciding on the program of works and changes in existing arrangements the participants in the conference, and particularly the members of the Lights Advisory Committee, have regard to the effect which new works or changes in existing arrangements would have on the level of light dues.

The basis on which light dues are levied was set out in the Second Schedule to the Merchant Shipping (Mercantile Marine

Fund) Act of 1898.[8] Modifications to the level of the dues and in
certain other respects have been made since then by Order in
Council but the present method of charging is essentially that
established in 1898. The dues are so much per net ton payable per
voyage for all vessels arriving at, or departing from, ports in
Britain. In the case of "Home Trade" ships, there is no further
liability for light dues after the first 10 voyages in a year and in the
case of "Foreign-going" ships, there is no further liability after 6
voyages. The light dues are different for these two categories of
ship and are such that, for a ship of given size, 10 voyages for a
"Home Trade" ship yield approximately the same sum as 6 voyages
for a "Foreign-going" ship. Some categories of ship pay at a lower
rate per net ton: sailing vessels of more than 100 tons and cruise
ships. Tugs and pleasure yachts make an annual payment rather
than a payment per voyage. In addition, some ships are exempt
from light dues: ships belonging to the British or Foreign Governments (unless carrying cargo or passengers for remuneration),
fishing vessels, hoppers and dredges, sailing vessels (except pleasure yachts) of less than 100 tons, all ships (including pleasure
yachts) of less than 20 tons, vessels (other than tugs or pleasure
yachts) in ballast, or putting in for bunker fuel or stores or because
of the hazards of the sea. All these statements are subject to
qualification. But they make clear the general nature of the scheme.

The present position is that the expenses of the British lighthouse service are met out of the General Lighthouse Fund, the
income of which comes from light dues. In addition to expenditures on lighthouses in Great Britain and Ireland, the Fund is also
used to pay for the maintenance of some colonial lighthouses and
to meet the cost of marking and clearing wrecks (to the extent that
these are not reimbursed by a salvaging firm), although these
payments amount to only a very small proportion of total expenditures. There are also expenditures on lighthouses which are not
met out of the Fund. The expenses of building and maintaining
"local lights," those which are only of benefit to ships using
particular ports, are not paid for out of the Fund, which is restricted to the finance of lighthouses which are useful for "general
navigation." The expenditures for "local lights" are normally made
by harbour authorities, and are recovered out of port dues.

[8]61 & 62 Vic., c.44, sch.2.

The Evolution of the British Lighthouse System

Mill, writing in 1848, and Sidgwick, in 1883, to the extent that they had in mind the actual British lighthouse system, would obviously be thinking of earlier arrangements. To understand Mill and Sidgwick, we need to know something of the lighthouse system in the 19th century and of the way in which it had evolved. But a study of the history of the British lighthouse system is not only useful because it helps us to understand Mill and Sidgwick but also because it serves to enlarge our vision of the range of alternative institutional arrangements available for operating a lighthouse service. In discussing the history of the British lighthouse service, I will confine myself to England and Wales, which is, presumably, the part of the system with which Mill and Sidgwick would have been most familiar.

The principal lighthouse authority in England and Wales is Trinity House. It is also the principal pilotage authority for the United Kingdom. It maintains Homes and administers charitable trusts for mariners, their wives, widows, and orphans. It has also many miscellaneous responsibilities, for example, the inspection and regulation of "local lights" and the provision of Nautical Assessors or Trinity Masters at the hearing of marine cases in the Law Courts. It is represented on a number of harbour boards, including the Port of London Authority, and members of Trinity House serve on many committees (including government committees) dealing with maritime matters.

Trinity House is an ancient institution. It seems to have evolved out of a medieval seamen's guild. A petition asking for incorporation was presented to Henry VIII in 1513 and letters patent were granted in 1514.[9] The charter gave Trinity House the right to regulate pilotage, and this, together with its charitable work, represented its main activity for many years. It did not concern itself with lighthouses until much later.

There seem to have been few lighthouses in Britain before the seventeenth century and not many until the eighteenth century. There were, however, seamarks of various kinds. Most of these were on land and were not designed as aids to mariners, consisting of church steeples, houses, clumps of trees, etc. Buoys and beacons

[9] G. G. Harris, *Trinity House of Deptford 1515–1660,* at 19–20 (1969). My sketch of the early history of Trinity House is largely based on this work, particularly ch. 7, "Beacons, Markes and Signes for the Sea," and ch. 8, "An Uncertaine Light."

were also used as aids to navigation. Harris explains that these beacons were not lighthouses but "poles set in the seabed, or on the seashore, with perhaps an old lantern affixed to the top."[10] The regulation of seamarks and the provision of buoys and beacons in the early sixteenth century was the responsibility of the Lord High Admiral. To provide buoys and beacons, he appointed deputies, who collected dues from ships presumed to have benefitted from the marks. In 1566 Trinity House was given the right to provide and also to regulate seamarks. They had the responsibility of seeing that privately owned seamarks were maintained. As an example, a merchant who had cut down, without permission, a clump of trees which had served as a seamark, was upbraided for "preferring a tryfle of private benefitt to your selfe before a great and generall good to the publique."[11] He could have been fined £100 (with the proceeds divided equally between the Crown and Trinity House). There seems to have been some doubt as to whether the Act of 1566 gave Trinity House the right to place seamarks in the water. This doubt was removed in 1594, when the rights of beaconage and buoyage were surrendered by the Lord High Admiral and were granted to Trinity House. How things worked out in practice is not clear since the Lord High Admiral continued to regulate buoyage and beaconage after 1594 but gradually the authority of Trinity House in this area seems to have been acknowledged.

Early in the seventeenth century, Trinity House established lighthouses at Caister and Lowestoft.[12] But it was not until late in the century that it built another lighthouse. In the meantime the building of lighthouses had been taken over by private individuals. As Harris says: "A characteristic element in Elizabethan society were the promoters of projects advanced ostensibly for the public benefit but in reality intended for private gain. Lighthouses did not escape their attention."[13] Later he says: "With the completion of the lighthouse at Lowestoft, the Brethren rested content and did no more . . . when in February 1614 they were asked to do something positive, and erect lighthouses at Winterton in response to a petition by some three hundred shipmasters, owners and

[10]*Id.* at 153.

[11]*Id.* at 161.

[12]*Id.* at 183–87.

[13]*Id.* at 180–81.

fisherman, they seem to have done nothing. Failure to respond to demands of this sort not only shook confidence in the Corporation; since there was a prospect of profit, it was tantamount to inviting private speculators to intervene. They soon did so."[14] In the period 1610–1675, no lighthouses were erected by Trinity House. At least 10 were built by private individuals.[15] Of course, the desire of private individuals to erect lighthouses put Trinity House in a quandary. On the one hand it wanted to be recognized as the only body with authority to construct lighthouses; on the other, it was reluctant to invest its own funds in lighthouses. It therefore opposed the efforts of private individuals to construct lighthouses but, as we have seen, without success. Harris comments: "The lighthouse projectors were typical of the speculators of the period: they were not primarily motivated by considerations of public service. . . . There was a strong foundation of truth in what Sir Edward Coke told Parliament in 1621: 'Protectours like wattermen looke one waye and rowe another: they pretend publique profit, intende private.' "[16] The difficulty was that those who were motivated by a sense of public service did not build the lighthouses. As Harris says later: "Admittedly the primary motive of the lighthouse projectors was personal gain, but at least they got things done."[17]

The method used by private individuals to avoid infringing Trinity House's statutory authority was to obtain a patent from the Crown which empowered them to build a lighthouse and to levy tolls on ships presumed to have benefitted from it. The way this was done was to present a petition from shipowners and shippers in which they said that they would greatly benefit from the lighthouse and were willing to pay the toll. Signatures were, I assume, obtained in the way signatures to petitions are normally obtained but no doubt they often represented a genuine expression of opinion. The King presumably used these grants of patents on occasion as a means of rewarding those who had served him. Later, the right to operate a lighthouse and to levy tolls was granted to individuals by Acts of Parliament.

The tolls were collected at the ports by agents (who might act

[14]Id. at 187.

[15]D. Alan Stevenson, *The World's Lighthouses Before 1820*, at 259 (1959).

[16]G. G. Harris, *supra* note 9, at 214.

[17]Id. at 264.

for several lighthouses), who might be private individuals but were commonly customs officials. The toll varied with the lighthouse and ships paid a toll, varying with the size of the vessel, for each lighthouse passed. It was normally a rate per ton (say ¼d or ½d) for each voyage. Later, books were published setting out the lighthouses passed on different voyages and the charges that would be made.

In the meantime, Trinity House came to adopt a policy which maintained its rights while preserving its money (and even increasing it). Trinity House would apply for a patent to operate a lighthouse and would then grant a lease, for a rental, to a private individual who would then build the lighthouse with his own money. The advantage to a private individual of such a procedure would be that he would secure the co-operation rather than the opposition of Trinity House.

An example of this is afforded by the building, and rebuilding, of what is probably the most celebrated British lighthouse, the Eddystone, on a reef of rocks some 14 miles offshore from Plymouth. D. Alan Stevenson comments: "The construction of 4 lighthouses in succession on the Eddystone Rocks by 1759 provides the most dramatic chapter in lighthouse history: in striving to withstand the force of the waves, their builders showed enterprise, ingenuity and courage of a high order."[18] In 1665, a petition for a lighthouse on the Eddystone Rocks was received by the British Admiralty. Trinity House commented that, though desirable, it "could hardly be accomplished."[19] As Samuel Smiles, that chronicler of private enterprise, says, "It was long before any private adventurer was found ready to undertake so daring an enterprise as the erection of a lighthouse on the Eddystone, where only a little crest of rock was visible at high water, scarcely capable of affording foothold for a structure of the very narrowest basis."[20] In 1692, a proposal was put forward by Walter Whitfield, and Trinity House made an agreement with him under which he was to build the lighthouse and Trinity House was to share equally in whatever profits were made. Whitfield did not, however, undertake the work. His rights were transferred to Henry Winstanley, who, after negotiating with Trinity House, made an agreement in 1696 under

[18]D. Alan Stevenson, *supra* note 15, at 113.

[19]*Id.*

[20]2 Samuel Smiles, *Lives of the Engineers* 16 (1861).

which he was to receive the profits for the first five years, after which Trinity House was to share equally in whatever profits were earned for 50 years. Winstanley built one tower and then replaced it with another, the lighthouse being completed in 1699. However, in a great storm in 1703, the lighthouse was swept away, and Winstanley, the lighthousekeepers, and some of his workmen, lost their lives. The total cost up to this time had been £8,000 (all of which had been borne by Winstanley) and the receipts had been £4,000. The government gave Winstanley's widow £200 and a pension of £100 per annum. If the construction of lighthouses had been left solely to men with the public interest at heart, the Eddystone would have remained for a long time without a light-house. But the prospect of private gain once more reared its ugly head. Two men, Lovett and Rudyerd, decided to build another lighthouse. Trinity House agreed to apply for an Act of Parliament authorizing the rebuilding and the imposition of tolls and to lease their rights to the new builders. The terms were better than had been granted to Winstanley—a 99 year lease at an annual rent of £100 with 100 per cent of the profits going to the builders. The lighthouse was completed in 1709 and remained in operation until 1755 when it was destroyed by fire. The lease still had some 50 years to run and the interest in the lighthouse had passed into other hands. The new owners decided to rebuild and engaged one of the great engineers of the time, John Smeaton. He determined to build the lighthouse entirely of stone, the previous structure having been made of wood. The lighthouse was completed by 1759. It continued in operation until 1882, when it was replaced by a new structure built by Trinity House.[21]

We may understand the significance of the part played by private individuals and organizations in the provision of lighthouses in Britain if we consider the position at the beginning of the nine-teenth century. The 1834 Committee on Lighthouses stated in their report that at that time there were in England and Wales (excluding floating lights) 42 lighthouses belonging to Trinity House, 3 light-houses leased by Trinity House and in charge of individuals; 7 lighthouses leased by the Crown to individuals; 4 lighthouses in the hands of proprietors, held originally under patents and subsequently sanctioned by Acts of Parliament; or 56 in total, of which

---

[21]This account of the building and rebuilding of the Eddystone lighthouse is based on Stevenson, *supra* note 15, at 113–26.

14 were run by private individuals and organizations.[22] Between 1820 and 1834, Trinity House had built 9 new lighthouses, had purchased 5 lighthouses leased to individuals (in the case of Burnham, replacing the one purchased by building two lighthouses not counted in the 9 new built lighthouses) and had purchased 3 lighthouses owned by Greenwich Hospital (which acquired the lighthouses by bequest in 1719, they having been built by Sir John Meldrum about 1634). The position in 1820 was that there were 24 lighthouses operated by Trinity House and 22 by private individuals or organizations.[23] But many of the Trinity House lighthouses had not been built originally by them but had been acquired by purchase or as the result of the expiration of a lease (of which the Eddystone Lighthouse is an example, the lease having expired in 1804). Of the 24 lighthouses operated by Trinity House in 1820, 12 had been acquired as a result of the falling in of the lease while one had been taken over from the Chester Council in 1816, so that only 11 out of the 46 lighthouses in existence in 1820 had been originally built by Trinity House while 34 had been built by private individuals.[24]

Since the main building activity of Trinity House, started at the end of the eighteenth century, the dominance of private lighthouses was even more marked in earlier periods. Writing of the position in 1786, D. A. Stevenson says: "It is difficult to assess the attitude of Trinity House towards the English coastal lighthouses at this time. Judging by its actions and not by its protestations, the determination of the Corporation to erect lighthouses had never been strong: before 1806, whenever possible it had passed on to lessees the duty of erecting them. In 1786 it controlled lighthouses at 4 places: at Caister and Lowestoft (both managed in virtue of its local buoyage dues), and at Winterton and Scilly (both erected by

[22]See Report from the Select Committee on Lighthouses, in *Parl. Papers* Sess. 1834, vol. 12, at vi (*Reports from Committees*, vol. 8) [hereinafter cited as "1834 Report"].

[23]*Id.* at vii.

[24]Of the 24 lighthouses operated by Trinity House in 1820, Foulness (1), Portland (2), Caskets (3), Eddystone (1), Lizard (2), St. Bees (1) and Milford (2), appear to have been acquired by the falling in of the leases and to have been built, as well as operated, by private individuals. This is based on information contained in D. Alan Stevenson, *supra* note 15. I have assumed, when a patent for a lighthouse was obtained by Trinity House and was then leased to a private individual, that the construction was undertaken and paid for by that individual, which appears to have been the case. See *id.* at 253 & 261.

the Corporation to thwart individuals keen to profit from dues under Crown patents)."[25]

However, by 1834, as we have seen, there were 56 lighthouses in total and Trinity House operated 42 of them. And there was strong support in Parliament for the proposal that Trinity House purchase the remaining lighthouses in private hands. This had been suggested by a Select Committee of the House of Commons in 1822, and Trinity House began shortly afterwards to buy out certain of the private interests in lighthouses. In 1836, an Act of Parliament vested all lighthouses in England in Trinity House, which was empowered to purchase the remaining lighthouses in private hands.[26] This was accomplished by 1842, after which date there were no longer any privately owned lighthouses, apart from "local lights," in England.

The purchase by Trinity House between 1823 and 1832 of the remainder of the leases that it had granted for Flatholm, Ferns, Burnham and North and South Forelands cost about £74,000.[27] The rest of the private lighthouses were purchased following the 1836 Act for just under £1,200,000, the largest sums being paid for the Smalls lighthouse, for which the lease had 41 years to run and for three lighthouses, Tynemouth, Spurn, and Skerries, for which the grant had been made in perpetuity by Act of Parliament. The sums paid for these four lighthouses were: Smalls, £170,000; Tynemouth, £125,000; Spurn, £330,000; Skerries, £445,000.[28] These are large sums, the £445,000 paid for Skerries being equivalent (according to a high authority) to $7–10 million today, which would probably have produced (owing to the lower level of taxation) a considerably higher income than today. Thus we find examples of men who were not only, in Samuelson's words, "odd enough to try to make a fortune running a lighthouse business," but actually succeeded in doing so.

The reasons why there was such strong support for this consolidation of lighthouses in the hands of Trinity House can be learned from the Report of the Select Committee of the House of Commons of 1834:

[25]*Id.* at 65.

[26]An Act for vesting Lighthouses, Lights, and Sea Marks on the Coasts of England in the Corporation of Trinity House of Deptford Strond, 6 & 7 Will. 4, c.79 (1836).

[27]1834 Report, at vii.

[28]Report from the Select Committee on Lighthouses, in *Parl. Papers* Sess. 1845, vol. 9, at vi [hereinafter cited at "1845 Report"].

Your committee have learned with some surprise that the Light-house Establishments have been conducted in the several parts of the United Kingdom under entirely different systems; different as regards the constitution of the Boards of Management, different as regards the Rates or Amount of the Light Dues, and different in the principle on which they are levied. They have found that these Establishments, of such importance to the extensive Naval and Commercial Interests of the Kingdom, instead of being conducted under the immediate superintendence of the Government, upon one uniform system, and under responsible Public Servants, with proper foresight to provide for the safety of the Shipping in the most efficient manner, and on the most economical plans, have been left to spring up, as it were by slow degrees, as the local wants required, often after disastrous losses at sea; and it may, perhaps, be considered as matter of reproach to this great country, that for ages past, as well as at the present time, a considerable portion of the establishments of Lighthouses have been made the means of heavily taxing the Trade of the country, for the benefit of a few private individuals, who have been favoured with that advantage by the Ministers and the Sovereign of the day.

Your Committee cannot consider it warrantable in Government, at any time, unnecessarily to tax any branch of the Industry of the Country; and particularly unwarrantable to tax the Shipping, which lies under many disadvantages, in being obliged to support unequal competition with the Shipping of other countries. Your Committee are of opinion that the Shipping ought, on very special grounds, to be relieved from every local and unequal tax not absolutely necessary for the services for which it is ostensibly levied.

Your Committee, therefore, strongly recommend that the Light Dues should in every case be reduced to the smallest sums requisite to maintain the existing Lighthouses and Floating Lights, or to establish and maintain such new Establishments as shall be required for the benefit of the Commerce and Shipping of the country.

Your Committee have, further to express their regret that so little attention should have been paid by the competent authorities to the continued exaction, contrary to the principle just expressed, of very large sums which have been annually levied, avowedly, as Light Dues, to defray the expenses of Lighthouses but, in reality, to be applied to the use of a few favoured individuals, and for other purposes not contemplated at the time of the establishment of the Lighthouses. It further appears particularly objectionable to have continued these abuses by the renewal of the Leases of several Lighthouses, after a Select Committee of this House had called the particular attention of Parliament, 12 years ago, to the subject.[29]

Although there was emphasis in this report on the untidiness of the then existing arrangements and suggestions (here and elsewhere) that some of the private lighthouses were not run efficiently, there can be little doubt that the main reason why the consolidation of lighthouses under Trinity House received such strong support was that it was thought that it would lead to lower light dues. The suggestion was, of course, made that lighthouses should be paid for out of the public treasury,[30] which would lead to the abolition of light dues, but this was not done and we need not discuss it here.

It is not apparent why it was thought that the consolidation of lighthouses under Trinity House would lower light dues. There is some basis for this view in the theory of complementary monopolies, but Cournot did not publish his analysis until 1838 and it could not have affected the views of those concerned with British lighthouses even if they were quicker to appreciate the significance of Cournot's analysis than the economics profession itself.[31] In any case, there were good reasons for thinking that little, if any, reduction in light dues would follow the consolidation. Since compensation was to be paid to the former owners of lighthouses, the same amount of money would need to be raised as before. And, as was pointed out by Trinity House, since "the Dues were mortgaged as security for the repayment of the money borrowed . . . the Dues cannot be taken off until the debt shall be discharged."[32] In fact, the light dues were not reduced until after 1848, when the loans were paid off.[33]

[29]1834 Report, at iii–iv.

[30]For example, the Select Committee on Lighthouses of 1845 recommended "That all expenses for the erection and maintenance of Lighthouses . . . be henceforth defrayed out of the public revenue." 1845 Report, at xii.

[31]See Augustin Cournot, *Researches into the Mathematical Principles of the Theory of Wealth* 99–104 (Nathaniel T. Bacon, trans., 1897). See also Marshall's discussion of Cournot's analysis, 1 *Principles of Economics* 493–95 (9th (Variorum) ed., 1961).

[32]1845 Report, at vii.

[33]T. Golding, *Trinity House from Within* 63 (1929).

Another way in which some reduction in light dues could have been achieved would have been for Trinity House not to earn a net income from the operation of its own lighthouses. This money was, of course, devoted to charitable purposes, mainly the support of retired seamen, their widows and orphans. Such a use of funds derived ultimately from the light dues had been found objectionable by Parliamentary Committees in 1822 and 1834. The 1834 Committee, noting that 142 persons were supported in almshouses and that 8,431 men, women and children received sums ranging from 36 shillings to 30 pounds per annum, proposed that all pensions cease with the lives of those then receiving them and that no new pensioners be appointed, but this was not done.[34]

In 1853, the Government proposed that the proceeds of the light dues no longer be used for charitable purposes. Trinity House responded, in a representation to Her Majesty, claiming that this income was as much its property as it was for private proprietors of lighthouses (to whom compensation was paid):

> The management of lighthouses has been entrusted to [Trinity House], from time to time, by special grants from the Crown or the Legislature. But the acceptance of such grants has in no respect changed the legal position of the Corporation as a private guild, except in so far as it has necessitated the maintenance of lights as a condition of retaining such grants. The legal position of the Corporation with regard to the Crown and the public has in no respect differed from that of individual grantees of light dues or other franchises, as markets, ports, fairs, etc. The argument that the Corporation was ever legally bound to reduce the light dues to the amount of the expenses of maintenance, inclusive or exclusive of interest on the cost of erection, and that they had no right to make any other appropriation, is altogether unfounded in reason or law . . . a grant is valid, if the dues granted are reasonable at the time of the grant, and continues so valid, notwithstanding that from a subsequent increase of shipping the dues may afford a profit. The Crown in these cases acts on behalf of the public; and if it makes a bargain, reasonable at the time, it cannot afterwards retract. . . . The title of the Corporation to the lighthouses erected by them is equally valid with the titles [of private proprietors] . . . , and the charitable purposes to which a portion of those revenues is applied, render the claims of the Corporation at least as deserving of favourable

[34]1834 Report, at xiii.

consideration as those of individuals. . . . The lighthouses and light dues belong to [Trinity House], for the purposes of the Corporation, and are, in the strictest sense, their property for those purposes. . . . The proposal of Her Majesty's Government appears to be that the use of the whole of this vast mass of property shall be given to the shipowners, without any charge beyond the expense of maintaining the lights. It is, as affecting the Corporation's charities, an alienation of property, devoted to the benefit of the decayed masters and seamen of the merchant's service, and their families, and a gift of that property to the shipowners.[35]

This representation was referred to the Board of Trade, which found the arguments of Trinity House without merit:

The Lords of the Committee do not call in question the title of the Corporation of the Trinity House to the property so alleged to be vested in them; but there is . . . this distinction between the case of the Corporation and that of the individuals referred to, that the property so vested in the Corporation has been held and is held by them, so far at least as relates to the light dues in question, in trust for public purposes, and liable, therefore, to be dealt with upon considerations of public policy. Their Lordships cannot admit that is any violation of the principle of property in the reduction of a tax levied for public purposes, where no vested interests have been acquired in the proceeds of the tax; and where the tax in question is one levied upon a particular class of Your Majesty's subjects, without that class deriving any adequate advantage in return (and any excess of light dues beyond the amount necessary to maintain the lights is a tax of this character), the reduction of such a tax not only involves no violation of the principle of property, but is in the highest degree just and expedient. Their Lordships cannot recognise any vested interests in the expectants of the bounty dealt out to poor mariners and their families, at the pleasure of the Corporation, from the surplus revenues of the lights; since it is of the essence of a vested interest that the individuals to whom the privilege is secured are ascertained and known to the law; and while their Lordships would religiously abstain from interfering in the slightest degree with the pensions or other benefits already conferred upon any

[35]Trinity House Charities: Representation from the Corporation of the Trinity House to Her Majesty in Council, on proposal of Government to prevent the Application of Light and Other Dues to Charitable Purposes," in *Parl. Papers* Sess. 1852–53, vol. 98, at 601, 602–03.

person whatsoever, they can acknowledge no injustice in resolving, upon grounds of public policy, to confer upon no new persons a right, to which at present no individual can advance any claim or title. . . . Their Lordships consider that the lights should be maintained by the light dues; and that what the providence of former generations has done in applying dues levied upon ships to the erection of lights for the preservation of ships from shipwreck, is the natural and just inheritance of those who navigate the coasts of the United Kingdom at the present time, and ought to be freely enjoyed by them at the lowest possible charge which the circumstances of the case may permit, and that no other consideration whatever should on any account be suffered to enter into the question.[36]

The use of the proceeds of the light dues for charitable purposes ceased in 1853. As a result, some reduction in the light dues was made possible, price moved closer to marginal cost and numerous ancient mariners and their families, unknown to the law and to us, were worse provided for. But it will be observed that it was not necessary to have a consolidation of all lighthouses under Trinity House to bring about this result.

This change was part of the reorganisation which, in 1853, established the Mercantile Marine Fund, into which the light dues (and certain other monies) were paid and out of which the expenses of running the lighthouse service and some other expenses incurred on behalf of shipping were met.[37] In 1898, the system was again changed. The Mercantile Marine Fund was abolished and the General Lighthouse Fund was set up. The light dues (and only the light dues) were paid into this fund, which was to be used solely for the maintenance of the lighthouse service. At the same time, the system for computing the light dues was simplified, the charge made on each voyage no longer depending, as it had before, on the number of lighthouses which a ship passed or from which it could be presumed to derive a benefit.[38] What was

[36]*Id*. at 605–06.

[37]The Merchant Shipping Law Amendment Act of 1853, 16 & 17 Vic., c.131 §§3–30.

[38]Merchant Shipping (Mercantile Marine Fund) Act of 1898, 61 & 62 Vic., c.44. See the Committee of Inquiry into the Mercantile Marine Fund, Report, Cd. No. 8167 (1896), also found in *Parl. Papers* Sess. 1896, vol. 41, at 113, for the reasons why this change was made in the way light dues were computed. The recommendations of this Committee were adopted by the Government and were incorporated

established in 1898 was essentially the present system of lighthouse finance and administration described in Section II. There
have, of course, been changes in detail but the general character of
the system has remained the same since 1898.

Conclusion

The sketch of the British lighthouse system and its evolution
above shows how limited are the lessons to be drawn from the
remarks of Mill, Sidgwick and Pigou. Mill seems to be saying that
if something like the British system for the finance and administration of lighthouses is not instituted, private operation of lighthouses would be impossible (which is not how most modern
readers would be likely to interpret him). Sidgwick and Pigou
argue that if there are ships which benefit from the lighthouse but
on which tolls cannot be levied, then government intervention
may be called for. But the ships which benefit from British lighthouses but do not pay would presumably be, in the main, those
operated by foreign shipowners which do not call at British ports.
In which case, it is not clear what the character of the required
government action is or what governments are supposed to act.
Should, for example, the Russian, Norwegian, German and French
governments compel their nationals to pay the toll even though
their ships do not call at British ports or should these governments
take action by paying a sum raised out of general taxation into the
British General Lighthouse Fund? Or is the British government
supposed to take action by raising revenue out of general taxation
to be paid into the Lighthouse Fund to offset the failure of these
foreign governments to compel their nationals to contribute to the
Lighthouse Fund?

Now consider what would be likely to happen if support out of
general taxation were substituted for the light dues (which seems
to be what Samuelson would like). First of all, it would increase
the extent to which the British Government and particularly the
Treasury would feel obliged to supervise the operations of the
lighthouse service, in order to keep under control the amount of

---

in the 1898 Act. Objections to the old system arose because the list of lighthouses
from which ships were presumed to benefit on a given voyage was based on the
course of a sailing ship rather than that of a steamship, because the foreign rate
was charged to the last port reached in the United Kingdom in the course of a
voyage and not to the first, while much was made of the complexity of the old
method of calculating the dues.

the subsidy. This intervention of the Treasury would tend to reduce somewhat the efficiency with which the lighthouse service was administered. And it would have another effect. Because the revenue is now raised from the consumers of the service, a committee has been established, the Lights Advisory Committee, representing Shipowners, Underwriters and Shippers, which is consulted about the budget, the operations of the service and particularly about new works. In this way, the lighthouse service is made more responsive to those who make use of its service and because it is the shipping industry which actually pays for additional services, they will presumably support changes in the arrangements only when the value of the additional benefits received is greater than the cost. This administrative arrangement would presumably be discarded if the service were financed out of general taxation and the service would therefore become somewhat less efficient.[39] In general, it would seem to be a safe conclusion that the move to support the lighthouse service out of general taxation would result in a less appropriate administrative structure. And what is the gain which Samuelson sees as coming from this change in the way in which the lighthouse service is financed? It is that some ships which are now discouraged from making a voyage to

[39]The Chairman of the Committee of Inquiry into the Mercantile Marine Fund (see *supra* note 38), was Leonard Courtney, M.P. Mr. Courtney, who was an economist, made essentially the same point in the debate in the House of Commons. Replying to those who had suggested that the lighthouse service should be supported out of general taxation, Mr. Courtney commented: "There is one substantial argument in favour of our maintaining the service as it is, and that is that there is an impression among shipowners—and it is a very useful one—that they have to bear the burden, and they are extremely jealous of the expenditure, and they would claim hereafter, if not now, a share in the administration; that is to say, that they being the people called upon to pay in the first instance, scrutinise the expenditure in which they are interested, and jealously guard it. This is a great advantage, and I conceive that by it economy and efficiency in the coast light service are obtained, and I think that to change a system which secures a frugal and yet sufficient administration of the service would be most inexpedient. The shipowners are jealously watching the whole of the administration, and they claim, I think justly, to have a voice in the matter conceded them. If the cost of lighting the coasts were thrown directly upon the Votes every year, there would not be the same check as is now existing upon unbounded demands which might be made in those ebullitions of feeling to which the nation is always exposed after some great maritime calamity." 40 *Parl. Deb.* (4th Ser.) 186–87 (1898). That is to say, Mr. Courtney was arguing that the method of finance meant that the shipowners were led to exercise at this early date the same influence over expenditures as is now exercised through the Lights Advisory Committee.

Britain because of the light dues would in future do so. As it happens, the form of the toll and the exemptions mean that for most ships the number of voyages will not be affected by the fact that light dues are paid.[40] There may be some ships somewhere which are laid up or broken up because of the light dues, but the number cannot be great, if indeed there are any ships in this category.[41] It is difficult for me to resist the conclusion that the benefit which would come from the abandonment of the light dues would be very unimportant and that there would be some loss from the change in the administrative structure.

The question remains: how is it that these great men have, in their economic writings, been led to make statements about lighthouses which are misleading as to the facts, whose meaning, if thought about in a concrete fashion, is quite unclear, and which, to the extent that they imply a policy conclusion, are very likely wrong? The explanation is that these references by economists to lighthouses are not the result of their having made a study of lighthouses or having read a detailed study by some other econo-

[40]There is no further liability for light dues after the first 10 voyages in a year for "home-trade" ships and the first 6 voyages for "foreign-going" ships. It seems to be the opinion of those conversant with the shipping industry that the vast majority of ships will not need to pay light dues on their last voyages in the year. A cross-channel ferry could probably meet the requisite number of journeys in a few days. Ships trading with Europe or North America will normally not be required to pay light dues on their last voyages. However, the ships trading with Australia will usually not be able to complete the number of voyages necessary to avoid light dues.

[41]I have not been able to secure any precise figures but all indications are that light dues form a very small proportion of the costs of running a ship trading with the United Kingdom. Such statistics as exist support this view. Payments into the General Lighthouse Fund in 1971–1972 were £8,900,000. "General Lighthouse Fund 1971–1972," H.C. Paper No. 301 (in cont. of H.C. Paper No. 211) at 2 (July 3, 1973). In 1971, the earnings of ships owned by U.K. operators and of ships on charter to them for carrying U.K. imports and exports, visitors to the U.K. and U.K. residents were about £700 million. In addition, about £50 million was earned in the U.K. coastal trade. Payments to foreign shipowners for carrying U.K. imports and exports were probably of the order of £600 million in 1971. This suggests that the annual costs of running ships trading with the U.K. must have been about £1,400 million. These estimates are based on figures kindly supplied to me by the Department of Trade. Some of the separate figures brought together to obtain these totals are very rough estimates but they give the order of magnitude and whatever error they contain would not affect the conclusion that payments into the General Lighthouse Fund form a very small proportion of the cost of running a ship trading with the U.K.

mist. Despite the extensive use of the lighthouse example in the literature, no economist, to my knowledge, has ever made a comprehensive study of lighthouse finance and administration. The lighthouse is simply plucked out of the air to serve as an illustration. The purpose of the lighthouse example is to provide "corroborative detail, intended to give artistic verisimilitude to an otherwise bald and unconvincing narrative."[42]

This seems to me to be the wrong approach. I think we should try to develop generalisations which would give us guidance as to how various activities should best be organised and financed. But such generalisations are not likely to be helpful unless they are derived from studies of how such activities are actually carried out within different institutional frameworks. Such studies would enable us to discover which factors are important and which are not in determining the outcome and would lead to generalisations which have a solid base. They are also likely to serve another purpose, by showing us the richness of the social alternatives between which we can choose.

The account in this paper of the British lighthouse system does little more than reveal some of the possibilities. The early history shows that, contrary to the belief of many economists, a lighthouse service can be provided by private enterprise. In those days, shipowners and shippers could petition the Crown to allow a private individual to construct a lighthouse and to levy a (specified) toll on ships benefitting from it. The lighthouses were built, operated, financed and owned by private individuals, who could sell the lighthouse or dispose of it by bequest. The role of the government was limited to the establishment and enforcement of property rights in the lighthouse. The charges were collected at the ports by agents for the lighthouses. The problem of enforcement was no different for them than for other suppliers of goods and services to the shipowner. The property rights were unusual only in that they stipulated the price that could be charged.[43]

---

[42]William S. Gilbert, *The Mikado*.

[43]This arrangement avoided a problem raised by Arrow in discussing the lighthouse example. Arrow says: "In my view, the standard lighthouse example is best analyzed as a problem of small numbers rather than of the difficulty of exclusion though both elements are present. To simplify matters, I will abstract from uncertainty so that the lighthouse keeper knows exactly when each ship will need its services, and also abstract from indivisibility (since the light is either on or off). Assume further that only one ship will be within range of the lighthouse at any

Later, the provision of lighthouses in England and Wales was entrusted to Trinity House, a private organisation with public duties, but the service continued to be financed by tolls levied on ships. The system apparently favoured by Samuelson, finance by the government out of general taxation, has never been tried in Britain. Such a government-financed system does not necessarily exclude the participation of private enterprise in the building or operation of lighthouses but it would seem to preclude private ownership of lighthouses, except in a very attenuated form and would certainly be quite different from the system in Britain which came to an end in the 1830's. Of course, government finance would be very likely to involve both government operation and government ownership of lighthouses. How such governmental systems actually operate I do not know. Bierce's definition of an American lighthouse—"A tall building on the seashore in which the government maintains a lamp and the friend of a politician"[44]—presumably does not tell the whole story.

We may conclude that economists should not use the lighthouse as an example of a service which could only be provided by the government. But this paper is not intended to settle the question of how lighthouse service ought to be organised and financed. This must await more detailed studies. In the meantime, economists wishing to point to a service which is best provided by the government should use an example which has a more solid backing.

---

moment. Then exclusion is perfectly possible; the lighthouse need only shut off its light when a nonpaying ship is coming into range. But there would be only one buyer and one seller and no competitive forces to drive the two into a competitive equilibrium. If in addition the costs of bargaining are high, then it may be most efficient to offer the service free." See Kenneth J. Arrow, "The Organization of Economic Activity: Issues Pertinent to the Choice of Market Versus Nonmarket Allocation," in U.S. Cong. Comm., Subcomm. on Economy in Government, 91st Cong., 1st Sess., The Analysis and Evaluation of Public Expenditures: the PPB System, vol. 1, at 47, 58 (J. Comm. Print, 1969). Arrow's surrealist picture of a lighthousekeeper shutting off the light as soon as it became useful while arguing with the captain about the charge to be made (assuming that the vessel has not run on the rocks in the meantime) bears no relation to the situation faced by those responsible for lighthouse policy. In Britain, no negotiation has been required to determine individual charges and no lighthousekeeper has ever turned off the light for this purpose. Arrow's conclusion that "it may be most efficient to offer the service free" is unexceptionable but also unhelpful since it is equally true that it may not.

[44]Ambrose Bierce, The Devil's Dictionary 193 (1925).

14. The Fable of the Bees: An Economic Investigation

Steven N. S. Cheung

Economists possess their full share of the common ability to invent and commit errors. . . . Perhaps their most common error is to believe other economists.

—George J. Stigler

Ever since A. C. Pigou wrote his books on "welfare,"[1] a divergence between private and social costs has provided the main argument for instituting government action to correct allegedly inefficient market activities. The analysis in such cases has been designed less to aid our understanding of how the economic system operates than to find flaws in it to justify policy recommendations. Both to illustrate the argument and to demonstrate the nature of the actual situation, the quest has been for real-world examples of such defects.

Surprisingly enough, aside from Pigou's polluting factory and Sidgwick's lighthouse, convincing examples were hard to come

Reprinted, by permission, from *Journal of Law and Economics* 16 (April 1973): 11–33.

Facts, like jade, are not only costly to obtain but also difficult to authenticate. I am therefore most grateful to the following beekeepers and farmers: Leonard Almquist, Nat Giacomini, Ancel Goolsbey, L. W. Groves, Rex Haueter, Harold Lange, Lavar Peterson, Elwood Sires, Clarence Smith, Ken Smith, John Steg, P. F. Thurber, and Mrs. Gerald Weddle. All of them provided me with valuable information; some of them made available to me their accounting records and contracts. R. H. Coase inspired the investigation, Yoram Barzel saw that it was conducted thoroughly, and Mrs. Lina Tong rendered her assistance. The investigation is part of a proposed research in the general area of contracts, financially supported by the National Science Foundation.

[1]A. C. Pigou, *Wealth and Welfare* (1912); and *The Economics of Welfare* (1920).

by.[2] It was not until 1952, more than thirty years after Pigou's initial analysis, that J. E. Meade proposed further examples and revitalized the argument for corrective government actions.[3] Meade's prime example, which soon became classic, concerned the case of the apple farmer and the beekeeper. In his own words:

> Suppose that in a given region there is a certain amount of apple-growing and a certain amount of bee-keeping and that the bees feed on the apple blossom. If the apple-farmers apply 10% more labour, land and capital to apple-farming they will increase the output of apples by 10%; but they will also provide more food for the bees. On the other hand, the bee-keepers will not increase the output of honey by 10% by increasing the amount of land, labour and capital to bee-keeping by 10% unless at the same time the apple-farmers also increase their output and so the food of the bees by 10%. . . . We call this a case of an unpaid factor, because the situation is due simply and solely to the fact that the apple-farmer cannot charge the beekeeper for the bees' food.[4]

And Meade applied a similar argument to a reciprocal situation:

> While the apples may provide the food of the bees, the bees may fertilize the apples. . . . By a process similar to that adopted in the previous case we can obtain formulae to show what subsidies and taxes must be imposed.[5]

In another well-known work, Francis M. Bator used Meade's example to infer "market failure":

> It is easy to show that if apple blossoms have a positive effect on honey production . . . any Pareto-efficient solution . . . will associate with apple blossoms a positive Lagrangean shadow-price. If, then, apple producers are unable to protect their equity in apple-nectar and markets do not impute to apple blossoms

[2]Pigou had offered other examples. The example of two roads was deleted from later editions of *The Economics of Welfare*, presumably in an attempt to avoid the criticism by F. H. Knight in "Some Fallacies in the Interpretation of Social Cost," 38 *Q. J. Econ.* 582 (1924). The railroad example has not enjoyed popularity. Most of Pigou's examples, however, were drawn from land tenure arrangements in agriculture, but an exhaustive check of his source references has revealed no hard evidence at all to support his claim of inefficient tenure arrangements.

[3]See J. E. Meade, "External Economies and Diseconomies in a Competitive Situation," 52 *Econ. J.* 54 (1952).

[4]*Id.* at 56–57.

[5]*Id.* at 58.

their correct shadow value, profit-maximizing decisions will fail correctly to allocate resources . . . at the margin. There will be failure "by enforcement." This is what I would call an *ownership* externality.[6]

It is easy to understand why the "apples and bees" example has enjoyed widespread popularity. It has freshness and charm: the pastoral scene, with its elfin image of bees collecting nectar from apple blossoms, has captured the imagination of economists and students alike. However, the universal credence given to the light-hearted fable is surprising; for in the United States, at least, contractual arrangements between farmers and beekeepers have long been routine. This paper investigates the pricing and contractual arrangements of the beekeeping industry in the state of Washington, the location having been selected because the Pacific Northwest is one of the largest apple-growing areas in the world.

Contrary to what most of us have thought, apple blossoms yield little or no honey.[7] But it is true that bees provide valuable pollination services for apples and other plants, and that many other plants do yield lucrative honey crops. In any event, it will be shown that the observed pricing and contractual arrangements governing nectar and pollination services are consistent with efficient allocation of resources.

Some Relevant Facts of Beekeeping

Although various types of bees pollinate plants, beekeeping is confined almost exclusively to honeybees.[8] The hive used by bee-

[6]Francis M. Bator, "The Anatomy of Market Failure," 72 *Q. J. Econ.* 351, 364 (1958).

[7]The presence of apple honey in the market is therefore somewhat mysterious. While occasionally apple orchards in the Northwest do yield negligible amounts of nectar, beekeepers are frank to point out that the dandelion and other wild plants in the orchard are often the sources of "apple" honey, so called. Elsewhere, as in New York, it was reported that apple orchards yielded slightly more nectar. See, for example, A. I. & E. R. Root, *The ABC and XYZ of Bee Culture* 386 (1923). The explanation for this divergence of facts, to my mind, lies in the different lengths of time in which the hives are placed in the apple orchards: in Root's day the hives were probably left in the orchards for longer periods than today.

[8]See George E. Bohart, "Management of Wild Bees," in U.S. Dep't of Agriculture, *Beekeeping in the United States* 109 (Ag. Handbook No. 335, 1971, hereinafter cited as *Beekeeping . . .*). Leafcutters, for example, have recently been introduced for the pollination of alfalfa and clover seeds. But these bees yield no honey crop and are seldom kept.

keepers in the state of Washington is of the Langstroth design which consists of one or two brood chambers, a queen excluder, and from zero to six supers. A brood chamber is a wooden box large enough to contain eight or ten movable frames, each measuring 9-1/8 by 17-5/8 by 1-3/8 inches. Within each frame is a wax honeycomb built by the bees. In the hexagonal cells of this comb the queen lays her eggs and the young bees, or "brood," are raised. It is here also that the bees store the nectar and pollen which they use for food. Honey is not usually extracted from this chamber but from the frames of a shallower box, called a super, placed above the brood chamber. The queen excluder, placed between the super and the brood chamber, prevents the laying of eggs in the upper section.[9]

The bees, and consequently the beekeepers, work according to a yearly cycle. Around the beginning of March, a Washington beekeeper will decide whether he wants to prepare for the pollination season by ordering booster packages of bees from California to strengthen his colonies, depleted and weakened during the winter and early spring. Alternatively, he may decide to build up the colony by transporting the hives to farms or pastures in warmer areas, such as Oregon and California. The colony hatches continuously from spring to fall, and the growth rate is rapid. Reared on pollen, the infant bees remain in the brood stage for about three weeks before entering the productive life of the colony for five or six weeks. Active workers spend three weeks cleaning and repairing the brood cells and nursing the young, then live out the remainder of their short lives foraging for pollen and nectar.[10]

Because of the bees' quick growth, the working "strength" of a colony includes both brood and workers, and increases from about five frames in early spring to about twelve by late summer. Spring is the primary season for fruit pollination, and beekeepers usually market a standard colony strength of roughly four frames of bees and two to three frames of brood for pollination services. But since empty frames are needed to accommodate the expanding colony,

[9]For further details see Spencer M. Riedel, Jr., "Development of American Beehive," in *Beekeeping* . . . 8–9; A. I. & E. R. Root, *supra* note 7, at 440–58; Carl Johansen, "Beekeeping" (PNW Bulletin No. 79, rev. ed., March 1970).

[10]For further details see Carl Johansen, *supra* note 9; F. E. Moeller, "Managing Colonies for High Honey Yields," in *Beekeeping* . . . 23; E. Oertel, "Nectar and Pollen Plants," in *Beekeeping* . . . 10.

two-story hives, with 16 or 20 frames, are used. The swarming period, beginning in mid-summer and lasting until early fall, is the peak honey season, and the yield per hive will vary positively with the colony strength. Because the maximization of honey yield requires that the colonies be of equal strength, they are usually reassorted in preparation for the major honey season, so that the number of colonies at the "peak" is generally larger than the number in spring.[11]

When pollen fails in late fall, the hives become broodless and the bee population begins to decline. During the idle winter months adult bees live considerably longer than in the active season, and they can survive the winter if about 60 pounds of nectar are left in the hive. But in the northern part of the state and in Canada, where cold weather makes the overwintering of bees more costly, the common practice is to eliminate the bees and extract the remaining honey. It should be noted here that bees can be captured, and that they can be easily eliminated by any of a large number of pesticide sprays.[12] The cost of enforcing property rights in nectar is therefore much lower than economists have been led to believe.

Few agricultural crops, to my knowledge, exhibit a higher year-to-year variance of yield than does the honey crop. Several natural factors contribute. Cold weather and rain discourage the bees from working, and winds alter their direction of flight. Also, the nectar flows of plants are susceptible to shocks of heat and cold.[13] The

[11]According to a survey conducted by Robert K. Lesser in 1968, based on a sample of 30 out of 60 commercial beekeepers in the state of Washington, the total number of peak colonies is 14.6% higher than that of spring colonies. See Robert K. Lesser, "An Investigation of the Elements of Income from Beekeeping in the State of Washington" 74 (unpublished thesis, Sch. of Bus. Admin., Gonzaga Univ., 1969).

[12]See, for example, A. I. & E. R. Root, *supra* note 9, at 97–103; Eugene Keyarts, "Bee Hunting, Gleanings in Bee Culture" 329–33 (June 1960); U.S. Dep't of Agriculture, *Protecting Honey Bees from Pesticides* (Leaflet 544, 1972); Carl A. Johansen, *How to Reduce Poisoning of Bees from Pesticides* (Pamphlet EM 3473, Wash. St. Univ., College of Ag., May 1971); Philip F. Torchio, "Pesticides," in *Beekeeping* . . . 97.

[13]See E. Oertel, *supra* note 10; C. R. Ribbands, *The Behaviour and Social Life of Honeybees* 69–75 (1953); Roger A. Morse, "Placing Bees in Apple Orchards," *Gleanings in Bee Culture* 230–33 (April 1960). Owing to its weather, Washington is not one of the better honey yielding states in the Union. Data made available to me by the U.S. Dep't of Agriculture indicates that over the years (1955–1971) Washington ranks 24th among 48 states in yield per colony and 20th in the total number of colonies. The U.S. Dep't of Agriculture data, like those obtained by Lesser, provide

plants yielding most honey are mint, fireweed, and the legumes, such as alfalfa and the clovers. Fruit trees usually have low nectar flows, although orange blossoms (in California) are excellent. Indeed, the pollination of fruits, especially the cherry in early spring, may actually detract from the yield of honey: less honey may be in the hive after pollination than was there initially, owing to the bees' own consumption. Another reason for the low honey yield from fruit trees is the relatively short time that the hives are left in the orchards.

Cross-pollination is accidentally effected as the bees forage for nectar and pollen. Pollination services were not marketed before World War I, primarily because small farms had enough flowering plants and trees to attract wild insects. It was not until 1910 and the advent of modern orcharding, with its large acreage and orderly planting, that markets for pollination services began to grow rapidly.[14] Today, the services are demanded not only for production of fruits but also for the setting (fertilizing) of seeds for legumes and vegetables. Evidence is incontrovertible that the setting of fruits and seeds increases with the number of hives per acre, that the pollination productivity of bees is subject to diminishing returns, and, despite some beekeepers' claims to the contrary, beyond some point the marginal productivity may even be negative.[15] There is also strong evidence that pollination yield will improve if the hives are placed strategically throughout the farm rather than set in one spot.[16] The closer a particular area is to a

---

no information on the different honey yields and pollination requirements of various plants and are therefore of little use for our present purpose. It should be noted that the U.S. Dep't of Agriculture overall yield data are significantly lower than those obtained by Lesser and by me. See Robert K. Lesser, *supra* note 11.

[14]See M. D. Levin, "Pollination," in *Beekeeping . . . 77.*

[15]*Id.;* 9th Pollination Conference, Report, *The Indispensable Pollinators* (Ag. Extension Serv., Hot Springs, Ark., October 12–15, 1970); G. E. Bohart, "Insect Pollination of Forage Legumes," 41 *Bee World* 57–64, 85–97 (1960); J. B. Free, "Pollination of Fruit Trees," 41 *Bee World* 141–51, 169–86 (1960); U.S. Dep't of Agriculture, *Using Honey Bees to Pollinate Crops* (Leaflet 549, 1968); *Get More Fruit with Honey Bee Pollinators* (Pamphlet EM 2922, Wash. St. Univ., March 1968); *Protect Berry Pollinating Bees* (Pamphlet EM 3341, Wash. St. Univ., February 1970); *Increase Clover Seed Yields with Adequate Pollination* (Pamphlet EM 3444, Wash. St. Univ., April 1971); *Honey Bees Increase Cranberry Production* (Pamphlet EM 3468, Wash. St. Univ., April 1971).

[16]See, for example, Douglas Oldershaw, "The Pollination of High Bush Blueberries," in *The Indispensable Pollinators, supra* note 15, at 171–76; Roger A. Morse, *supra* note 13.

hive, the more effective will be the pollination within that area. Although each individual bee will forage only a few square yards, the bees from one hive will collectively pollinate a large circular area,[17] and this gives rise to a problem: given a high cost to control fully the foraging behavior of bees, if similar orchards are located close to one another, one who hires bees to pollinate his own orchard will in some degree benefit his neighbors. This complication will be further discussed in the next section.

In the state of Washington, about 60 beekeepers each own 100 colonies or more; at the peak season the state's grand total of colonies is about 90,000. My investigation, conducted in the spring of 1972, covered a sample of nine beekeepers and a total of approximately 10,000 spring colonies. (One of these beekeepers specialized in cut-comb honey and he will be treated separately in a footnote.) Table 1 lists the bee-related plants covered by my investigation. As seen from Columns (3) and (4), some plants (such as cherry trees) require pollination services for fruit setting but yield no honey; some (such as mint) yield honey while requiring no pollination service; and some (such as alfalfa) are of a reciprocal nature. Note that when alfalfa and the clovers are grown only for hay, pollination services are not required, although these plants yield honey.

The practice of relocating hives from farm to farm, by truck, enables the beekeeper to obtain multiple crops a year, either in rendering pollination service or in extracting honey. However, while the maximum observed number of crops per hive per year is four and the minimum is two, my estimate is that a hive averages only 2.2 crops a year. More frequent rotation not only involves greater costs of moving and of standardizing hives, but abbreviates the honey yield per crop. In the southern part of the state, where the relatively warm climate permits an early working season, beekeepers usually begin by pollinating either cherry or almond (in California) in early spring. The hives may or may not then be moved northward in late spring, when apple and soft fruits (and some late cherry) begin to bloom.[18]

---

[17]There is, however, little agreement as to how far a bee could fly: estimated range is from one to three miles. For general foraging behavior, see M. D. Levin, *supra* note 14, at 79; O. W. Park, "Activities of Honeybees", in *The Hive and the Honeybee* 125, 149–206 (Roy A. Grout ed., 1946); C. R. Ribbands, *supra* note 13.

[18]Following the practice of local beekeepers, we use the term "soft fruit" to refer

Table 1

BEE-RELATED PLANTS INVESTIGATED (STATE OF WASHINGTON, 1971)

(1) Plants	(2) Number of Beekeepers	(3) Pollination Services Rendered	(4) Surplus Honey Expected	(5) Approximate Season	(6) Number of Hives per Acre (Range)
Fruits & nuts					
Apple & soft fruits[a]	7	Yes	No	Mid-April–mid-May	0.4 to 2
Blueberry (with maple)	1	Yes	Yes	May	2
Cherry (early)	1	Yes	No	March–early April	0.5 to 2
Cherry	2	Yes	No	April	0.5 to 2
Cranberry	2	Yes	Negligible	June	1.5
Almond (Calif.)	2	Yes	No	February–March	2
Legumes					
Alfalfa	5	Yes and no[c]	Yes	June–September	0.3 to 3
Red clover	4	Yes and no	Yes	June–September	0.5 to 5
Sweet clover	1	No[d]	Yes	June–September	0.5 to 1
Pasture[b]	4	No	Yes	Late May–September	0.3 to 1
Other plants					
Cabbage	1	Yes	Yes	Early April–May	1
Fireweed	2	No	Yes	July–September	n.a.
Mint	3	No	Yes	July–September	0.4 to 1

[a]Soft fruits include pears, apricots, and peaches.

[b]Pasture includes a mixture of plants, notably the legumes and other wild flowers such as dandelions.

[c]Pollination services are rendered for alfalfa and the clovers if their seeds are intended to be harvested; when they are grown only for hay, hives will still be employed for nectar extraction.

[d]Sweet clover may also require pollination services, but such a case is not covered by this investigation.

The lease period for effective pollination during spring bloom is no more than a week. But then, for a month or two between the end of fruit pollination and the beginning of summer nectar flow, the hives have little alternative usage. Since this period is substantially longer than the time needed for the beekeeper to check and standardize his hives for the honey crops, he will generally be in no hurry to move them and will prefer to leave them in the orchards with no extra charge, unless the farmer is planning to spray with insecticide. The appropriate seasons for the various plants listed in Column (5) of Table 1, may not, therefore, match the lengths of hive leases. Lease periods are generally longer for honey crops, for the collection of nectar takes more time.

The sixth column in Table 1 indicates the various hive-densities employed. The number of hives per acre depends upon the size of the area to be serviced, the density of planting, and, in the case of fruit pollination, the age of the orchards. For the pollination of fruits, the hives are scattered throughout the farm, usually with higher densities employed in older orchards because the trees are not strategically placed to facilitate the crossing of pollen. The most popular choices are one hive per acre and one hive per two acres. It is interesting, and easily understood, that farmers demand significantly fewer hives for pollination than the number recommended by entomologists:[19] both are interested in the maximization of yield, but for the farmer such maximization is subject to the constraint of hive rentals. When bees are employed to produce honey only, the hives are placed together in one location, called an apiary, for greater ease of handling.[20] The relatively large variation in hive densities required if legumes are, or are not, to be pollinated is discussed in the next section.

Before we turn to an analysis of the pricing and contractual behavior of beekeepers and farmers, I must point out that the two government programs which support the beekeeping industry did not constitute relevant constraints for the period under investigation. The honey price-support program, initiated in 1949, involves

---

to peaches, pears, and apricots, generally grown in the same area, and often in the same orchard, as apples. (By standard usage, the term refers only to the various berry plants.)

[19]See note 15 *supra*.

[20]See, for example, W. P. Nye, "Beekeeping Regions in the United States," in *Beekeeping . . . 17.*

purchase of honey at supported prices by the Commodity Credit Corporation.[21] For the period under investigation, however, the supported price was about 20 per cent lower than the market price.[22] Section 804 of the Agricultural Act of 1970, effectuated in 1971 and designed to reimburse beekeepers for any loss due to pesticide sprays, has been largely ignored by beekeepers because of the difficulty of filing effective claims with the federal government.[23]

The Observed Pricing and Contractual Behavior

It is easy to find conclusive evidence showing that both nectar and pollination services are transacted in the marketplace: in some cities one need look no further than the yellow pages of the Telephone Directory. But the existence of prices does not in itself imply an efficient allocation of resources. It is, therefore, necessary to demonstrate the effectiveness of the market in dictating the use even of those resources—bees, nectar, and pollen—which, admittedly, are elusive in character and relatively insignificant in value. In doing so, I shall not attempt to estimate the standard sets of marginal values which an efficient market is said to equate: the burden of such a task must rest upon those who believe the government can costlessly and accurately make these estimates for the imposition of the "ideal" tax-subsidy schemes. Rather, I offer below an analysis based on the equimarginal principle. To the extent that the observed pricing and contractual behavior fails to falsify the implications derived from this analysis we conclude that (1) the observed behavior is explained, and (2) the observations are consistent with efficient allocation of resources.

The Analysis

The reciprocal situation in which a beekeeper is able to extract honey from the same farm to which he renders pollination services

[21]See Harry A. Sullivan, "Honey Price Support Program," in *Beekeeping* . . . 136.

[22]From 1970 to 1972 the supported prices were near 11.5 cents per pound, whereas the market wholesale price was above 14 cents per pound. Between 1950 and 1965 were seven years in which the CCC purchased no honey, and two years of negligible amounts. See Harry A. Sullivan, *supra* note 21, at 137.

[23]See 7 U.S.C. § 135 b, note (1970); Pub. L. No. 91-524 § 804. My judgment is based both on the behavior of beekeepers (see next section) after the initiation of the Act and on the complexity of relevant claim forms which I have at hand. In April 1972 beekeepers associations were still lobbying for easier claiming conditions.

poses an interesting theoretic riddle. The traditional analysis of such a condition relies on some interdependent production functions, and is, I think, unnecessarily complex.[24] The method employed here simply treats pollination services and honey yield as components of a joint product generated by the hive. That is, the rental price per hive received by a beekeeper for placing his hives on a farm may be paid in terms of honey, of a money fee, or of a combination of both. The money fee or the honey yield may be either positive or negative, but their total measures the rental value of the hive.

The solution is illustrated in Figure 1. We assume that the hives are always strategically placed. In Figure 1a the curve $(\partial N/\partial h)_a$ depicts the value of the marginal nectar product of a farm in which beehives are used *only* for the extraction of nectar (as with fireweed, mint, or alfalfa grown only for hay), with the farming assets held constant. Given the market-determined rental price of OA per hive, constrained wealth maximization implies that OQ' of hives will be employed. In this case, the beekeeper will be remunerated only in honey, and will pay an *apiary rent* equal to area ABC (or DB per hive) to the farmer. The curve $(\partial P/\partial h)_b$, on the other hand, depicts the value of the marginal pollination product for a farm which employs hives for pollination *only* (as with cherry or apple orchards). Here the number of hives employed will be OQ, which again is the result of wealth maximization. With zero honey yield, the money pollination fee per hive is again OA, and the *orchard rent* is represented by the area AGH.

We now turn to the joint product case in Figure 1b, where hives are used both for pollination and for the extraction of nectar (as in the setting of alfalfa and clover seeds). The curves $(\partial P/\partial h)_c$ and $(\partial N/\partial h)_c$ respectively are the values of marginal pollination and of marginal nectar products. Their *vertical* summation, the solid line $(\partial V/\partial h)_c$, is the total marginal value. Wealth maximization implies the employment of OQ" of hives, the point where the rental price per hive equals the aggregate marginal value. As drawn, area HIJ

[24]In J. E. Meade, *supra* note 3, at 58, this problem is set up in terms of the interdependent functions $x_1 = H_1 (l_1, c_1, x_2)$ and $x_2 = H_2 (l_2, c_2, x_1)$. I find Meade's analysis difficult to follow. Elsewhere Otto A. Davis and Andrew Whinston employ the functions $C_1 = C_1 (q_1, q_2)$ and $C_2 = C_2 (q_1, q_2)$ in their treatment of certain "externalities." It is not clear, however, that the authors had the bee example in mind. See Otto A. Davis & Andrew Whinston, "Externalities, Welfare, and the Theory of Games," 70 *J. Pol. Econ.* 241 (1962).

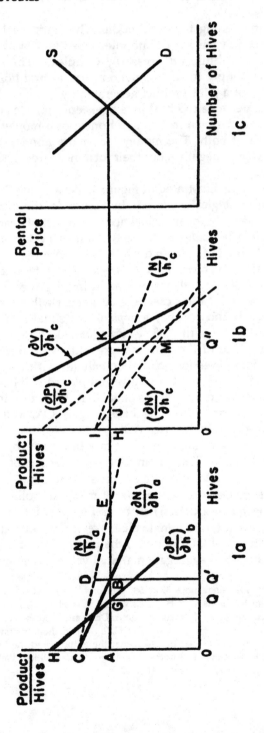

FIGURE 1

is smaller than area JKM. This implies that the value of the *average* nectar product, $(N/h)_c$, must pass below point K, as it does here at L. In this case the rental price per hive, KQ", will consist of LQ" in honey yield and KL in pollination fee. For this joint product situation, of course, it is possible to construct a case in which $(N/h)_c$ passes above point K, thus yielding an apiary rent. It is also possible to construct cases where the number of hives employed yields zero or negative marginal productivity, in either nectar or pollination. In other words, *zero or negative marginal productivity in one component of the joint product is consistent with efficient allocation of resources.*

Under open competition, there are large numbers of potential participants in each of the cases above. The aggregate total marginal value curve for the market, or the market demand for hives, is therefore the horizontal summation of a large number of the *solid* curves in Figures 1a and 1b. Similarly, the market supply of hives is the horizontal summation of the marginal costs of producing and keeping hives of all actual and potential beekeepers. Both market curves are shown in Figure 1c.[25] Assuming no costs for collating bids and asks or for forming rental contracts among all actual and potential participants, the price per hive, OA, is determined in the market. The Pareto condition is satisfied: the value of the marginal product of a hive is the same on every farm, and in turn equals the rental price and the marginal opportunity cost of producing the hive.

Tests of Implications

Before we derive and test some implications of the above analysis, it is necessary to point out the limitations of the information at hand. Since no attempt is made to estimate the marginal values or the elasticities of the marginal products, we will seek to confirm the marginal equalities with some observed average values. These include apiary rent, pollination fees, honey yields per hive, and the wholesale price of honey. We also have information on the number of hives employed on different farms, and some other numerical data. My choice of data for the honey yield per hive, however, must be qualifed. The large fluctuations in yield from year to year and even from farm to farm caused by uncontrollable

---

[25]More variables are usually used in the derivation of these curves, but for our present purpose little is gained by incorporating them.

natural phenomena makes the use of the actual observed yields of a particular year, or even of a few years, irrelevant for our purposes. Take, for example, the exceptionally poor year of 1971 when, in many cases, the yield per hive was just one-third of that in a normal year. This windfall loss is irrelevant for decision-making (although the expected variance is relevant), and it cannot be attributed to market "failure." Lacking sufficient data to compute the honey yield per hive extracted from various plants over time, I resort to the expected yields as reported by beekeepers. Fortunately, their estimates for yields under comparable conditions exhibit remarkable consistency.

An overall view of the pricing structure is shown in Table 2. Since a hive has different rental values for different seasons, we divide the time period into three productive seasons: early spring, late spring, and the honey season (summer to fall). Surplus honey is not expected in the early spring season, although nectar may accumulate in the brood chamber and there may be a gain in brood strength. Most beekeepers in the state are idle during this season, and pollination is confined to almond in California or cherry in the southern part of Washington. The rental value of hives is the highest in the major pollination season of late spring (April to June), second highest in the major honey season, and lowest in the early spring (March).

The pollination fees listed in Table 2 are based on 1971 data, but they have remained roughly constant from 1970 to 1972. The wholesale honey prices, however, are based on 1970 and early 1971 data, as the unexpectedly low honey yield throughout the country in 1971 generated a sharp rise in prices (from 14 cents a pound in April 1971 to 32 cents a pound in March 1972). The apiary rents are paid mostly in refined and bottled honey, and are therefore converted into money values according to 1970 retail honey prices. To maintain consistency with pollination fees, the apiary rents are computed per hive, although in the latter contracts the number of hives is not stipulated.

The following test implications are derived from our analysis:

1. Our first implication is that, at the same season and with colonies of the same strength, the rental price per hive obtained from different farms or by different beekeepers will be roughly the same whether the hive is employed for pollination, for honey production, or for a combination of both. By "roughly the same" I do not mean that hive rentals are invariable among different bee-

Table 2

PRICING SCHEMES AND EXPECTED HONEY YIELDS OF BEE-RELATED PLANTS (STATE OF WASHINGTON, 1970–1971)

Seasons	Plants	Surplus Honey Expected (Pounds per Hive)	Honey Prices per Pound (Wholesale, 1970)	Pollination Fees (Range, 1971)	Approximate Apiary Rent per Hive (Range, 1970–1)
Early spring	Almond (Calif.)	0	—	$5–$8	0
	Cherry	0	—	$6–$8	0
Late spring (major pollination season)	Apple & soft fruits	0	—	$9–$10	0
	Blueberry (with maple)	40	14¢	$5	0
	Cabbage	15	13¢	$8	0
	Cherry	0	—	$9–$10	0
	Cranberry	5	13¢	$9	0
Summer and early fall (major honey season)	Alfalfa	60	14.5¢	0	13¢–60¢
	Alfalfa (with pollination)	25–35	14.5¢	$3–$5	0
	Fireweed	60	14.5¢	0	25¢–63¢
	Mint	70–75	11¢	0	15¢–65¢
	Pasture	60	14¢	0	15¢–65¢
	Red clover	60	14¢	0	65¢
	Red clover (with pollination)	0–35	14¢	$3–$6	0
	Sweet clover	60	14¢	0	20¢–25¢

keepers. Rather, I mean that (a) any differences which do occur are statistically no more significant than those for most other commodities in the market, and that (b) there is a strong *negative* correlation between the pollination fee (hive rental in money) and the expected honey yield (hive rental in kind).

Data from the early spring season are not suitable to test this implication because during this period there are great variations in colony strength, in the gains in brood and unextracted nectar, and in distances travelled by beekeepers to deliver the hives.[26] Lacking sufficient information to make appropriate adjustments for these variations in calculating the rental price per hive, we concentrate on data from the late spring and summer seasons.

In contracting for pollination services, beekeepers offer discounts for larger numbers of hives and for less elaborate hive dispersals. Of the four beekeepers from whom detailed records are available, for example, each served from 10 to 14 farms of apples and soft fruits; their mean hive rentals in the major pollination season ranged from $9.20 to $9.68 and their coefficients of variation from 0.025 to 0.053.[27] To reduce the effects on price generated by discounts, we use the mean rentals for the above four beekeepers and the reported means from beekeepers who did not maintain records. Our data thus comprise separate observations of the mean hive rental of each beekeeper, of each different plant, and (for the summer season) of each different expected honey yield for the same plant. The latter separation is requisite because the expectation of honey yield varies greatly depending on whether pollination is, or is not, required in the case of such plants as alfalfa.

The coefficient of variation of the mean hive rentals among beekeepers who engaged in the pollination of apples (including soft fruits) and cherries (9 observations in total) is 0.035. The

[26]In the pollination of almond, for example, $5.00 is charged for a one-story hive and $6.00 to $8.00 for a two-story hive. On the one hand, Washington beekeepers have to travel to California to obtain this amount when they could have earned the same fee locally in the pollination of early cherry. On the other hand, however, the brood gain is greater with almond than with cherry; also, unextracted nectar in the brood chamber gains significantly in the case of almond but is likely to suffer a net loss with early cherry.

[27]An analysis of variance performed for these four beekeepers shows no significant difference in their mean rentals in the pollination of apple and soft fruits. However, the coefficient of variation of their means, 0.018, is lower than those computed from a larger body of data. This simply indicates a very low variation among the four who provided detailed records.

expected honey yield for these observations is zero. When we extend the computation to include cranberry, blueberry and cabbage pollination (13 observations in total), with expected honey yields converted into monetary terms and added to the pollination fees, the coefficient of variation is 0.042. We may meaningfully compare our coefficients of variations with those cited by George Stigler:[28] automobile prices (0.017) and anthracite coal prices (0.068).

Another, and more illuminating, way of testing our implication is through the relationship

$$x_0 = x_1 + x_2, \tag{1}$$

where x_0 is the total rent per hive, x_1 is the rent paid in money, and x_2 is the expected rent paid in nectar. During the major pollination season, x_1 is positive for all our observations, but during the summer honey season negative values for x_1 (that is, payments in apiary rents) are common. As noted earlier, x_2 may also be positive or negative, but it is generally either zero or positive for the late spring and summer seasons. In the major pollination season, the mean values of equation (1) are \$9.65 = \$9.02 + \$0.64.

The variance of x_0 can be broken down to

$$\sigma^2_{x_0} = \sigma^2_{x_1} + \sigma^2_{x_2} + 2 \operatorname{Cov}(x_1, x_2). \tag{2}$$

With a total of 13 observations in late spring, the corresponding values are

$$0.166 = 1.620 + 2.317 - 3.771.$$

The variability in x_1 is almost entirely accounted for by the variability in x_2, as reflected by the large negative covariance term. The coefficient of correlation between x_1 and x_2 is -0.973.

Turning to the summer honey season, we have a total of 23 observations, covering mint (3), fireweed (2), pasture (4), sweet clover (1), red clover (6), and alfalfa (7). The mean values of equation (1) are \$8.07 = \$1.30 + \$6.77. The values corresponding to equation (2) are

$$0.806 = 5.414 + 6.182 - 10.791.$$

Again, most of the variability in x_1 is strongly and negatively correlated with that of x_2. The remaining variance of x_0 (with a coefficient of variation of 0.111) is larger here than in the major

[28]George J. Stigler, "The Economics of Information," 69 *J. Pol. Econ.* 213 (1961).

pollination season. This can be explained as follows. First, high risks are associated with the expected honey yields, and beekeepers seem willing to settle for lower, but more certain, incomes. Since x_1 is more certain than x_2, beekeepers seem willing to accept a lower x_0 with a higher ratio of x_1 to x_2,[29] and the variability in this ratio is larger in summer than in spring. Similarly, they will accept a lower expected mean of x_2 for mint than for other honey crops, since mint is generally known to have the smallest variance in expected honey yield of any crop in the state.[30] A second, and more important, factor contributing to the larger variance of x_0 is the premium paid to beekeepers to assume the risk of pollinating crops (notably red clover) where the use of pesticide sprays on neighboring farms poses the danger of loss of bees. Since our information is inadequate to support adjustments for these factors, the resultant distortions must remain. Even so, the coefficient of correlation between x_1 and x_2 computed from the data is -0.933.

2. The preceding evidence confirms that the rental prices of hives employed in different uses by different beekeepers lie on a roughly horizontal line. However, it does not confirm that these prices are equated to the marginal productivities. Refer to Figure 1, for example: the employment of hives might be at a point such as E rather than at G, B, or K. We now turn to some testable implications regarding the tendency toward the equalization of price and marginal productivity.

One obvious implication is that, if the employment of hives renders no valuable pollination services, then an apiary rent will always be observed. In the entire body of evidence available to me,

[29]This statement is drawn only from casual conversations with beekeepers; no attempt was made to seek refuting evidence.

[30]Inconclusive evidence indicates that hive rentals (paid in honey) obtained from mint is about 40 cents less than those obtained from other honey-yielding plants. Although available information is insufficient for us to compute the year-to-year variances of the honey yields of different plants, ranges of yields as recalled by beekeepers are larger than most agricultural crops.

Because honey from mint has an undesirably strong flavor that excludes it from the retail market, it is either sold to bakeries or used to feed bees during the winter. Quite understandably, onion honey shares the distinction of being much cheaper than any other. Generally rated as the best is orange honey, which commands a wholesale premium of about 1 to 2 cents a pound. Between the extremes, different varieties of honey have roughly the same value and are graded more by clarity than by taste.

there is not a single observation to the contrary,[31] and this means, referring to Figure 1a, that the employment of hives is to the left of point E. It should be noted here that even in the absence of demand for pollination some is effected when bees forage for nectar from alfalfa and the clovers, but this is not to be treated as a service unless the seeds are harvested.

Less obvious implications can be obtained from the case of a farm where hives may be employed for nectar extraction only *or* jointly with pollination services. When we discussed the reciprocal case, as depicted in Figure 1b, it was noted that either an apiary rent or a pollination fee may be paid. With simple manipulation, the following implications are evident:

a. If an apiary rent is paid in the case of a joint product, and if the marginal pollination product is positive, the number of hives employed per acre is necessarily greater than where bees are used only for nectar extraction on the same or a similar farm.

b. If a pollination fee is paid in the case of a joint product, the number of hives employed per acre is necessarily greater than where bees are used only for nectar extraction on the same or a similar farm.

While both implications indicate a tendency toward point K (in Figure 1b), we lack sufficient information regarding the marginal pollination product to test (a) above. But since in every available observation involving pollination and nectar extraction a pollination fee is paid, only implication (b) is relevant for our purposes.

---

[31]One beekeeper specializing in cut-comb honey reported that he pays apiary rents even though no surplus honey is expected, provided that gains in brood strength and in unextracted nectar are expected to be substantial, as when the hives are placed in a farm with maples. This beekeeper is excluded from our first test of implication because he did not engage in pollination and his colonies were of greater strengths.

Cut-comb honey is more expensive than ordinary honey because the comb wax, which goes with the honey, is about three times the price of honey per pound. Only honey of top grades (very clear) will be extracted. This observation is implied by the law of demand, since with the comb top-grade honey becomes relatively cheap. Implied by the same law also is that this beekeeper chooses to forgo pollination contracts so that a higher honey yield can be obtained (see evidence in implication test 2). Even during the major pollination season, when little honey can be expected, he prefers to place his hives in farms where the colonies will gain greater strength than would occur if they were used for pollination. For a related discussion on similar implications of the law of demand, see Armen A. Alchian & William R. Allen, *Exchange and Production: Theory in Use* 78–79 (1969). These implications are accepted here in spite of the criticisms in John P. Gould & Joel Segall, "The Substitution Effects of Transportation Costs," 77 *J. Pol. Econ.* 130 (1969).

The evidence, obtained from red clover and alfalfa farms, strongly confirms the implication. The density of hives employed is at least twice as great when the bees are used for both pollination service and nectar extraction as when used for nectar extraction only. As a rule, this increase in hive density leads to a sharp decrease in the expected honey yield per hive. In the typical case, the density of hives in alfalfa and clover farms for pollination services is about 2.5 times what would be employed for nectar extraction only, and the expected honey yield per hive is reduced by 50 per cent. This indicates the marginal nectar product of a hive is close to zero and possibly negative. In one extreme case, in a red clover farm the hive density with pollination services is reported at about seven or eight times that for nectar extraction only; since the expected honey yield is then reduced to zero, the marginal nectar product of the hive is clearly negative! But, as noted earlier, zero or negative marginal product in one component of a joint product is consistent with efficient allocation of resources.

3. It remains for us to show that the rental price of a hive is roughly equal to the marginal cost of keeping it. Lacking data on marginal cost, we will show that the price approximates the average cost, as implied by competition. We will make the comparison in terms of some general considerations. The expected annual income of a spring colony under a normal rate of utilization, as of 1970–1971, is about $19.00. This includes rentals from a pollination crop, a honey crop, an occasional extra crop (for some hives), and a small amount from the sale of beeswax.[32] The costs of delivering or moving a hive and of finding and contracting the farmers for its use are estimated to total about $9.00 per year.[33] This figure is obtained as follows. Some beekeepers lease some of their hives to other beekeepers on a share contract basis; the lessor receives 50 to 55 per cent of whatever income in money and in kind the lessee

[32]In Lesser's investigation (*supra* note 11) the actual mean annual income of a spring colony for the year 1967 was estimated to be $14.71, and the actual honey yields of that year were slightly larger than our expected honey yields. But in 1967 the price of honey was about 16% lower than that in 1970; and Lesser's estimate of pollination income per hive is about 37% lower than mine, owing both to a rise in pollination fees in recent years and to different samplings of beekeepers. According to Lesser's estimate, beeswax constitutes 4.4% of the beekeeper's total income.

[33]The moving costs cover labor, truck, and other hive-handling equipment. Depending on the time of the year, a complete hive (with supers) weighs somewhere between 80 and 250 pounds.

obtains from the farmers. Since the lessor could have contracted to serve the farmers himself and obtained the entire income of the $19.00, the fact that he has chosen to take 45 to 50 per cent less indicates that $9.00 must approximate such costs. The interest forgone in keeping a hive is about $3.00 per year.[34] The cost of renewing the colony strength in early spring is about $4.50, the price of a standard booster package of bees.[35] This leaves about $2.50 to cover the costs of depreciation of the hive value, the labor involved in checking and standardizing hives, space for keeping hives in the winter, and the equipment used for honey extraction.

Characteristics of the Contractual Arrangements

Contracts between beekeepers and farmers may be oral or written. I have at hand two types of written contracts. One is formally printed by an association of beekeepers; another is designed for specific beekeepers, with a few printed headings and space for stipulations to be filled in by hand.[36] Aside from situations where a third party demands documented proof of the contract (as when a beekeeper seeks a business loan), written contracts are used primarily for the initial arrangement between parties; otherwise oral agreements are made. Although a written contract is more easily enforceable in a court of law, extra-legal constraints are present: information travels quickly through the closely knit society of beekeepers and farmers,[37] and the market will penalize any party who does not honor his contracts. Oral contracts are rarely broken.

Pollination contracts usually include stipulations regarding the number and strength of the colonies, the rental fee per hive, the time of delivery and removal of hives, the protection of bees from pesticide sprays, and the strategic placing of hives. Apiary lease

[34]A complete hive, used but in good condition, sells for about $35.00. The borrowing rate of interest for the beekeepers is around 8%.

[35]The nectar left unextracted in the brood chamber, which constitutes the major cost of overwintering, is not counted as part of income and therefore is not counted as part of the cost.

[36]Some beekeepers use just postal cards. The general contractual details reported below are similar to those briefly mentioned in Grant D. Morse, "How About Pollination," *Gleanings in Bee Culture* 73–78 (February 1970).

[37]During my conversations with beekeepers, I was impressed by their personal knowledge of one another, including details such as the number of hives owned, the kinds of farms served, and the rents received.

contracts differ from pollination contracts in two essential aspects. One is, predictably, that the amount of apiary rent seldom depends on the number of colonies, since the farmer is interested only in obtaining the rent per apiary offered by the highest bidder. Second, the amount of apiary rent is not necessarily fixed. Paid mostly in honey, it may vary according to either the current honey yield or the honey yield of the preceding year.[38]

In general, contractual arrangements between beekeepers and farmers do not materially differ from other lease contracts. However, some peculiar arrangements resulting from certain complications are worth noting. First, because of the foraging behavior of the bees a farmer who hires bees may benefit his neighbors. Second, the use of pesticide sprays by one farmer may cause damage to the bees on an adjacent farm. And third, fireweed, which yields good honey, grows wild in forests. Let us discuss each in turn.

The Custom of the Orchards. As noted earlier, if a number of similar orchards are located close to one another, one who hires bees to pollinate his own orchard will in some degree benefit his neighbors. Of course, the strategic placing of the hives will reduce the spillover of bees. But in the absence of any social constraint on behavior, each farmer will tend to take advantage of what spillover does occur and to employ fewer hives himself. Of course, contractual arrangements could be made among all farmers in an area to determine collectively the number of hives to be employed by each, but no such effort is observed.

Acknowledging the complication, beekeepers and farmers are quick to point out that a social rule, or custom of the orchards, takes the place of explicit contracting: during the pollination period the owner of an orchard either keeps bees himself or hires as many hives per area as are employed in neighboring orchards of the same type. One failing to comply would be rated as a "bad neighbor," it is said, and could expect a number of inconveniences

---

[38]While we may attribute this behavior to the aversion of risks, the apiary contracts are not the same as share contracts. Rather, they resemble fixed-rent contracts with what I have called "escape clauses." For discussion of the "escape clause" and the stipulations of the share contract, see Steven N. S. Cheung, *The Theory of Share Tenancy,* ch. 2 & 4 (1969). One impression I obtain is that apiary rents generally involve such low values in Washington that elaborate formations and enforcements of apiary contracts are not worthwhile. In further investigations of these contracts, states with higher honey yields are recommended.

imposed on him by other orchard owners.[39] This customary matching of hive densities involves the exchange of gifts of the same kind, which apparently entails lower transaction costs than would be incurred under explicit contracting, where farmers would have to negotiate and make money payments to one another for the bee spillover.[40]

The Case of Pesticide Sprays. At the outset, we must remember that to minimize the loss of bees from insecticide usage is not necessarily consistent with efficient allocation of resources. The relevant consideration is whether the gain from using the pesticide is greater than the associated loss of bees, in total and at the margin. Provided that the costs of forming contracts permits, beekeepers and farmers will seek cooperative arrangements such that the expected marginal gain from using the pesticide is equal to the value of the expected marginal bee loss. In the absence of the arrangements, however, the total gain from using the pesticide may still be greater than the associated loss; the greater the expected damage done to bees, the greater will be the gain from the cooperative arrangements.[41]

When a pollination contract is formed, the farmer usually agrees to inform the beekeeper before spraying his crop, but this assurance will not protect the bees from pesticide used on neighboring farms. In areas dominated by orchards which require pollination at roughly the same time, such as the apple-growing districts, this

[39]The distinction between an oral or an implicit contract and a custom is not always clear. A common practice in some areas is that each farmer lets his neighbors know how many hives he employs. Perhaps the absence of a court of law to enforce what could in fact be a highly informal agreement is the reason why farmers deny the existence of any contract among them governing the employment of hives.

[40]Since with a sufficiently high reward the notoriety of being a "bad neighbor" will be tolerated, the likelihood of explicit contracting rises with increasing rental values of hives. Alternatively and concurrently, with a high enough rental price of hives the average size of orchards may increase through outright purchases, or the shapes of the orchards may be so tailored as to match the foraging behavior of the bees. By definition, given the gains the least costly arrangement will be chosen.

Some beekeepers reported that there are peculiar situations where the foraging behavior of the bees forces a one-way gift, but these situations are not covered by the present investigation. Even under these rare situations, the absence of both contractual and customary restraints may not result in a different allocation of resources. See Steven N. S. Cheung, "The Theory of Inter-individual Effects and The Demand for Contracts" (Univ. of Washington, Inst. of Econ. Res.).

[41]For a fuller discussion, see Steven N. S. Cheung, *supra* note 40.

agreement will suffice, for no farmer will apply the spray during the pollination period. But in regions where adjacent farms require bee pollination at different times, or do not require it at all, a farmer with no present obligation to any beekeeper may spray his fields and inflict damages to the bees rented by other farms. In this situation, only cooperation over a large geographic area can avoid bee loss, and we find just such arrangements in the pollination of cranberries but not of red clover.

Cranberry farms near Seattle are usually found in clusters, and spraying is conducted shortly after the bloom, which may vary by as much as a week or two among neighboring farms. Although each cranberry grower agrees not to spray until the contracted beekeeper removes the bees from his farm, this does not protect bees which may still remain on adjacent farms. Therefore the beekeepers make a further arrangement among themselves to remove all hives on the same date, thus insuring that all the bees are protected.

Red clover presents a different situation. Since the plant is often grown in areas where neighboring farms require no bee pollination, the pesticide danger is reportedly high and beekeepers demand an additional $1.00 to $2.00 per hive to assume the risk. But just as the beekeepers cooperate with one another during cranberry pollination, a clover farmer could make arrangements with his neighbors. Given that neighboring farmers have the legal right to use pesticide, the clover farmer would be willing to pay them an amount not exceeding the beekeeper's risk premium if they would refrain from spraying during the pollination period. Although no such arrangements are observed, it would seem that the costs of reaching an agreement would be no higher than those encountered in the case of the cranberries, and we must infer, pending empirical confirmation, that the gain from using the sprays is greater than the associated loss. This would particularly apply when a single farm requiring pollination is located amidst a large number of farms which require spraying during that same period.

The Case of Fireweed. I have at hand two types of apiary contract pertaining to fireweed, a honey plant which grows wild in the forest. The first is between a beekeeper and the Weyerhaeuser Company, owner of private timber land; the second is between a beekeeper and the Water Department of the City of Seattle. Two distinctions between them are worth noting. First, while both contracts stipulate 25 cents per hive, Weyerhaeuser asks a minimum charge of $100, and the Water Department a minimum of $25. In the apiary for fireweed honey, the number of hives used by a beekeeper is more than 100 but less than 400. Thus it happens that in the case of Weyerhaeuser, the apiary rent is independent of the number of hives, whereas with the Water Department it is dependent. The "underpriced" rent levied by the Water Department would have implied some sort of queuing except that a second unique feature is incorporated in its apiary contracts: no beekeeper is granted the exclusive right to the fireweed nectar in a particular area. The implication is that competition among beekeepers will reduce the honey yield per hive until its apiary rent is no more than 25 cents; while no beekeeper attempts to exclude entrants, the parties do seek a mutual division of the total area to avoid chaotic hive placement. Finally, fireweed also grows wild in the national forests and for this case I have no contract at hand. My information is that apiary rent is measured by the hive, is subject to competitive bidding among beekeepers, and has a reported range of 25 to 63 cents with the winner being granted exclusive right to a particular area.

Conclusions

Whether or not Keynes was correct in his claim that policy makers are "distilling their frenzy" from economists, it appears evident that some economists have been distilling their policy implications from fables. In a desire to promote government intervention, they have been prone to advance, without the support of careful investigation, the notion of "market failure." Some have dismissed in cavalier fashion the possibility of market operations in matters of environmental degradation, as witnesses the assertion of E. J. Mishan:

> With respect to bodies of land and water, extension of property rights may effectively internalize what would otherwise remain externalities. But the possibilities of protecting the citizen against such common environmental blights as filth, fume, stench, noise, visual distractions, etc. by a market in property rights are too remote to be taken seriously.[42]

[42] E. J. Mishan, "A Reply to Professor Worcester," 10 J. Econ. Lit. 59, 62 (1972). As immediate refutation of Professor Mishan's claim, I refer the reader to a factual example: Professor John McGee has just purchased a house, separated from that of his neighbor by a vacant lot. That the space would remain vacant had been assured

Similarly, it has been assumed that private property rights cannot be enforced in the case of fisheries, wildlife, and whatever other resources economists have chosen to call "natural." Land tenure contracts are routinely taken as inefficient, and to some the market will fail in the areas of education, medical care, and the like.

Then, of course, there is the fable of the bees.

In each case, it is true that costs involved in enforcement of property rights and in the formation of contracts will cause the market to function differently than it would without such costs. And few will deny that government does afford economic advantages. But it is equally true that any government action can be justified on efficiency grounds by the simple expedient of hypothesizing high enough transaction costs in the marketplace and low enough costs for government control. Thus to assume the state of the world to be as one sees fit is not even to compare the ideal with the actual but, rather, to compare the ideal with a fable.

I have no grounds for criticizing Meade and other economists who follow the Pigovian tradition for their use of the bee example to illustrate a theoretical point: certainly, resource allocation would in general differ from what is observed if the factors were "unpaid." My main criticism, rather, concerns their approach to economic inquiry in failing to investigate the real-world situation and in arriving at policy implications out of sheer imagination. As a result, their work contributes little to our understanding of the actual economic system.

---

by the previous owner who (upon learning that a third party was planning to buy the lot and construct a house there) had negotiated with the neighbor to make a joint purchase of the ground, thus protecting their two households from the "filth, fumes, stench, noise, visual distractions, etc." which would be generated by a new neighbor.

15. Fire Protection

Robert W. Poole, Jr.

Most people think of fire protection as a typical public good—a service that must be paid for by taxes and provided by a government agency. But there is far more to fire protection than simply waiting for a fire to occur and then dousing it with water. A great deal of fire protection is inherently a private, rather than a public, responsibility. The way a building is designed, built, and maintained is important. The owner's investment in protective features (e.g., alarms, sprinklers) has a great deal to do with the probability and seriousness of fires. Analysts like William Pollack at the Urban Institute have concluded that the provision of fire protection by government—that is, produced by a bureaucracy and offered to the public at no direct charge—has led to an overinvestment in fire *suppression* and an underinvestment in fire *prevention*. A 1974 study by Public Technology Inc. of the fire department grading system administered by the insurance industry reached the same conclusion.[1]

Pollack seems to have been the first to propose that this situation be remedied by means of user charges. The typical city fire department is supported by property taxes. Consequently, each owner's bill is proportional only to the assessed value of the property, regardless of how fire resistant it may or may not be. Pollack proposed a fee based on a formula including the property value, size, number of occupants, and probability of fire. The latter would be based on the building's structural characteristics, age, and use of protective systems (fire doors, smoke detectors, sprinklers). Under this system owners would have an economic incentive to invest in improvements that reduce the risk and severity of fire.

Reprinted, by permission, from *Cutting Back City Hall* (New York: Universe Books, 1980), pp. 62–78.

[1]*New Provisions of ISO Grading Schedule.* Washington, D.C.: Public Technology, Inc., 1974.

Proposition 13 helped spur the first actual use of such a fee in 1978. The pioneering city was Inglewood, California. Threatened with a loss of revenue because of property-tax cuts, its fire department analyzed its operating costs and came up with a new financing plan. Some $1.6 million of the fire department's budget was necessitated solely by the additional personnel and equipment needed to cope with large-scale blazes in the city's commercial and industrial buildings. (This determination was based on well-established analytical procedures whereby the required "fire flow" for a particular building can be computed, based on its size, materials, fire-resistive features, etc.). Thus, it was decided to fund only the "basic" level of fire protection—fire flow adequate for single-family houses—from the property tax. The remaining $1.6 million would come from a fire-service fee, based on each building's excess fire-flow requirement.

The fire-service fee went into effect in the second half of 1978. Some property owners, whose net cost went up, challenged the fee system in court. Others, however, whose commercial structures are fire resistant, benefited handsomely. The Forum, a large auditorium-stadium, for instance, used to pay $60,000 in property taxes for fire protection. After the change it paid only $3,700 in fees. "We're encouraging people to invest in their own fire protection," said Fire Chief Dale Hill.

Nearby Culver City and Commerce also adopted user-fee ordinances. And a number of other California cities have considered doing so. The 1979 legislature passed a bill to permit fire protection districts to enact such fees—with a two-thirds vote of their citizens. But the fees have proved politically unpopular thus far. With the apartment owners' suit still pending, Inglewood suspended use of the fee system after the 1978/79 fiscal year. The Culver City and Commerce fees, though on the books, have not yet been implemented. Thus, tradition is proving to be stronger than many people anticipated.

Nevertheless, we can see how far removed fire protection actually is from being a public good. Not only can fire protection be charged for, it can also be provided by the private sector. In fact, the traditional tax-funded government fire department is the rule only in a minority of American communities (though they contain the majority of the population). The many forms of privatization—volunteer departments, subscription service, contracting, etc.—vary considerably in organization and sophistication but share one characteristic in common: *Almost without exception they are less costly than conventional government fire departments.* Nor is this lower cost an accident. We shall see how and why it comes about, and how a few government fire departments have learned some things from their private competitors.

Volunteer Fire Departments

According to the National Fire Protection Association, 87% of America's 24,500 fire departments are manned by volunteers. Volunteers supplement the paid employees at many of the remaining departments, to the point where 91% of the nation's 2.2 million firefighters are volunteers. Most volunteer departments are in rural or semirural areas, but in some states many small and medium-size towns and cities have volunteer departments. New York State, for example, has only 62 paid fire departments—and more than 1,800 volunteer departments. In Iowa there are 900 volunteer departments and only 23 paid ones. California is one of the few states with more paid than volunteer departments—571 to 462.

Volunteer departments vary greatly in the quality of service they provide. Some are highly professional, with a high level of personnel, extensive training, and modern equipment. Others are little more than social clubs with a hand-me-down 1940s pumper. Some form of objective comparison *can* be made, however, thanks to the rating service developed by the fire insurance industry. The Insurance Services Office sends teams of fire engineers to inspect the level of fire protection in every community in the country. Each is graded on a four-part scale which rates its water supply, fire department, communications system, and prevention efforts. The community's total score determines which ratings class it ends up in, from Class 1 (best) to Class 10 (worst). Most cities with paid departments are in Classes 3 to 6. Despite the fact that for many years ISO's Grading Schedule was biased against volunteer departments (e.g., it counted *three* volunteers or paid reservists as equivalent to *one* regular firefighter), many of them rank as high as paid departments. Unfortunately for our purposes, however, there are no overall statistics comparing the ISO ratings of paid and volunteer departments. Individual case studies, however, provide numerous examples of volunteer departments every bit the equal of paid departments, even in cities as large as Reading, Pennsylvania (pop. 300,000).[2]

---

[2]*The Volunteer Fire Company*, by Ernest Earnest. New York: Stein & Day, 1979.

Auburn, California, provides an example of a professional volunteer department. This community of 7,000 has a 75-member fire department dating back to 1852. It has three stations and $350,000 worth of modern equipment. Chief Henry Gietzen reports that the department has a waiting list, and always has had, since serving in the department is a mark of prestige in the community. Auburn has a Class 5 rating from ISO. Similarly well qualified is the McMinnville, Oregon, volunteer fire department. This department operates with a core of six paid men plus 72 volunteers. Its volunteers are alerted by portable radio paging units, to assure rapid response. And its extensive training program requires volunteers to train for a full year before getting a permanent assignment. McMinnville has a Class 4 rating.

Volunteer fire departments are substantial money savers for the taxpayers in their communities. About 90% of the budget of a typical paid department is spent on salaries and fringe benefits. Since volunteer departments for the most part eliminate this expense, they need only about 10% of the budget of paid departments—for facilities, equipment, and maintenance. A few raise this amount by taxation, as does Auburn. But most are financed voluntarily, either by direct contributions or via fund-raising events.

Anthropologist John Lozier studied volunteer fire departments in rural West Virginia.[3] He found that the more professional ones are highly skilled at fund-raising while the more traditional ones rely on community activities to raise funds. Members of the traditionalist Gray's Forge volunteer department take part in a wide variety of community service activities. The department is financed by dances, bake sales, and a major summer festival (which also raises funds for other community organizations).

The more professional departments, like that of Foster, West Virginia, stress technical excellence and virtually eliminate social fund-raising activities. Instead, the Foster department calculates an annual fee for each household in the area and sends its members door to door asking citizens to contribute. Each paid-up household receives a license-plate-size sign bearing a house number keyed to the department's custom-designed response system. In a rural area these signs are helpful in locating the house in the

[3]"Volunteer Fire Departments and Community Mobilization," by John Lozier. *Human Organization*, Vol. 35, No. 4, Winter 1976.

event of a fire call. In addition, they are evidence of which house-holders have met their "obligation" to support the community's fire department.

Door-to-door solicitation provides a way for the firefighters to become familiar with each building and resident in the community. It also makes it more difficult for residents to refuse their support. But coercion is not involved. Reports John Lozier, "The ultimate sanction, a threat to refuse fire service, is occasionally implied but never applied. The effective sanction is a threat of damage to an individual's standing in the community." And interestingly, poor people in towns like Foster, though they can't contribute as much as others, are often among the most regular contributors.

Thus, volunteer fire departments *can* be professionally run, highly rated, and financed entirely by voluntary means. Far from being a thing of the past, volunteer departments remain a vital force in American fire protection. Indeed, there are signs of a swing *back* to volunteer departments. "I'm sure some cities can and must get back to on-call and volunteer firefighters," says McMinnville Chief Jerry Smith. "It's becoming more obvious every year that the people cannot and will not pay for some of the services they feel they should get." Indeed, in 1975 the town of Orcutt, California (pop. 27,000), switched to an "on-call" fire department. Up until then it had contracted with the Santa Barbara County Fire Department for a paid engine company to supplement its 23-man, four-truck on-call force (trained men who are paid only for time spent responding to calls). But Orcutt's taxpayers decided that the $67,000 annual contract cost was excessive and that they could do the job more economically themselves. Now they use only their paid reservists. Other departments with a mix of paid and on-call men may well decide likewise, as the tax revolt contin-ues.

Private Subscription Services

In some rural and unincorporated suburban areas—especially areas of rapid growth—a different kind of fire service exists. This is paid subscription service, provided to individual customers by a private, profit-making fire protection company. Fire service of this type exists in at least five states: Arizona, Georgia, Oregon, Mon-tana, and Tennessee. Counties in these states do not automatically provide fire departments in unincorporated areas, as is the case in many other states. Hence, a market for such service exists.

In Arizona that market is well served by Rural/Metro Fire Department, Inc.—a company that also provides contract security and police service. Since 1948 Rural/Metro has been providing fire protection to individual subscribers in Arizona. It currently operates out of 30 locations in five counties. As of 1979 Rural/Metro had 55,000 subscription customers, most of them homeowners.

It's little wonder that Rural/Metro's customers are satisfied. Thanks to many efficiencies developed by the company (which we will discuss later in this chapter), its costs of operation are amazingly low. A typical 1,200-sq.-ft. house pays only $23 per year for fire protection—even though it may be out in the country far from any fire hydrant. The 1977 national average cost for city fire protection is $35.39 per person, or about $103 per house (since there is an average of 2.9 persons per household). Thus, Rural/Metro customers pay only 22% of the national average. Rates for commercial and industrial property are based on square footage, except that schools and hospitals are served at no charge. All subscribers also receive, free of charge, emergency first aid service, rescue and resuscitation service, fire-safety inspections, inspection service when on vacation, emergency utility shutoff and removal of excess water in event of burst pipes, and "removal of desert reptiles from your premises."

If a nonsubscriber's property catches fire, the company's policy is one of professional public service: protect life and property first and ask questions later. The state Corporation Commission permits the company to send nonsubscribers a bill for its services. The charge is 14 times what the annual subscription rate for the property would have been, plus $50/hour for each firefighting vehicle, $10/hour for each command vehicle, and $15/hour for each firefighter. This policy has the effect of deterring free riders. At the same time, though, no one is forced to subscribe. Those who prefer to take their own protective measures or trust their luck are still free to do so.

In many cases individual subscriber service occurs for a limited number of years, as an area develops. When it reaches a certain stage, citizens often wish to incorporate it as a city, enacting local property taxes and setting up government services. Once this occurs, of course, everyone receives fire protection and pays for it via taxes. Although this has happened in several of Rural/Metro's former service areas, it is a tribute to the quality of the company's service that in two newly incorporated cities—Oro Valley and

Paradise Valley—such a high percentage of people were subscribers at the time the city incorporated, and were satisfied with the service, that they saw no need to get the newly formed city government into the act.

Rural/Metro achieves its amazingly low costs by thinking smarter. As noted earlier, labor-related expenses constitute about 90% of a fire department's costs. Hence, the greatest potential for saving lies in reducing the cost of personnel. R/M's philosophy is that it is unnecessary and wasteful to have only full-time firefighters, who must sit around and wait for a fire to occur. It therefore relies on a relatively small core staff of paid regulars, supplemented by a well-trained group of paid reservists called Auxiliary Firefighters.

In its home city of Scottsdale, Arizona, the Auxiliaries are 25 employees from various city departments—mostly from parks and public works—trained to double as on-call firefighters. They must pass the same initial tests and go through the first 20 hours of regular firefighting training. Once trained, the Auxiliaries are paid a monthly retainer of from $35 to $70 plus $6.34 per hour for any on-duty time outside normal working hours. Each Auxiliary is assigned to one of four shifts, which are on duty one week out of four. During working hours of his on-duty week, the Auxiliary is authorized (and required) to leave his regular city job when summoned by a portable radio pager to respond to a fire. He is also required to respond after hours, 24 hours a day, during his on-duty week.

The Auxiliary program is an outstanding success. The Auxiliaries are trained as general-purpose firefighters, proficient at from half to two-thirds of the fireground tasks—laying lines, doing nozzle work, and conducting salvage and ladder work. They are required by contract to respond, just like full-time employees. And statistics demonstrate that they do. In a recent study, Auxiliaries accounted for 44% of the total personnel responding to alarms. That same study showed that during a six-month period each Auxiliary was required to be away from his normal city job only 6.28 hours—only a bit over one hour per month. Thus, the city loses a negligible amount of employee time, while saving substantial sums on its fire protection costs.

Besides using a mix of full-time and part-time people, the company uses a number of other "manpower multiplication" techniques to reduce the need for excessive staffing. First, some of the off-duty paid Auxiliaries are provided with paging radios, so that they can be called for major fires, even though not on duty. Second, since the company serves a number of adjacent areas outside Scottsdale, it can call on a large number of additional *on-duty* personnel, trained to the same standards and using the same type of equipment but not paid for by Scottsdale residents. This points out another advantage of the private firm over government fire departments; even though the latter frequently render "mutual aid," their equipment, procedures, radio frequencies, training, and even terminology are often very different, leading to significant coordination problems.

The company has also developed a number of technological innovations that reduce the number of personnel needed to perform a given function. For example, R/M has pioneered the use of attack trucks (mini-pumpers). They are smaller, lighter, and more maneuverable than regular pumpers and respond with regular pumpers to most fires. For the 75% of incidents that are minor, the attack truck (with its onboard water tank, pump, and hose) can handle the job alone, permitting the pumper and its crew to return to "available" status. If the incident is major, the faster attack truck usually gets there first, carrying an officer who can size up the situation before the other units arrive, organize the placement of pumpers and hose lines, and thereby save time and make more efficient use of the men and equipment.

Another R/M innovation is the Snail—a tread-mounted, remote-controlled robot which can drag a 2½-inch hose line into areas too hot (up to 700°F) or too dangerous for firefighers to enter. The Snail, which cost only $3,000 to build, is controlled by one firefighter but can do the work of four.

Rural/Metro makes its dollars go further when it comes to equipment acquisition, as well. It is a licensed manufacturer of fire apparatus, building pumpers and attack trucks both for its own use and occasionally for sale to other fire departments. This enables it to obtain its equipment for about half the price of commercial, overly chromed engines, while also incorporating the company's own design innovations. One of R/M's most impressive vehicles is Engine 21, flagship of the Scottsdale fleet. It was designed "as if we had never seen a fire truck, but knew water in the proper quantities at the proper pressure would put out a fire," says Louis A. Witzeman, president of the company. Unique in the industry, Engine 21 carries a portable pump that can be dropped off at one hydrant, while the truck continues on to a second hydrant (thereby serving as two pumpers in one). Its design is modular, with interchangeable equipment bays for water tanks, ladders, or hose lines. Engine 21 was designed and built by Rural/Metro for only $25,000, compared with $50,000–$75,000 for a conventional 1,000-gallon-per-minute pumper (at that time—today's pumpers cost more than $90,000).

Engine 21 makes use of lightweight plastic 4-inch hose, rather than the heavy canvas 2½-inch hose most common in the fire service. The 4-inch hose permits fewer firefighters to deliver a quantity of water to a fire. It has also permitted fire hydrant spacing twice as great as usual in residential areas, at considerable saving to the taxpayers. To save valuable time at fires, the hose is equipped with quarter-turn, quick-disconnect couplings, instead of garden-hose-type threaded couplings. Four-inch hose and quarter-turn couplings are beginning to be used by other American fire departments, but originally Rural/Metro had to import both from Germany.

Rural/Metro, although the largest, is not the only firm engaged in private fire protection. Another is the Grant's Pass Rural Fire Department and Ambulance Service. This firm serves all of unincorporated Josephine County, Oregon, outside the city limits of Grant's Pass. The company serves 10,000 subscribers and is growing rapidly. It charges $35 a year for single-family residences and from $50 to $300 a year for businesses. Nonsubscribers are charged $100/hour plus $5 per firefighter. For their basic annual fee, subscribers also receive free ambulance service.

The company operates from six stations with 12 full-time, paid employees and a large number of volunteers. It is rated class 9 by ISO. The neighboring Grant's Pass Fire Department has "no comment" about the quality of the company's service, and refuses to conduct mutual aid operations with it. "The politicians don't like us," says owner and Chief Bertha Miller, "but every time they speak out against us, we pick up more customers."

Outside Billings, Montana, a similar friction exists between the O'Donnell Fire Service and the city fire department. O'Donnell serves 5,000 subscribers from three stations, using 11 full-time, paid staff and 10 reservists. It charges homeowners $42 per year; nonsubscribers pay $75 per hour for each fire unit involved. The company has a Class 6 ISO rating in areas with water supply and Class 8 elsewhere.

O'Donnell offers residents a considerable cost advantage. Citizens of nearby Billings pay about $250 per household to support their city fire department, compared with the company's $42 annual charge. O'Donnell gains its cost advantage in two ways: paying fewer full-time firefighters and using innovative equipment (custom-designed trucks, high expansion foam). The firm's major problem is that the city keeps expanding outward, annexing away its customer base. Consequently, it must continually seek new customers just to stay even. Despite this obstacle, it has more than doubled its customer base in the past three years.

Tennessee provides the setting for additional subscription service. Five small subscription fire-service firms were recently merged to form the Tennessee Rural/Metro Fire Department, Inc. The new company, partially owned by Rural/Metro of Arizona, serves 6,000 subscribers on the outskirts of Knoxville. In its first two years of operation it upgraded the largely rural service from Class 10 to Class 9, giving its customers significant fire insurance savings. Another subscription company serves about 6,500 customers in East Ridge, Tennessee. It has signed up over 90% of the homes in its area, charging only $15 per year. Altogether, there are ten subscription fire companies in various parts of Tennessee.

Subscription fire service is also thriving in Georgia. There are five subscription firms in Chatham County. The largest of these is the Southside Fire Department, located in the suburbs of Savannah. Begun in 1962, Southside serves some 8,000 subscribers and is growing rapidly. Its service area encompasses 220 square miles. It covers this area from five stations, using a force of 20 paid and 110 volunteer firefighters and 18 vehicles. Single-family homes under $20,000 in value pay $30 per year; over that value the rate is $35 per year. Much of Southside's service area is graded Class 6, though some areas without fire hydrants are Class 8 or Class 9. Over the years the company has been asked to take over several areas formerly served by volunteer departments. When this occurs, the firm moves in its own personnel and equipment and recruits the existing volunteers as well.

Another Georgia firm is the West Richmond County Fire Department just outside Augusta. Begun in 1975 with 6,000 customers the first year, the firm ended 1977 with more than 10,000 subscribers and continues to grow rapidly. In most areas it has a Class 6 rating and is working to upgrade it to Class 5. The company charges homeowners $1 per $1,000 of valuation. Thus, on a $30,000 home the annual charge is $30. The company's Class 6 rating results in an insurance premium saving of $65 a year on a $30,000 home. By subscribing, then, an owner saves $35 a year. Not surprisingly, a high percentage of homeowners in the county subscribe.

The existence of subscription fire protection provides additional evidence that fire protection is not a public good. As we have seen, in five states individual homeowners and businesses find it to their advantage to pay for professional, private fire-protection services. Problems with free riders are minimal; the firms' principal problem is city-government annexation or incorporation that takes away their customer base.

A further example of private fire protection is the industrial fire department. Many large industrial installations, instead of socializing the cost of their unusually large fire-protection needs by demanding an oversize city fire department, choose to provide their own protection. Some are even getting together to provide shared protection. In Bayway, New Jersey, seven large firms have joined together to create the Linden Industrial Mutual Aid Council. The driving force behind the council is Exxon, whose Bayway refinery has long had its own 12-man fire department. Another large industrial fire service is the 57-member Channel Industries Mutual Aid (CIMA) organization, to which all the major plants on the Houston Ship Channel belong. CIMA represents the largest collection of petroleum and petrochemical fire-fighting expertise and equipment in the world. Its resources include 25 fire trucks, two fire boats, numerous pieces of special equipment, and hundreds of trained industrial firefighters. Citizens in cities with large industrial installations should take a careful look at how much of their fire department's size and cost are due to the special requirements of these industries. The public good argument can be rhetoric that disguises a large and unnecessary subsidy.

Private Contracting by Government

If you live in an incorporated city which collects taxes and views fire protection as a public good, there are ways to minimize the cost and maximize the efficiency of the fire service. One way is to contract with a private firm, instead of operating a city fire department. As in the case of police protection, contracting provides a city with a choice among suppliers and gives the providing company an incentive to be efficient. The leader in fire-service contracting is our old friend, Rural/Metro Fire Department, Inc. Its service within the Scottsdale city limits is via contract with the city, and it also provides contractual fire service to four fire districts and two developer-owned new towns in Arizona.

Scottsdale, the company's home base, is a showcase of the benefits of private fire protection. Rural/Metro grew up with the city, providing subscriber service before the city incorporated. When Scottsdale became a city in 1952, city officials decided that there was no need to create a city fire department. Instead, following the example of the many cities which contract for such services as garbage collection and street sweeping, they decided to use the city tax funds to hire Rural/Metro on a renewable contract basis. Over the succeeding years the contract has been renegotiated and renewed a number of times. Both parties continue to be highly satisfied with the arrangement.

The bottom line when it comes to evaluating Rural/Metro is its cost and performance. First of all its low cost is quite impressive. The per capita cost of fire protection in Scottsdale, a city of over 90,000 people, is about one-fourth the national average for cities of 50,000–100,000. Because the costs of fire protection vary, depending on the types of structures, their age, and weather conditions, it is more meaningful to compare cities that are as similar as possible. Economist Roger Ahlbrandt, Jr., made a theoretical study of this sort in 1972.[4] In 1976 the Institute for Local Self-Government (ILSG) made an actual on-the-scene, side-by-side evaluation.[5]

As part of a research project on contract public services, ILSG made a detailed comparison of fire protection in Scottsdale and its three very similar neighbors—Glendale, Mesa, and Tempe—all of which have conventional city fire departments. Over the years 1971–75, the average per capita cost in Scottsdale was only $6.48, about half as much as in Glendale ($12.62), Mesa ($11.43), and Tempe ($10.68).

But is it as good as its neighbors' fire service? The Institute examined this question in detail. A key indicator of fire department performance is response time. Although Scottsdale has twice the land area of the others (72 square miles versus 24.5 for Glendale,

[4]*Municipal Fire Protection Services: Comparison of Alternative Organizational Forms*, by Roger S. Ahlbrandt, Jr. Beverly Hills, Calif.: Sage Publications, 1973.

[5]*Alternatives to Traditional Public Safety Delivery Systems: Civilians in Public Safety Services*. Berkeley, Calif.: Institute for Local Self-Government, 1977.

48 for Mesa, and 30.2 for Tempe), Scottsdale had the best average response time: 2.96 minutes, compared with 3.0 for Glendale, 3.0 for Mesa, and 3.8 for Tempe. Another key indicator is the ISO grading. Scottsdale has earned a Class 5 rating, the same as Glendale, while Mesa is Class 3 and Tempe is Class 4. Thus, Scottsdale's fire protection is judged acceptable by ISO's conservative standards. And its residents pay no more for fire insurance since homeowners' policies cost the same in Classes 3, 4, and 5. Finally another indicator is the actual fire loss. The Institute found that the average annual per capita loss was $5.45 in Scottsdale—quite comparable to the $5.19 figure for Glendale and $5.26 for Mesa, and far below Tempe's $9.60.

Rural/Metro is not the only firm engaged in contracting with cities and fire districts. New contract service came into existence in 1977. When voters in the Nashville, Tennessee, area created a metro government, five small subscription fire companies were hired by the new government on contract to serve the formerly unincorporated county areas. Whether this will be just an interim step or a permanent move to contract service remains to be seen.

Two more contracts came into being in 1979. On January 1, American Emergency Services Corporation began operating Illinois's first private fire service. The 5,000 residents of Elk Grove Township, adjacent to O'Hare Airport, had voted the previous month by a 9-to-1 margin to contract with the private firm rather than to renew their 22-year contract with adjacent Mount Prospect. Like Rural/Metro (on which it is modeled), Gary Jensen's firm relies on 25 paid reservists to supplement his nine full-time firefighters. All of the latter have Emergency Medical Technician certificates and two are trained as full-fledged paramedics. The firm operates two fully equipped emergency ambulances as well as two pumpers and a ladder truck. Based on the industrial/commercial township's average daily population of 20,000, the first-year cost was $15 per capita—compared with an estimated 1979 national average of more than $29 for cities that size.

Also in January 1979, Rural/Metro was hired by the county commission of Hall County, Georgia, to replace its county fire department. Delayed by a court challenge over the legality of contracting (which was upheld), operations began on March 1. The $862,000 first-year contract for fire and ambulance service saved county taxpayers $100,000, and Rural/Metro projected a somewhat greater saving for the second year. Angry fire union members, whose court challenge failed, next organized an election to recall the county commissioners. That move succeeded, but the new commissioners—impressed by the firm's performance and cost saving—made no move to change the contract. (Incidentally, R/M offered jobs to all the former firefighters, but only about 20% applied, and of those, all but one were hired.)

Contract fire protection is not limited to the United States. Denmark's Falck Company has been providing contract fire protection to Danish municipalities since 1926. It currently has fire equipment based in 90 stations across Denmark, providing fire protection for about half the country. Like Rural/Metro, Falck operates with a core staff of full-time paid men supplemented by paid reservists. Falck responds to about 30,000 fire calls per year, and derives 70% of its income from fire protection services. (The rest of its activities involve ambulance and rescue work.)

Intergovernmental Cooperation

In many states it is possible to contract with another governmental unit for fire service. As in the case of law enforcement, contracting with another government agency permits a city to take advantage of whatever economies of scale may exist. It also gives the purchasing city greater flexibility since it can negotiate for the type of service it desires and may switch to an alternative supplier (including a private firm, should one later become available) if not satisfied.

Government contracting for fire services is especially common in California. In Los Angeles County the county fire department contracts with 35 of the county's 77 cities, saving them the trouble and expense of operating their own departments. Since the program began (with the city of Lakewood, in 1954), only three cities have dropped out and started their own departments. In Orange County eight cities, including the "new town" of Irvine, have for many years contracted for fire service with the California Division of Forestry (CDF). The contracting arrangements were considered as long-term, stable relationships rather than as interim steps. One of the eight cities, Placentia, made history in 1975 by abolishing its city fire department, in response to a wildcat strike by firefighters, and contracting with CDF. But late in 1978 CDF gave notice that it would no longer provide urban fire protection in Orange County after June 30, 1980. As this book went to press, city and county officials were considering whether to (1) create new departments, (2) contract with other cities, or (3) contract with the private sector.

Other California counties with intergovernmental contract fire service include Monterey, San Bernardino, Santa Barbara, Riverside, and Ventura. Such contracting also exists in Kentucky, Maryland, Minnesota, New Jersey, Ohio, Tennessee, and Virginia.

Some of the cost advantages of contracting can be obtained by consolidating adjacent small fire departments in urbanized areas. The potential advantages include elimination of overlapping or redundant response areas, reduced administrative positions, centralized dispatch, and greater flexibility in using personnel and equipment. All of these translate into hard dollar savings. Huntington Beach, California, in 1968 enacted a joint powers agreement with three adjacent cities to consolidate dispatching and to coordinate fire station location policies. The joint operation requires 14 rather than 18 stations and six rather than eight ladder companies. The savings total over $1 million a year. A similar functional consolidation was achieved among six cities in California's Contra Costa County.

Sprucing Up the City Department

Many innovative methods have been developed by private fire-protection companies and a handful of progressive municipal fire departments. These can be applied by any city or county fire department. For the most part they have *not* been tried because the fire service over the years has become the most tradition-bound of all local public services. This is partly because of its being, like the police, a sacred-cow function of government and therefore not subject to critical scrutiny at budget time. It is also because of the conservatism of the insurance industry and its relatively unchanging ISO standards. These have tended, like building codes, to retard innovation rather than to encourage it. Whatever the reason, the fire service has lagged far behind the technological state of the art. What follows is a sampling of these innovative ideas.

Personnel Utilization

Although Rural/Metro pioneered the large-scale use of paid reservists, there is no inherent reason why this approach cannot be used in any fire department—government or private. The use of portable radio-paging units (about $300 each) makes this idea more feasible in both urban and rural areas. And while the exact mix of full-timers and reservists may vary with local conditions, the reservist concept makes technical and economic sense across the board.

Cottage Grove, Oregon, is a small community 25 miles from Eugene. The city's fire department operates with a mix of paid men and volunteers but had the problem of reduced volunteer turnout during working hours. It recently organized its 13 public works employees into a paid reservist unit—the Public Works Fire Department Support Unit. The Support Unit's members are required to respond during regular working hours, thus solving the turnout problem. The members each receive four hours of fire training every six months, covering hose and nozzle work, salvage, traffic control, etc.

Other departments that utilize paid reservists include Orange County (California Division of Forestry), Riverside County, Visalia, Santa Maria, and Lompoc in California, and Denison, Texas. In each case the reservists receive regular fire training but are paid only for the time spent actually responding (plus, in some cases, a small monthly retainer). Savings to the city, depending on the extent of reservist use, range from 20% to 40%.

Other personnel changes can lead to additional cost savings. Using volunteers or reservists at night can provide important cost reductions. The Citrus Heights Fire Protection District in Sacramento County, California, uses college students as night reservists. They attend school during the day, pay rent for city-owned living quarters, and receive the minimum wage for on-duty time at night. Downers Grove, Illinois, uses a similar concept for its night staff and estimates its savings at 33% of all personnel costs. Orange, California, does not fully staff its six fire stations. Instead, it operates a two-person "flying squad," based at the central station, which is sent as needed throughout the city to supplement each station's assigned personnel. Savings are estimated at $50,000 a year.

Productive use of firefighters' on-duty time is another avenue for savings. The Rural/Metro employees in Scottsdale spend some of their time building new fire engines, repairing city water meters, and assembling the specialized refuse containers used by the city. Glenview, Illinois, and Visalia, California, firefighters operate the city's printing department. In other cities firefighters issue bicycle licenses or carry out city inspections.

Facilities

Although fire stations and other facilities account for only a small fraction of a fire department's average annual cost, significant economies are possible here as well. One California department has found a way to build stations for less than half price by converting ordinary tract houses. In 1971 the city of Garden Grove purchased a surplus house in a street-widening project. Rather than construct a needed fire station at 1211 Chapman Avenue, the city moved the house to the site, enlarged its garage to fit a pumper, and added a hose rack in the backyard. The total cost for what became Station No. 6 was only $42,000, compared with about $135,000 for building a new station, at 1971 prices. When another station was needed the following year, the department went shopping for a suitable tract house in the area to be served. A three-bedroom, two-bath house at 14162 Forsyth Lane was purchased new for $25,625. Adding a garage and hose rack plus furnishing and landscaping brought the total cost to $58,629. Firefighters find the tract homes more comfortable than typical fire station dormitories, and the neighbors like the way the station blends in with its surroundings.

Major economies can result from more careful placement of fire stations. Eliminating an unnecessary station saves not only the construction and maintenance costs, but also the far larger costs of unneeded personnel and equipment. In large metropolitan areas, adjacent jurisdictions often have fire stations located quite close together. Mutual-aid agreements can sometimes permit one city's border station to be closed. In other cases, stations may be located too close together within a city, possibly due to changing land-use patterns. By agreeing to make joint use of an Arlington Heights, Illinois, fire station, the city of Rolling Meadows saved the $350,000 cost of constructing a second station of its own.

Some larger cities are now using a sophisticated computer program to determine the optimum number and location of fire stations. Developed by nonprofit Public Technology, Inc. (PTI), the program uses such factors as street layouts and alarm histories to specify how many stations are necessary, where they should best be located, the predicted response time, and the predicted number of alarms at each. The PTI program is being used by several dozen cities, including New Orleans, Dallas, Long Beach, San Diego, Wichita, and Eugene, Oregon. Not all are using it to reduce costs, but those that are, such as San Bernardino, California, expect "major" savings in both capital and operating costs.

In Denver, researchers from the University of Colorado and the Denver Urban Observatory developed their own mathematical model to determine optimum station location. Their results showed that the present level of service could be maintained with a reduction of two engine companies and three ladder companies, by suitable rearrangement of equipment and stations. The city/county Budget and Management Office has prepared a multi-year fire-service plan which calls for phasing out the surplus companies, saving $2.8 million over the six-year phase-out period, and $1.2 million a year thereafter.

Another area for cost savings is removal of obsolescent firebox alarm systems. Many years ago the firebox on the street corner was the principal means of reporting a fire. Today, though, most fires are reported by telephone (and pay phones generally outnumber fireboxes on the streets). Moreover, in most cities the firebox has become a target for pranksters, who delight in turning in false alarms.

As a result, many cities have begun to reevaluate the need for a firebox alarm system. Los Angeles took the lead in this area several years ago. Poring over departmental records in an intensive study, the city fire department found that 92% of the alarms received via street boxes were false. Moreover, nearly 89% of the valid box alarms were also reported by telephone. Further analysis showed that only 1.4% of the box alarms were for *real* fires that were not also reported by telephone.

Despite the meager benefits of the system, it was costing the taxpayers a lot of money. Simple maintenance cost over $100,000 a year. And every response to a false alarm led to $80 in direct costs, besides tying up personnel and equipment and increasing the risk of accidents involving responding units. Because 7,000 false alarms were being turned in annually, the needless response cost was running $560,000 per year. Based on these figures the department decided to scrap the entire system. Some 300 boxes had already been removed from areas of chronic false alarms, and the remaining 1,400 were taken out in 1975. As antiques, the boxes themselves proved extremely popular. The city salvage department priced them at $73 each, and all were quickly sold. Rumor has it that many were immediately resold at much higher prices.

Removing fireboxes is a step that some cities still hesitate to take, despite the impressive cost savings. They have two worries: public safety and insurance rates. As far as public safety is concerned, the Los Angeles statistics are fairly typical. Most firebox alarm systems bring in mostly false alarms, and nearly all true alarms are reported by telephone. Public access to telephones for emergency reporting is being upgraded all across the country, as phone companies introduce the three-digit "911" emergency number. In many cases pay phones are then modified to permit dialing 911 without having to insert a coin.

It is true that the ISO grading system penalizes a city for not having a box alarm system. But the penalty affects only 100 out of a possible 5,000 points of the grading scales. Other improvements—in communications or in other aspects of fire protection—can offset any penalty for removing the boxes. And it is only a matter of time until ISO revises its standards to reflect the reality of modern-day telephone communications.

These facts are becoming apparent to city officials. In 1977 San Diego and Santa Barbara, California, decided to scrap their box alarm systems. Both cities are putting in "911" telephone systems. Joining the parade in 1978, Oakland, California, removed its 1,250 alarm boxes at an annual saving of $80,000.

Equipment Innovations

Most fire trucks and equipment have changed little since the 1920s when motorized trucks completed the replacement of horse-drawn wagons. Most departments rely exclusively on two types of trucks, pumpers and ladder trucks, produced virtually custom-made to each city's specifications at $75,000–$100,000 each. As we have seen, Rural/Metro and several other private firms have led the way in producing less expensive, standardized fire engines using many off-the-shelf components and innovative design ideas. Not many of these ideas have yet found favor with municipal fire departments.

One that *is* slowly making headway is the mini-pumper or attack truck.[6] Depending on the locality, anywhere from 40% to 80% of all calls can be handled with two firefighters and a minimum of equipment—a van or one-ton truck with its own water tank and hose. Use of a mini-pumper at small incidents (grass and rubbish fires, lock-out calls, auto fires) tends to reduce overall personnel requirements and costs a lot less—anywhere from $6,000 to $29,000 for a complete mini-pumper.

Besides Rural/Metro, one of the pioneers in using mini-pumpers

[6]*Municipal Innovations 1: The Mini-Pumper.* Washington, D.C.: International City Management Association, February 1975.

is Syracuse, New York. In 1974 Syracuse's fire department completely reorganized, in response to a state law mandating a 40-hour firefighter work week. Retaining its traditional pattern of staff and equipment would have required adding 125 firefighters to comply with the law. The new concept, based on using a mix of mini-pumpers and full-size trucks, required only 62 new employees—an annual saving of $600,000. Most Syracuse engine companies now consist of a two-person mini-pumper and a three-person maxi-pumper. Depending on the type of call, the response will be the mini alone, both together, or the maxi with all five firefighters. Other departments now using mini-pumpers include Des Moines, Iowa; Cayce, South Carolina; and University City, Missouri. The former two have constructed their minis on pickup truck chassis, while the latter converted a 1973 Dodge van.

Public Technology, Inc., has developed an infrared viewer for use by the fire service. Called Probeye, and now in production by Hughes Aircraft, the viewer permits location of fire victims and hidden fire sources by "seeing" their heat through solid walls. It is also useful in overhaul and salvage work and in routine fire inspections. Probeye costs $3,500.

PTI and Rural/Metro have separately worked on two other technical problems: control of water flow and improved breathing apparatus. Rural/Metro has spent several years working on a radio-controlled fire hydrant valve. With the unit mounted on the hydrant, the flow of water can be controlled by one of the men on the hose, rather than by an extra firefighter stationed at the hydrant. Rural/Metro's system is still under development. The PTI system provides for radio control of the pump on the pumper, from a transmitter at the hose nozzle, again eliminating the need for an extra person. It is in production at Grumman Allied Industries, Inc.

PTI has also developed a lighter-weight, longer-duration, easier-to-use, self-contained breathing apparatus for firefighters. The system was developed with NASA assistance and is entering production as this is written. Rural/Metro has taken a different approach to the limitations of present breathing gear (which typically have less than 30 minutes' air supply). At a cost of under $2,500, it has developed a firefighters' umbilical consisting of a fire-resistant Nomex braid hose ½ inch in diameter. The hose provides not only air but also a two-way communications line and an electric power line for operating hand-held lights. If the air supply fails, the firefighter can hit a quick-release latch with one hand and then rely on an auxiliary air tank bottle.

These exciting technological advances were not developed by city fire departments. Some were developed by a private firm, others by a foundation-supported nonprofit corporation. This fact only serves to underline what we've learned about the inherent disadvantages of municipal monopolies in providing public services.

16. Leisure and Recreational Services

Robert W. Poole, Jr.

Cities and counties have traditionally provided a host of leisure-oriented facilities such as parks, golf courses, beaches, marinas, athletic fields, stadiums, auditoriums, museums, and libraries. It is not at all clear *why* provision of such services came to be viewed as the business of local government. Going back to our discussion of public goods versus private goods, it is difficult to consider any of these services as public goods, per se. Each tends to be used by only a minority of the residents of the community. When these facilities are paid for by tax money, nonusers end up helping to pay, so that users can get in "for free." This is hardly equitable. Moreover, in the case of larger cities within a metropolitan area, many of the users of a particular facility are nonresidents, and hence not even among the taxpayers indirectly paying for the facility.

Perhaps it is as a result of such considerations that leisure and recreational services are among those most often subject to user charges by local governments. Yet the extent of user charges varies widely among communities and types of facilities, with no apparent rhyme or reason. Some cities, such as Washington, D.C., impose virtually no charges for any of these services. Others charge for some types (e.g., swimming pools) but not others (e.g., museums). Yet another city may do just the opposite. Even within a single city the user charge philosophy is not always consistent. The whole subject is one that needs a thorough overhaul, with a view toward making these special-interest facilities as nearly as possible self-supporting. Doing so will increase equity and help to reduce the tax burden.

Private vs. Public

Municipal recreational services are actually only a small proportion of the total recreational expenditures made by Americans. In

Reprinted, by permission, from *Cutting Back City Hall* (New York: Universe Books, 1980), pp. 99–109.

1978 expenditures on recreation totaled $180 billion, compared with only about $4 billion spent by cities and counties. It takes only a little thought to see where the private spending goes: movie theaters, private museums, concert halls, auditoriums, golf courses, bowling alleys, stadiums, campgrounds, and amusement parks (ranging from miniature golf to such giants as Disneyland). The huge market for recreation is being met largely by the private sector.

Tradition may be the immediate explanation for why municipalities are involved at all. But that will not suffice as a justification for continued governmental involvement. And we have already seen that the public-good argument is not valid for this type of service since it is used by only a limited number of readily identifiable beneficiaries. One argument may be that privatization or charging is viewed as impractical.

One reason given why parks, for instance, must be provided by government and made available free of charge is that it would be impractical to restrict admission to paying customers. We can all imagine walling in a city park and stationing a ticket taker at the gate. The change in esthetics and convenience, as well as the high cost of the ticket taker, pretty clearly rules out this approach. But, the argument goes, if we cannot exclude nonpayers and charge users, how can the costs of the park (payments for the land and facilities, and ongoing maintenance) be met—unless, that is, the government owns it and taxes everyone?

There is no single answer to this oversimplified argument. Different cases must be dealt with differently. To begin with, there's a world of difference between a large county park facility offering specific attractions (rides, exhibits, swimming) and small city parks whose principal benefit is to provide esthetic relief in the midst of the city's concrete. The former are already designed in such a way as to facilitate exclusion of nonpayers and generally support enough business (due to their specific attractions) to justify ticket booths or coin-operated turnstiles. So we are left with only city parks that offer merely a pleasant walkway, a place to sit, and a nice view.

An interesting perspective on this case can be gained by asking the following question: What if the city suddenly no longer had the funds to maintain such parks? Who would then value their presence enough to come up with the funds to do so? This type of thought experiment helps us to see more clearly who the primary beneficiaries of such parks are. It's unlikely that the entire city's taxpayers would band together to support a park maintenance fund. To be sure, everyone may benefit at least a little from the existence of properly maintained parks, but it is readily apparent that some people benefit far more than others. The people whose homes and businesses are nearest to a park are the primary beneficiaries. They have ready access to it, they can see it every day, and their property value most likely reflects the benefit of having the park nearby. Thus, if any group would band together to maintain a city park, it's the neighborhood nearby, to preserve the park as an asset to their neighborhood (and incidentally, to maintain their property values).

This isn't just wishful thinking. Such a spontaneous demonstration of mutual local self-interest has come into being in Houston. The Houston Anti-Litter Team, Inc. (HALT) was organized in 1976 to clean up and maintain the city's freeway interchanges. When developer Howard Rambin III complained to the state highway department about the "mounting tide of litter" at these intersections, he was told that the state simply did not have the funds. Rambin thereupon decided to get the job done himself by organizing HALT.

The organization's *modus operandi* is as follows. Once an interchange has been targeted for cleanup (litter removal and grass cutting), HALT locates a business person near the intersection to serve as a team captain. With the help of HALT literature, the captain then solicits financial support from neighboring businesses—generally from $10 to $30 per month. HALT then contracts with a landscaping or grounds maintenance firm for initial cleanup and regular maintenance, and posts antilittering signs bearing HALT's name. The very first HALT project—the interchange of Interstate 610 and Westheimer Road—got the support of 63 of the 65 nearby owners or proprietors.

Rambin considers keeping the streets and sidewalks near his office building clean to be a normal business expense, and HALT is trying to promote general acceptance of this position. The group has found that initial cleanup of an interchange costs from $1,000 to $2,300, with ongoing maintenance costs of $750–$1,000 per month. HALT's operations have been so successful that it is able to support a full-time director to promote and administer the organization. Thus, we see how even small city parks could be maintained by their principal beneficiaries rather than by all tax-payers.

The same type of thing occurred in Oakland, California, after Proposition 13 was passed. Faced with a large amount of park acreage and serious budget cutbacks (from $19 million down to $13 million), the East Bay Regional Parks District set up an "adopt-a-park" program. The first participant was Kaiser Aluminum & Chemical Corp., based in Oakland, which agreed to adopt 88-acre Roberts Regional Recreation Area. (Kaiser Vice President for Public Affairs Richard Spees lives in the area and jogs in the park every day.) Under the agreement, Kaiser is making regular payments to the district to keep the park properly maintained—and getting a tax deduction in the process. Among other firms helping support park maintenance in California are Clorox Corporation, Atlantic Richfield Co., and *Sunset* Magazine.

National Journal columnist Neal Peirce reports that several non-profit friends-of-the-parks organizations have been formed in large cities, to help parks departments cope with smaller budgets. The New York City Parks Council raises private and grant money and mobilizes adult and teenage volunteers to help with park mainte-nance. In 1977 it built a new waterfront park in Brooklyn's Wil-liamsburg section. Using volunteer labor from local residents and donations of material from local firms, it kept the cost below $10,000.

A park support group is really just an extension of an idea big cities have long been accustomed to: the nonprofit "friends of the zoo" or "friends of the library" or "friends of the art museum." These groups, which traditionally include many leading (and wealthy) members of the community, raise money and provide volunteer services to support their favorite leisure-time facilities. For example, the Los Angeles zoo society provides the funds for all capital expenditures at the city's huge Griffith Park Zoo. The city pays only the operating expenses, one-third of which come from user fees and the balance from taxes. The Oakland zoo society recently signed a contract to take over operation of the zoo from that financially troubled California city.

Another reason why it is argued that cities must operate leisure services is so that poor people won't be denied access to them by lack of money. The same logic is frequently applied to other publicly operated facilities, such as mass-transit systems. Nobody, however, seems to apply it to the fast food restaurants, record stores, or shoe stores used by the poor. But for some reason, when it comes to the services supplied by the public sector, the prime criterion of pricing policy is access for the poor.

This kind of approach is mistaken. Prices serve several valuable functions, which apply to the public sector's services as well as to those of the private sector. Besides producing revenues to pay the costs of the operation (and thereby avoiding unfairly charging nonusers), a price serves to ration demand so as to prevent overcrowding. When the city of Oakland, California, eliminated admission charges at two pools serving partly low-income neighborhoods in 1968, attendance soared—by 29% in one case and by 67% in the other. The pools quickly became overcrowded and unpleasant to use. This is an expected consequence of providing a desired service at a price of zero. Prices also serve to measure people's relative demand for various types of services, thereby giving the providers valuable feedback as to the quantity and quality desired. If, for example, small quantities of lawn chairs, umbrellas, and baby strollers are all made available for rental in a park, their relative popularity—measured by the income received—will tell the park manager which types of equipment are most wanted. They may even experiment with more expensive chairs (at a higher price, of course) to see if there's a demand for such diversity. Were the equipment made available "for free," whatever was there would be used, and most likely abused, and such experimentation would most likely never take place.

Consequently, the decision not to put prices on public services is an implicit decision to produce them inefficiently. The taxpayers are then doubly victimized. They have to pay for services they may not use and they pay more than is necessary to produce the services. If the political process decides that the poor (or the elderly, or any other favored group) must have better access to recreational services, it is far less costly to make this special privilege explicit, by such devices as giving out free or reduced-rate passes to persons meeting certain criteria, or relying on income-supplement programs which let the poor make their own expenditure decisions. That way at least all *other* users will pay a price for the services, and many of the efficiency-promoting benefits of the price system will still be realized.

The *Fees and Charges Handbook* of the Heritage Conservation and

Recreation Service[1] suggests a number of ways of reducing the impact of user fees on low-income groups:

- Define differential fee structures.
- Waive fees on an individual basis.
- Have local citizens, businesses, or service clubs provide scholarships or subsidize programs.
- Adjust fee structure according to income level of neighborhood.
- Allow extended payment schedules.
- Provide work exchange ("sweat equity") for admission.
- Allow equipment or supply donations in lieu of fees.

Some agencies are already making use of these ideas. The Fairfax County, Virginia, recreation agency distributes sports complex passes to low-income children identified through the county's school lunch program. The Los Angeles County Art Museum provides free admission one day per month so that senior citizens and others who can't afford the new (post-Proposition 13) $1.50 admission fee can be allowed entry. The San Juan School District in Sacramento, California, arranges for local businesses to give money for "scholarships" for low-income children to attend recreation facilities.

The point of this discussion is that it is not necessary to give up the many benefits of pricing recreational services, simply because some people are poor. Many creative ways can be found to aid the poor—while ensuring that everyone else pays his or her way.

Recreation User Fees

There are many types of user fees. The American Insitute of Park Executives and the National Recreation and Parks Association classify them as follows:

- *Entrance fees*—to parks, gardens, zoos, beaches, campgrounds, or their parking lots
- *Admission fees*—to enter a specific building or attraction within a recreational area

[1]*Fees and Charges Handbook: Guidelines for Recreation and Heritage Conservation Agencies*. Washington, D.C.: Heritage Conservation and Recreation Service, 1979.

- *Rental fees*—to use a piece of property or equipment, e.g., a boat, tennis racquets, golf clubs, ice skates, baby stroller
- *Use fees*—to make use of a specific facility or take part in an activity, e.g., an archery range, boat race, reserved picnic area
- *License or permit fees*—to gain seasonal access for hunting, fishing, boating, or similar activity
- *Sales revenues*—derived from proprietors of concession stands, which, in turn, charge their customers
- *Special services fees*

Entrance or admission fees are not usually charged for city parks, playgrounds, and community centers. In contrast, at least nominal fees are often charged for those facilities that are more costly to maintain, more subject to congestion, and easier to fence off. These might include golf courses, pools, tennis courts, and zoos. In some cases, these facilities also charge higher rates during times of high demand, thus shifting some of the demand for the services to off-peak hours and reducing congestion, maintenance, and deterioration.

Several new ideas in park and recreation user charges have been suggested in recent years. One is the annual permit, similar to the Golden Eagle passes one can purchase for access to the National Parks. A 1967 study by the Arthur D. Little consulting firm recommended extending this concept to other recreational facilities, and some cities have been doing just that. Santa Barbara, California, for example, now charges residents $18 a year for a tennis permit that grants preferential admission to the city's popular tennis courts. A permit is not required to play, but permit holders can bump nonholders at any time.

In other cases a permit can be required for access to the facility. To keep administrative costs to a minimum, the permits can be obtainable by mail, and enforcement need not require a tended admission gate. Instead, signs and spot checking can be used to deter use by nonpermit holders.

Another relatively recent development is setting higher user charges for nonresidents because residents already pay for part of the park and recreation program via taxes. Dallas; Fairfax County, Virginia; and Santa Barbara are three of the most recent jurisdictions to introduce a nonresident differential in their recreation pricing. In Santa Barbara the fees for nonresidents are 25% higher in many programs, such as weaving and yoga classes. But for all those that involve the use of major facilities—tennis courts, pools, gymnasiums—nonresidents pay twice as much as residents.

Cincinnati's new pay fountain is one of the most unusual forms of user charges on record. The fountain is part of a $2.8-million structure (including a parking garage) in that city's Yeatman's Cove Park on the banks of the Ohio River. Although water flows in the fountain at all times, insertion of a quarter turns on a spectacular three-minute display. If the fountain is activated only five times an hour, eight hours a day, it will bring in over $4,500 a year, to be used for park (and fountain) maintenance.

There is no reason why leisure and recreational services cannot be made self-supporting by means of user fees. Apart from political obstacles, that is. Private recreation facilities, after all, *have* to be self-supporting or they go out of business. Not only is it *possible* to make these public programs self-supporting—it is actually happening in some communities. The park and recreation agency of Wheeling, West Virginia, is now 98% self-supporting. Its fee programs support nonfee programs to bring overall income nearly into balance with expenses. The famed San Diego zoo is virtually self-supporting from user fees. The recreation programs of Newark and El Cerrito, California, were both made 100% self-supporting in 1979, to cope with Proposition 13 constraints. Santa Barbara's Park Departments in 1978 adopted a five-year goal of reaching self-sufficiency. Among the measures being taken are the introduction of parking fees at beaches and expansion of private concessions to provide more revenues. San Diego's Mission Bay Park includes hotels and restaurants as concessionaires; rents from these facilities pay for the public facilities in the rest of the park.

Thus, even if an individual neighborhood park cannot be self-supporting, a city's park and recreation *system* can be, if enough attention is given to finding sources of income and developing appropriate user charges.

Park Contracting

Regardless of how a park is financed, the cost of operating it can generally be reduced. An increasingly popular way to do this is to turn over park maintenance to a professional landscape-maintenance firm, on a contract basis. All the advantages of private-sector contracting that we have discussed in previous chapters apply equally well to park-maintenance contracting—and the number of potential suppliers is large (in contrast to such services as police and fire protection).[2]

Park-maintenance contracting has caught on rapidly in California over the past several years. Downey reports saving 20% on upkeep of its golf course since the work was contracted out. Ventura County, north of Los Angeles, is also saving 20% by contracting for its park maintenance, with performance incentives written into the contract. Lynwood's first week with contract tree trimming resulted in 500 trees being trimmed. "People around City Hall were stunned," notes administration analyst Gerard Goldhart. "Our city crew did 500 trees in an entire year, literally." The 1979 contract was for $87,000, compared with the previous budget of $125,000 for the city crew it replaced. Reportedly, there are "hundreds" of landscaping firms in California—many of them small, local outfits—that now market their services to local government.

Even before Proposition 13, a number of California cities had begun to contract for some of their park and recreation services. A 1976 survey by the League of California Cities found that seven cities had hired private firms to do their park maintenance; eight, to maintain their street trees and median strips; and eight, to take care of the landscaping around city buildings. Another four used private firms rather than city staff to design and develop new parks. Five cities had private firms running some or all of their recreation programs, and 13 had contracted out their golf course operations.

Since passage of Proposition 13 this trend has accelerated. Alameda, for example, is trying out contract maintenance at its newest park. Rohnert Park has contracted out maintenance of two of its parks, and of the landscaping at city hall and on median strips. San Jose awarded its first two-year contract for maintenance of its downtown parks. Compared with city costs of $12,500 per month, the bids it received ranged from $4,800 to $13,000.

While the operation of parks by private firms is not yet common, golf course operation is a runaway success, especially in Southern California. When Fullerton decided to contract out its golf course

[2]*Contract Services Handbook.* Washington, D.C.: Heritage Conservation and Recreation Service, October 1979.

in 1974, the winning bidder cut operating costs by 21%—and extended the playing time by five weeks a year. After several years, though, that firm lost out to a competitor which was willing to invest in capital improvements and take over the restaurant and pro shop as well.

Rohnert Park's eight-year-old golf course was losing about $60,000 a year when city officials decided to privatize. The winning bidder, California Golf, signed a 30-year lease contract, rebuilt the course, and guaranteed the city a minimum income of $60,000 a year. Increasingly, like Rohnert Park, cities are turning to long-term leases, under which the contractor takes over the entire operation, leaving the city nothing to do but sit back and collect revenues.

A few California cities are turning other facilities over to private contractors, as well. Fremont and Walnut Creek have contractors operating tennis facilities in city parks. San Joaquin County has contracted out the operation and maintenance of some of its parks, swimming pools, and zoo.

The rapid growth of interest in contracting became evident in April 1979 when California State University at Hayward held a conference on the subject in Oakland. With only minimal advance publicity, more than 100 people attended—park and recreation professionals from all over the state. They eagerly exchanged information on this rapidly growing means of saving money in the operation of park and recreation programs.

Park Efficiency

Besides using private contracting, officials can make park maintenance more efficient by various analytical and technological improvements. A scheduling technique known as *work measurement* can produce substantial savings by utilizing park-maintenance personnel more efficiently. Wilmington, Delaware, realized an annual saving of 27% thanks to a new work-scheduling system based on this type of analysis. Other cities which have used the technique include Santa Rosa, California; Syracuse, New York; and Honolulu, Hawaii.

Labor-saving equipment can also cut costs, more than paying for itself in subsequent labor-cost savings. For example, a surprising number of cities still rely extensively on hand watering. Automated sprinkler systems offer many benefits. They use only about half as much water as hand watering and they generally increase a park's availability since, unlike gardeners, they work at night. Generally a sprinkler system will pay for itself in labor-cost savings in less than seven years. Other types of equipment can also save time. Chula Vista, California's $10,000 automated swimming pool chemical-treatment system paid for itself in just 13 months due to savings in time, chemicals, and mileage. Winston-Salem, North Carolina, park employees save time applying insecticides by using a centrifugal-force spraying unit. In some applications, instead of cutting and trimming, St. Petersburg, Florida's park crews are using residual herbicides whose effect is much longer lasting; and application of the herbicides takes less time than trimming, thus producing substantial man-hour savings.

Further maintenance savings can be realized by proper design or redesign of the parks themselves. Parks should be planned from the start for automated sprinkler systems. Other time-saving design features include tree-planting configurations that make mowing and trimming easier, avoidance of grass areas that are inaccessible to large mowers, and bordering flower beds with walkways instead of grass. St. Petersburg is an exemplar of such park-design techniques.

Libraries and Museums

Libraries and museums can represent large drains on the taxpayers or can be made efficient and self-supporting. Both represent services used mostly by an elite minority of the community which tends to be vocal about "public" (taxpayer) support. Hence, major changes are likely to be slow in coming. But coming they are.

Museums, both public and private, seem to be showing the way. Faced with the decline of wealthy patrons and limitations on what can be drawn from the public purse, museums across the country are deriving increasing revenue from the sale of related products. Former "sales desks" have become full-fledged retail stores and mail order operations offering a considerable assortment of goods, from art prints and statuary to tote bags. New York's Metropolitan Museum of Art, which pioneered museum retailing, took in $12.5 million in 1977, three-fourths of it from catalog mailings to a million households. The Smithsonian Institution sold goods valued at $5.5 million in 1976, New York's Museum of Modern Art $1.5 million, the Los Angeles County Art Museum $800,000. Profits on such sales, which average about 15%, help pay the museums' ongoing expenses.

Most museums are also increasing their admission fees—or beginning to charge them where they never did before. (Some have begun simply by asking for donations—which is better than not charging at all!) Traditionalists have a hard time accepting even modest fees if the museum has been "free" for many years, and some museums report sharp declines in attendance—at first. But after awhile people get used to the idea of pay-as-you-go. A prime success in this regard is the Oregon Museum of Science and Industry in Portland. Rated as one of the four best science centers in the nation, the museum is completely self-supporting. Its $2-million-a-year budget comes entirely from donations, memberships, an annual auction, admission fees, educational program fees, and a periodic fund drive.

Whether or not they sell products, libraries, too, are beginning to charge money. Some now charge a fee for library cards, and a few charge admission. The Los Angeles public libraries charge a daily fee for checking out best sellers, thereby helping to keep these popular books in circulation. They have also doubled their fine for overdue books from 5¢ to 10¢ per day. The public library in Indianapolis is conducting a research project to gauge user reaction to fees for computer searches and interlibrary loans. The Minneapolis Public Library is offering a sophisticated computerized reference service called "Inform." The users, most of which are large firms headquartered in the city, pay $35 an hour for access to the system.

"The user fee idea is cropping up all over," writes Fay Blake: "in public libraries in Minneapolis, in academic libraries for data base services and for interlibrary loans, and in the small freelance operations which provide information for those who can pay." Like quite a few librarians, Blake is opposed to the whole idea, having been schooled in the tradition of "free public libraries." The 1977 convention of the American Library Association witnessed sharp debate on the user-charge issue and ended up passing a resolution in support of "free" libraries—although the organization's governing council had previously defeated a similar resolution.

But the precedent for setting user fees is being solidly established by the growth of computerized information services. In many cases the only way a library can afford to get into these increasingly popular services is to offset the costs via user charges. Several years ago Eugene Garfield, board chairman of the Information Industry Association, told the National Commission on Libraries and Information Science that pay libraries are inevitable. *Library Journal* editor John Berry III, although opposing the trend, seems to agree: "If a city manager is looking for a way to cut the municipal budget, he might look at a library and say, 'Well, if you charge for this (computerized) research, why don't you charge for the story hour for the kids? Why don't you charge for using the catalog?' " Adds Fay Blake, "No hard-pressed city auditor or mayor or council is going to approve a budget for a library's free services once he smells user fees in the offing."

Library administrators also save money for taxpayers by automation. Macon, Georgia, has installed an automated book checkout and check-in system using supermarket-type bar codes on the books and light-wand reading devices. The new system's computer also replaced the huge clerical task of filing and unfiling about a million 3×5 cards each year. It automatically prepares overdue book notices and bills for lost books, maintains reserve book lists, and produces various statistical reports. Library Director Charles J. Schmidt reports that the system has doubled the productivity of his personnel, from an average of 11,000 annual check-outs per staff member to nearly 22,000. The system is now being adapted for the Albany, Georgia, library, as well.

Sunnyvale, California, has automated the process of cataloging new books. Following a study by Public Technology, Inc., library officials there decided to tie into the Ohio College Library Center's automated cataloging system. More than 300 public, university, and federal libraries now participate in the system via time-sharing computer terminals. Previously the library had to wait four to six weeks after a book was received for catalog cards to arrive from the Library of Congress. Now the cards are printed on Sunnyvale Library's printer by the OCLC computer. The system has reduced the cost per card set from 50¢ plus typist's time to a net cost of 21¢. Book processing time has been cut from five weeks to two weeks, and backroom storage space has been reduced 60%. Overall savings work out to $4,000–$6,000 per year.

Like most other public services, libraries and museums provide something of value to identifiable beneficiaries. They can be run well, or poorly, like any service business. Modern management and technological tools can make these institutions efficient, and user charges can begin matching up those who pay with those who benefit. Together, these techniques can eventually remove yet another burden from the backs of the local taxpayer.

17. Private Solutions to Conservation Problems

Robert J. Smith

Whales provide a classic example of the wanton waste generated by a common property resource system. Part of the "common heritage of mankind" and owned by no individual, whales have been rapidly exploited, to the near extinction of some species. Under the system of nonownership, even the most conservation-minded whaler is unlikely to stop overharvesting; if he didn't take the whales, someone else would.

However, what if we extended the concept of private property ownership to the California gray whale herd so that the first users of that resource obtained property rights in it, just as if whales were like any other renewable resource? Self-interest and an economic incentive would then tend to encourage the whalers to conserve the species. Because each whaler could capture the capital value of his property, he would attempt to maintain its value and would harvest the whales at a rate that would produce a sustained yield.

Private ownership could bring about other benefits as well. A patrol ship could travel back and forth with the whales on their annual migrations from Alaska to Baja California, protecting and caring for the herd. Killer whales could be driven away, the young and the ailing could be given antibiotics, and whales stranded in the shallow lagoons of Baja could be freed. The whaling companies could supply boats and facilities for visiting the Baja lagoons and viewing the whales as they migrated off the U.S. coast, thus providing the public, environmentalists, and naturalists with a unique educational and aesthetic experience. Moreover, biological and communications studies could be carried out by private interests instead of being funded by further burdening the taxpayers.

Other species of great whales that migrate in distinct herds could be treated similarly, and the knowledge gained through managing them might enable us to extend the private property concept to species that appear to migrate randomly, perhaps by tagging them and then caring for them or harvesting them only when they appeared in their recognizable summer and winter ranges.

But whales continue to be treated as a common property resource. Whaling nations—and, increasingly, nonwhaling nations—have attempted to limit or resolve the tragedy of the commons, most notably by creating the International Whaling Commission and mandating it to impose quotas and bans on the taking of various species. With little effective policing power, the IWC has been hard-pressed to enforce its decisions. Some countries have openly circumvented the quota system. For a while there was a burgeoning pirate whaling fleet that sailed under various flags of convenience and was therefore beyond the reach of IWC restrictions. However, the radical environmental organization Greenpeace undertook guerrilla activities, including the ramming, sinking, and scuttling of pirate whaling ships. That tactic had the effect of dampening the enthusiasm of the pirate whalers as well as raising their insurance premiums to exorbitant levels, and it effectively eliminated pirate whaling.

Although almost every nation has at least tacitly agreed to discontinue whaling and observe a moratorium, both to conserve the various species and to allow their populations and population growth rates to be ascertained, the survival of the world's whales is still chancy. The major whaling nations view the moratorium as a mere hiatus in their activities, whereas the environmentalists hope that world opinion will make a return to whaling politically impossible and that the aging whaling fleets will rust away and not be replaced. Yet with nearly all legal commercial whaling already suspended and a full moratorium on the horizon, a few nations have begun to circumvent the new rules by conducting "research" whaling—killing whales and using them in biological experiments, then consuming or selling the products. That development simply underscores the difficulty of managing the commons.

It is unfortunate that so many environmentalists are emotionally and philosophically opposed to private enterprises' attempting to make a profit by harvesting wildlife. It is not private ownership that has led to the near extinction of many species of whales but rather the very concept that most environmentalists endorse: common property "ownership"—the idea that whales belong to everyone.

The tragedy of the commons applies to all of the ocean fisheries, and the daily accounts of waste, overfishing, and depletion of marine resources are a strong testament to the failure of common property resource "management." As long as that system is in force, we will continue to witness the overharvesting of tuna, salmon, striped bass, haddock, and other species. As the demands on the marine fisheries continue to grow, the problems will continue to worsen. Recent years have seen "fish wars" between nations—Iceland vs. Great Britain, the Bahamas vs. the United States, Peru and Mexico vs. the United States. Such wars have led many nations to extend their fishing limit to 200 miles out (and are part of the basis for the United Nations-sponsored Law of the Seas conferences). Eliminating the presence of foreign fishermen, however, is at best a partial solution to the problems inherent in common property resource use. Economic and political struggles among all of the competing users continue.

The future of the marine fisheries is shaky. Although the total world fish catch has begun to rise—after a decade-long pattern of no growth or little growth that elicited Global 2000–type forecasts of doom—the reason for that increase may be a shift to formerly underutilized species rather than the return of overfished species. But at least a few highly valued species appear to have made a remarkable recovery in the short time since various bans on catching and selling them were enacted. Among them are the striped bass, known locally as the rockfish, in the Chesapeake Bay, whose decline was attributed in part to acid rain. Because acid rain has obviously not disappeared, it seems likely that their decline was a classic instance of the tragedy of the commons. If more attention was given to ending the tragedy of the commons by creating property rights and other incentives to manage natural resources wisely—instead of using wildlife population declines to "prove" the evils of human population growth or the free enterprise system—the world's environment would be in much better condition.

A classic example of the conflicts inherent in common property resource use is provided by the salmon fishery of the northwestern United States, where commercial fishermen, sport fishermen in boats near river mouths, upstream rod fishermen, Indians, and managers of hydroelectric projects are all at odds, and foreign fleets persist in taking salmon beyond the 200-mile limit. Unless private property rights are developed, the only means of resolving such conflicts will continue to lie in the political process or in the economic incentive to take all the fish one can before someone else does.

There has been considerable development of private and quasi-private property rights in the fields of aquaculture and mariculture. Examples include the Japanese pearl oyster industry; lobster and shrimp farms at utility plants, where "thermal pollution" is used to accelerate growth; and private oyster, clam, scallop, and mussel farms, which are run by firms that own or lease portions of the sea or the sea bottom and care for the shellfish by providing proper bedding material and eliminating predators such as starfish.

The abalone, a shellfish highly prized on the West Coast and in the Orient, has suffered from rising demand and the overfishing that is a consequence of common property resource use. Moreover, it has nearly been exterminated along the central California coast by an endangered but strongly resurgent population of sea otters. That situation has led to a near war between abalone fishermen and pro–sea otter environmentalists. The latter allege that the former are killing sea otters, which are protected by federal law, to halt their huge intake of abalone. The environmentalists have responded by launching boycotts against abalone, and each side is seeking governmental assistance in protecting its interests. Once again a multiple-use conflict has been thrown into the political arena. A more satisfactory solution may result from recent attempts to develop abalone farming programs by various groups.

Those pioneering efforts came to fruition with the creation of Pacific Ocean-Farms, Ltd., an open-ocean shellfish farming company that has leased 50 acres 2½ miles offshore in Monterey Bay and anchored fiberglass boxes called condominiums in 100-foot-deep water. The boxes protect the company's abalone from predators such as starfish and sea otters, and they are growing twice as fast as they would in the wild. Because it is a commercial farming operation, the abalone do not come under certain governmental regulations and thus can be marketed at an earlier age and a smaller size. They can also be exported to prime seafood markets in the eastern United States and Japan. California law prohibits the export of wild abalone. Because decades of mismanagement under the common property system have caused the price of abalone to rise from $1.50 a pound in 1960 to $17 a pound today, the success of the venture seems assured. In addition, the company's breeding efforts cause a large number of fertilized eggs to be transported into the ocean, thereby providing a positive externality to the marine food chain, including the voracious sea otters. One of the company's officers said, "Such conservationist groups as the Friends of the Sea Otter really like us because we could be providing a lot of new abalones in the open sea."[1]

Unfortunately, George Lockwood, the major entrepreneurial spirit behind the development of the new industry, had overlooked the extreme zealousness of the governmental bureaucracy. Scores of federal and state agencies, departments, and bureaus continually subjected his fledgling enterprise to a crazy quilt of regulations, permits, restrictions, and licenses.

The state nearly prevented the expansion of Lockwood's operation by rejecting his request to install more abalone condominiums because his plan did not provide for garages to accompany them. Federal regulators argued that his abalone were relieving themselves in the bay, a practice from which the wild abalone presumably refrained. OSHA representatives ruled that because his was an underwater business, his employees, who could easily skindive the short distance involved in order to inspect and service the condominiums, had to be outfitted with the extremely expensive state-of-the-art diving gear required for deep-sea operations such as offshore oil platform work.

As the years of experimentation and costly private investment finally began to pay off in a successful, productive farm, the governmental harassment continued. California officials attempted to place Lockwood's farmed, commercial product under state fish and game regulations. The state demanded access to his most closely held proprietary secrets (the invertebrate biology of mariculture is an exceedingly complex subject), then allegedly used those secrets to construct and run a tax-supported operation to compete with him and hired away one of his key biologists.

Having finally recognized that even California's mildly conservative Republican administration had no interest in fostering private solutions to the abalone shortage or the growth of new industries, fisheries employment, and profitable ventures, Lockwood closed down his Monterey Abalone Farms. He moved the entire operation—tanks, condominiums (with no garages), aba-

---

[1]Gordon Grant, "Expensive Shellfish Commercially Farmed: Condos Built for Abalone at Sea but No Garages," *Los Angeles Times*, June 11, 1979.

lone, and so on—to Kona, Hawaii, where he reopened it as Hawaiian Abalone Farms. The state government welcomed his arrival and was enthusiastic about the prospect of hosting a thriving mariculture industry.

Such persistent governmental interference with and resistance to the development of private solutions to environmental problems are all too characteristic of the prevailing mindset.

Aquaculture programs on land involving highly productive freshwater fish farms have been developed in many parts of the United States and are increasingly becoming a major source of inexpensive protein in Third World countries. The principal fish involved in the U.S. operations are carp and catfish in the South (the latter supplying restaurant chains) and trout in the Northwest and in many parts of the East that have cool waters. Fountain Rock Springs Trout Farm, a fish-for-a-fee enterprise near Washington, D.C., advertised year-round trout fishing and "all the trout you can catch, open every day, no limit, no season, and no license." Private trout farms in Idaho supply most of the frozen trout sold by the nation's grocery stores. The survival of the farms was threatened, however, when the Environmental Protection Agency discovered that the fish had a tendency to deposit their droppings in the water and maintained that the resulting discharge into streams and rivers violated the zero-runoff requirements. However, the "fertilization" of water near the outflow pipes of some of the trout farms resulted in the growth of aquatic life and therefore the presence of larger numbers of wild fish, which attracted many fishermen to those areas. Apparently it was a problem only in the offices of Washington, D.C.'s regulatory agencies.

(A similar absurdity affected logging operations in some of the watershed regions above reservoirs in the Northwest. The companies were required to use horses to get into the logging areas and to haul out logs; the use of motorized equipment was banned because of the chance that petroleum wastes would enter the water and the likelihood that siltation would result from the erosion of roads. However, it later occurred to some bureaucrat that horses produce waste. The result? A requirement that the horses wear diapers. That created the quaint possibility of an army of rugged cowboys heading into the hills with a supply of Vaseline and safety pins.)

A number of promising developments in sea farming have involved salmon. Bay Center Mariculture Company of Washington

State has been experimenting with oyster and crayfish cultures as well. Until very recently raising salmon in ponds with the aim of marketing them for profit was not permitted in Washington, although taxpayer-supported state fish hatcheries were fine. Bay Center Mariculture described the benefits of its methods as follows:

> It has been discovered in recent years that salmon go through their early development and growth much faster in brackish water than in the fresh water we are accustomed to expect them in during their early life. . . . [We] take advantage of this by both sea-farming salmon and raising them to market size in controlled ponds. Because of the specificity of salmon to return to the spot of their birth, it is possible to release them at an early age and allow them to mature in the sea and return to the hatchery site a year earlier than they would if raised in nature in fresh water streams. The expected return is a very small percentage, but still very profitable.[2]

In 1977 Weyerhaeuser initiated a similar system in southern Oregon; the young salmon were to be raised in ponds at the head of a bay and then released into the bay. The company expected to make a profit if 1 percent of the adult salmon returned to its fish ladders. In the wild, approximately 2 to 5 percent of the salmon survive to return to their breeding grounds.

Such programs not only solve conservation problems at private interests' expense rather than at taxpayers' expense but reduce the take on wildlife populations and provide a positive externality to the wild food chain.

Another interesting experiment is being conducted by Maine Sea Farms, whose salmon are raised in a fenced seawater cove, are fed a special diet of ground shrimp and crab, and achieve a survival rate of nearly 50 percent. They are marketed 20 months later as 9- to 12-ounce "yearlings" in the luxury fresh fish markets of the Northeast.

In spite of the tremendous profit potential of the mariculture industry and the willingness of venture capitalists to enter the field, its development has been slow. Governmental regulations and restrictions continue to be a problem. Environmentalists often oppose such ventures on the grounds that farmed fish interbreed with and "pollute" the wild strains (although they have not been equally vociferous in their objections to state and federal fish

---

[2]Bay Center Mariculture Company, n.d.

farms). Furthermore, there is an instinctive bias by environmental activists against big businesses' and profit-seekers' entering the field. Many groups have maintained that because Weyerhaeuser's salmon farming operation, Ore-Aqua, is a large venture, it competes with the rugged individualists working their commercial fishing boats in the nearby storm-tossed Pacific. Early in its history, when Ore-Aqua was a center of controversy and the subject of a "Nova" episode on PBS television, there were even rumors in Oregon that Weyerhaeuser was conditioning its salmon to avoid fishing boats by running diesel engines at one end of the rearing ponds to give them an electric shock and then feeding them salmon chow at the other end of the ponds.

Faced with high costs, cumbersome regulations, and an often-hostile public, the mariculture industry in the United States has been characterized by a high rate of turnover and instability. Salmon farms appear to be thriving only in northern European countries such as Scotland and Norway, where they benefit from a long tradition of private ownership of fishing streams, shellfisheries, and so on.

In Nova Scotia, giant Atlantic bluefin tuna, which often enter shallow bays to feed on herring and subsequently get caught in herring traps, used to be wastefully slaughtered and discarded by herring fishermen. But now enterprising entrepreneurs are transferring the tuna into fenced enclosures and raising them until they have a high fat content; in the late fall they are harvested and shipped to Japan, where they are considered a great delicacy and command a high price.

What we need now are legal changes that make private ownership of marine waters possible. The process could be started most readily by allowing private ownership of lagoons, shallow bays, sounds, and the waters near islands. Strips of different sizes along the Atlantic coast could be owned by lobster fishermen and strips along the Pacific coast by abalone fishermen.

Under the common property resource use system, a fisherman has little incentive to practice conservation and farming methods. Any attempt to enrich the sea on his part would simply allow free-riders to benefit from his expenditures. Gordon Tullock reported the following example:

> The present legal situation can well be illustrated by an account of the misfortunes of Captain Mikuletsky, the owner and opera-

tor of a boat engaged in taking parties of New Yorkers out for a day's fishing. One day Captain Mikuletsky took a party of fishermen to a likely spot and there threw several hundred pounds of chopped herring into the water in order to attract the fish, who would then be caught by his passengers.

To the good Captain's annoyance, three other boats proceeded to fish in the area in which he was "investing capital." After trying out some seaman-like oaths, Captain Mikuletsky fired across the bows of the three intruders with his shotgun. In the course of the resulting legal proceedings a Coast Guard spokesman, quite rightly, said that the action of the three intruding boats was unsportsmanlike, but not illegal.[3]

The need for private ownership is also evident in the case of the reefs that are created by dumping junk in shallow coastal waters. In the past wrecked cars were widely used; however, they tend to rust away too rapidly to result in long-lived reefs. Today the preferred material is used tires, which create a serious waste disposal problem on land; burning them produces highly toxic residues, and they have a tendency to shift around in landfill areas. But because tires are nearly indestructible, they have proved to be ideal for reef building. Artificial reefs thus provide a solution to the waste disposal problem; moreover, as Richard B. Stone, director of the National Marine Fisheries Service's reef program, has explained, they benefit ocean life and produce astonishing concentrations of fish.

[M]ost of the American continental shelf, especially from New York through Virginia to Florida and around the Gulf of Texas, is a real desert—flat and sandy, with little shelter or food to attract fish. But once rock or anything else hard becomes available to furnish an anchor, barnacles, hydroids, corals and mussels attach themselves. As soon as these growths flourish, bottom-dwelling fish and crustaceans congregate to graze on the plant and animal life and to hide in the holes and cracks. Then the free-swimming predators come to feed on this rich bounty, and a thriving colony of fish is born.[4]

Artificial reefs therefore create vastly improved catches for the billion-dollar sport fisheries industry. They achieve that result not

---

[3]Gordon Tullock, "The Fisheries: Some Radical Proposals" (Ph.D. diss., University of South Carolina, 1962), p. 21.

[4]Don Carl Steffen, "Life-Giving Junk, Man-Made Reefs," *Northern Virginia People*, January/February 1977, p. 31.

by luring fish away from other areas but by providing homes for fish that otherwise would not be able to survive.

Once the productivity of artificial reefs had been demonstrated and interest in them had grown, the Dingell-Johnson Federal Aid in Fish Restoration Act was passed to provide tax revenues to the states for reef construction. Broward County, Florida, even passed a law requiring that used tires be turned in for that purpose. Artificial reef creation could clearly be accomplished by the market. Unfortunately, the common property resource use system would not allow private reef builders to prevent free-riders from benefiting from their reefs. If private ownership was extended to the seabed, their property rights could be enforced. Fishing fleets operating out of harbors could create their own reefs, thereby ensuring successful sport fishing trips for their customers or successful catches for fish factories.

Offshore oil rigs serve as temporary artificial reefs, and it is common to see large numbers of sport fishing boats gathered in the vicinity of such platforms off the Gulf coast. Under current federal regulations, once offshore oil platforms have completed their productive life, they must be removed—at considerable expense to the oil companies. They are usually towed ashore, where they are cut up and sold for scrap metal. But the petroleum industry is exploring the possibility of towing the platforms to deep water and then sinking them to create permanent artificial reefs. That would result in substantial savings for the oil companies and would benefit the fishing public as well. Although it is not an ideal solution, it is better than the present one.

Perhaps the most important example of a private approach to conservation is that of Cayman Turtle Farm, Ltd. on the Cayman Islands in the British West Indies. It was formed in 1968, as Mariculture, Ltd., by Irvin Naylor, a Pennsylvania businessman, and Antony Fisher, an English businessman and the founder of a noted free-market study center, the Institute of Economic Affairs. Operating under the motto "Conservation via Commerce," they began a program of breeding the green sea turtle in captivity by gathering eggs from the wild (generally from beaches where the eggs would have been lost because of high tides, predation, or harvesting). They were then able to get the eggs to hatch and the hatchlings to reach maturity at far higher rates than occurred in nature.

All of the world's sea turtles can probably be considered either threatened or endangered—a result of ages of overharvesting under the common property use system, the commercial development of breeding beaches, and such incidental causes of death as entrapment in shrimp trawlers' nets. The response of the conservation community has been to seek a ban on all trade in sea turtle products. However, that prohibition would do very little, if anything, to aid the various species in their recovery. With populations so reduced, the mortality rates of eggs and hatchlings so high, and the pace of beachfront development so rapid, it would seem that sea turtles can only continue down the slope to extinction.

A number of eminent scientists have maintained that farming operations are the only hope for the survival of the green turtle. Jacques Yves Cousteau said, "If the sea turtle is to survive, it must be farmed."[5] Harold F. Hirth, in a report to the United Nations' Food and Agricultural Organization, said, "The green sea turtle is the world's most important reptile, and sea farms for turtles are a necessity."[6] Even Archie Carr, who has been a prominent opponent of Cayman Turtle Farm, was quoted by the International Union for Conservation of Nature and Natural Resources as saying, "There seems no inherent reason why *Chelonia mydas* should not become a semi-domesticated meat animal of great value. . . . Successful evolution of such a culture would not only extend the means of taking food from the sea, but would quickly take the pressure off the wild sea turtle populations, and thus help save the species for the distant future."[7]

Unfortunately, from the very beginning Cayman Turtle Farm's efforts were met with disapproval or even hostility by most environmentalists and some biologists. Among their objections were the philosophical or emotional argument that it was wrong to seek to profit from exploiting wildlife, the economic argument that the farm had overinvested in its physical plant, and the biological argument that its conservation methods were unsound and would harm the green sea turtle. Eventually, under the weight of all the opposition, the company went into receivership; it was reorganized under new owners and given its present name in 1975.

One might have expected the conservation community to wel-

---

[5]"New Hope for the Green Turtle" (Mariculture, Ltd., Cayman Islands, B.W.I., n.d.).

[6]Ibid.

[7]Ibid.

come the turtle farm, as its only demand upon wild populations was to collect eggs until its program became self-sufficient. Having achieved very high rates of hatching, the farmers began to release hatchlings and, later, yearlings off the beaches where they had collected the eggs. Moreover, all of the farm's operations were aimed at reducing the market's reliance on green turtles from the wild. It hired some of the remaining turtle hunters in the Caymans and attempted to undersell wild turtle meat with its farmed meat. (The products from farmed turtles—meat, calipee for soup, oil, shell jewelry, and leather goods—are labeled as farmed products under trade law.) The farm also required its customers to sign contracts stating that they would refrain from purchasing wild turtle products on pain of losing their guaranteed source of farmed products. Of course, the steady supply of farmed products also served to reduce the market's reliance on wild populations. In addition, relatively little had been known about the life cycle and breeding behavior of the sea turtle, and the farm's biologists were accumulating a considerable amount of information—at no expense to taxpayers.

In May 1975 the Department of Commerce proposed that farmed green turtle products be allowed to enter the United States for a specific trial period or until the farm could prove that it was self-sufficient. During the following three years environmentalists continued to press to have the green turtle listed as endangered by the Department of the Interior and trade in its products thus banned in the United States. (Interestingly enough, sea turtles are controlled by Interior when they are on land and by Commerce when they are in the water. In an attempt to resolve the dispute over that split jurisdiction, $500,000 was wasted.) Finally, in July 1978, Commerce joined Interior in placing all sea turtles on the endangered species list. It also banned the importation of all farmed sea turtle products, even though the company was at most a year away from achieving self-sufficiency and was even willing to forgo egg collection.

Because about half of Cayman Turtle Farm's market was in the United States, the company found it difficult to survive, although the ban did not affect its trade with countries that made an exception for farmed turtle products. Many environmentalists gleefully welcomed the decision and eagerly awaited the demise of the farm. It would be ironic if instead they were hearing the death knell of the green turtle.

The most striking example of the farm's conservation achievements is the fact that its stock grew to about 80,000 green turtles, whereas the wild population in the western Caribbean and the Gulf of Mexico is little more than 5,000. Because much of the stock would not have lived if the farm had left the eggs in the wild, the net contribution to the survival of the green turtle has been enormous.

Cayman Turtle Farm was supplying the luxury goods market with products that conservationists want to ban worldwide. Moreover, the preservation of sea turtles was funded through the voluntary patronage of the well-to-do, not through the coercion of overburdened taxpayers. And once again a legislative ban on trade in products that people desire only served to bring the economics of prohibition into operation. The National Wildlife Federation reported that there was a thriving black market in which sea turtles brought up to $200.[8] There were also reports of turtle nets that entangled and drowned female green turtles approaching the beaches of Little Cayman and any other turtles that entered them, including the highly endangered hawksbill.

Cayman Turtle Farm's owners and the Cayman government made vigorous attempts to get the United States to repeal the import ban or grant an exemption for products from the farm. The farm even offered to cover the expenses of having U.S. officials inspect its operations and institute a system of certificates of origin proving that sea turtle products entering the United States were derived from farmed turtles rather than from threatened or endangered populations. The entry of such products could have been restricted to the Port of Miami, where the certificates of origin could have been verified. But the environmentalists' shortsighted, counterproductive objections to the farm and its profit-seeking nature prevailed. As a congressional assistant remarked, "The farm's mistake was probably in not applying for a federal subsidy for their program. Then they would have been an environmentalist's delight."

With the U.S. market closed to tourist purchases as well as to commercial imports, and with transshipment in bond through Miami to nations that permit trade in farmed sea turtle products

[8] Rosanne Hallowell, "Life's a Shell Game," *International Wildlife*, July/August 1979, p. 12. The article also states, "Now, the green turtle is in danger of extinction because of relentless poaching."

also banned, Cayman Turtle Farm fell on hard times. The second owners sold out to the Cayman government, which now operates the farm on a greatly reduced scale; it has a very small breeding stock and serves as little more than a major tourist attraction and a source of green sea turtle meat for the local restaurants.

The sea turtle continues to be heavily exploited in many areas of the world; on the beaches of Mexican resort communities, for example, sea turtle products are still sold in sizable numbers. Sadly, the thriving illicit trade could have been replaced by legal, carefully regulated trade in certified farmed sea turtle products.

Captive breeding programs for a wide variety of wildlife may become the last chance for other endangered and threatened species, especially in the Third World countries, whose rapidly expanding populations are placing ever-greater pressure on natural habitats. Although the developed countries' environmentalists have expressed their concern by requesting, for example, that Brazil not develop the Amazon jungles, the Brazilians, understandably, are much more interested in obtaining housing, air conditioning, and automobiles than in keeping their country in undeveloped splendor for the pleasure of foreign conservationists.

Private farms, ranches, preserves, and parks have begun to present exciting possibilities for the preservation of rare and endangered species. At hunting preserves on large ranches and estates throughout the American West, highly desired big-game animals from many countries are raised; the conservation of their species is funded by the fees charged to hunters for limited cropping of the herds. Although such programs are opposed by many environmentalists, they are preserving wildlife (many species of which are threatened in their native countries) and doing so at private expense. Some of the herds contain trophy animals superior to any in the wild. Such animals may provide a nucleus for stocking sanctuaries in their native habitats when Third World countries can afford the environmental conscience so evident in the developed countries.

There are also promising private programs such as the Big Horn Wildlife and Habitat Research Project on a 20,000-acre ranch in Montana, which was created for the sole purpose of developing habitat management techniques. Native plant species are used in an attempt to sustain maximum numbers of big-game animals and upland game birds.

Many African countries are exploring the possibility of raising game animals on large ranches for their meat, hides, and horns, which not only is less environmentally destructive than converting wildlife habitats to cattle pastures but generates greater revenue from each acre. There is also a trend toward moving away from intensive cattle ranching and grain farming throughout the western United States. Instead, landowners are allowing their property to return to a native grass and brush habitat and raising game mammals and birds for hunting. That alternative requires less-intensive management of the land and less application of agricultural chemicals and still permits landowners to earn a profit. The return to a native habitat also permits a wide range of nongame species to thrive in areas that otherwise would be relatively wildlife-barren.

Some species have actually been saved from extinction by being represented in private preserves and collections, which serve as modern Noah's arks. Many species of birds that are rare, threatened, or endangered in the wild are being raised in captivity at private aviaries and conservatories. Such programs have been particularly active in preserving waterfowl (such as ducks, geese, and swans) and gallinaceous birds (such as quail, grouse, and pheasants); at least six species of pheasants that are endangered throughout their native ranges are being raised in captivity by private enterprises in the United States.

Private zoos, game parks, and drive-through safarilike theme parks are experiencing a population explosion. They're breeding more great cats than the market can use and are being forced to resort to birth control techniques to control the glut (they hope to develop a reversible birth control method for tigers). Some parks have even attempted to ship their excess lions back to Africa. Conservationists do not seem to be particularly opposed to ranch-bred mink and fox, so why not extend the concept to the spotted cats in order to supply the fur trade and thus reduce the demand on wild populations?

Until the midcentury nearly all of the raptors—birds of prey such as eagles, hawks, falcons, and owls—were unprotected by federal or state law. The notable exceptions were the nation's emblem, the bald eagle, which received federal protection in 1940, and the golden eagle, which received protection in 1962. The other birds of prey were essentially treated as vermin, and throughout much of the nation, government bounties were paid for their corpses. Raptors were killed not only by bounty hunters and sport shooters but by farmers and ranchers, who considered them major predators of chickens, lambs, and other livestock.

As a result of the massive slaughter, a number of species were seriously reduced in numbers and became threatened. Additional causes of various raptors' decline were egg collecting and other human interference, loss of habitat due to changes in land use patterns, and the use of agricultural chemicals.

The most notable and dramatic decline was that of the peregrine falcon, once called the duck hawk. A widespread but never common species, the peregrine is considered one of the most spectacular birds. It is one of the fastest-flying birds, reaching nearly 200 miles an hour in its swoops on prey, is a fierce predator, and usually inhabits wild and inaccessible places. Throughout the ages it has often been the species most favored by falconers; in many areas its use was reserved exclusively for the nobility.

A drastic, seemingly overnight decline in the peregrine populations of North America and Europe occurred after World War II. By the early 1950s it was noted that peregrine eggs were failing to hatch, and by 1960 there were no active eyries in the northeastern United States. By the mid-1960s the peregrine had disappeared from much of its northern range. It had been extirpated from the eastern United States and Canada and greatly reduced in the Rockies and along the Pacific coast. Only in the Arctic and in the humid coastal belt of British Columbia and southeastern Alaska was its population relatively stable. Its numbers had also plummeted in Europe. Many scientists predicted extinction for the peregrine.

Eventually, after years of study, scientists determined that the major cause of the peregrine's decline was DDT. Most of the developed nations subsequently banned the use of DDT; the U.S. Environmental Protection Agency did so in 1972. The ban was intended to preclude a further accumulation of DDT residues, which become concentrated in the tissues of the peregrine and other predatory species at the top of long, complex food chains. It was largely successful, but of course it did nothing to reestablish the peregrine in the areas where the species had been extirpated.

Also in 1972, federal protection was finally extended to all of the birds of prey; the Migratory Bird Treaty Act made it illegal to kill them, capture them, or take them from the wild without a permit or other authorization. In 1973 the Endangered Species Act was passed to protect and help restore threatened and endangered species—such as the peregrine falcon.

However, it was the private sector that played the leading role in the restoration of the nation's peregrine populations. There is a special irony in the fact that this was accomplished largely through the techniques and efforts of falconers, because falconry has long been aggressively opposed by most conservationists as well as by many employees of the U.S. Fish and Wildlife Service. Such opponents consider it dreadfully wrong for the small number of government-licensed falconers to take a few young birds from the nests in order to fly them for pleasure, even though far more die each year from striking broadcast towers, skyscrapers, airplanes, and power lines. It is estimated that 67 percent of the first-year peregrines die and that 20 percent of the subadults die.

In the late 1960s, when they saw that the species was rapidly disappearing, falconers began attempting to breed large numbers of peregrines in captivity. Their interest in having a continuous supply of peregrines for use in their sport was a sufficient incentive. By the early 1970s falconers had their own breeding stock. Yet their efforts were often belittled by the conservation community.

In 1970 Tom J. Cade, a professor of ornithology at Cornell University and the Cornell Laboratory of Ornithology, established the Peregrine Fund, a private, nonprofit organization affiliated with the laboratory. Building on and later improving on the techniques of falconers, Cade and his colleagues developed a program of captive propagation and reintroduction of the peregrine.

Essentially, Cade's concept was to institute a regular breeding operation that would eventually produce enough peregrines to restore the species throughout its former range. His efforts, like those of the falconers, were met with hostility from naysayers, detractors, and opponents. His breeding stock initially consisted of birds donated or lent by falconers and wild birds from the Arctic, the Pacific Northwest, Europe, South America, and Australia. The fact that he was crossing peregrines from different populations in an attempt to breed a bird that was ideal for introduction into the wild caused great consternation among the genetic purists in the environmental community. Apparently they thought it was better to have no peregrines in the wild than to have peregrines of mixed parentage there.

The Peregrine Fund has been supported by contributions from thousands of individuals and hundreds of companies and private foundations. State and federal agencies have also contributed, but most of its funding has been nongovernmental. However, the organization has had to work closely with governmental agencies because the peregrine falcon is on the endangered species list.

The success of the Peregrine Fund's program has been striking. The fund produced its first peregrine chick in 1973 and released its first birds in the wild in 1974. It has since raised nearly 2,000 young peregrines, of which over 80 percent were successfully released in the wild. In 1980 its birds began to nest in the wild in the East—it was the first time peregrines had done so in over 20 years. Those captive-bred birds and their progeny are now breeding in the wild throughout the peregrine's historic eastern range. The fund's goals have largely been accomplished in the East (there are more peregrines breeding in New Jersey now than before the extirpation of the species), and considerable progress has been made in the West.

The fund has expanded its facilities and operations and moved its world headquarters to Boise, Idaho, where it is studying and breeding a wide range of threatened and endangered raptors, including some that are native to other countries. Additionally, it is now attempting to reintroduce falcons other than the peregrine, hawks, and owls in various states where they have become extirpated.

The propagation and reintroduction techniques developed and perfected by the Peregrine Fund have been so successful that both other conservation organizations and governmental agencies are applying them in programs aimed at restoring such raptors as the bald eagle and the osprey. It can be hoped that Cade will eventually receive his due and that environmentalists opposed to falconry will recognize his signal contributions to the conservation of endangered species.

One of the major achievements in the history of wildlife conservation was the creation of a sanctuary for raptors by a private group, Hawk Mountain Sanctuary Association. Located along the ridges of the Appalachian Mountains in eastern Pennsylvania, the sanctuary is one of the points of highest concentration for most of the hawks, falcons, and eagles of eastern North America as they migrate south each autumn. As a consequence, it used to be frequented by gunners, who would gather by the hundreds and kill hundreds or even thousands of hawks a day. Shooting hawks not only was considered a sport but was actively encouraged by the state government's payment of bounties for dead hawks. During the peak period Pennsylvania paid $90,000 worth of bounties; it estimated that hawks had killed $1,875 worth of chickens. Although a few chickens may have been saved, the state later estimated that its farmers had lost nearly $4 million worth of grain crops because of the increased rodent population resulting from the decreased number of hawks.

In 1934 conservationists, led by Rosalie Edge, quietly purchased 1,398 acres for a mere $3,500 and established the Hawk Mountain Sanctuary Association. Since expanded to over 2,000 acres, the sanctuary accepts no government aid and is completely self-supporting. Besides serving as a mecca for birders, it conducts research and educational programs on the biology and economic value of hawks. So effective have its educational efforts been that many farmers in nearby valleys maintain nesting boxes that attract the American kestrel in order to help control the rodent population.

Today the sanctuary is world-famous, and 50,000 visitors a year travel there to view one of the most spectacular sights in nature. Crowds of over 2,000 people gather and are able to watch as many as 7,000 hawks pass in a single day at the peak of the fall migration. The sanctuary has therefore been an economic boon to the area by bringing capacity business to small boarding houses, motels, and restaurants. Moreover, the single piece of private action that created the sanctuary has probably done more to preserve birds of prey and change the public's attitude toward them than all of the subsequent legislation against killing them.

One last example of an extremely successful private conservation program is that of Ducks Unlimited, a nonprofit corporation dedicated to the preservation of waterfowl. DU has over 600,000 members in over 38,000 chapters in the United States, Canada, Mexico, and New Zealand. It raised over $386 million between 1937 and 1986 (with contributions growing rapidly in recent years). Most of the money has been spent on the preservation, restoration, and creation of wetlands in Canada, where approximately 70 percent of North America's waterfowl are hatched. Instead of purchasing land, DU has rented or leased it, obtaining long-term conservation easements from individual landowners as well as from Canada's federal and provincial governments. It is currently maintaining over 3,000 wetlands management projects that provide over 4 million acres of habitat for waterfowl as well as about 250 other species of birds, 60 species of mammals, and 19 species of fish.

Although DU has received considerable criticism from environmentalists who oppose hunting, some of whom charge that its programs are motivated solely by a selfish interest in producing more ducks to be hunted, its privately funded projects have enabled North America's nature lovers to benefit from the sight and enjoyment of waterfowl and other wildlife. Moreover, most of DU's efforts have been directed toward preserving wetlands in the prairie provinces; because of the demand for agricultural products, much of that land might otherwise have been drained and put to the plow.

Thus, a wide variety of private conservation programs have been carried on by birders, hunters, land and wildlife preservation organizations, and commercial farming operations. They have been preserving wildlife and natural resources through private land purchases and easements, user fees, membership dues, contributions, and business investments. The superiority of those programs lies primarily in the fact that because their resources are privately owned, they manage to overcome the tragedy of the commons and the multiple-use dilemma. But they have the additional virtue of preserving nature through voluntary efforts, not through the taxation of people who would rather pursue other goals.

18. The Private Supply of Education: Some Historical Evidence

Jack High and Jerome Ellig

Introduction

Education is often cited as a good that exemplifies "market failure": if education is left to the voluntary choices of consumers and educators, it is maintained, an "inadequate" supply of education will result.

Historically, economists have advanced many arguments to support the view that the market fails to adequately supply education.[1] The most common modern argument centers on the "external benefits" of education: Because education benefits persons other than those being educated, there is supposedly insufficient incentive to call forth the requisite investment in it. Therefore, government should act to stimulate the provision of education. This argument can be traced back at least as far as Adam Smith and J. B. Say (Smith [1776] 1937, p. 768; Say [1880] 1964, p. 433), but the most influential modern statement of it comes from Milton Friedman in his classic 1955 article "The Role of Government in Education."[2]

The present study examines the private supply of education in Great Britain and the United States prior to and just after the onset of extensive government involvement in education. The historical record clearly points to several conclusions that confute the conventional wisdom of market failure in education:

---

[1]See High (1985) for a survey.

[2]The essentials of Friedman's argument appear in the writings of Benson (1968), Cohn (1979), Garms (1978), Papi (1966), Rowley and Peacock (1975), Weisbrod (1964), and Wiseman (1959). Friedman later changed his mind about externalities justifying government intervention in education, after considering E. G. West's argument against state education. See West 1976, pp. 92–93.

- In both Great Britain and the United States, education was widely demanded and supplied.

- Government action not merely increased the supply of public education, it displaced private education, sometimes deliberately stifling it.

- Private education was more diverse and responsive to the demands of consumers.

- Government involvement altered the kind of education that was offered, mainly to the detriment of the poorer working classes.

The paper begins with an examination of the supply of education in Britain from 1800 to 1870, for which a readily accessible body of evidence is available due to the pioneering efforts of E. G. West. An examination of a number of historical instances of private education in the United States follows: New York and New England in the late 18th century; and New York, the Ohio Territories, Chicago, and St. Louis in the 19th century. While not as complete as the case for Britain, the American examples still give a fairly clear picture of the extent and kinds of education offered through the market at the time.

Great Britain

The relatively detailed historical evidence on private education in Great Britain makes the British experience a particularly important case study. The data indicate that education was widespread and rapidly growing prior to the beginning of significant government involvement in the late 19th century. The prevalence of private education is especially meaningful in light of the widespread poverty of the period. In real terms, average per capita GNP in 1833 was $84 in 1890 dollars (West 1975, p. 201). Given this low income, the wages of children were often important to the family. Sending a child to school involved not only out-of-pocket expenses but forgone earnings.

Scotland established a system of subsidized parochial schools in 1696, but the subsidy was only partial. Almost all working parents paid fees. In England, where limited state aid was introduced in 1833, government subsidies usually paid about one-quarter of the cost of erecting buildings for designated schools, with the remainder of construction and operating expenses met from voluntary sources (Baines 1848, p. 36). Compulsory and "free"—i.e., fully tax-supported—education was introduced in Scotland in 1872 and in England in 1881. Both countries initiated widespread free schooling in 1891 (West 1970b, pp. 74–75).

There is ample evidence of substantial growth in both the demand for and the supply of education in England during the pre-subsidy period. According to West (1975, p. 75), Lord Henry Brougham's Select Parliamentary Committee report of 1820 "revealed that in 1818 about one in 14 or 15 of the [total] population was being schooled. This considerable improvement since the beginning of the century was attributable partly to the energy of ecclesiastical groups, but more importantly . . . to the willingness of parents to pay fees, which indeed in most cases at this time covered the whole of the cost." A private survey conducted by Brougham in 1828 indicated that there were twice as many children in school then as there had been 10 years earlier, even though the population had increased by only one-fifth. An 1833 English government report stated that the number of children in school had increased 73 percent between 1818 and 1833, from 748,000 to 1,294,000, "without any interposition of the Government or public authorities," according to Brougham (speech in House of Lords, May 21, 1835, quoted in West 1975, p. 75). The Kerry Report, named for its sponsor in the House of Lords, was criticized by the Manchester, Birmingham, and Bristol statistical societies for under-reporting the number of children in school in 1833 in many cities (West 1970b, pp. 83–84).

From statistics in Lord Kerry's report, West (1975, p. 86) calculated that 58 percent of day-school pupils in 1833 paid fees that entirely covered the cost of their education. Another 15 percent paid partial fees. The remaining 27 percent attended schools supported by endowment and/or subscription.

Even after 1833, the bulk of English educational expenses were met out of fees and voluntary donations. "By 1841, they [subsidies to education] were so small that they amounted to a sum considerably less than that collected from parents for schooling in the City of Bristol alone" (West and McKee 1983, p. 1118). In 1843 Edward Baines undertook a survey of the manufacturing districts of Yorkshire, Lancashire, Cheshire, and Derbyshire to determine the moral and educational state of the working classes. After adjusting for errors, he determined that 1 person in 10 living in those districts was enrolled in day school. In addition, slightly more than 1 in 5 attended Sunday school, where 66,000 volunteers taught both reading and religion. "It ought to be borne in mind," he states, "that more than four years of severe manufacturing distress have considerably reduced the means of the working classes of paying for week-education, or even clothing their children decently to attend the Sunday School. In better times the attendance at both classes of schools would have been much larger" (Baines 1843, pp. 25–28).

In an 1847 letter to Lord John Russell, Baines (1847, pp. 25–27) pointed out that there was enough schooling capacity in England to allow every child to attend a day school for five years. He admitted, moreover, that his conclusion was based on a conservative estimate of space in schools for 1,879,947 pupils, whereas several other authors had estimated that there was space for over 2 million. New schools to accommodate 600,000–650,000 students had been built since 1833, at a cost of £1.5 million, without any government aid (Baines 1847, p. 34).

Progress continued over the next several decades. The 1851 census put the day-school attendance figure at 2,144,378, 1 person in 8.36 of the population. In the City of London, B. I. Coleman reports, the census showed that 8.6 percent of the 0–4 year olds, 56 percent of the 5–9 year olds, and 46.3 percent of the 10–14 year olds were in school. This finding is consistent with the estimate that nearly every child received an average of five years of schooling (West 1975, pp. 95–96).

By the time the Newcastle Commission on Popular Education issued its report in 1861, the number of day scholars had risen to 2,535,462, 1 in 7.7 of the population. "Moreover, the Commissioners' information from the specimen districts showed that the actual average duration at school was in fact 5.7 years. . . . In other words the figures indicated that nearly all the children were having some schooling" (West 1975, p. 97). These figures are significant because Horace Mann, British registrar-general assistant in charge of the 1851 Census Report's section on education, promulgated in that report the "one in six" rule—i.e., that 1 person in 6 should be enrolled in school—as the goal of British educational policy.[3] Commenting in 1869 on the Census and Newcastle Commission

---

[3] The goal has never been reached. In 1975, only 1 in 6.4 of the British population was in school (West 1975, pp. 22–23).

reports, Mann (quoted in West 1975, p. 108) said,

> Of schools and teachers in the aggregate therefore there is no great lack, and the deficiency as to scholars is less a deficiency in general than in certain crowded centres, and less of numbers than of the time passed in school. New schools are wanted in some populous places, and better schools and a better distribution of schools in other parts of the country; but the statements which are frequently made by eminent persons as to the enormous number of children (sometimes put at from 1,000,000 to 2,000,000) growing up wholly without education, rest upon an obvious arithmetical fallacy.

The decline of private schooling for the masses in England was initiated with the passage of the Education Act of 1870. The act provided for the establishment of tax-supported "board schools" under the control of local boards of education. These schools were originally intended to fill gaps in the existing system, but they often crowded out privately provided education. While 4,402 board schools came into being between 1870 and 1886, 1,124 of them were previously subsidized establishments run by churches and charitable societies and were simply taken over and renamed by school boards. The boards also acquired an undetermined but apparently substantial number of private profit-making schools (West 1970a, p. 150). The "free" board schools obviously had a large competitive advantage over fee-charging schools. And unlike private schools, board schools could never go bankrupt because they could draw upon the public treasury. Further weakening the private educational market, the Education Department's interpretation of the 1870 legislation allowed it to restrict the entry of new entrepreneurs into the schooling business (West 1970a, pp. 152–55).

As early as 1835, Henry Brougham had warned that state aid to education would come at the expense of, rather than in addition to, private efforts. "Today over a century later," West (1970a, p. 139) comments, "Brougham would no doubt look for support for his prophecy in the fact that with our total population of nearly four times bigger there are less than 500,000 pupils in unsubsidized and unendowed independent schools compared with the 1,144,000 in 1833."

Scotland's experience with public and private education provides an example of how the market responds to consumer demand for education. The Act of 1696 mandated the establishment of a school in every Scottish parish. Local taxes were to pay construction costs and, in some instances, part of the teacher's salary. Since parental fees provided for the rest of the expenses and attendance was voluntary, schoolmasters had a strong incentive to pay attention to the wishes of their customers (West 1975, p. 59).

By the 19th century, however, population growth had rendered the parochial system insufficient to meet demand, particularly in the industrial towns, and private suppliers of education proliferated. In 1818, there were 106,627 pupils in 2,222 private, unendowed schools, compared with 54,161 in the 942 parochial schools. According to West (1970b, p. 74),

> These figures would seem to show that the population "explosion" of the late eighteenth century had proved far too much of a strain for the system to carry, since by 1818 "non-legislated" private schools were bearing the main burden. The figures exclude the Sunday schools, Dame schools, and schools for the education of the rich. It is worth noting that very little of this education was free; nearly all the working-class parents paid fees whether they used the parochial schools or the more numerous private establishments.

In 1827, the *Edinburgh Review* observed that it was in the new industrial areas "that education is the most necessary and the most easy to be got" and that the parish schools were making a relatively insignificant contribution to the educational effort there (West 1975, p. 66). A report by the Scottish Factory Inquiry Commissioners in 1834 revealed that fully 96 percent of a sample of 28,000 mill workers could read and 56 percent could write (West 1975, p. 68).

The following picture emerges, therefore, of education in Great Britain in the early and mid-19th century: The supply side of the market was dominated by nongovernment providers, the majority of which received no public funds. Attendance was not compulsory, yet most children received five years of schooling. Poor and working-class parents effectively exercised their demand for education, often paying fees that fully covered costs. In light of the relative poverty of the time, the investment in education was impressive.

But were expenditures on education in any sense optimal? Much as economists might like to answer this question, they cannot do so without "some notion as to the 'correct' share of resources that 'should have' been employed. Such a figure has never, so far as is known, been derived or suggested" (West 1975, p. 84). Nevertheless, it is possible to estimate the share of national income devoted to education in Great Britain during this period and compare it with the relevant figures for other times and places. West (1975, pp. 89, 201–2) estimates that approximately 1 percent of net national income in England and Wales was expended on the day-school education of children of all ages in 1833. In 1920, only 0.7 percent was spent on children's day schooling; by 1965, the figure had risen to 2 percent. The British figure for 1833 compares favorably with the figures for the United States in 1860 (compulsion rare, fees common), Germany in 1860 (education free and compulsory), France in 1880 (education free and compulsory), and Italy in 1883 (education 80 percent public, provided primarily by local governments). Dividing the percentage of GNP devoted to education by the number of children in the population, the figure for Britain in 1833 still exceeds those for Germany, the United States, and France for the years mentioned.

Early American Schools and Academies

A thriving educational marketplace likewise existed in the United States prior to large-scale government involvement in the provision of education. From the colonial period into the mid-1800s, private schools existed both alongside and in the absence of tax-supported schools. In fact, the early 19th century saw the rise of a new educational institution, the academy. The following section briefly examines some accounts of private American education during the colonial period and the early years of the republic and then discusses the growth of the American academies.

The Colonial and Early Republic Period

Two features of private education during the colonial period and the early years of the republic are noteworthy. First, private education was highly responsive to the demands of its consumers. Second, in light of the relatively low standard of living of many of those consumers, the number of people educated was very high.

Several historians have commented on the degree to which self-interest forced private schoolmasters, in contrast to their counterparts in tax-supported schools, to pay close attention to the demands of their customers. Speaking of schools during the colonial period, historian Robert Seybolt (1971, pp. 101–2) notes:

> It is a significant fact in American education that the curriculum developed most rapidly in the private schools, that the curricular response to popular educational demands was initiated by private, rather than public enterprise. With the development of the economic life of the colonists, their vocational needs increased, and because most people were engaged in occupational activities, these needs were of more immediate importance than their purely cultural requirements.
>
> In the hands of private schoolmasters the curriculum expanded rapidly. Their schools were commercial ventures, and, consequently, competition was keen. . . . Popular demands, and the element of competition forced them not only to add new courses of instruction, but constantly to improve their methods and technique of instruction.

Private schoolmasters had to offer instruction at hours convenient to their customers; classes were offered in the early morning, at the noon lunch hour, in the late afternoon, and in the evening (Seybolt 1971, p. 100). They also had to be willing to offer not just the elements of a standard classical education but also instruction in more advanced or practical subjects.

For example, in New York City in 1749, John Clarke's school taught French, "Reading, Writing, Vulgar and Decimal Arithmetick, the Extraction of the Square and Cube Root, Navigation, Surveying . . . Spanish . . . Book-keeping after the true Italian Method." The following year, Michael C. Knoll's school in the same city offered "Latin . . . Greek, and Hebrew, and Philosophy, and . . . Merchant's Accounts after the Italian fashion" (quoted in Seybolt 1971, p. 13). In the New York of 1765, Thomas Carroll offered "Vulgar and Decimal Arithmetic; the extraction of roots; Simple and Compound Interest; how to purchase or sell Annuities; Leases for Lives, or in Reversion, Freehold Estates, & c. at Simple and Compound Interest" (quoted in Seybolt 1971, p. 45).

According to Carl F. Kaestle, New York City was well served by its decentralized network of private schools from the later colonial period through the 1790s. This fact is significant because the first government funding for schools in New York did not occur until 1795, and compulsory attendance laws were not enacted until 1874.

The private nature of market-supplied schooling makes historical information on private education more difficult to locate than in the case of a legislated school system. Some evidence, though, is available. Kaestle's examination of private schoolmasters' receipt books from 1760 to 1780 led him to conclude (1973, pp. 4–5) that tuition charges averaged 8–10 shillings per quarter, "low enough to be within the means of many workers of the middling sort." Eighty percent of New Yorkers leaving wills could sign their names, implying that "literacy was quite general in the middle reaches of society and above. The best generalization possible is that New York, like other American towns of the Revolutionary period, had a high literacy rate relative to other places in the world, and that literacy did not depend primarily upon schools."

Tuition in the city's common pay schools averaged 16 shillings. These schools served children from families with a diverse mixture of income and occupations (Kaestle 1973, pp. 41–42). Even in the absence of compulsory-attendance laws, fully 52 percent, Kaestle estimates, of children between the ages of 5 and 15 were enrolled in the city's common pay and charity schools in 1795. He points out (1973, pp. 51–53) that 80 or 90 percent of the population must have received some schooling, since few people actually attended school for 12 years. At this level, every child would have received an average of 6 years of schooling.

Colonial Boston provides an interesting comparison with New York. Private schools flourished in Boston, despite the city's long history of tax-supported grammar schools. According to Seybolt (1969, p. 92), the grammar schools apparently contented themselves with offering the three R's, catechism, and classics:

> The public schools made no attempt to meet the educational needs of all. They continued in their old-accustomed ways. The private schools were free to originate, and to adapt their courses of instruction to the interests of the students. The masters sought always to keep strictly abreast of the time, for their livelihood depended on the success with which they met those needs. No such freedom or incentive was offered the masters of the public schools.

The subjects offered in Boston's private schools included geography, bookkeeping, geometry, trigonometry, surveying, French, German, history, and, when legal, dancing.

Private schools were so prevalent that many cities, including Boston, sought to regulate them. Often the town's permission was required before a private school could open. Boston's selectmen issued the following permit in 1736: "Voted the said Mr. Joseph Kent have liberty to keep a school in this town for the teaching and instructing youth &c. in mathematical arts and sciences, whilst he continues to behave himself to the approbation of the selectmen of the town for the time being" (quoted in Small 1969, p. 318). As early as 1670 the town of Stamford, Connecticut, agreed "to put down all petty schools that are or may be kept in the town which may be prejudicial to the general school" (quoted in Small 1969, p. 312). In 1742, the Connecticut assembly passed a law stipulating that no one could establish a school in the colony without the assembly's approval (Small 1969, p. 318).

The Age of the Academies

As America moved from the colonial period into the early 19th century, the most significant development in private American education was the rise of the academies. Academies were private educational institutions that were often granted state charters prohibiting government control. They were usually run by independent boards of trustees (Sizer 1964, pp. 2–3). In some states, academies were eligible to receive grants of state lands or money, but many received no state aid at all, covering their expenses by means of tuition charges, subscription, lotteries, and sale of stock. Government "assistance to the academies most often took the form of public encouragement and sporadic aid rather than continuing full financial support. Relative laissez faire seemed a reasonable policy for corporate business; it was applied as well to the academies and colleges" (Sizer 1964, p. 21; see also Middlekauff 1971, pp. 145–46 and Knight 1919, p. 6). The academy movement, moreover, was not confined to states that had a history of government support for education and compulsory-attendance laws; it was national in scope.

The growth of academies in New England was spurred by a cutback in local government support for schools. Burdened by war debt after the Revolution, Massachusetts and New Hampshire sought to curtail state expenditures in any manner possible. In 1789, Massachusetts enacted a law requiring only towns of 200 families or more to support a town grammar school; previously, towns of 100 families or more had been obligated to do so. This measure reduced the number of Massachusetts towns required to support grammar schools by more than half, from 230 to 110 (Brown 1970, p. 216). Also in 1789, New Hampshire relieved most of its towns from a requirement that they support Latin (secondary) schools, although the state did mandate that each town and parish support a grammar school, expanding a policy that had earlier applied only to towns of 50 or more families. The net effect was a reduction in local requirements (Middlekauff 1971, pp. 133–36).

Parents responded to cutbacks in government support by turning to private schools. "They hired more private masters than ever before, and established academies with fat endowments, fine buildings, and complicated administrative apparatus. In short, their zeal for education seems to have been greater than ever, but it was a zeal now channeled into private education" (Middlekauff 1971, p. 136).

Though some of the academies received government aid, all charged tuition. Indeed, some were supported solely by tuition (Middlekauff 1971, pp. 145–46). But even when state aid was offered, it was not always accepted. In New York, academies receiving state funds had to submit to inspection by the Board of Regents and offer specified courses. Theodore Sizer (1964, pp. 25–26) reports, "Many obviously preferred to forgo government money and maintain their independence." The independence of the academies seems also to have been attractive to teachers in tax-supported schools, drawing many into the academy movement. "Many of the prominent New England schoolmasters," Emit D. Grizzell (1923, p. 28) states, "were attracted by the spirit of freedom of the academy and left the public Latin grammar school and district school, starting private schools or academies."

By 1830, there were 163 academies in New England; by 1850, the number had grown to 1,007 (Grizzell 1923, p. 31). In contrast to most modern "academies," which are viewed as college-preparatory schools for the rich, 19th-century academies were "the most significant organ of popular education" (Fish, quoted in Lottich 1962, p. 240). While their historical roots go back to John Milton and to academies set up by dissenting religious sects in England (see Brown 1970, pp. 155–78), the American academies are most closely connected with the rise of the middle class (Brown 1970, pp. 228–29):

> The academy age was, in fact, the age of transition from the partially stratified colonial society to modern democracy. Perhaps the most marked feature of that transition was the growing importance of a strong middle class. The rise of the academies was closely connected with the rise of this middle class. The

academies were by no means exclusively middle-class schools at the start, and they became something very different from that at a later period. But it is one of their glories that they were in the earlier days so bound up with the higher interests of the common people.

Academies led the way in providing wider educational opportunities for women, enlarged curricula, teacher training, and extracurricular activities (Brown 1970, p. 251; see also Mock 1949, p. 164 and Sizer 1964, pp. 32–33). In Massachusetts in the 1830s, the academies offered instruction in Latin, French, Italian, Greek, Spanish, German, English, mathematics, geography, arithmetic, orthography, history, rhetoric, philosophy, surveying, astronomy, composition, navigation, surveying, algebra, geometry, trigonometry, grammar, reading, declamation, writing, and needlework (Lottich 1962, p. 250). In Tallmadge, Ohio, a private academy for the deaf was established in 1827 (Lottich 1962, pp. 244–45), and in the Ohio Valley an academy served Choctaw, Creek, and Pottawatamie Indians for 18 years before the Civil War (Sizer 1964, p. 34).

As settlers from the East moved into the Northwest Territory, they took their tradition of private educational institutions with them. Academies were particularly prominent in the Western Reserve (northeast Ohio), where many pioneers from Connecticut settled. Between 1803 and 1851, 210 academies and private schools received charters to operate in Ohio. The census of 1850 reported 206 private secondary institutions in the state, serving 15,052 students. These schools were founded by religious denominations, itinerant preachers, wealthy persons, and others (Lottich 1962, pp. 240–41). Further west, Indiana had 131 academies by 1850, located in 78 of the state's 92 counties (Mock 1949, p. 4).

Writing in 1936 Charles W. Dabney (1969, p. 61) commented that Northern writers "assumed that because, before the Civil War, the South had no complete system of public schools, it had no education of any kind." In reality, the South had its share of private academies as well. Large numbers of Scottish and Scotch-Irish Presbyterians settled in the South, and they were joined in their enthusiasm for education by Quakers, Baptists, and Methodists (Dabney 1969, p. 47; Knight 1919, p. 13). By 1850, there were 1,815 academies in 11 southern states, serving 70,546 students (Knight 1919, pp. 23–32). According to Edgar W. Knight (1953, p. vi), "The prestige and popularity of these private and denominational efforts accounted in large part for the long delay in establishing public high schools in the Southern States."

In short, although the historical data on private education in 18th- and 19th-century America are incomplete, the available evidence strongly indicates that Americans of the period took an active interest in education. Their demand for reading, writing, arithmetic, and other skills called forth a responsive supply from private educators whose income depended on satisfied customers. This private supply was extensive, not only in the number of children served but in the spectrum of social classes involved.

Government played no large role in American education in the period under consideration. Government funding, even when present, was meager and sporadic; and compulsory-attendance laws, where they existed, do not appear to have been a binding constraint. Moreover, government involvement sometimes aimed, as it did in Massachusetts and Connecticut, at stifling the development of private education.

Urban Catholic Schools in the United States

Many economic discussions of government aid to education assume that the educational product remains the same regardless of who provides schooling. Experience with public education in the United States shows, however, that government provision of schooling results in a standardized product that is often quite different from—and inferior to—the various educational alternatives provided in a free market.

During the 19th century in both England and America, a philosophical and political movement existed that opposed any state aid to education. These "Voluntaryists," as they were called, saw a free market in education as the best way to preserve religious and political liberty and cultural pluralism and predicted that "government would employ education for its own ends, especially to instill the habit of obedience in its subjects" (Smith 1982, p. 124).

Recent work by revisionist historians confirms the accuracy of the Voluntaryist prediction of government manipulation of education. According to Michael Katz (1971, p. xviii), "The purpose [of the public school system] has been, basically, the inculcation of attitudes that reflect dominant social and industrial values; the structure has been bureaucracy. The result has been school systems that treat children as units to be processed into particular shapes and dropped into slots roughly congruent with the status of their parents." Joel Spring (1972, p. 89) writes of the "hard shell of bureaucracy" that protects public school systems from the obligation to pay attention to the desires of the people they ostensibly serve.

The development and growth of Catholic schools in New York, St. Louis, and Chicago provide examples of a minority's efforts to preserve a religious and cultural heritage threatened by systematized public schooling. The 1840s and 1850s saw a vast influx of Irish and German Catholic immigrants into America. They were soon followed by fellow church members from Eastern Europe. While one of the commonly avowed purposes of tax-supported public schools is to assist in the assimilation of immigrants, the Catholic immigrants saw the schools in a different light—as vehicles for nondenominational Protestantism (Ravitch 1974, p. 35). They objected to the schools' use of the King James version of the Bible rather than the Douay version. They also objected to the practice of Bible reading without instruction, which was based on the Protestant idea that the individual is capable of interpreting the Bible without the guidance of religious authorities. Perhaps most troubling to parents, though, was the Protestant and nativist bias of some texts and teachers (Kaestle 1973, pp. 151–54). Robert Cross (1965, pp. 197–98) reports the statement of Archbishop John Hughes of New York in 1852

> that education, as perpetrated in America was "Socialism, Red Republicanism, Universalism, Deism, Atheism, and Pantheism—anything, everything, but religionism and patriotism." Such a fantastic image of public education in the era of Horace Mann and William McGuffey reflected how deeply this prominent Irish-American was alienated from American institutions.

It is important to note that poor Catholics—recent immigrants and unskilled laborers—were the ones most heavily in favor of Catholic schools, in spite of the additional financial burden that private education entailed (Cross 1965, pp. 202–3). Hughes's archdiocese was a case in point. The financial condition of New York's Catholics was, according to Kaestle (1973, p. 147), probably worse than that of the city's Protestants because the Catholics were predominantly poor immigrants. Although by 1850 it was clear that no denominational school in New York City would receive any financial assistance from state or local authorities, the Catholics continued to establish parochial schools with the help of religious teaching orders. In that year, Hughes enunciated his principle of "the school before the church" and had it enacted into diocesan legislation: "Let parochial schools be established and maintained everywhere; the days have come, and the place, in which the school is more necessary than the church" (Lannie 1968, p. 225).

In 1854, 10,061 children were being educated in 28 New York Catholic schools. Enrollment rose to 12,938 in 1857 and to 15,000 in 1862 (Lannie 1968, p. 256). Population figures for the city's Catholics are not available for these years, but the Roman Catholic population of New York in 1850 has been estimated at 100,000, of whom 20,000 were between the ages of 5 and 15 (Kaestle 1973, p. 146).

In St. Louis, the growth of parochial schools was closely connected to the desire of German immigrants to preserve their language and culture. Between the early 1850s and 1890, Germans comprised the largest single group of immigrants in the United States. The approximately one-third of them who were Catholic set the pace for their coreligionists in the development of schools, even before the advent of compulsory education (Cross 1965, p. 199). According to Selwyn Troen (1975, pp. 55–56), "The situation in St. Louis was similar to that in other midwestern cities in the triangular area defined by Cincinnati, Milwaukee, and St. Louis. Throughout this area Germans were sufficiently numerous and well organized to demand concessions of the community at large and, if these were not granted, to develop and maintain independent cultural institutions." They were, however, neither sufficiently numerous nor well-enough organized to ever obtain government subsidies for religious schools.

Because the St. Louis public schools refused to teach German until 1864, both Catholic and non-Catholic citizens of German descent turned to private and parochial schools to meet their educational needs. In 1860, St. Louis Germans sent their children to their own schools rather than to the city's by a ratio of four to one (Troen 1975, p. 57).

The vast majority of the city's religious-ethnic schools were Catholic. It was not until 1850 that public school enrollment exceeded enrollment in Catholic schools, 2,570 pupils to 2,488. In 1860, 48 Catholic schools educated 6,972 students, 36.5 percent of the combined Catholic and public school populations. The fraction of students in Catholic schools remained roughly constant at about 20 percent between 1880 and 1920 (Troen 1975, pp. 33–34).

Not all the city's schools were founded by Catholics, however. A nonsectarian school offering instruction in English and German was established in St. Louis in 1837, one year before the first two public schools opened there (Troen 1975, p. 56). In addition, there were about 2,000 students in St. Louis Lutheran parish schools by 1900 (Troen 1975, p. 33). The Lutheran Church-Missouri Synod, which covered several states in the Midwest, was operating 179 schools in those states for 11,653 students by 1860.

The influence of ethnicity in the expansion of Catholic education perhaps reached its apex in Chicago in the late 19th and early 20th centuries, where both religious services and schooling were offered in a variety of languages. Some churches and their schools served particular geographic parishes; others served particular ethnic groups. In 1890, Germans and Irish made up 80 percent of Chicago parish-school enrollment (Sanders 1977, p. 57). By 1930, there were also Catholic elementary schools affiliated with Polish, Bohemian, French, Lithuanian, Italian, Slovak, Negro, Croatian, and Slovene churches (Sanders 1977, p. 45). The Poles were the most energetic in founding their own high schools, and in 1908 they even planned to establish in Chicago a Polish National University affiliated with the Catholic University of America (Sanders 1977, pp. 61–62).

In 1890, one-half to two-thirds of the city's Catholic children were being educated in parochial schools (Sanders 1977, p. 85). As in other cities, it was the poorer Catholics who were most likely to send their children to parochial, rather than public, schools. According to James W. Sanders (1977, p. 80), "In every poverty zone, the proportion in Catholic schools exceeded that for Chicago as a whole in 1890." Seventy-seven percent of Catholic schoolchildren in 1890 lived in "poor workingman's areas." Sanders (1977, p. 79) observes,

> The workers settled near industrial and commercial sites. Here, in the shadow of belching smoke stacks and near the squeal of dying pigs the laborer could slog without cost through the mud of unpaved streets to his long day's work. In these areas—the older, residentially blighted commercial sections surrounding the city center, along the branches of the river, near the noisy railroads, around the stockyards, and in the southeast Chicago industrial areas adjoining the Calumet River—one found most of the Catholic population.

It was on this infertile soil, where people lived in "conditions as bad as any in the world," according to contemporary accounts, that the Catholic parochial school system had its roots.

In wards 5–9, where many of the poor lived, 17 Catholic schools educated 14,000 pupils, "40 percent of the public–Catholic school total in the area, more than twice the city-wide average, and almost one-half of all the Catholic school children in the entire city" (Sanders 1977, pp. 79–80). The poverty of the Catholic poor apparently inhibited neither the establishment of parochial elementary schools nor attendance, even though free public schooling was available. In 1912, interviews with Catholic families in the stockyard district revealed that 90 percent of them sent their children to parochial schools. By 1930, more than 90 percent of the Catholic congregations in Chicago and the surrounding suburban area had schools (Sanders 1977, p. 85).

Urban Catholic education in the 19th century displays two significant features. First, the poorer working classes demonstrated a remarkable commitment to securing education for their children. Second, government involvement in education did not merely increase the supply of education; it altered the product to the detriment of the working classes.

Both these features call into question any rationale for government involvement in education on the grounds of external benefits. First, the extensive private supply of and demand for education, especially among the poor, renders doubtful the contention that there were marginal, or Pareto-relevant, external benefits to be gained, and inframarginal benefits provide no basis for government involvement. If the market supplies education in sufficient quantity so that an additional supply of schooling does not yield benefits greater than costs, then government does not increase the social welfare by increasing the supply of education (see Buchanan and Stubblebine 1962).

Second, a change that lowers the quality of education and imposes an inferior educational product on people who, because of their poverty, can resist only with difficulty undermines the logic of the external-benefits argument. The argument takes the quality of the educational product that people demand as fixed: if "ethnic" or "cultural" values are demanded, then they will be provided in the education the government supplies. The historical evidence demonstrates that this assumption is false.

Of course, proponents of state-provided education might argue that education is a "merit good," meaning that a group of elite officials knows better than poor persons which kind of education is best (see West 1970b, pp. xxx–xxxii and Musgrave 1959). This argument dates back at least as far as John Stuart Mill. Besides containing the paradoxical element that people are competent to judge and elect the officials who choose education but are incompetent to judge education itself, the argument goes beyond the strictly economic. Economics provides no basis for passing judgment on the kinds of education that people want (see Friedman 1953, p. 5). In any case, a merit good, by definition, is one that must be imposed only temporarily, until consumers "learn" to acquire a taste for it. E. G. West and Michael McKee (1983, p. 1114) argue that the existence of free, compulsory education for more than three generations is enough to disqualify any merit-good theory of education.

The history of urban Catholic education points up still another ill effect of imposing unwanted goods on consumers: to the extent that persons can undo the effects of unwanted acculturation from public education, the resources devoted to imposing values through public education will be wasted. That is, even if some children have no choice but to attend public schools and learn values their parents oppose, parents can counter by undermining those values in their homes and churches.[4] The level of commitment that poor urban Catholics demonstrated in preserving their cultural values through private schools indeed suggests that they may also have used educational methods other than schools to resist the imposition of undesirable ideas. To the extent that the resources devoted to acculturation by the public schools were offset by private resources devoted to opposing it, there was a net "deadweight loss" in social welfare.

Conclusion

The historical evidence clearly supports the four conclusions stated at the beginning of this paper. Private education was widely demanded in the late 18th and 19th centuries in Great Britain and America. The private supply of education was highly responsive

[4]This observation is the converse of Gary S. Becker's argument (1981, pp. 125–26) that public provision of an education that parents view as a positive good results in a redistribution of family resources away from the children so educated.

to that demand, with the consequence that large numbers of children from all classes of society received several years of education. The effect of government intervention in the private educational market was not unambiguously beneficial. Government education displaced, and sometimes stifled, private education. In addition, compulsory-education laws in America forced a kind of education on poor people that they saw as threatening to their ethnic cultures and values. The historical evidence strongly suggests that economists should rethink the view that education is a market failure.

References

Bailyn, Bernard. 1960. *Education in the Forming of American Society*. Chapel Hill: University of North Carolina Press.

Baines, Edward. [1843] 1969. *The Social, Educational, and Religious State of the Manufacturing Districts*. 2d ed. New York: Augustus M. Kelley.

———. 1847. *Letters to the Right Hon. Lord John Russell . . . on State Education*. London: Ward and Co.

———. 1848. "On the Progress and Efficiency of Voluntary Education in England." In *Crosby-Hall Lectures on Education*, pp. 2–47. London: John Snow.

Becker, Gary S. 1981. *A Treatise on the Family*. Cambridge: Harvard University Press.

Benson, Charles. 1968. *The Economics of Public Education*. 2d ed. Boston: Houghton Mifflin Co.

Brown, Elmer E. [1902] 1970. *The Making of Our Middle Schools*. Totowa, N.J.: Littlefield, Adams and Co.

Buchanan, James, and W. Craig Stubblebine. 1962. "Externality." *Economica* (November): 371–84.

Burns, James A. [1912] 1969a. *The Growth and Development of the Catholic School System in the United States*. New York: Arno Press.

———. [1912] 1969b. *The Principles, Origin, and Establishment of the Catholic School System in the United States*. New York: Arno Press.

Butler, Vera M. [1935] 1969. *Education as Revealed by New England Newspapers Prior to 1860*. New York: Arno Press.

Coase, Ronald H. "The Lighthouse in Economics." *Journal of Law and Economics* 17, no. 2 (October): 357–76.

Cohn, Elchanan. 1979. *The Economics of Education*. Cambridge: Ballinger Publishing Co.

Cross, Robert D. 1965. "Origins of the Catholic Parochial Schools in America." *American Benedictine Review* 16: 194–209.

Dabney, Charles W. [1936] 1969. *Universal Education in the South, Vol. I*. New York: Arno Press.

Friedman, Milton. 1953. "The Methodology of Positive Economics." In *Essays in Positive Economics*. Chicago: University of Chicago Press.

———. 1955. "The Role of Government in Education." In *Economics and the Public Interest*, ed. Robert A. Solo. New Brunswick: Rutgers University Press.

Friedman, Milton, and Rose Friedman. 1980. *Free to Choose*. New York: Harcourt Brace Jovanovich, 1980.

Garms, Walter, James Guthrie, and Walter Pierce. 1978. *The Economics and Politics of Public Education*. Englewood Cliffs, N.J.: Prentice-Hall.

Grizzell, Emit D. 1923. *Origin and Development of the High School in New England before 1865*. Philadelphia: Macmillan and Co.

High, Jack. 1985. "State Education: Have Economists Made a Case?" *Cato Journal* 5, no. 1 (Spring/Summer): 305–23.

Kaestle, Carl F. 1973. *The Evolution of an Urban School System: New York City 1750–1850*. Cambridge: Harvard University Press.

———. 1978. "Social Reform and the Urban School: An Essay Review." In *History, Education, and Public Policy*, ed. Donald Warren, pp. 127–47. Berkeley: McCutchan Publishing Corp.

Katz, Michael B. *The Irony of Early School Reform*. Cambridge: Harvard University Press.

———. 1971. *Class, Bureaucracy and Schools*. New York: Praeger Publishing Co.

Kiesling, H. J. 1983. "19th Century Education According to West: A Comment." *Economic History Review* 2d ser. 36, no. 3 (August): 416–25.

Knight, Edgar W., ed. 1953. *A Documentary History of Education in the South before 1860, Vol. IV*. Chapel Hill: University of North Carolina Press.

Knight, Edgar W. [1919(?)] *The Academy Movement in the South*. Chapel Hill, N.C. Reprint. *High School Journal* 2, no. 78 and 3, no. 1.

Kraushaar, Otto F. 1976. *Private Schooling: From the Puritans to the Present*. Bloomington, Ind.: Phi Delta Kappa Educational Foundation.

Lannie, Vincent P. 1968. *Public Money and Parochial Education*. Cleveland: Case Western Reserve University Press.

———. 1976. "Church and School Triumphant: The Sources of American Catholic Historiography." *History of Education Quarterly* 16, no. 2 (Summer): 131–45.

Lazerson, Marvin. 1977. "Understanding American Catholic Educational History." *History of Education Quarterly* 17, no. 3 (Fall): 297–317.

Lottich, Kenneth V. 1962. "Democracy and Education in the Early American Northwest." *Paedigogica Historica* 2, no. 2: 234–54.

Middlekauff, Robert. [1963] 1971. *Ancients and Axioms*. New York: Arno Press.

Mock, Albert. 1949. "The Midwestern Academy Movement: A Composite Picture of 514 Indiana Academies, 1810–1900." Butler University. Unpublished ms.

Musgrave, R. A. 1959. *The Theory of Public Finance*. New York: McGraw-Hill.

Papi, G. U. 1966. "General Problems of the Economics of Education." In *The Economics of Education*, ed. E. A. G. Robinson and John Vaizey. London: Macmillan and Co.

Ravitch, Diane. 1974. *The Great School Wars: New York City 1805–1973*. New York: Basic Books.

Richard, Henry. 1848. "On the Progress and Efficacy of Voluntary Education, as Exemplified in Wales." In *Crosby-Hall Lectures on Education*. London: John Snow.

Rowley, Charles, and Alan Peacock. 1975. *Welfare Economics*. New York: John Wiley and Sons.

Sanders, James W. 1977. *The Education of an Urban Minority: Catholics in Chicago, 1833–1965*. New York: Oxford University Press.

Say, Jean Baptiste. [1880] 1964. *A Treatise on Political Economy*. New York: Augustus M. Kelley.

Seybolt, Robert F. [1925] 1971. *Source Studies in American Colonial Education: The Private School*. New York: Arno Press.

———. [1936] 1969. *The Private Schools of Colonial Boston*. New York: Arno Press.

Sizer, Theodore, ed. 1964. *The Age of the Academies*. New York: Columbia Teachers College.

Small, Walter H. [1914] 1969. *Early New England Schools*. New York: Arno Press.

Smith, Adam. [1776] 1937. *An Inquiry into the Nature and Causes of the Wealth of Nations*. New York: Modern Library.

Smith, George H. 1982. "19th Century Opponents of State Education." In *The Public School Monopoly*, ed. Robert Everhart. Cambridge: Ballinger Publishing Co.

Spring, Joel. 1972. *Education and the Rise of the Corporate State*. Boston: Beacon Press.

Troen, Selwyn R. 1975. *The Public and the Schools: Shaping the St. Louis System, 1838–1920*. Columbia: University of Missouri Press.

Weisbrod, Burton. 1964. *External Benefits of Public Education*. Princeton: Princeton University Press.

West, E. G. 1967. "The Political Economy of American Public School Legislation." *Journal of Law and Economics* (October): 102–28.

———. 1970a. "Resource Allocation and Growth in Early 19th-Century British Education." *Economic History Review*. 2d ser. (April): 68–95.

———. 1970b. *Education and the State*. London: Institute of Economic Affairs.

———. 1975. *Education and the Industrial Revolution*. New York: Barnes and Noble.

———. 1976. *Nonpublic School Aid*. Lexington, Mass.: D. C. Heath and Co.

————. 1983. "19th Century Educational History: The Kiesling Critique." *Economic History Review*. 2d ser. 36, no. 3 (August): 426–34.

West, E. G., and Michael McKee. 1983. "De Gustibus *Est* Disputandum: The Phenomenon of 'Merit Wants' Revisited." *American Economic Review* 73, no. 5 (December): 1110–21.

Wiseman, Jack. 1959. "The Economics of Education." *Scottish Journal of Political Economy*. (February).

Contributors

Tyler Cowen is assistant professor of economics at the University of California, Irvine, and an adjunct scholar of the Cato Institute.

Robert Axelrod is professor of political science and public policy at the University of Michigan.

Francis M. Bator is professor of political economy at the John F. Kennedy School of Government at Harvard University.

Earl R. Brubaker is professor of economics at the Naval Postgraduate School in Monterey, California.

James M. Buchanan, Harris University Professor of Economics and general director of the Center for Study of Public Choice at George Mason University, won the Nobel Prize in Economic Science in 1986.

Steven N. S. Cheung is professor of economics at the University of Hong Kong.

Ronald H. Coase is emeritus professor of law at the University of Chicago.

Carl J. Dahlman is deputy assistant secretary for income security policy in the U.S. Department of Health and Human Services.

Harold Demsetz is professor of economics at the University of California, Los Angeles.

Jerome Ellig is research director of Citizens for a Sound Economy Foundation.

Kenneth D. Goldin is professor of economics and associate dean of the School of Business Administration and Economics at California State University, Fullerton.

Jack High is professor of economics and director of the Center for the Study of Market Processes at George Mason University.

Robert W. Poole, Jr., is president of the Reason Foundation.

Paul A. Samuelson, professor of economics at the Massachusetts Institute of Technology, won the Nobel Prize in Economic Science in 1970.

Andrew Schotter is associate professor of economics and co-director of the C. V. Starr Center for Applied Economics at New York University.

Robert J. Smith is senior environmental consultant at the Competitive Enterprise Institute.

Charles M. Tiebout taught economics at the University of Washington until his death in 1969.

Printed in the United States
by Baker & Taylor Publisher Services